S0-AGD-132

Get Out of My Room!

Get Out of My Room!

A History of Teen Bedrooms in America

JASON REID

The University of Chicago Press Chicago and London

The University of Chicago Press, Chicago 60637
The University of Chicago Press, Ltd., London

Printed in the United States of America

26 25 24 23 22 21 20 19 18 17   1 2 3 4 5

ISBN-13: 978-0-226-40921-4 (cloth)
ISBN-13: 978-0-226-40935-1 (e-book)
DOI: 10.7208/chicago/9780226409351.001.0001

Library of Congress Cataloging-in-Publication Data

Names: Reid, Jason, 1974– author.
Title: Get out of my room! : a history of teen bedrooms in America / Jason Reid.
Description: Chicago ; London : The University of Chicago Press, 2017. | Includes bibliographical references and index.
Identifiers: LCCN 2016027827 | ISBN 9780226409214 (cloth : alk. paper) | ISBN 9780226409351 (e-book)
Subjects: LCSH: Teenagers' rooms—United States. | Teenagers—United States—Social conditions. | Bedrooms—United States. | Teenagers—Conduct of life. | Teenage consumers—United States. | United States—Social life and customs—20th century. | Self-realization.
Classification: LCC NK2117.T44 R45 2017 | DDC 747.7/70835—dc23 LC record available at https://lccn.loc.gov/2016027827

∞ This paper meets the requirements of ANSI/NISO Z39.48–1992 (Permanence of Paper).

Contents

Acknowledgments

I'd like to begin by thanking my parents, Wayne and Linda, and my brother, Jamie. They have been extremely supportive of my efforts, and, since I lived with them for the first nineteen years of my life, it perhaps goes without saying that they played a significant role in shaping my earliest experiences with teen bedroom culture.

Several of my peers in the history profession deserve recognition as well. Molly Ladd-Taylor, Marc Stein, Marlene Shore, and Leslie Paris gave me the guidance and tools necessary to produce a publishable (and hopefully compelling) work of history. The same can also be said of the two anonymous readers who went through my original manuscript and offered me invaluable advice on how to improve it. Similarly, Todd Webb, Alexis Lachaine, Peter Stevens, and Geoff Read deserve recognition for providing me with a wealth of encouragement and support. Indeed, their views on history and how it should be written can be found on nearly every page of this book.

I'd also like to thank the dozens of people who were gracious enough to respond to my surveys and share memories and photos of their own bedrooms. Their firsthand accounts not only gave shape to my arguments; they also added a certain amount of flair and color to my work. In short, they were key contributors in my attempt to bring the teen bedroom to life.

I'd be remiss if I didn't acknowledge the long list of friends who supported my efforts by simply establishing a warm presence in my life, including Rob Vandenbrink, Anthony Alviano, Brett Poirier, Catharine Ackert, Troy Robinson, Kim

Wulterkens, Brent Jesney, Tim Packham, Isabel Matwawana, Sharlet Esho, Rob Worsoff, Scott Hutchinson, Kevin Mertens, Razmeen Joya, Marc Tinney, and Mike Graham.

Lastly, I'd like to thank the various institutions that helped get this book published. Of course, I am forever grateful to the University of Chicago Press for agreeing to publish my work. I can safely say that its reputation as a world-class press is wholly deserved and that the people who work there have been nothing but friendly and helpful during this entire process. I'd also like to thank the library staff at York University, the University of Toronto, and Ryerson University. Although the Internet has certainly had a profound effect on how scholars do research nowadays, we would be lost without the people who ensure that the old brick-and-mortar libraries run as smoothly as possible.

Introduction

A bedroom is a teenager's sanctuary, dressing room, dance studio, study hall, entertainment room, meeting place, therapy room, and so many other things, but mostly it is *home*.

CASEY CALLOWAY, TEEN BEDROOM SURVEY PARTICIPANT (2013)

Given the somewhat personal and intimate nature of the topic at hand, I'll begin by confessing that I only began to contemplate the significance of my own teen bedroom once it was nearly wiped from existence. During my second year of university, I received a call from my mother explaining that she and my father were selling the house we had lived in for much of my teenage years. Though I was saddened at the prospect of not being able to spend one more night in my old shag-carpeted bedroom, I knew that my parents' decision made perfect sense; my older brother and I were no longer living at home, and the new place was simply much better suited for two empty nesters like my parents. Unfortunately, I didn't get a chance to even see the new house before the ownership papers were signed. This bothered me somewhat, but I knew that my opinions on such matters would no longer be taken into consideration to the same extent as they were when I was still living at home. My parents, more importantly, seemed satisfied with their decision, even though they understood that their immediate future would be marked by a series of time-consuming renovation projects.

My first opportunity to see the new place arrived a few months later, when I came home for the summer. Situated on a double lot, the new house had a swimming pool in the backyard, a fully furnished basement rec room, and three bedrooms. The big shock came when I actually saw "my" bedroom for the first time. My parents had lived in the new place for only a few months, but already my mother had taken complete control of the room I'd be sleeping in whenever I came to visit. The Metallica and Iron Maiden posters that had dotted the walls of my old bedroom were gone, replaced by a black-and-white picture of my father as a young man and a portrait of my eight-year-old self that had been drawn years earlier by a semi-talented caricaturist from Marineland. My collection of home electronics was gone too, including my color television set, my computer, my telephone, and my stereo. The clothes hamper I had used to hide an array of contraband goods was also nowhere to be found—along with, presumably, any contraband that may have still been around when moving day arrived. Even my amazing queen-size bed had been dispatched with in record time, traded to a relative because it was too big to be carried downstairs. The new bed, a "cozy" double, was covered in flowery bedding; at its foot sat an old cedar chest that housed my mother's collection of quilts.

My new bedroom, in short, no longer belonged to me. I did not decorate it, I rarely spent time in it, and it was shamefully bereft of home electronics, save for a cheap clock radio that was tuned to an oldies station of my mother's choosing. Although my parents weren't consciously trying to erase my presence from their newly purchased home, the somewhat jarring nature of the move got me thinking about how my experiences were part and parcel of what Sonia Livingstone, a media studies professor at the London School of Economics, dubs "teen bedroom culture"—a decidedly Western phenomenon in which the sleeping quarters of youth are expected to assume a prominent role in socializing teens and shaping their identities. I recalled how, as a moody teenager, I would slink off to my room in order to hang out with friends, listen to music, do homework, or play video games without worrying about being interrupted by my parents or my brother. I recalled the time and energy I devoted to plastering the walls of my room with pinups and store-bought posters, many of which reflected my ever-shifting taste in music and movies. Lastly, I recalled the lengths to which my parents went in order to respect my privacy there—for example, knocking before entering and announcing their presence outside the door—while also recognizing that these rules were established in a somewhat informal manner. I'm sure I complained mightily whenever my privacy was violated, but at no point did my parents and I sit down to formulate a basic set of rules that would govern social interaction in my room. We had an unspoken understanding, as though the sanctity of my bedroom was simply beyond debate.[1]

My own experiences, to make a long story short, played a definitive role in influencing my decision to examine the historical roots of teen bedroom culture. This led me to formulate two questions that would serve as the basis of this book:

1. When did the idea of the autonomous teen bedroom emerge and become normative in American culture?
2. What individuals, institutions, and other social and cultural factors helped bring this ideal to the fore?

Get Out of My Room! represents the culmination of my efforts in answering these questions, bringing focus to a neglected, yet seemingly ubiquitous, feature of the modern family home.

Teen bedroom culture has its roots in an era that actually predated the very concept of "teens" and "teenagers," finding expression among affluent, urban-dwelling families in the Northeast and Midwest during the decades leading up to the Civil War, a by-product of the rise of modern capitalism and the sweeping social, demographic, and cultural changes that emerged in its wake. However, the bedrooms occupied by American youth during this time bore only a fleeting resemblance to the ones that emerged after the Second World War. Indeed, the earliest manifestations of the autonomous teen bedroom were shaped in large part by an evangelical spirit that emphasized piety, character building, literacy, and the value of privacy in establishing a one-on-one relationship with God. Although these ideas would continue to inform the sleeping space of youth in subsequent decades, teen bedroom culture would begin to assume a much more secular identity during the late nineteenth and early twentieth centuries, when scientific ways of thinking began to permeate the culture.

Boys, as it turns out, didn't play a vital role in the earliest expressions of teen bedroom culture. Nineteenth-century bedrooms were often geared toward middle-class girls—many of whom, historian Jane Hunter argues, used their sleeping quarters for "private rumination of self." Though there is no doubt that boys enjoyed rooms of their own, their leisure activities were rarely centered in the bedroom. As Sally McMurry notes in her study of nineteenth-century farmsteads, rooms for boys were rarely given a second thought because the children who were expected to assume control of this space were simply "not often there." Whereas the activities of girls were often oriented toward the lush parlors and private chambers of the middle-class Victorian home, boys were expected to come of age among the hills and rivers immortalized by Mark Twain and the clogged byways and bustling street corners of Horatio Alger. Associated as it was with home décor, housekeeping, and other so-called womanly pursuits, the bedroom was simply much too feminine a place for adventurous boys on the cusp of manhood. At nearly every turn, then, teen bedroom culture was shaped by the "separate spheres" argument and other long-standing ideas on gender.[2]

The late nineteenth and early twentieth centuries represent an important turning point for teen bedroom culture. Though it was still largely limited to affluent families, the teen bedroom was subjected to a slow process of democratization as the Victorian era drew to a close. By the 1920s and 1930s, for example, working-class girls and boys were increasingly being given rooms of their own, a trend that was noted favorably by many observers. In explaining why this was so, we must once again look at socioeconomic trends—most notably, shrinking family size and a rising standard of living—as well as the contributions of the academically trained child development experts who championed the separate bedroom ideal. If the nineteenth-century bedroom can be characterized as a feminine, middle-class, Protestant space, the version that emerged during the early twentieth century can be regarded in much more broad and secular terms. Social scientists from a wide array of disciplines basically medicalized the teen bedroom, transforming a space that had once been defined by ideas on religion and spirituality into a space marked by scientific ways of thinking. This was an extension of a process noted by Joan Jacobs Brumberg in *The Body Project*, as doctors and other medical professionals began to colonize various aspects of adolescent experience. Whereas *The Body Project* discusses the extent to which doctors established authority over the bodies of young girls, *Get Out of My Room!* examines how similar forces staked a claim inside the bedrooms of teens from both sexes. To deny American teens the privilege of presiding over rooms of their own, many child development experts argued, was to risk erecting a roadblock to proper development, which could in turn lead to pathology and criminality.[3]

The expansion of teen bedroom culture during the late nineteenth and early twentieth centuries was also hastened by the rise of youth-oriented consumerism. Just as many working-class and middle-class teens used their growing economic clout to while away the hours in dance halls and movie theaters, so too did they welcome the opportunity to express their consumer preferences in the comfort of their own rooms. Indeed, the material culture of teenagers changed drastically during the late-Victorian era, as the teen bedroom became a storage space for a host of mass-produced, store-bought items, including toys, clothing, reading material, and games. The culture's growing acceptance of youth-oriented consumerism had an especially pronounced effect on how teenagers decorated their bedrooms. Although nineteenth-century youths weren't entirely excluded from determining the basic appearance of their rooms, most décor decisions were made by parents—particularly mothers. The teen bedroom was often treated as an extension of the parlor or master bedroom, featuring a middle-class aesthetic in which ideas of order, gentility, and domesticity were paramount. By the 1920s, 1930s, and 1940s, however, the rise of the teen consumer afforded American youths the opportunity to reshape their bedrooms according to their own sensibilities. Owing to its proximity to the family home and the opportunities it provided for accommodating some measure of parental supervision, the teen bedroom may have helped legitimize youth-oriented consumption in ways that poorly supervised public leisure venues simply could not. Unlike the penny arcade, the teen bedroom was seen as a relatively safe place in which teens could express their consumer preferences without straying too far from the comfort and safety of home.[4]

The autonomous teen bedroom would eventually become normative during the years following the Second World War. By the 1960s, 1970s, and 1980s in particular, the teen bedroom was seen as a safe haven that adolescents from nearly all points on the socioeconomic spectrum could benefit from and enjoy. Parental input and oversight were downplayed to an extent not seen in previous eras of American history, all in the hopes of encouraging self-expression, pride of ownership, and autonomy among teenagers. Once again, prominent socioeconomic trends played a role in bringing this version of the teen bedroom into being: the standard of living continued to rise during the postwar years; family size, despite a brief spike upward during the years immediately following the war, continued to shrink; homes became larger and home ownership became more common; and teenagers became a driving force in the postwar economy. Under these circumstances, the autonomous teen bedroom became an enshrined part of the postwar suburban consensus, an adolescent expression of the homeowner ideal that could be indulged without swallowing up too much of the family's resources.

Similarly, academically trained child development experts continued to offer support for providing teens with rooms of their own, receiving additional help from the scores of advice columnists who emerged during the postwar years as powerful cultural arbiters. By the 1950s and 1960s, for instance, popular experts such as Ann Landers and Abigail Van Buren established themselves as the teen bedroom's biggest cheerleaders. Besides reinforcing the child development community's earlier claims regarding the teen bedroom's value as a child-rearing tool, popular experts codified a host of practical measures that promised to minimize parent-child conflict while further reinforcing the teen bedroom's reputation as a space within the home where unannounced visits and other forms of trespass were frowned upon. If parents were resistant to the idea of giving their offspring rooms of their own, privacy-starved teens could rest assured in knowing that the likes of Dr. Spock and Dr. Joyce Brothers were in their corner, urging parents to grant teens a measure of autonomy that previous generations might have found alien.

Though earlier manifestations of the teen bedroom were often defined by various acts of consumption, the rooms that emerged after the Second World War brought this idea to its logical conclusion. Home décor experts, furniture manufacturers, and other businesses that trafficked in teen-oriented products courted youth in an intense manner, encouraging teens to fill their bedrooms with big-ticket items such as beds, dressers, and desks, as well as rock posters, stuffed animals, and other inexpensive knickknacks. However, companies that catered to teens also found out how difficult it was to market their products to a demographic that was often defined by opposing various forms of adult authority. The *New York Times* and *Good Housekeeping* could offer suggestions on how to decorate the teen bedroom, but by the 1960s, 1970s, and 1980s, many teens preferred to fill their rooms with found items such as beer cans, cutouts from magazines and newspapers, and other detritus from the world of pop culture. That many of these found items were also produced by corporate interests didn't matter much; all that mattered was that teens had a free hand to decorate their rooms as they saw fit. In many respects, this trend reflects the extent to which the teen bedroom had moved beyond its Victorian, middle-class roots. Earlier design strategies, after all, were capital intensive and geared toward replicating a feminine, middle-class aesthetic; the do-it-yourself (DIY) approach, by contrast, could be employed by even the poorest of teens, offering anyone who could afford to buy a rock magazine and some Scotch tape the means to personalize their rooms. The genteel designs of old were essentially replaced by a concert-poster aesthetic, as teen bedrooms just as often resembled a chaotic, Warhol-inspired art experiment than a tasteful Victorian parlor.

The proliferation of home electronics had a similarly profound effect on teen bedroom culture during the postwar years. Stereo equipment, telephones, televisions, personal computers, and video game consoles flooded the bedrooms of youth during this time, greatly affecting the manner in which parents and children socialized with each other. Initially marketed as a means of providing entertainment for the entire family, many of these items found their way into the teen bedroom during the 1960s, 1970s, and 1980s. Products that originally entertained the entire family soon migrated into the bedrooms of parents and children alike, into spaces that encouraged solitary forms of leisure. This trend served only to strengthen the teen bedroom's reputation as a means of "getting away from it all" because teens no longer needed to leave their rooms in order to entertain themselves or their friends; they could now use their rooms to watch TV, listen to music, or talk on the phone relatively free from intrusion. Parents who felt that this trend was contributing to the fragmentation of family life were told by various experts that home electronics ownership could actually help keep youth off the streets. Indeed, just as the domestic containment of women during the early years of the Cold War was aided by a bevy of so-called time-saving appliances, the containment of youth was similarly encouraged by an array of inexpensive gadgets that offered teens a wide range of entertainment options in the comfort of their own rooms—an idea that may have taken on even greater significance during the 1970s and 1980s, when women began reentering the workforce in droves. Under these circumstances, the technologically well-appointed teen bedroom may have served as a makeshift babysitting service, a means of keeping teens distracted and in the home while both parents were at work.[5]

The various filmmakers, television writers, and musicians who provided content for many of these home electronics devices also made significant contributions to teen bedroom culture during the postwar years. Members of the cultural industry—be they creators of respectable literary fiction or groan-worthy television sitcoms—used the teen bedroom as a prominent setting or motif in their works, oftentimes referring to this space in terms that reinforced decades-old ideas on child development expertise, the importance of consumer forces in defining the basic appearance of the teen bedroom, and the bedroom's role as a potential source of parent-child conflict. However, many of these same artists also envisioned the teen bedroom in ways that undermined some of the more optimistic characterizations being offered by child development experts and other supporters of the separate bedroom ideal. The teen bedroom found in film, song, television, and literature continued to be portrayed as a space for personal development, self-expression, and leisure, but it also came to be seen as a site of profound loneliness and romantic longing. If the Beach Boys' 1963 hit song "In My Room" is any guide, then it is safe to say that the teen bedroom featured just as much "sighing and crying" as it did "scheming and dreaming."[6]

The teen bedrooms that emerged in popular memory nicely illustrate the extent to which this space was thought of as contested terrain. The history of teen bedrooms is riddled with culture-wide expressions of fear and anxiety, as Americans came to recognize that giving teenagers rooms of their own could create just as many problems as it supposedly solved. Some nineteenth-century families, for example, romanticized shared beds and bedrooms to such an extent that separate bedrooms came to be seen as a threat to family togetherness. Similarly, child development experts during the late nineteenth and early twentieth centuries often felt that separate bedrooms, though they could potentially minimize instances of incest among siblings, might also encourage masturbation, which was thought to be a source of pathology and degeneration. Fears of unchecked expressions of teen sexuality reappeared time and again throughout much of the twentieth century, with many observers suggesting that adolescents could get into trouble in their rooms by consuming pornography or participating in clandestine sex acts with their peers. The teen bedroom inspired anxiety among many Americans because it supposedly encouraged the consumption of drugs, alcohol, and forbidden forms of popular culture, while also serving as a stage upon which depression, suicidal behavior, and other psychiatric maladies could be expressed. A closed door—particularly one with a lock on it—was often seen as a potential threat to the well-being of both teenagers and the family unit as a whole.

Ultimately, *Get Out of My Room!* offers us ways in which to understand how the rise of teen bedroom culture affected (and was affected by) some of the seismic shifts that have taken place in American culture over the previous two hundred–plus years. For instance, it takes no great leap of logic to suggest that giving teens greater autonomy in their rooms was related to significant changes in the parent-child relationship. The autonomous teen bedroom represents a serious attack on traditional parenting ideas—particularly, older strategies that emphasized strict surveillance and unbending deference to parental authority. Indeed, it might be useful to regard the autonomous teen bedroom as a spatial expression of how the stern, patriarchal approaches to parenting that dominated before the American Revolution eventually gave way to more egalitarian strategies.[7] The autonomous teen bedroom fits nicely into this narrative because it not only represented a clear-cut victory for advocates of liberal parenting strategies (these types of sleeping arrangements could not have come about when corporal punishment, rigid surveillance, and elder worship were the norm); it also acted as a lightning rod for advocates of traditional parenting methods who felt that the family unit was being threatened by selfishness and rampant individualism. The teen bedroom, in short, served as a venue in which progressive and conservative ideas on child-rearing could do battle on a regular basis.

We also see in the rise of teen bedroom culture a reminder that even the most egalitarian parenting strategies are capable of accommodating parental power. Although it is often marketed as a means of providing children on the cusp of adulthood with greater freedom and independence, the autonomous teen bedroom offers parents a subtle yet effective form of surveillance. To borrow a phrase or two from Michel Foucault, the teen bedroom should be best understood as "a design of subtle coercion," a means of improving the exercise of parental power by "making it lighter, more rapid, more effective." It is well to remember, after all, that parents are never too far away from their offspring at any given moment, and that parental snooping is possible anytime the child leaves the home for extended periods of time. One could even argue that the autonomous teen bedroom offers nothing more than the illusion of privacy, encouraging a host of teen-friendly experiences while other forms of authority linger nearby.[8]

The emergence of teen bedroom culture also, of course, touches upon prominent issues in the history of housing and domestic architecture. Whereas the average home in the colonial era consisted of two or three heavily populated rooms in which privacy concerns were rarely addressed, modern homes, as architectural historian Christine Hunter points out, often include "separated sleeping areas and places for day and evening activities, so that family members can have some privacy from one another." Single-family dwellings—particularly those owned by middle-class suburbanites—became much more attuned to the needs of the individual during the nineteenth and twentieth centuries, providing occupants with opportunities to escape from the pressures associated with the outside world and the family itself. *Get Out of My Room!* situates the teen bedroom within this larger narrative, suggesting that it was no coincidence that the idea of giving teens rooms of their own emerged at a time when privacy-oriented housing found favor among many affluent families.[9]

Perhaps the most valuable point of reference in explaining the autonomous teen bedroom's place within American culture is Steven Mintz's recent book, *Huck's Raft: A History of American Childhood* (2004). Mintz's study ends with a discussion of child-rearing strategies during the 1970s, an era he characterizes as a struggle between parents who sought to protect children and those who wished to prepare children. The protective parent, Mintz explains, assumed that mothers and fathers should act as safeguards between children and the dangers of the outside world. The prepared parent, by contrast, opted to educate children rather than shield them from the world's many dangers. *Get Out of My Room!* tweaks Mintz's argument by suggesting that ideas on preparing and protecting children were being applied to the teen bedroom as far back as the nineteenth century. On the one hand, protection was promised by offering teens a safe alternative to urban street culture and commercial amusements; on the other hand, the teen bedroom was often conceived as a means of preparing adolescents for adulthood, offering them a space geared toward self-expression and cognitive growth, the development of personal autonomy, and the creation of a stable identity. The teen bedroom, in sum, often embodies the myriad hopes and fears associated with modern child-rearing, providing parents with a space that was expected to both keep children safe from the outside world and simultaneously prepare youth to assume their place in it.[10]

Terminology

Teen, *teenager*, *adolescent*, *youth*, and *child* will be used to describe the people who occupied teen bedrooms during the period under study. My decision to employ such a broad vocabulary is due in part to aesthetic concerns. Given the subject matter of my book, the opportunity to use these words comes up quite often; using just one or two of them exclusively would become overly repetitive and distracting after a while. More important, however, is the fact that there isn't any one phrase specific enough to use with any accuracy. *Youth* and *child* are simply much too vague and are often applied to younger children whose experiences don't fall into my field of view. Similarly, *teen* and *teenager* are much too specific, encompassing all children between the ages of thirteen and nineteen, while neglecting those who are slightly older and slightly younger. The term *adolescent*, meanwhile, is problematic because the people who use it most—psychologists, anthropologists, and other social scientists—have been unable to decide on when it begins or ends. Jean Piaget and Barbel Inhelder, for example, suggested in the late 1950s that the adolescent phase begins with the development of advanced reasoning skills and logic, regardless of the teen's physical age, while others have suggested that adolescence corresponds roughly with the onset of puberty—a stage in the life cycle that has no firm beginning or end.[11]

Nonetheless, I recognize that my own inability to settle on a single term that describes the people who sit at the center of my research does not give me license to abandon boundaries altogether. Even as I stand firm in my decision to use a variety of words and phrases that describe adolescents and the adolescent stage, I have decided to limit my research to the bedrooms of children between the ages of ten and twenty who lived exclusively in the family home (college dorms will not be examined). Though I'm mindful of the subtle and not-so-subtle differences between a ten-year-old and a twenty-year-old, the adolescent stage merits a rather flexible approach that will allow me to take into account stages of the life cycle—preadolescence and early adulthood—that bump up against the so-called adolescent stage and acknowledge that adolescence has been subject to numerous revisions since G. Stanley Hall first popularized the concept in the early 1900s. Boundaries must be drawn, but they should be drawn in a manner that recognizes the amorphous nature of adolescence. To quote Helen Flanders Dunbar, a prominent child-rearing expert after the Second World War: "Teenage is not a boundary, nor is it a demarcation line that parents sitting on the sideline can watch a child step across. It is a zone. It is like dusk or dawn. Everyone knows when it is day or night but no one can tell for certain when, exactly where, day turns into evening or night turns into day."[12]

ONE

A Little Wholesome Neglect

No man prefers to sleep two in a bed. In fact, you would a good deal rather not sleep with your own brother. I don't know how it is, but people like to be private when they are sleeping. HERMAN MELVILLE, *MOBY DICK* (1851)

In 1868 Anna Stanton, a thirty-six-year-old woman from Indiana, took on a teaching assignment four miles outside of Le Mars, Iowa, a sparsely settled prairie town that was in dire need of qualified educators. As was customary at the time, a portion of Stanton's $2.50 weekly salary went to a family who offered her room and board for the length of her teaching assignment. Though Stanton was thankful for her hosts' generosity, the house she stayed in offered little in the way of privacy. "Size of house 16 x 18, all one room," she wrote in her autobiography. "The single brother has his bed on his side of the house, the married brother on his side. For me a cot was made and it was so near the cookstove I could put my hand on it. It took a great deal of maneuvering to get in and out of bed." Stanton was similarly troubled by the fact that her hosts often took in travelers. "On one occasion," she explained, "a family stopped, spread their bedding on the floor for six or eight, did their cooking on the stove, and next morning were up early, ate their breakfast and started on. I did not hear a word of complaint from either side." For Stanton, who had presided over a room of her own as a child, the cramped living arrangements produced a certain amount of discomfort and unease. "They were good, pure minded people and I got along very well," she noted, "but to those used to their own private room it was a little hard to reconcile."[1]

Though one might expect frontier homes to be somewhat lacking in terms of personal privacy, housing in more established parts of the country was similarly cramped. Many urban-dwelling Americans—particularly those from large and/or poor families—shared beds and bedrooms with siblings, parents, and even total strangers. John Gough, a British-born temperance advocate who came to America as a ten-year-old, recalled sharing a bed with a gravely ill man after moving in to a New York City boardinghouse in 1831. "To my surprise," he recalled in his autobiography, "I found, when the hour of rest approached, that I was to share a bed with an Irishman, who was lying very sick of a fever and ague. The poor fellow told me his little history; and I experienced the truth of the saying, that 'Poverty makes us acquainted with strange bedfellows.'" These stories continued to flourish after the Civil War, when America's urban centers grew at an unprecedented rate. Famed novelist Upton Sinclair, for instance, recalled sharing a bedroom with his parents in Baltimore during the 1870s and 1880s. "We never had but one room at a time," Sinclair wrote in his memoirs, "and I slept on a sofa or crossways at the foot of my parents' bed." Though Sinclair was bothered by the fact that most of the dwellings he and his parents occupied were run down and teeming with bedbugs, he admitted that sharing a bedroom with his parents caused him "no discomfort," all things considered.[2]

For many nineteenth-century Americans, then, home life was often characterized by a lack of privacy, by a measure of proximity among blood relatives, acquaintances, and strangers that contemporary Americans might find off-putting. Some Americans, however, made a concerted attempt to buck this trend, as a select group of middle-class, urban-dwelling families ushered in a privacy-oriented approach to housing that shaped teen bedroom culture in a wide-ranging manner. As the teen bedroom was just one space among many expected to act as a refuge from both the outside world and other family members, its earliest expressions were part of a larger process in which, to quote two prominent twentieth-century architects, the "forced togetherness" of early American homes was replaced by an approach emphasizing privacy and "voluntary communality." Though one would be hard pressed to argue that the nineteenth century witnessed the creation of a fully formed teen bedroom culture, the bedrooms Americans are familiar with nowadays certainly had their origins during this period, offering youngsters a space within the home that stressed, among other things, character building, intellectual growth, spiritual awareness, and personal responsibility.[3]

Socioeconomic Change during the Antebellum Era

In order to best understand the emergence of teen bedroom culture, one must examine the extent to which economic changes during the early nineteenth century altered both basic family structures and the layout of the average middle-class home. The economy during the antebellum era became less agrarian in nature as commercial and industrial capitalism began to transform American society in a far-reaching manner. The urban middle-class families who benefited most from these socioeconomic transformations tended to differentiate themselves from their rural/working-class counterparts by placing much greater emphasis on personal privacy in the home. Dubbed the "isolated household" by historian Dolores Hayden, this new approach to housing became a prominent feature of middle-class identity during the Victorian era, acting as a bellwether for the health and success of the family as a whole. A successful family, after all, was expected to live in a detached or semidetached home with enough square footage to accommodate the privacy demands of parents and children alike, while cramped tenements, boardinghouses, and other dwellings associated with the poor were to be avoided at all costs. The isolated household was considered superior because it created a buffer against the outside world, offering its occupants a means of nourishing their individuality in, as architectural historian Clifford Clark describes them, a host of "separate but interdependent spaces." For affluent Americans who could afford to embrace this ideal, togetherness was to be a matter of choice rather than an imposition.[4]

Of course, the privacy demands associated with the isolated household could not have been met without a steep decline in family size. In 1800 the typical American mother could expect to give birth to an average of 7.0 children in her lifetime; by 1900, however, that number had dipped to 3.6. In a span of a hundred years, then, the birthrate was essentially cut in half, meaning that parents often had fewer children to consider when determining basic living arrangements. Lower birthrates became the norm among middle-class families in particular, due to the decline of the family economy and the transformation of children into consumers rather than producers of wealth. The costs of raising children, in short, began to far outweigh their economic benefits. Although rural and working-class families often found themselves at odds with this particular mode of living due to their continued reliance on child labor, the growing prevalence of small, tight-knit nuclear families played a significant role in bringing about the emergence of the autonomous teen bedroom because the custom of combining siblings in beds and bedrooms became less necessary as family size shrank. The decision to provide children with rooms of their own was a matter of simple arithmetic, as a family of four or five was much more capable of living up to this ideal than a family of eight or nine.[5]

As with nurseries, playrooms, and other child-oriented spaces during the Victorian era, the teen bedroom was shaped by Americans' ever-changing views on childhood and child-rearing. The privacy offered by separate sleeping quarters was thought to have a beneficial effect on the basic character of youth—a notion that first found expression in the early nineteenth century with the emergence of sheltered childhood, an approach to child-rearing that used segregation within the home as a means of creating firm distinctions between the lived experiences of adults and children. Characterized by a particularly romantic view of children, the sheltered childhood ideal emphasized educational goals, leisure, and the innate goodness of children. Whereas earlier generations of parents tended to regard children as miniature adults who were expected to work and form a family at a relatively young age, this new approach prolonged the period of childish dependency by limiting a child's interaction with the adult world. Indeed, by the latter decades of the nineteenth century, the sheltered childhood ideal was so prevalent among affluent families that it was often used as a centerpiece in the fight against child labor. The average middle-class child, to adopt the parlance of sociologist Viviana Zelizer, was expected to be "economically useless" yet "emotionally priceless," a beloved creature with distinct needs and interests whom parents were obliged to protect from some of the less palatable aspects of the adult world.[6]

The sheltered childhood ideal complemented the emergence of the isolated household in several ways. For starters, both concepts were premised on the idea that a certain amount of privacy was beneficial to one's health and well-being. The inward-looking nuclear family, for example, was often regarded as the best means of shielding family members from the chaos and uncertainty of the outside world, with the home itself acting as a physical embodiment of the average family's attempts to create clearly delineated boundaries between the private and public spheres. The sheltered childhood ideal, meanwhile, projected these distinctions into the realm of child-rearing. The decision to prolong the educational process and keep children at home for a longer period of time was based on the idea—popularized by John Locke and Jean Jacques Rousseau—that children were cheerful innocents who needed to be kept apart from the adult world, lest it corrupt their character or dull their spirit. This growing emphasis on generational separation would have a profound effect on the emergence of teen bedroom culture during the antebellum era. For instance, the desire to accommodate privacy demands within the home helped establish an environment in which the teen bedroom, as both an idea and a concrete entity, could flourish. Indeed, the early teen bedroom should be seen as the isolated household in microcosm, a means of reinforcing the uniqueness of children—and securing some much-needed privacy for parents—by, in effect, separating the generations for extended periods of time.[7]

The separate bedroom ideal first emerged during the early 1800s, proving somewhat popular among smaller, affluent families from the towns and cities of the Northeast. That the first instances of teen bedroom culture should emerge in New York or Massachusetts rather than South Carolina or Mississippi is not particularly surprising. Economically speaking, the northern states were simply better suited to accommodate these types of living arrangements. The southern economy was largely agrarian in nature and had not yet produced a powerful urban bourgeoisie that could sustain these types of living arrangements; its economy and culture had not yet been commandeered by the very people who tended to embrace the idea of privatized homes and separate bedrooms for children. The Northeast was also better suited to experiment with privacy-oriented living arrangements due to the simple fact that the educational options available to children there were much more extensive than in the South. Between 1838 and 1853 every northern state established a common school system, thus ensuring that children had access to schooling that was free of charge and (theoretically) nonsectarian. By contrast, the states that would eventually rally around the Confederate flag did not establish common school systems of their own until long after the Civil War had drawn to a close. This is important to note because teen bedrooms, as we will see below, were often defined by the extent to which they encouraged scholarly excellence and intellectual growth.[8]

Climate also played an important role in nurturing the growth of teen bedroom culture in the northern states during the early 1800s. Unlike their fellow countrymen south of the Mason-Dixon line, residents of northern states were often, as Henry Adams would have it, victims of "winter confinement" for months at a time—housebound creatures who endured the cold season knowing that there would be no respite from "daily life in winter gloom." Under these circumstances, young and old alike could be forgiven for placing far greater attention to the various rooms they occupied within the home than, say, their peers in warmer climes. Every room in the house took on greater significance during the winter, especially spaces that were meant to accommodate the boundless energy of youth.[9]

Nonetheless, much of the prescriptive literature that was directed at middle-class families offers us mixed messages insofar as the "own room" concept is concerned. Very few commentators denounced the separate bedroom ideal, but one can't help but notice that these types of living arrangements inspired a certain amount of ambivalence among the chattering classes. Some experts, for instance, were satisfied with merely separating parents and children during hours of rest. In 1819 educator William Mavor claimed that "it is esteemed unwholesome for children to sleep with old persons," adding that "even if two persons of any age sleep together, the bed should be large." This type of advice suggests that providing children with rooms of their own wasn't an especially pressing issue during this time. Experts like Mavor may have taken issue with shared beds and bedrooms, but the purported dangers of these arrangements were not pronounced enough to recommend radical change. Indeed, it is telling to note that the most vocal supporters of the separate bedroom ideal tended to be builders who stood to benefit economically from these types of arrangements and middle-class housing reformers, many of whom were active participants in the housing industry.[10]

One of the most widely read reformers during the antebellum era was O. S. Fowler, an architect whose appreciation for separate bedrooms set him apart from many of his peers. In 1854 he claimed that separate suites could help "promote the development of children" by preventing the transmission of illness—"imbibing anything wrong from other children"—and ensuring that children avoid having "their slumbers disturbed by a restless bed-fellow" or a talkative roommate. Fowler similarly argued that separate bedrooms complemented a host of important middle-class values, including self-reliance, personal responsibility, and an appreciation for private property:

> Where two or three children occupy the same room, neither feel their personal responsibility to keep it in order, and hence grow up habituated to slatternly disorder, whereas, if each had a room "all alone to themselves," they would be emulous to keep it in perfect order, would feel personally responsible for its appearance, would feel ashamed of its disarrangement, would often find themselves alone for writing or meditation, but especially will feel a perfect satisfaction of the home element.

Conservative ideas on domesticity also informed Fowler's advice, as he claimed that separate bedrooms could help young girls "cultivate the housekeeping arts." This was to be accomplished by allowing girls to invite their parents up to their rooms in order to sip tea and "taste her cakes and dainties." Ultimately, Fowler's arguments were based on the notion that separate rooms for children would "contribute immeasurably" to their love of home. "Without it," he added, "it is only their father's home, not theirs. . . . By giving them their own apartment, they themselves become personally identified with it, and hence love to adorn and perfect all parts."[11]

Though Fowler's ideas were not particularly controversial, it would be a mistake to assume that they were broadly accepted within American culture during the antebellum era. It is striking to note, for instance, that *Godey's Lady's Book*, the most popular middle-class magazine of the time, had nothing to say about providing children with rooms of their own, despite offering its readers reams of advice on related aspects of family living. In fact, a case can be made that the "own room" concept failed to take off because communal living arrangements continued to be of value to rich and poor alike. On a practical level, shared beds and bedrooms were useful in colder parts of the country because they kept family members warm in an age before central heating. Perhaps more importantly, shared bedrooms also provided parents with a practical means of keeping an eye on children when traditional surveillance methods were not always effective. In 1831 Lydia Maria Child, an abolitionist and women's rights activist, claimed that young girls should share a room with a "well-principled, amiable elder sister," a "safe and interesting companion" who might act as a "great safeguard to a girl's purity of thought and propriety of behavior." If Child is to be believed, older children were useful in these types of situations because they could act as parental surrogates, ersatz authority figures who ensured that nightly prayers were performed while preventing late-night reading, acts of self-love, and other immoral behavior. Even if an older child desired a room of his or her own, he or she may have been prevented from doing so due to parental demands to stand watch over younger siblings whenever parents were unable to do it themselves.[12]

Of course, many families during the early nineteenth century were also reluctant to abandon shared bedrooms because they simply enjoyed the companionship they afforded. Benjamin Hallowell, a Quaker boy who was born in Pennsylvania in 1799, felt that sharing a bedroom with his ailing grandfather was a comforting experience, noting that he "always felt safe in his presence." Sleeping alone, by contrast, was seen by some Americans as a source of alienation and, at times, terror. Samuel Goodrich found this out firsthand in 1811, when he became an apprentice at a dry goods store in Hartford, Connecticut, shortly after his eighteenth birthday. Wrenched from his family and crippled by religious angst, Samuel "slept in an upper room of a large block of brick buildings, without another human being in them." The prospect of sleeping alone terrified Samuel. "Never have I known the nights so black, so long, so dismal, as during the periods when I awoke from sleep," he noted glumly, "and in the solitude of my chamber, wrestled with the tormenting questions . . . which came like Inquisitors, to put me upon the rack of anxiety and doubt." Though homesickness may have contributed to Goodrich's feelings of despair, one suspects that his anxiety levels would have been much less pronounced had he been sleeping alongside one or more members of his immediate family.[13]

Goodrich wasn't alone in thinking that separate bedrooms left much to be desired. Indeed, writers of children's literature occasionally used the fear of sleeping alone as a prominent plot device. An excellent example of this is Elizabeth Bruce's *Aunt Eleanor's Childhood Memories* (1863), a best-selling collection of stories about a twelve-year-old girl who, in one vignette, was "compelled one night to sleep in an upper room alone." The story begins with Eleanor, who normally shares a room with her four older sisters, being asked to sleep alone for the evening when one of them became ill. Although Eleanor "begged very hard to be allowed to stay with them," her mother is having none of it. After one last attempt to convince her mother to allow her to sleep on the lounge in the sitting room, Eleanor begins to make her way upstairs shortly after 11:00 p.m. "I put on an appearance of submission," she adds, "and opening the door leading to the staircase, I stepped on the first stair, and closed the door behind me." Instead of going up to her room, however, Eleanor sits on the staircase for more than an hour, mulling the benefits of sleeping near kin. "I was now cut off from the family, by the door," she thinks to herself while shivering in the cold stairwell, "and yet near enough to them to feel that magnetic influence, which gives us a mysterious sense of protection, when we are surrounded by human beings." When she eventually makes her way up to the guest room, Eleanor's anxiety levels rise precipitously. "I laid my hand on the latch, but had not the courage to raise it. Terrible as the darkness of the hall seemed to be, an additional fear seized me at thought of putting another wall between myself and all human aid."[14]

The remainder of the story addresses Eleanor's attempts to fall asleep in her cold and lonely bedroom. Shortly after climbing into bed, she spots a pair of glowing eyes staring blankly at her. Inspired by her mother's advice to "walk bravely up to anything that you see," Eleanor jumps from her bed in order to investigate the ghostly apparition. She eventually concludes that the glowing eyes are nothing more than moonlight shining through two holes in a curtain. Although Bruce's story has an instructive purpose, offering its young readers a lesson about facing and overcoming one's fears—Eleanor eventually pledges to "never again be the slave to such weakness, and fears, as I had shown that night"—it also illustrates

There were two bright eyes right opposite me looking directly into my own. Page 21.

Figure 1 A sketch from *Aunt Eleanor's Childhood Memories* explains why many nineteenth-century children were not always so eager to sleep alone at night. E. M. Bruce, *Aunt Eleanor's Childhood Memories* (Boston: R. A. Ballou, 1866), inset.

how separate sleeping quarters continued to be seen as a source of dread. Sharing a bed or a bedroom may not have been the best option in terms of securing reasonable amounts of privacy and personal autonomy, but these types of arrangements seemed to have provided a measure of emotional comfort that separate sleeping quarters simply couldn't provide.[15]

The comforts associated with sleeping with others might help explain why, in some instances, spare bedrooms stood empty for extended periods of time. Benjamin Hallowell, for example, slept alongside his grandfather, despite the fact that his family had a guest bedroom that was rarely ever used during his preteen and teen years. In fact, the only time he recalled using the guest room was when he was eleven years old and he arranged a sleepover with a friend. "It was delightful to me," Hallowell explained; "he was the first guest I had ever had. We were put to sleep in the guest chamber, over grandfather's room, and enjoyed it greatly." In many cases, moreover, the excess space required to provide children with rooms of their own was often claimed by parents. In his autobiography, *The Bark Covered House* (1876), William Nowlin pointed out that his father built an addition on to their home in Dearborn, Michigan, during the 1830s. Although William shared both a bed and a bedroom with his little brother, his father decided that the new addition would be used as a sitting room for William's mother. "In one corner stood a bed surrounded by curtains as white as snow; this mother called her spare-day bed," Nowlin recalled. "Two chests and a few chairs completed the furniture of this room; it was mother's sitting room and parlor." In Nowlin's childhood home, then, excess space was subjected to a strict hierarchy in which parental needs took precedent over the needs of children.[16]

Firsthand Accounts

Although most families adopted shared sleeping arrangements in their homes during the first half of the nineteenth century, diaries and memoirs provide us with evidence that a growing number of youngsters were able to secure rooms of their own. Perhaps the earliest example of this phenomenon comes courtesy of Sarah Connell Ayer, a resident of Newburyport, Massachusetts. Born in 1791, Ayer, an only child, began keeping a diary in 1805 when she was fourteen years old. The entries from her teen years reveal that her bedroom fostered numerous creative and intellectual pursuits, providing her with a space to read and write poetry and engage in various forms of self-reflection. "It has been a wet, disagreeable day," an entry from Sunday, June 18, 1809 reads. "I have set in my chamber, writing and reading alternately. After tea, I felt in rather a contemplative mood, and retiring to my room, I indulged in a long series of reflections. They were not of the most pleasant kind, but they soothed my heart." On Sunday, April 22, 1810, Ayer decided to forgo her literary activities altogether, opting instead to simply meditate. "I have risen early, my heart calm, and unruffled," she declared, "and retired to my little bed-room to enjoy an hour of serious meditation." Though Ayer didn't explain what the focus of her meditation was, all signs point to boy trouble. A mere two days after engaging in "serious meditation" in her room, Ayer expressed concern that a prospective suitor had not written to her. "I retired to my little dark bed room, and my reflections were none of the most pleasant. Has A. . . . forgotten me? Has absence obliterated all those sentiments of affection he once so warmly professed for me?" Though Ayer enjoyed a warm relationship with both of her parents, perhaps the walls of her bedroom and the pages of her diary were more likely to hear of her experiences with unrequited love than were her mother or father. Ayer's room seems to have had a therapeutic value that cannot be underestimated.[17]

Mary Gove Nichols, a free-love and women's rights advocate, also wrote extensively about the bedroom she occupied while growing up in Vermont during the 1820s. Though the Nichols family was large by today's standards, featuring six children from two marriages, Mary was given the opportunity to preside over a room of her own due to several deaths in the family and the fact that her siblings no longer lived in the family home when Nichols entered into adolescence. Her autobiographical novel, *Mary Lyndon, or Revelations of a Life* (1855), reveals that her experience with early teen bedroom culture was much darker than Ayer's. Whereas Ayer occasionally relished the prospect of spending time alone in her room, Nichols—though admitting that "it is well" to "set ourselves apart for use"—felt that "neither man, woman, nor angel can live alone." Complicating matters somewhat was the fact that Nichols had isolation thrust upon her by a recurring illness and a mother who placed intense emphasis on the dominant culture's views on domesticity. "All my work was done in confinement," Mary explained. "My mother abhorred romping, and was never satisfied unless little girls were miniature women. I was constantly ill from want of exercise, want of sympathy, and want of all things healthful for my body and spirit." A gloomy and self-conscious girl, Nichols often associated her room with sadness. She not only "awoke in tears" for several months after moving into their new house, but she also used her bedroom to sidestep her mother's ban on unnecessary expressions of sadness after her Italian greyhound, Carlo, was poisoned by a neighbor. "Night was precious to me," she explained, "for then I could weep."[18]

Nichols's room shouldn't be characterized solely as a site of misery, though. Unable to enjoy the out of doors with her friends, Mary managed to experience the many splendors of nature inside her bedroom. At one point she owned a pet crow named Scipio, who introduced himself by bringing her a metal cup as she stood in her bedroom window. He returned often to Mary's windowsill in the coming weeks, whereupon she would reward him with a penny or some "bright buttons." Mary also captured a pheasant that ended up sleeping in her room for a brief spell. "If, weary or ill, I lay down upon the bed," she noted, "unlike any bird I ever saw before or since, he would nestle beside me, and remain while I slept." Unfortunately, Mary's bedroom menagerie was eventually shut down when her pheasant was killed by a rooster, thus providing the young girl with yet another opportunity to return to her gloomy ways. "My bright-winged angel was gone," she lamented. "I buried him under a rose bush, and the roses seemed a fit inscription for his tomb. I thought then that every creature I loved must die in some dreadful way."[19]

One of the most expansive accounts of early teen bedroom culture can be found in the journals of Elizabeth Payson, a young girl from Maine who would eventually become a popular novelist and hymn writer. Born in 1818, Elizabeth was the fifth of eight children, the daughter of Edward Payson, an eminent Congregationalist pastor. Elizabeth's experiences were similar to Nichols's in that they were shaped in large part by family tragedy, as six of her siblings did not make it past infancy. Unlike Nichols, however, Elizabeth found much joy in her bedroom because it offered her a quiet place to indulge her love of reading. "I have not been down in season once this week," she explained in an entry from April 25, 1831. "I have persuaded mother to let me read some of Scott's novels, and have sat up late and been sleepy in the morning." According to an entry dated February 21, 1834, Elizabeth's late-night reading habits only intensified as she grew older. "I was getting to dislike all other books," Elizabeth explained, "and night after night sat up late, devouring everything exciting I could get hold of. One Saturday night I sat up till the clock struck twelve to finish one, and the next morning I was so sleepy that I had to stay at home from church." Although Payson's mother didn't appreciate the late hours her daughter was keeping—especially when it interfered with church attendance—she seemed more concerned with the secular nature of Elizabeth's reading material. To combat this trend, she decided to bribe her daughter with a brand-new reading desk, reminding the young girl that it ought to be used for reading holy texts rather than novels. "A little note, full of love, said it was from mother, and begged me to read and reflect upon a few verses of a tastefully bound copy of the Bible which accompanied it every day of my life." Although Elizabeth didn't know it at the time, her mother's attempts to steer her away from secular literature represents an early attempt by parents to regulate the types of popular culture teenagers enjoyed in the privacy of their own bedrooms.[20]

Payson, as it turns out, seems to have taken her mother's advice seriously, as her bedroom acted as an important site of religious expression, a sacred space in which feelings of jubilation and despair were expressed in equal measure. She wrestled with Kierkegaardian levels of despair throughout much of her youth, expressing confusion as to whether God loved her, whether she loved God, and whether she would ever get into heaven. A diary entry from February 20, 1831, when she was thirteen years old, explains her problems in a typically anguished manner:

> I think God has been very good to me in making me well again, and wish I loved Him better. But, oh, I am not sure I do love Him! I hate to own it to myself, and write it down here, but I will. I do not love to pray. I am always eager to get it over with and out of the way so as to have leisure to enjoy myself. I mean that this is usually so. This morning I cried a good deal while I was on my knees, and felt sorry for my quick temper and all my bad ways.

In February 1834, after years of pondering her spirituality and accepting religious counseling from a local minister named Dr. Cabot, Elizabeth had a conversion experience in her bedroom. "I knelt down to pray," she wrote, "and all my wasted, childish, wicked life came and stared me in the face. I looked at it, and said with tears of joy, 'But He loves me!'" Payson's bedroom in this instance acted as something more than a mere sleeping space; it was a conduit through which at least one middle-class girl could grasp the power and scope of God's love. Although evidence is lacking, one could argue that Payson's bedroom conversion inspired her to write one of the best-known hymns of the nineteenth century, "More Love to Thee, O Christ."[21]

Payson's accounts are also remarkable because they illustrate the extent to which her bedroom played host to behavior that contemporary teens and parents might find achingly familiar. For starters, Elizabeth and her mother often argued about the messy state of her bedroom. In an entry dated February 24, 1834, Elizabeth complained that her mother spoke to her "for the fiftieth time" about her "disorderly habits." Though she failed to note how she responded to her mother's scolding, Elizabeth freely admitted that her room was a mess, claiming that it was the result of "always being in a hurry and a ferment about something." She adds, "I wish I was not so eager and impatient. But I mean to try to keep my room and drawers in order, to please mother." Like many contemporary teens, Payson also used her room as a space in which to address emotional turmoil. For instance, Elizabeth once hid in her bedroom after a relationship with a potential suitor ended abruptly. Her room proved to be an especially valuable place in which to vent her feelings of frustration and wrestle with issues of love and loss, free from the scrutiny of her parents and siblings. "I have shut myself up in my room today to think over things," she remarked in an entry dated January 26, 1834. "The end of it is that I am full of mortification and confusion of face. If I had only had confidence in mother's judgment I should never get entangled in this silly engagement." Although Elizabeth regretted ignoring her mother's advice in this particular instance, there were other times when her mother's attempts to interfere in her personal affairs sent the young girl into self-imposed exile in her room. The most notable example took place in July 1831, when Elizabeth's mother arranged to have Dr. Cabot drop by for a visit in order to discuss the young girl's various spiritual issues. Intent on going to a friend's house when Dr. Cabot arrived, Elizabeth expressed resentment toward her mother for prying into her personal affairs. Her response has been emulated by many a teenager ever since. "I brushed past her," Payson noted, "ran into my room, and locked my door." Thus, even in its earliest manifestations, the teen bedroom was used to keep other members of the family at a safe remove during times of trouble.[22]

Julia Ward Howe, the famous abolitionist leader and author of "The Battle Hymn of the Republic," encountered similar experiences in her bedroom. Born in 1819, Howe was one of seven children, a pious girl who enjoyed significant amounts of personal privacy due to the sheer wealth of the Ward family. Indeed, the Wards were so wealthy that Julia was given access to both a room of her own and a separate suite that was decorated in yellow silk and equipped with a grand piano. Regardless, although the "yellow room" provided Howe with many fond memories (she seemed especially proud of the fact that she could "occupy it at will"), it did not play as significant a role in enlarging her "horizon of thought and faith" as her bedroom did. Like Sarah Connell Ayer and Elizabeth Payson, Julia developed an appreciation for the great works of Western literature in her room, providing her with the opportunity to familiarize herself with Milton's *Paradise Lost* and the collected works of the German poet Matthias Claudius. Given her Protestant background and the religious thrust of her reading material, it should come as no surprise to find that Howe also used her room to wrestle with a host of theological issues. Her experience with *Paradise Lost*, for example, led her to reject the idea of an all-powerful Satan and the "thought of a terrible hell that which till then had formed part of my belief." Described as "a great emancipation for me," Howe's epiphany revealed the extent to which teen bedroom culture complemented the religious fervor that emerged during the Second Great Awakening, granting her the opportunity to reflect upon the basic tenets of Christianity and cultivate a direct and personal relationship with God.[23]

One aspect of early teen bedroom culture that is somewhat difficult to flesh out is determining how the parent-child dynamic helped bring the separate bedroom ideal into being. The many memoirs and diaries that are available from this period, though they help explain what types of activities were taking place in the sleeping quarters of children, offer very little information in terms of determining whether the separate bedroom ideal was a product of parental indulgence or the demands of youth, or a mixture of both. Given the economic dependence of middle-class children during the antebellum era, as well as the somewhat firm hold Victorian parents had over their offspring, it is safe to say that early teen bedroom culture was in large part a top-down process that depended greatly on parental indulgence. However, there is also evidence to suggest that the process wasn't entirely one-sided, that some American youths played an active role in securing rooms of their own. Interestingly enough, the preeminent voice for privacy-starved teens during this period belonged to a young girl who would eventually go on to become one of the best-selling authors of the nineteenth century: Louisa May Alcott.

Well before she wrote her immensely popular novel *Little Women* (1868–69), Louisa May Alcott made it known that she was no longer happy sharing a bedroom with her sisters. According to an early biographer, one of Louisa's "strongest desires" as a young girl "was for a room of her own where she might have the solitude she craved to dream her dreams and work out her fancies." Though Louisa's parents were not opposed to the idea, her requests went unfulfilled due to fact that her father was often jobless, in debt, and thus unable to purchase a large enough home to satisfy his daughter's demands. This didn't stop Louisa from engaging in an intense lobbying campaign, one that was aimed squarely at the young girl's mother. In 1843 Louisa, then ten years old, began dropping hints to her mother, emphasizing the extent to which a separate suite could encourage several creative and intellectual endeavors. "Dearest mother," one of her more passive-aggressive missives began, "I have tried to be more contented, and I think I have been more so. I have been thinking about my little room, which I suppose I never shall have. I should want to be there about all the time, and I should go there and sing and think." By all accounts an incredibly kind and patient woman, Louisa's mother responded in as gentle a manner as possible. "Patience, dear, will give us content, if nothing else," she wrote. "Be assured the little room you long for will come, if it is necessary to your peace and well-being. Till then try to be happy with the good things you have."[24]

A headstrong and stubborn child, Louisa continued on in this vein for the next three years. She even wrote a poem, entitled "To Mother," which clearly explained how a separate suite was something that could benefit both children *and* parents:[25]

I hope that soon, dear mother,
You and I may be
In the quiet room my fancy
Has so often made for thee,—

The pleasant, sunny chamber,
The cushioned easy-chair,
The book laid for your reading,
The vase of flowers fair;

The desk beside the window
Where the sun shines warm and bright;
And there in ease and quiet
The promised book you write;

While I sit close beside you,
Content at last to see
That you can rest, dear mother,
And I can cherish thee.

Louisa's efforts eventually paid off in 1846, shortly after her father came into some money and was able to move the family into a more spacious home. Upon learning the news, thirteen-year-old Louisa wrote in her diary that the privacy she gained would encourage all manner of creative expression and personal growth. "I have at last got the little room I have wanted so long, and am very happy about it," she stated triumphantly. "It does me good to be alone, and mother has made it very pretty and neat for me." Alcott concluded her rather jubilant diary entry by noting both the beauty of her new room as well as its proximity to the natural world. "My work-basket and desk are by the window, and my closet is full of dried herbs that smell very nice," she bragged. "The door that opens into the garden will be very pretty in summer, and I can run off to the woods when I like." If Alcott is to be believed, a room of one's own was something more than a mere sleeping space—it was a means of encouraging a measure of personal growth and contentment.[26]

Alcott's new living arrangements seemed to have been the result of three things: her parents' improved finances, their willingness to accommodate their daughter's request, and Louisa's various attempts to convince her mother and father that a separate bedroom could benefit her intellectually. This last point is especially important because Alcott had a strange habit of drawing comparisons between her intellectual capabilities and her immediate physical surroundings, oftentimes conceiving of her own mind as a messy room that needed to be cleaned and maintained. In an extremely telling journal entry from August 1850, Alcott—then seventeen years old—explained that intellectual growth was a matter of simple housekeeping. "I used to imagine my mind a room in confusion, and I was to put it in order," she noted, "so I swept out useless thoughts and dusted foolish fancies away, and furnished it with good resolutions and began again." The problem, of course, was that Louisa often fell behind in her chores. "But cobwebs get in," she confessed. "I'm not a good housekeeper and never get my room in nice order." Alcott's metaphor reinforces two very important features of early teen bedroom culture: it both comments on the bedroom's value as an educational tool and ties it into long-held ideas on domesticity and the proper role of women, both of which retained their strength among supporters of the "own room" concept for much of the next 150 years.[27]

Boys

As the accounts cited above illustrate, early teen bedroom culture seemed to have taken root more so among girls than boys. There is much to be said for this argument, as firsthand accounts of boys' bedrooms are exceedingly rare during the run-up to the Civil War. Although culture-wide fears about male masturbation may have played a role in limiting male participation in the "own room" custom, the public nature of boys' culture should not be ignored either. After all, many nineteenth-century Americans would have agreed with abolitionist Thomas Wentworth Higginson's claim that "the most important portion of a boy's life is perhaps his outdoor training, since to live out of doors is to be forever in some respects a boy." Indeed, in those rare instances when boys' bedrooms do make an appearance in the literature, they are often portrayed as being secondary to the world outside the home. William Foulke, an only child who came of age during the 1850s, was not alone in thinking that the room he presided over while living in Long Branch, New York, simply didn't compare to the pleasures available to him outside the home. "I had a little attic room where I studied and wrote," he noted, "though my life was mostly out of doors, and I recall with delight the bathing, the sailing, the fishing, the picnic in the woods, the clambake by the river, the dance at night in the hotel, the tete-a-tete upon the beach." Foulke certainly appreciated his bedroom, but it didn't capture his imagination to the same extent as did, say, the rooms of Sarah Connell Ayer or Louisa May Alcott. Foulke and his boyhood chums were expected to broaden their vistas well removed from the corridors and private suites of the Victorian home.[28]

Similarly, boys' bedrooms were often regarded as transitory spaces—as mere gateways to the outside world. Born in Connecticut in 1840, A. D. Rockwell, an early innovator in the development of the electric chair, was not alone in admitting that he "loved to play, to tramp the fields and woods, and to fish the streams." On a few occasions, Rockwell and his cousin Steve used their love of the great outdoors to run away from home, a playful act of rebellion that was planned out in his attic bedroom. "Our vision of freedom was that of hunters," he explained. "There was an old shotgun in our garret, and we conceived the delectable idea of starting for the wilds, wherever they were, and subsisting mainly on the proceeds of the chase." Rockwell's bedroom was an ideal place to concoct these types of schemes because it allowed him and his cousin to sidestep parental oversight. Unfortunately, the privacy they enjoyed there may have also placed them in grave danger:

> So we burnished up the gun and bought a pound of powder and a quantity of shot. We found an old powderhorn, and in the evening went to my room with a lighted candle, placed it on the soft, well-rounded feather bed—about as insecure a foundation for a candlestick as could well be found—and within a foot of the flame proceeded to fill our powderhorn. Could any boy do more senseless thing than this? It is a wonder that we were not both blown up, and that we were not is strong evidence of a special Providence that protects the weak, foolish, and ignorant.

As with so many grand plans concocted during the heady days of youth, Rockwell's sojourn began with a test of nerves and ended in failure. By the time the boys embarked on their midnight adventure, the weather had taken a turn for the worse, forcing Rockwell and his cousin to return home. Nonetheless, Rockwell's aborted quest sheds light on the dangers that can arise whenever youngsters are granted too much privacy in their rooms—an aspect of teen bedroom culture that continues to vex contemporary observers.[29]

One of the more humorous anecdotes regarding boys' rooms involves David Ripley, a young southerner who was born in New Orleans in the early 1830s. Tellingly, the details of David's room were brought to light by his younger sister Eliza, who noted that David began keeping a bust of Queen Victoria on the shelf in his bedroom during the 1840s. She claimed in her memoirs that David's unusual trinket was "idealized beyond all reason or recognition," despite the fact that the United States had twice warred with Britain in the previous sixty years. Suffice it to say that David's taste in décor wasn't the result of any Anglophilic tendencies; rather, the bust served as a fantasy object, owing to the fact that it resembled a girl he liked. "He adored it," Eliza argued, "because he saw a resemblance to beautiful Emma Shields," a "noted beauty" who lived in their neighborhood. However, shortly after Emma got married and "dropped suddenly out of sight," David's bust was mysteriously broken when "an accidental flourish of a feather duster knocked Queen Victoria off the shelf." A symbol of heartbreak and lost love, David's trinket illustrates how the early teen bedroom may have been as influenced by the sexual fantasies of its occupant as the Internet-equipped rooms that prevail nowadays. Erotic material certainly took on different forms back then, but in an age before photographic technology became ubiquitous, David's bust of Queen Victoria may have been used as a masturbatory aid, acting as an antebellum equivalent of the Farrah Fawcett posters that popped up on the walls of numerous teen bedrooms during the 1970s and 1980s.[30]

Despite the lack of male representation in early accounts of teen bedroom culture, there is little doubt that some boys were unhappy with shared bedrooms. John Allen Wood, for example, used his burgeoning interest in evangelical Christianity to criticize the custom of sharing a bedroom with others. Born in Fishkill, New York, in 1828, Wood underwent a powerful conversion experience when he was quite young. "I was led to see myself a sinner and gave my heart to the Savior at ten years of age," Wood recalled in his autobiography, "the first in my father's family." He soon found out, however, that forging a personal relationship with Christ was difficult while surrounded by ten brothers and two sisters, many of whom failed to appreciate their brother's newfound religiosity. Making matters worse was the fact that Wood was the eldest child, which meant that he had no hope of ever inheriting a room of his own. Since his daily devotions required some degree of privacy, Wood decided to improvise. "To get away from my brothers and sisters, who annoyed me in my devotions," Wood declared, "I made the barn my closet of prayer." Although Wood didn't sleep in his newfound devotional space, his decision to commandeer a no-doubt filthy barn in order to attend to his spiritual needs suggests that boys were just as eager as their female counterparts to enjoy the privacy and autonomy that shared bedrooms fail to provide. The demand for separate bedrooms was there, but demographic and economic factors excluded boys like Wood from taking part in this custom.[31]

John Braly used similarly ingenious means to carve out a space of his own while growing up in California during the 1850s. Braly—who would later go on to become one of the wealthiest real estate developers in Los Angeles—was forced to share a room with his brothers throughout much of his childhood, an arrangement that supposedly hindered his studies. As he explained in his autobiography, "I labored under the adverse condition of having no suitable place to study, no quiet or private room away from the rest of the family." Braly refused to be deterred, and his subsequent course of action lends credence to the old adage about necessity being the mother of all invention. In the summer of 1854, when he was nineteen years old, Braly built a room of his own in an affordable yet labor-intensive manner: "I took down a deserted squatter's shanty, some miles away, hauled it home and built a studio for myself." If his autobiography is to be believed, Braly's efforts seemed to have paid off handsomely, as he claimed that his new room worked wonders for his intellectual development. "After this I made better progress," Braly recalled, "developing with every effort a greater thirst for knowledge—a craving which so grew upon me that at last I prevailed upon father and mother to allow me a few years in an Eastern college." Braly's improvised study space was thus invested with great significance, acting as an important contributor to a brand of intellectual growth that, under different circumstances, may have been nurtured in a bedroom rather than an abandoned shanty that had once housed transients.[32]

Continuity and Change after the Civil War

Teen bedroom culture after the Civil War was marked by both the continued strength of antebellum ideas and the transformative socioeconomic changes associated with the Gilded Age. The persistence of antebellum norms is illustrated by noting that support for separate bedrooms in the prescriptive literature remained somewhat lukewarm after Lee surrendered to Grant. Unlike the nursery (a space within the home that was deemed "a necessity" and "a blessing in disguise" by many late nineteenth-century child-rearing experts), the teen bedroom received only sporadic attention from those who claimed expertise on such matters. Indeed, the most popular child-rearing tract of the nineteenth century, L. Emmett Holt's

The Care and Feeding of Children (1894), offered little in the way of support for the "own room" concept, as Holt suggested that sleeping alone was only necessary when "symptoms of serious illness" arrive—when it became necessary, in other words, to prevent other family members from being exposed to various transmittable diseases.[33]

Nonetheless, the value of separate bedrooms continued to find support among a select group of observers. In 1877, for instance, housekeeping expert Phyllis Browne claimed it a "splendid thing" to give children "a room all to themselves," using ideas associated with the sheltered childhood ideal to support her claims. Though Browne acknowledged that parents "should not choose a room with an open fire or a window that opened upon the leads for their delectation," she also pointed out that attics and other spaces that were "far away from the haunts of the family" were preferable. Creating a space in which children could "shout, and jump, and run to their heart's content" was also thought to be beneficial, Browne argued, because "healthy romping saves many a doctor's bill." The appeal of this type of advice is obvious; after all, what forward-thinking parent could find fault with a custom that assured the physical and emotional well-being of children without undermining the financial security of the family as a whole?[34]

Rigid ideas on gender also continued to shape teen bedroom culture after the Civil War. In February 1893, for instance, a writer for the *Mother's Nursery Guide* claimed that "every girl over seven years old should have her own little bedroom, wherever that is possible." Boys, meanwhile, were to be given access to other spaces in or around the home that could encourage the development of various occupational skills. "Boys, if they have any taste for mechanics," the writer argued, "should be allowed some corner of the house, basement, or outhouse, for a workshop; and should also be provided with carpenter's tools and material to work on." The author buttressed her arguments by reminding readers that taking a keen interest in one's bedroom could protect young girls from the purported violence and squalor associated with modern cities. Described as "little sanctum[s] of their very own to which they may retire," separate rooms for girls were expected to keep them safe from "runaway horses, rabid or vicious dogs, [and] wicked or insane men or women [who] may attack or kidnap or otherwise injure them." These types of arguments were meant to strike a nerve among white, middle-class Anglo-Saxons, many of whom feared the growth of cities and the foreign-born people who often flocked there looking for work. The separate bedroom ideal may not have been a product of nativist sentiment per se, but its supporters were not above using xenophobic arguments to spread the gospel.[35]

While some experts used fears associated with city living to win support for the "own room" concept, others focused on winning over well-to-do farmers. In fact, birthrates in agricultural communities in the North and the Midwest declined to such an extent after the Civil War that more and more farm families were able to take part in the "own room" custom. Progressive farm magazines picked up on this trend during the 1870s and 1880s, arguing that separate bedrooms helped minimize sibling conflict, inspired a greater appreciation of family, and kept children out of trouble. Though many farm families in the South and the West were still unable to live up to this ideal, the fact that these ideas were now being directed at a demographic that had long been excluded from the discourse suggests that teen bedroom culture was starting to broaden its base beyond the urban middle-class milieu that had initially embraced it. The appeal of teen bedroom culture was still quite limited during the latter parts of the Victorian era, but it doesn't require a particularly keen eye to notice that change was most certainly afoot.[36]

Firsthand accounts, meanwhile, suggest that the most important feature of the "own room" was its role in educating youth. During the 1880s, for instance, Annie Cooper, a fifteen-year-old from Sag Harbor, New York, believed that the privacy and introspection she enjoyed in her own bedroom was an integral part of her intellectual and moral development. "Oh! How I love my room," she exclaimed in a diary entry from January 1885, "this room in which I am now writing, it is a great comfort and a great blessing. If it were not for the refuge of my room, I fear I should not ever be able to be good, or think of serious things." Theodore Roosevelt made similar claims in his memoirs. Born in 1858 to one of the most wealthy and powerful families in the state of New York, Roosevelt spent much of his childhood and adolescence in bed, his sleeping quarters acting as a sickroom whenever his asthma flared up. "One of my memories is of my father walking up and down the room with me in his arms at night when I was a very small person," he recalled in his autobiography, "and of sitting up in bed gasping, with my father and mother trying to help me." Although Roosevelt admitted that he didn't gravitate toward too many great works of literature, he often read books on natural history and the occasional dime novel in his room. His parents, of course, approved of his interest in natural history, but the dime novels were another matter altogether. Roosevelt, it seems, used the privacy of his bedroom to read *Under Two Flags* (1867), an adventure story by novelist Maria Louise Ramé (pen name Ouida) that shocked the English-speaking world—including Roosevelt's parents—due to the homoerotic relationship between its main character and his servant.[37]

In some ways, Roosevelt's experiences with teen bedroom culture mirrored those of Mary Gove Nichols's during the 1820s, as his various illnesses kept him from enjoying the outside world in anything but a cursory manner. To compensate, Roosevelt brought the wonders of nature indoors, transforming his bedroom into a storage facility for all sorts of specimens from the world of nature. The future president's collection began when a local butcher gave him a seal skull. It underwent further expansion with the help of two of his cousins, both of whom brought back specimens that stoked the young boy's love of zoology, a field of study that had been energized in Teddy's time due to the discoveries of Charles Darwin. Roosevelt's room eventually housed so many specimens—including live mice, live squirrels, and several stuffed birds—that it was dubbed the "Roosevelt Museum of Natural History" by his family. Teddy's parents, of course, went out of their way to support their son's new hobby, citing its educational value and the positive effects it could have on one's character. "My father and mother encouraged me warmly in this," Roosevelt noted, "as they always did in anything that could give me wholesome pleasure or help to develop me." Unfortunately, his collection was eventually moved to another part of the house when a servant refused to clean his assortment of dead animals. Roosevelt recalled, "The collections were at first kept in my room, until a rebellion on the part of the chambermaid received the approval of the higher authorities of the household and the collection was moved up to a kind of bookcase in the back hall upstairs." This incident serves as an illustration of how teen bedroom culture during the nineteenth century was still, in many respects, being shaped by parental prerogatives. Teddy's collection of live and dead animals may have been a boon to his education, but ultimately one complaint from a servant was enough to convince his parents that the "Roosevelt Museum of Natural History" needed to find a new home.[38]

Though it would be tempting to argue that the scientific spirit of the late nineteenth century diminished the teen bedroom's value among evangelicals and others with a religious bent, there is simply not enough evidence to support this claim. Scientific authority certainly posed a significant challenge to religious ways of thinking during this time, but the teen bedroom still managed to maintain its reputation as a devotional space. In 1900, for instance, Harlow Gale, a Yale University–educated psychologist, reflected on how the privacy afforded to him in his bedroom as a fourteen-year-old was valuable in cultivating a lifelong relationship with Christ. Born in 1862 to affluent parents in Minneapolis, Minnesota, Gale claimed that his room put him at ease whenever he felt the urge to unburden himself to God. "How vividly my little bedroom still remains," he explained, "where I poured out my hyper-secret emotions in prayer and with unspeakable comfort. For thus I could unbosom my holy of holies as to no living person." One gets the impression that Gale's room acted as a Protestant version of the Roman Catholic confessional, a private space in which he could confess his sins without using a priest as an intermediary. Like the rooms enjoyed by Elizabeth Payson and Julia Ward Howe decades earlier, Gale's sleeping quarters offered him something that the latest scientific theory could not: a direct line of communication with God.[39]

Although spiritual matters didn't play a particularly prominent role in Mary Ellen Chase's early encounters with teen bedroom culture, her attempts to secure a room of her own act as a reminder that many middle-class families were still not that eager to abandon shared sleeping arrangements as the twentieth century neared. Born in Maine in 1887, Chase was the daughter of a classically trained school teacher and a prominent lawyer. In her autobiography, *The White Gate* (1954), Chase claimed that the bedroom she shared with two of her sisters during the first few years of her life was not unlike many other children's rooms at the time: cramped, impersonal, and shaped by practical concerns. "A bedroom in my childhood was a place to sleep in, not to escape or to enjoy," she argued. "It was not even a place to dress or undress in except in spring and summer; and the notion that it might hold other gifts for children than that of mere sleep would have astonished my parents." In 1897, shortly after her tenth birthday, Mary Ellen's father decided to turn a room that had previously been used for storing firewood into a sewing room for her mother, a decision the young girl later described as "the hour of my ultimate salvation."[40]

Unfortunately for Mary Ellen, the refurbished room sat unoccupied for nearly two years; her mother rarely used it for sewing, while her older sister was reluctant to assume ownership of it because—and this is worth noting—she did not want "to sleep so far away from folks." Sensing that an opportunity was slipping away, Mary Ellen, like Louisa May Alcott some fifty years earlier, worked up the courage to ask her parents if she might claim the room as her own. Her parents' response illustrates just how alien the concept of separate bedrooms was to many middle-class families:

> That they were stunned by my request is an understatement. My mother in particular was overcome, not alone by my question, I feel sure, but also by her genuine concern as what might conceivably be wrong with me. That a presumably normal and in no way unusual child of hers should of her own free will desire not only a room by herself, but one far away from the companionship and security of the family, was to her both incredible and alarming, and she at once asked me if I had completely lost my senses.

Mary Ellen's request was met with shock and dismay not because her parents feared having their authority challenged or were worried that she might use the increased privacy to get into trouble; rather, they were taken aback by the idea that she would want to create significant distance between her and the rest of the family. The request was considered odd because her parents saw great benefit in sharing a bed or a bedroom with loved ones and were reluctant, as a result, to consider alternate arrangements.[41]

Nonetheless, after much deliberation, Mary Ellen's parents allowed her to assume control of her mother's rarely used sewing room. The transition was not exactly smooth, though. Accustomed to sharing both a bed and a room for the first twelve years of her life, she admitted that the prospect of sleeping alone made her feel "beset by fears." Her bed looked "small and cold," while the location of her bedroom windows caused her to think that "anyone of a marauding nature might peer or even step" into her room. Though there were moments when she was tempted "to return, chastened and grateful, to the security of confusion and a double bed," Mary Ellen eventually decided that she was too proud to give up her space. Luckily for her, the acclimatization process was sped up with a little help from her father, who made a point of providing her with a key to her room. The key was "something more than just the means of locking a door," Mary Ellen noted, but rather a symbol of ownership, independence, and freedom.[42]

Her anxiety would continue for several weeks after the move, but Mary Ellen's spirits were eventually lifted by the knowledge that the bedroom was hers and hers alone, and that the distancing effects of her new room were merely products of her own fertile imagination:

> And when I at last knew that I must blow out the friendly lamp and snuggle beneath my covers, my hand happily brushed the wall behind my bed. The wall was warm. I suddenly realized that it was the back wall of our kitchen, which after all was near at hand and in which there would always be red circles of light around the black covers of the Rising Sub, and, in winter, the flame of our lantern on the table.

In summarizing her situation in such a sentimental manner, Mary Ellen helped reinforce the notion that personal privacy could benefit the family in many ways. Regrettably, her memoirs have little to say about what she actually did in her room in subsequent years, but she did count herself as a firm supporter of the separate bedroom ideal well into old age. "Among the many evidences of understanding shown by modern young parents in bringing up their children," she explained in 1954, "none is more wise than the allotment to a child, whenever possible, of a room of his own."[43]

Mary Ellen's views, though novel in her own time, would become more prevalent in subsequent decades due in part to the numerous socioeconomic changes that swept across American society during the Gilded Age. Home ownership rates, for example, rose substantially among both middle-class and select working-class families during this time. In 1850 approximately 26 percent of American homes were owner occupied; by 1900 home ownership rates rose to an all-time high of 36.5 percent. The expansion of the middle classes and the emergence of newer, more efficient construction techniques helped push home ownership rates higher, especially in America's ever-expanding suburbs. Though privacy was not unheard of in, say, a boardinghouse or an apartment, detached and semidetached suburban homes were thought to be better at meeting familial privacy demands due to their more spacious floor plans and larger lot sizes. Indeed, by century's end, the average middle-class suburban home was particularly well suited to solitude and introspection, featuring, as historian Gwendolyn Wright argues, separate bedrooms for children and parents and numerous "places for children to hide and for friends to visit."[44]

The Gilded Age also witnessed a steep decline in the number of nonblood relatives who took up space in the average American home. During much of the nineteenth century, working-class and middle-class families often took in boarders as a means of securing additional income for the family. Employers appreciated this practice because its family-oriented structure—which involved taking meals, doing chores, and socializing with the host family—was thought to ensure access to a disciplined pool of workers. During the final decades of the nineteenth century, however, boarding began to be supplanted by lodging, a new approach that was centered around the family home, but featured greater distance between tenant and host. Unlike boarders, lodgers ate their meals and engaged in leisure activities in restaurants, cafés, and bars, assuming a much less prominent place within the household of the family that hosted them. By the 1920s the split between tenant and host widened even further, as most lodgers began expressing a preference for rooming houses and apartments rather than private homes—a trend that was applauded by both workers and middle-class reformers who railed against the purported negative effects of sharing family space with strangers. Similarly, the practice of hiring live-in servants also went into steep decline during this time, as middle- and upper-class families increasingly opted to hire day workers who worked set hours and lived off-site. By the 1930s it was rare to see domestic servants living in the same dwelling as their employers—thereby freeing up even more space within the home. Suffice it to say that the growing popularity of teen bedrooms can be at least partly attributed to the fact that fewer people were taking up valuable space in the average American home.[45]

The impact of technological innovation on teen bedroom culture cannot be underestimated either. As child-rearing expert Mary Blake pointed out in 1883, the "own room" concept was difficult to accommodate because parents were required to "set apart and warm" peripheral areas of the home. The emergence of electricity and central heat, however, ensured that family members no longer had to spend much of their waking hours in the one or two rooms that had heat and power; parents and children could now detach themselves from communal areas of the home, resulting in a much more decentralized, privacy-oriented approach to leisure. Technological innovation also opened up additional space within the home by allowing rooms that had once been used for storage to be reconfigured for other functions. The best example of this is the basement, a dark and musty space that was often used during the eighteenth and nineteenth centuries for storing foodstuffs and fuel. The development of oil furnaces and more efficient forms of refrigeration changed all that by minimizing the basement's food-storage function and by doing away with the coal bins and firewood piles that ate up space in many a nineteenth-century cellar. Of course, it goes without saying that access to these technologies continued to be restricted by geography and class, as affluent families in urban and suburban areas of the Northeast and the Midwest were in a much better position, financially speaking, to embrace these technologies. Many working-class neighborhoods, after all, were forced to postpone the installation of power and telephone lines because families simply could not handle the increased property taxes that were necessary to offset installation costs. However, when these types of technological change eventually did find their way into less affluent neighborhoods during the early decades of the twentieth century, the separate bedroom ideal became much more feasible for even families of modest means.[46]

* * *

The earliest manifestations of teen bedroom culture were shaped in large part by the people who were excluded from taking part in this custom. The experiences of Lucy Larcom, the mill girl whose poetry shed light on working conditions in the Massachusetts textile industry during the 1830s and 1840s, nicely illustrate how economic concerns often quashed many teens' hopes of having rooms of their own. Lucy was the product of a large working-class family, one of ten children whose father died when she was eight years old. And yet, despite her impoverished background, she was ideologically suited to appreciate the benefits of separate bedrooms. For example, Lucy bought into the idea that spending time away from other family members was an important part of growing up, referring to the occasional flight from parental oversight as "a little wholesome neglect." She also characterized her bedroom as a venue for self-improvement, a space in which her creative drives could be nourished. Unable to afford hiring the services of a professional art teacher—"the cost of instruction would have been beyond my family means"—Lucy found inspiration instead on the panes of glass in her bedroom window. "Jack Frost was my most inspiring teacher," she explained. "His sketches on the bedroom window-pane in cold mornings were my ideal studies of Swiss scenery, crags and peaks and chalets and fir trees." Nonetheless, Lucy's experiences with teen bedroom culture were fitful at best, as her garden and "riverside playground" offered her much more privacy than her cramped bedroom ever could. If anything, the young mill girl's experiences remind us that the autonomous teen bedroom would become normative only when a more diverse array of teenagers were welcomed into the fold. Leading the charge to democratize the separate bedroom ideal were the various child development experts who emerged from the social scientific revolution of the late nineteenth and early twentieth centuries. These people will be the subject of our next chapter.[47]

TWO

A Site of Developmental Significance

What sort of place have you given him to live, to sleep and to think in? It may affect his destiny no matter whether it is the right kind of room or the wrong.
MOTHER'S MAGAZINE (1917)

By the latter decades of the nineteenth century, the feminized, God-infused versions of the teen bedroom began to give way to something quite different. Buoyed by a culture-wide embrace of scientific authority, medical professionals and social scientists took it upon themselves to reenvision the teen bedroom as a developmental tool, an integral part of the maturation process that parents simply could not ignore. Although these new forms of expertise often reinforced the biases of its middle-class creators and ignored how this custom played out in real life, they also played a decisive role in democratizing teen bedroom culture by encouraging families from all points on the socioeconomic spectrum to consider embracing the "own room" concept. Providing an adolescent child with a room of his or her own was thus transformed into something more than a bourgeois rite of passage, an expression of affluence among the urban middle classes; it was seen by child development experts as a means of producing rational, autonomous citizens who were well equipped to uphold the nation's liberal democratic traditions.

As many observers were quick to point out, however, this new approach was not without its fair share of problems. Many child development experts openly acknowledged that social class would continue to limit the teen bedroom's popularity to affluent families. Poorer families were better incorporated into discussions of teen bedroom culture, but their inclusion was often presented in such a way as to stigmatize their own ideas on child-rearing. If child development experts could agree that the autonomous teen bedroom aided the maturation process, it stands to reason that its absence posed a serious challenge to proper development—a phenomenon that affected larger, poorer families more so than their smaller, affluent counterparts. Some experts, moreover, expressed concern that the autonomy and privacy afforded to teens in their bedrooms would end up interfering with parents' ability to assert and maintain their authority within the home. Pronounced fin-de-siècle fears over masturbation, in particular, ensured that the teen bedroom would continue to be defined by a somewhat parent-centric approach, as supporters of the separate bedroom ideal found that scientific ways of thinking could not necessarily overcome the various social and cultural reservations that had prevented a more fully realized brand of teen bedroom culture from emerging during the nineteenth century.

It is also worth noting that these new ways of thinking continued to reinforce ideas that had dominated debates on teen bedroom culture throughout much of the nineteenth century. Teen bedrooms may have been regarded in a more scientific manner during the first half of the twentieth century, but few would argue that this new version was all that different, developmentally speaking, from the versions that arose in the previous century. Indeed, the bedrooms teens occupied during both eras were expected to achieve similar results: producing young adults who were well versed in the benefits of self-reliance, property ownership, personal autonomy, intellectual growth, love of home and family, and self-expression. In many respects, then, one could argue that child development experts were simply offering old wine in new bottles, as the religious arguments of the nineteenth century were replaced by scientific claims—very few of which were actually based on any amount of concrete evidence.[1]

* * *

One of the most striking aspects of the debates that arose among child development experts during the first few decades of the twentieth century was how quickly a consensus formed around the idea of providing adolescents with rooms of their own. In fact, using the word *debate* in this context is a bit misleading; though many child-rearing gurus were slow to address the supposed benefits of separate bedrooms, those who did offer an opinion tended to speak of them in overwhelmingly positive terms. On one level, this may have been the result of the child development community's socioeconomic status, a reminder that educated Americans probably supported these types of arrangements out of loyalty to their own middle-class backgrounds. What is most astounding about this phenomenon, however, is that many of the experts who agreed on the value of separate sleeping quarters formed their views within an intellectual environment in which consensus of any type was quite rare. Early child development experts couldn't agree on whether nature or nurture played the biggest role in development, much less determine the beginning and end points of adolescence. And yet a slew of experts from a variety of theoretical backgrounds found much to recommend in the idea of providing children with rooms of their own. Their reasons for supporting the separate bedroom ideal weren't always the same, but prominent psychoanalysts, behaviorists, and other child development experts agreed that it was something from which children from all walks of life could potentially benefit.

One of the earliest child development experts to address this issue was G. Stanley Hall, the acclaimed founder of the child study movement. Unfortunately, Hall's views on the matter were somewhat muted and contradictory. There is no doubt that he was in favor of providing adolescents with rooms of their own, but unlike many of the child development experts who followed him, Hall didn't seem particularly eager to abandon shared accommodations altogether. In *Adolescence* (1904), Hall adopted a pragmatic approach by pointing out that a separate bed would suffice if a separate bedroom could not be arranged. In other contexts, however, Hall's support for separate bedrooms was a bit more enthusiastic. His dual role as educator and child psychologist, for instance, led him to conclude that adolescents in both private homes and boarding schools could benefit from having access to well-designed, private sleeping quarters. Moreover, despite his overly masculinist views on adolescent development, Hall believed that both boys *and* girls could benefit from these types of arrangements.[2]

In many respects, Hall's views on the matter were shaped by traditional views on child-rearing that emphasized parental authority rather than the specific needs and demands of children. Hall had one foot in the nineteenth century and another in the twentieth, oftentimes regarding the teen bedroom as a predominantly parent-centric area of the home, a space in which teen liberties should be accommodated yet circumscribed. Although adolescents were expected to have a measure of privacy in their rooms, parents were encouraged to establish their authority there in ways that child development experts during the 1920s and 1930s would deem excessive. Hall believed that almost every feature of the teen bedroom should be decided by parents, including the firmness of his or her mattress, the type of bedding to be used, the room temperature, as well as the sleep schedule adolescents were to abide by. Most telling, though, were his ideas on how the bedroom's proximity to the master suite could fortify a somewhat forceful brand of parental surveillance. "Each should have at least a bed, if not a room to himself," he explained, "but it should not be too remote and not too secluded from adult observation." To do otherwise, he argued, risked encouraging a host of unsavory activities, including, most notably, self-love. Indeed, Hall's calls for cold rooms, light bedding, and avenues of surveillance can best be understood as an attempt to aid parents in eliminating the masturbatory habits of American teens, as his reluctance to abandon shared sleeping arrangements was undoubtedly a by-product of his belief that parental oversight could prevent teens from acting on their base instincts. Sleeping in the same bed or bedroom with other siblings might not discourage masturbatory acts altogether, but sleeping alongside an additional set of eyes might just act as a strong deterrent.[3]

Hall, of course, was not alone in believing that separate bedrooms afforded adolescents too much of an opportunity to engage in self-love. Louis Starr, a general practitioner from Philadelphia and an admirer of Hall, made similar claims in *The Adolescent Period* (1915). Perhaps the most conservative of the experts cited here, Starr felt that teens deserved rooms of their own, but not at the expense of parental authority and surveillance demands. "Living and sleeping rooms should be well ventilated and never over-heated," he argued, echoing Hall's suggestions. "Each child should have his or her own bed and, if possible, a separate bed-room not far removed from the watchful eyes of the mother or other really responsible person." Starr even urged parents to abandon the age-old practice of sending children to bed as punishment and, in extreme cases, insisted that parents insert themselves (or a surrogate) into their offspring's bedrooms while they slept, paying particular attention to "the child's hand and body movements" during the early-morning hours and right before bedtime. In the rare instance that the adolescent managed to masturbate in an unconscious state, Starr suggested "careful watching of the child throughout the night by a trained nurse who must take the hands from beneath the bed coverings when they are approached to the parts and check any suspicious movements of the legs or body." Such an approach, he continued, should be employed "for several weeks and must not be relaxed until sometime after all suspicious actions have ceased. It has proved very successful in my own experience."[4]

Masturbation issues aside, Hall's views on the teen bedroom were also problematic due to the fact that he rarely discussed the teen bedroom in strictly developmental terms. In both *Adolescence* (1904) and *Youth* (1907), Hall suggested that boarding school students be given rooms of their own not because this would encourage cognitive growth or help adolescents establish an identity free from parental authority, but because this could reaffirm cherished middle-class values, including property ownership, self-expression, and gentility. "Each student," he argued, "should have three rooms, for bath, sleep, and study, respectively, and be responsible for their care, with every encouragement for expressing individual tastes, but with an all-dominant idea of simplicity, convenience, refinement, and elegance, without luxury." In short, Hall's views on the teen bedroom may have been affected more by his upbringing and social status than by his various ideas on child development. It is worth noting, after all, that Hall was very much a part of the same Protestant, middle-class milieu that had been touting separate bedrooms during much of the nineteenth century. Like many of his peers in the child development profession, he may have been predisposed to support these types of arrangements because they were already a somewhat common feature of modern bourgeois living.[5]

While Hall rarely couched his support for teen bedrooms in a particularly theoretical context, many of his views on the maturation process complemented the separate bedroom ideal in interesting ways. For example, his great emphasis on "storm and stress" helped legitimize the idea that adolescence was marked by a rupture in the parent-child relationship. Hall often argued that it was normal for familial obligations to play second fiddle to the egotism and scheming of youth during the adolescent stage. "It is the time for large views and plans," he exclaimed in the first volume of *Adolescence*. "Life problems now press upon him; ambition and self-affirmation are never of such high selective value. His ego must be magnified and all in the new environment subordinated to it." Similarly, Hall suggested that intrusive, heavy-handed parenting methods be minimized during the adolescent stage in favor of more flexible strategies. Hall wasn't a supporter of permissive parenting strategies by any stretch of the imagination—his views on masturbation attest to that—but he did acknowledge that parents shouldn't expect to play as prevalent a role in the lives of their children as they did during earlier stages of the life cycle. "The time comes when parents are often shocked at the lack of respect suddenly shown by the child," he claimed. "They have ceased to be the highest ideals. The period of habituating morality and making it habitual is ceasing; and the passion to realize freedom, to act on personal experience, and to keep a private conscience is in order." As historian Leslie Paris puts it, Hall believed that adolescents, particularly boys, should "pull away" from adult society in order to better their chances of becoming a productive part of it—a process that the bedroom seemed particularly well suited to accommodate.[6]

Unfortunately, Hall's belief in recapitulation theory—the long since discredited idea that the development of individuals mirrors the development of the species as a whole—meant that there was very little parents could do to forgo adolescent withdrawal. The child's newfound "overassertion of individuality" was not really a conscious choice, he argued, but rather a lingering by-product of our primitive past: "This is germane to a state of nature, when the child no longer needs the parental protection but, in primitive life and warm countries, breaks away and shifts for himself." Breaking away from parental oversight was thus seen as a predictable, if not entirely unavoidable, expression of the maturation process, and one that parents would be wise to encourage rather than retard. "Parents still think of their offspring as mere children, and tighten the rein when they should loosen it," he claimed in 1907. "Many young people feel that they have the best of homes and yet that they will go crazy if they must remain in them."[7]

Given his overriding fears of masturbation, it is surprising to note Hall's belief that privacy was an integral part of the maturation process. "Aloneness," as two contemporary psychologists describe it, was always a defining feature of Hall's basic outlook on child development, one that would retain its popularity long after other aspects of his theories were deemed irrelevant by subsequent generations of child-rearing experts. Young people, Hall maintained, need solitude in order to establish a unique identity of their own and counteract the pressures of both the peer group and the family. "Normally this is the social age where friendships, interests, and sympathies with others ought to be at their strongest and best," he explained in 1907, "but many a normal youth is shy, solitary, bashful, and inclines to withdraw from the world and nourish his individuality in isolation." Solitary pursuits were common among youth due to "disappointed hunger for praise, wounded vanity, the reaction from over-assertion, or the nursings of some high ideals," allowing teens to regroup in the face of adversity while providing a playground of sorts for abstract thought and future strivings. These "solitary moods," Hall intoned in his memoirs, advanced the developmental process by allowing adolescents to "come to terms, not only with the great problems of the world but to understand and size himself up as to his fitness for the various departments of the world's work." For whatever reason, though, Hall declined to incorporate these ideas into his discussions of sleeping arrangements, despite the fact that the teen bedroom was a seemingly ideal space to enjoy the benefits of privacy.[8]

Though Hall may have been reluctant to connect his support of separate bedrooms with broader child development issues, many of his peers were more than willing to explore this terrain in the years leading up to and including the First World War. In 1912 James Kirtley, a Chicago-area preacher and follower of Hall, raved about the developmental possibilities of the separate bedroom, claiming that "the virtues of self-dependence, self-control, responsibility for one's own belongings, companionship, imagination, originality and cooperation will have been nurtured in that room." Similar arguments were directed toward farm families as well. In 1913 William McKeever, a professor of philosophy at Kansas State Agricultural College, encouraged rural parents to give their sons and daughters "a good room of their own," a space that could impart to their children the "beauty" of home life and provide them with "inner strength" and a "new endowment of power to go on with life's struggle and master the larger problems that come to [them]." Five years later, in 1918, Norman Richardson—yet another Hall-inspired man of the cloth—suggested that separate bedrooms encouraged cognitive growth and helped adolescents develop their own unique personalities by ostensibly freeing them from parental interference. "Here is another argument for giving the adolescent youth a room of his own," Richardson averred. "He needs a sanctuary, he needs a place to be by himself where he can think out his long, long thoughts. He needs a chance to get out of the influence of his gang and even of his parents, so that he may become a personality."[9]

These types of ideas became commonplace during the 1920s, as the wariness evinced by G. Stanley Hall and Louis Starr was replaced by a more optimistic, child-centered approach, one that reflected the sweeping changes taking place in the way child-rearing experts approached the issue of masturbation. In Hall's day, masturbation was treated as an excuse for parents to maintain a firm presence within their children's bedrooms. Though unsupervised adolescents were bound to produce a certain amount of anxiety among many parents, fears over masturbation acted as a flash point in determining who had ultimate authority over a child's personal space; so long as self-love was equated with degeneracy, the teen bedroom would continue to necessitate relatively high levels of parental oversight. However, once child development experts began to accept masturbation as a relatively harmless activity during the 1920s and 1930s, the way was paved for a much more liberal approach to teen space. Indeed, Hall and Starr may have represented the last generation of experts to argue that the problem of masturbation could be addressed by invading the privacy of adolescents. Future commentators would certainly pay a fair share of attention to the average teen's autoerotic behavior, but very few suggested addressing the problem by employing explicit forms of surveillance inside his or her bedroom.[10]

Support for a more child-centered version of the teen bedroom was also aided by the growing popularity of child-rearing strategies that emphasized freeing adolescents from parental control. Of particular importance was the emergence of "psychological weaning," a variation on Hall's storm-and-stress model in which generational separation came to be seen as integral to the formation of a unique and healthy identity. In 1920 Frederick Tracy, an ethicist and theologian from the University of Toronto, pointed out that the weaning process was most likely to manifest itself in resistance to the school curriculum, as adolescents begin to equate the demands of their teachers with those of their parents. "He is stronger than he was in childhood, and loves to assert his strength and show his independence," he argued, "and so, on the surface, he appears less reverential toward authority." Frankwood E. Williams, a follower of Sigmund Freud and one of the leading lights in the mental hygiene movement during the 1920s, even went so far as to claim that parents should expect to see their children come home drunk, their bones broken, the family car smashed to bits in their attempts to break free from parental influence: "So absolutely fundamental and vital is this emancipation that it were far better that we have smashed cars and broken bones and even alcohol on breaths—particularly in view of the adolescent circumstances under which these adolescents have alcohol upon their breaths—than that this boy should fail in the objective toward which he is directed." On the home front, meanwhile, Williams pointed to the use of coarse language and an "increasing intolerance of other children, particularly the younger children in the family," as common features of the weaning process.[11]

In responding to these types of behavioral changes, parents were encouraged to subtly disengage from their children—to give them space. Mothers and fathers were expected to stand on the sidelines like lifeguards at a public beach, ensuring, as one expert proclaimed in 1921, "that the hard-pressed soul does not get off the track or utterly run down." Parents were to become mentors to their teens, friendly figures who eschewed intrusive, authoritarian parenting methods in favor of a more companionate approach. As historian Kathleen Jones convincingly argues, child development experts essentially "turned parental feelings of impotency and loss of authority into a virtue." Lip service was still being paid to parental needs, but ultimately the tide was starting to shift in a decidedly child-centered direction. Leading this charge were two increasingly influential schools of thought: Watsonian behaviorism and Freud-inspired psychoanalysis.[12]

Founded by the University of Chicago's John Watson in 1913, the behaviorist approach was predicated on the idea that a child's behavior is shaped more by external stimuli than by introspection and other subjective processes. Behaviorists, as a result, placed special emphasis on how parents interacted with their children and how these interactions shaped the child's behavior. More often than not, this translated into a generally dim view of parents, as Watson and his followers believed that children were being put at risk by excessive amounts of parental indulgence. Mothers, in particular, were singled out for criticism due to their purported love of coddling and other forms of affection that supposedly interfered with the child's ability to become self-reliant. "The extent to which you devote time to petting and coddling," Watson warned young mothers in 1928, "and I have seen almost all of a child's waking hours devoted to it, just to that extent do you rob the child of the time which he should be devoting to the manipulation of his universe, acquiring a technique with fingers, hands, and arms." Something as benign as attending to a crying child, kissing them, or even bidding them goodnight was thought to result in poor developmental outcomes, including "years of Stygian darkness and fear" during the adolescent phase. A properly raised child, Watson argued, was a master of adapting to his or her environment, someone "who never cries unless actually struck by a pin, who loses himself in work and play, who quickly learns to overcome the small difficulties in his environment without running to mother, father, nurse or other adult." Watson even toyed with the idea of raising children completely separate from the rest of the family. "It is a serious question in my mind," he mused, "whether there should be individual homes for children—or even whether children should know their own parents. There are undoubtedly much more scientific ways of bringing up children which will probably mean finer and happier children."[13]

Perhaps not surprisingly, the behaviorist model often featured some rather withering attacks on parental authority. Two of the most strident voices in this respect belonged to Sidney Schwab and Borden Veeder, professors of clinical neurology and clinical pediatrics at Washington University's medical school. Whereas most child development experts suggested a simple revision of the parent-child relationship during adolescence, Schwab and Veeder practically declared war on the family, stopping just short of suggesting its total abolition. They argued that the family posed a significant threat to the weaning process by exposing adolescents to authoritarian ways of thinking, as parental control and state repression were regarded as being two sides of the same coin. "It is through the family that the adolescent sees the state and it is from the family that he vaguely interprets it," they argued.

"They are almost identical and his first experience in control, in the forces of tyrannical conduct, injustice, and punishment is through the power of the family." Though the authors freely admitted that this was a rather "warlike" interpretation of the maturation process, they also suggested that it was an appropriate one because the family, as a "rigid and unyielding obstacle" to adolescent development, was the "handiest structure of opposition" and a primary "objective for attack." The typical adolescent, they declared, was "a kind of prisoner, shut in and closed about by his environment." If Schwab and Veeder are to be believed, then, teenagers had no choice but to distance themselves from their family and its oppressive designs.[14]

Though Sigmund Freud and his followers were unable to match Watsonian behaviorists in their general hostility toward the family unit, the psychoanalytic project nonetheless helped validate some of the more parent-averse child-rearing strategies of the 1920s and beyond. Freud's basic worldview, after all, was premised on the belief that "the liberation of an individual, as he grows up, from the authority of his parents is one of the most necessary though one of the most painful results brought about by the course of his development." This process was "essential," Freud noted in 1909, because "everyone who has reached a normal state" will have broken free from parental dictates at some point in their lives. This process was not the result of atavistic pressures or environmental conditions, but was instead a by-product of something much more quotidian: pubertal change. Puberty was thought to profoundly alter the parent-child relationship by supplementing older forms of affection with, as Freud described it, a powerful "sensual current." Adolescents' attempts to separate themselves from the family was necessary, then, because this endeavor reflected a very real need among youth to direct their newfound sexual energies to an appropriate partner outside the family circle. If oedipal ties remained unchanged during adolescence, Freud and his followers argued, the incest taboo was in grave danger of being violated, which would in turn lead to the development of neuroses.[15]

Much of the psychoanalytic project was thus focused on freeing individuals from various forms of familial authority. As historian Eli Zaretsky suggests, psychoanalysis emphasized a process of "defamiliarization, the freeing of individuals from unconscious images of authority rooted in the family." Although Freud's emphasis on personal liberation would undergo several revisions during the twentieth century, its various manifestations were almost always predicated on the idea that individual growth was at risk of being stunted by parental overreach. During the 1920s, for instance, psychoanalysts tended to focus on the negative effects of maternal dependence, which gave rise to fears of "momism" during the years following the Second World War. By the 1960s, moreover, New Left writers such as Herbert Marcuse and Norman O. Brown similarly offered a "utopian reading of Freud" that "rejected the suffocating conformity of the family." In a passage that could very well be used to describe the teen bedroom itself, Zaretsky suggests that Freud and his followers basically urged their audiences to "leave behind their 'families'—the archaic images of early childhood—not to preach but to develop more genuine, that is, more personal relations."[16]

Perhaps not surprisingly, calls for adolescent privacy became much more sustained during the age of Watson and Freud. At times, the child development community's special emphasis on solitude took on an almost spiritual dimension, as the solitary adolescent was frequently portrayed as an enigmatic visionary in pursuit of some divine truth—a teenage version of Nietzsche's Zarathustra, who bides his time in a mountain cave before descending to the forest below in order to teach mankind all that he has learned. "Things come to have for him a sense of mystery," Ralph Pringle, an instructor at the Illinois State Normal University, proclaimed in 1922. "Sometimes he seems to exhibit the traits of the poet, sometimes those of the genius." Ella Lymon Cabot, a prominent social reformer and educator in Boston during the 1920s, expressed her appreciation of youthful solitude in terms that fans of New England transcendentalism could surely appreciate. "Adolescence is often driven into silent, deserted places," she explained in 1921. "The woods, the stars, and the firelight may be closer confidants than any human being." Cabot reinforced her claims by suggesting that solitude helped push her toward a career in writing. "In the years when my soul was most alone, most foolishly self-conscious, most veiled and blocked by reserve," she wistfully exclaimed, "I found in the pastures and under the stars, space that freed me from myself; companions that encircled my loneliness; peace to think, and a dawning, happy impulse to write."[17]

During the 1920s, then, child development experts offered a clear and concise message to parents of teens: to be too close to your adolescent—physically or emotionally—was to risk setting them on the road to pathology. Followers of Freud, for example, claimed that families that failed to revise oedipal ties risked producing a generation of emotionally stunted children, a veritable "class of neurotics." The social dangers of thwarting this process were also emphasized, as many Freudians claimed that generational conflict was not only an important contributor to individual growth, but also responsible for "the progress of civilization." The rebellious adolescent who questioned the authority of his or her parents was compared favorably to the Galileos and Darwins of the world, who challenged received truths in order to craft truths of their own. Meanwhile, Leta Hollingworth, a renowned feminist psychologist, pointed to more prosaic concerns, citing "occupational drifting," "matrimonial wrecks," and the creation of a generation of "mamma's boys" as predictable outcomes of unweaned adolescents.[18]

Discussions of the teen bedroom reflected the growing popularity of these parent-averse child-rearing strategies in interesting ways. John Watson, for one, had absolutely no doubts about the value of separate bedrooms, oftentimes suggesting that male and female children of *all* ages deserved to have rooms of their own. "If it can possibly be avoided," he argued in 1928, "never let children sleep together in the same room. Each child should have a separate room. No nurse or other adult should ever sleep in the same room with infant or child." Though he ultimately balked at the idea of creating a separate home in which to raise children, Watson opted for the next best thing—a room of one's own—because he saw it as valuable tool in which to encourage personal autonomy and keep overindulgent parents at bay. With parents out of the picture, he suggested, children would be forced to adapt to their environment on their own terms, thereby increasing the likelihood of engendering a seamless transition into adulthood.[19]

Psychoanalysts, too, offered several parent-averse rationales in support of the separate bedroom ideal. This was particularly evident in the works of Smiley and Margaret Blanton, the former a psychiatrist who studied directly under Freud, the latter a speech pathologist who studied under John Watson before embracing psychoanalysis in the early 1920s. In *Child Guidance* (1927), the Blantons claimed that separate bedrooms helped spatialize the liberation process, creating walls—both literally and figuratively—that parents and children could use to hasten proper identity formation. "In order that the child may have the best opportunity for development," they stated, "it is essential that he have his own living quarters, a room or rooms in which he may spend his sleeping and most of his waking hours. This room may be shared with another child but never with an adult. There are definite advantages not only in having his own room, but also in getting him out of the rooms in which the adults of the family live." The Blantons believed that the process of "defamiliarization" would be played out in the bedroom, offering children an excellent opportunity to gain much-needed autonomy and independence. A site of "physical" and "psychological security" that would help transform the child into an "independent social unit," the child's bedroom was "a den into which the young animal of our species may crawl for freedom and protection from unwanted interferences from the adult in his environment," a "sacred place" in which the child, "for once, is king of all he surveys." Separate bedrooms, the Blantons contended, were nothing less than tools of teen empowerment.[20]

Given the importance of the incest taboo to the psychoanalytic project, it should come as no surprise to find that the Blantons stressed proper sexual hygiene as a reason to give children rooms of their own. Indeed, by removing proximity from the equation, separate bedrooms were seen as a means of facilitating a healthy view of sex among children, one that was both heterosexual in nature and directed away from family members. "There is one absolutely hard and fast rule," the Blantons thundered. "The child should never sleep in the room with his parents after he is a year or a year and a half old, and he should not sleep in the same bed with an adult. He should not sleep with a child of the opposite sex, and it is better that he should not sleep with one of his own sex." To do otherwise, they concluded, would be to encourage "the worst sort of sex hygiene." In many respects, however, the Blantons were merely adding their own considerable authority to an already simmering social issue. The Blantons were just two of many observers during the late nineteenth and early twentieth centuries who saw room sharing, to quote one historian, as "invitations to incest."[21]

Followers of Watson and Freud undoubtedly offered some of the more confident justifications for providing children with rooms of their own during the 1920s, but firm support could also be found among unaffiliated child development experts. In fact, one could argue that the most fervent supporter of the teen bedroom during the 1920s was Leta Hollingworth, a former student of the famed behaviorist E. L. Thorndike. A staunch opponent of Hall's racialized take on adolescent development, Hollingworth made a name for herself during the First World War by refuting the variability hypothesis, the idea that women were inferior to men due to their fixed physical and mental traits. By the 1920s, however, Hollingworth began concentrating her energies on child development, culminating in *The Psychology of the Adolescent* (1928), a groundbreaking work that "replaced G. Stanley Hall's text . . . as the standard in the field."[22]

Despite Hollingworth's refusal to align herself with any particular theoretical perspective, her views on the teen bedroom were similar to those of Watson and the Blantons, as she argued that the teen bedroom was a site of "developmental significance," a privileged space where teens could establish an identity free from parental interference. "Part and parcel of the normal sundering of self from the rest of the world, and especially from the family," she explained, "is the delight of the adolescent in having a room of his own." The bedroom was expected to act as a sanctuary where adolescents could escape from the din of family life and pursue his or her own interests. "Here the developing self is master, can relax from vigilance, can live entrenched," she noted, "and can elaborate peculiar interests and ideas pertaining to decoration, hobbies, and so forth." Families who couldn't afford or were simply unwilling to foster these types of sleeping arrangements were doing their children a disservice by, in effect, hampering "the development of personal autonomy." Though she agreed that "a room may be hygienically shared by two or more children during the years of childhood," Hollingworth claimed that these types of arrangements were particularly dangerous during the adolescent stage due to the arrival of puberty. "It becomes especially desirable at adolescence," she concluded, "that each one have his own room, if possible."[23]

Perhaps suspecting that popular audiences might have a hard time processing some of the more abstract concepts featured in academically oriented child development texts, Hollingworth and her peers made a concerted effort to sell parents on the merits of the teen bedroom by mentioning some of its more practical benefits. Louis Starr, for instance, suggested that the bedroom could be used to help teenage girls deal with menstruation in an orderly manner. They should "rest in bed until the hemorrhage is completely over," he noted. "Subsequently, at least three days should be passed in bed, and two to four more idling about in her room, dressed but most of the time flat on a lounge." Winfield Hall, a professor of physiology at Northwestern University during the 1920s, pointed out that the bedroom could be also used as an exercise space for adolescent boys, but only, he warned, "if the weather is bad." Meanwhile, other experts cited the bedroom's value in attending to emotional matters, treating it as an excellent place in which to vent. Phyllis Blanchard, a follower of Freud, even suggested that teen girls could use their bedroom as a safe place to weep. "Sometimes she seeks the solitude of her room or of some outdoor nook to indulge in the luxury of tears," she argued in 1920, "especially if their flow is simply the result of nervous fatigue and tension."[24]

Parents, too, were told that they had much to gain from these types of arrangements. William Forbush, a juvenile welfare expert from Philadelphia, argued that separate bedrooms could help ease the workloads of mothers by providing children with a space in which they could quietly entertain themselves. "This is a good time also for collections and for quiet hospitality in the children's rooms," Forbush claimed, describing a typical Sunday afternoon in a typical middle-class home. "It will not tire the boys and it will rest their mothers if they form the regular habit of preparing and serving the Sunday evening meal." The Blantons, meanwhile, suggested that separate bedrooms could help minimize parent-child conflict by creating distinct zones in the home where children and adults could go about their daily business without bumping into each other. Citing an anecdote in which a father grew impatient with his daughter for roller-skating on the front porch, the Blantons suggested that this kind of tension and conflict could have been avoided "had the child's domain and the man's domain been clearly defined," adding that "such conflicts will arise when children and adults, with their varied interests and capacities, occupy continuously the same quarters." Separate bedrooms could also help ease the fears of parents who wanted to enjoy some time together without being constantly interrupted by nosy children. This was an especially popular topic of conversation during the 1920s and 1930s, when experts presented recreational sex as a defining feature of the companionate marriage ideal.[25]

One of the most important practical benefits of the teen bedroom, however, was its purported ability to contain the wanderlust of youth. Parents, law enforcement officials, and educators have worried about youngsters roaming around unsupervised in the public realm since at least the mid-1800s. These fears—which intensified with the rise of the automobile and the proliferation of commercial leisure venues—prompted experts and reformers during the early decades of the twentieth century to further stress the importance of playrooms and other spaces in the home that could facilitate more wholesome, domestic activities. "The question of leisure hours is a great problem," Norah March, a prominent eugenicist, wrote in 1919. "Where there is room for it, boys and girls should be encouraged to bring their friends home, and to feel that, in doing so, they have the sympathy and interest of their parents. They will not desire then, to make friends with any of whom their parents would disapprove." William McKeever similarly suggested that rural homes be turned into "social center[s] for the young" so as to both "keep down unbecoming conduct" and stifle the natural youthful desire to go into town. At times, experts resorted to the worst kind of fearmongering in order to scare parents into addressing this problem. H. W. Gibson, a former secretary of the YMCA, cited the story of a boy who ended up in the state reform school for stealing after his fastidious mother refused to let him entertain friends at home. "This is a terrible indictment against house-keeping instead of home-making," Gibson argued, once again singling out mothers as the culprit. "When home becomes more than a house with four walls and a roof, and is a genuine social center, then there will be fewer true tales like this to tell."[26]

These types of arguments placed child development experts in an awkward position. Many of these same experts had given themselves the task of encouraging parents to "let go" of their adolescent children, while a competing discourse warned of the dire consequences of allowing teenagers to escape parental supervision. The teen bedroom, however, may have represented a workable solution to this problem, a means of localizing adolescent leisure pursuits within the home and buttressing parental demands for some form of supervision over their offspring. In *That Boy of Yours* (1912) James Kirtley acknowledged as much when he urged parents to give boys rooms of their own on the grounds that it would encourage more home-oriented activities. "He needs a room of his own—needs it in his business of being a boy," he declared. "If he does not get it at home he always wants to establish headquarters somewhere else on the street corner, or a vacant lot, or in an old deserted house, or in some basement, or in another boy's home; which always lessens his attachment to his own home." William Byron Forbush made similar suggestions in *The Boy Problem in the Home* (1915): "The wise parent works with the 'gang' and not against it. The child may be allowed an almost uninterrupted relationship with his group so long as that relationship is conducted under wholesome conditions. This especially emphasizes the necessity of the young person's having a room of his own." Louis Starr, meanwhile, suggested that separate sleeping quarters could even act as a means of keeping adolescent girls resistant to the lures of prostitution by encouraging "modesty, self-respect, and the natural sense of shame which are the chief fortifications of virtue." Although many of these claims may seem dubious to contemporary observers, these types of arguments probably strengthened the teen bedroom's appeal by convincing parents that it was better to watch the maturation process unfold in the home rather than in front of a saloon keeper or a pimp.[27]

The teen bedroom's containment function was also shaped by longstanding ideas on gender, as experts often emphasized the value of separate bedrooms in bringing order to the social lives of boys rather than girls. Girls, of course, were still prominent figures in the various discussions of teen bedroom culture, but many experts argued that this in itself was a problem that needed to be rectified. Michael O'Shea, a professor of education at the University of Wisconsin, suggested in 1920 that teenage girls had a distinct advantage over boys because parents often went out of their way to "improve the environment of girls so as to keep their thoughts, feelings and conduct wholesome and sweet and refined." The girl always has "the choicest room in the house," he continued, "and the boy must take what is left after everyone else is provided for." James Kirtley similarly chastised parents for relegating male children to the worst room in the house. "His little sister, bless her dear heart, has the daintiest room in the house, and mamma and papa bring her all sorts of exquisite souvenirs and decorations, till she is like a pink rose in a garden of exotics. But he is often put into any kind of a corner, with instructions not to interfere with what little he finds there and not to make any noise, as he goes to his gloomy quarters." To compensate, Kirtley suggested turning the boy's bedroom into a miniature version of an Elks Lodge, "a place to which he can bring his friends, both informally as individuals and formally as a club or gang." The boy's room, the fiery pastor concluded, should be regarded as "a social centre training him for life."[28]

What these arguments amount to is a concerted effort by child-rearing experts to challenge the idea that the teen bedroom was a predominantly feminine space—a necessity for daughters, a mere afterthought for sons. Indeed, many experts during this time went out of their way to de-emphasize the feminine aspects of the teen bedroom, presenting it instead as an excellent space to cultivate a masculine identity. This was especially true in the case of James Kirtley, the man who in many respects became the standard bearer in the struggle to masculinize the bedrooms of American boys. According to Kirtley, the bedroom was especially valuable in preparing male children for work, property accumulation, and citizenship. "He has the proprietary instinct and that cannot be fully gratified without a room he can call his own," Kirtley explained. "The mere possession of that room may be the training that will make him a useful citizen and property holder and keep him from becoming improvident and a vagabond." Boys who were denied rooms of their own were at a distinct disadvantage, he continued, because they were more likely to live a life of want, resulting in a penchant for lawlessness. "The penalty for not having what he can call his own," he argued, "is that he never has anything to give to others, is thriftless, selfish, begging, borrowing and tempted to steal what he would like to have." By acting as a storage space for a boy's many possessions, the bedroom was thus expected to play a rather large role in producing a generation of upstanding, self-assured men. "He cannot take care of his own things unless he has a place for them which is his own," Kirtley concluded. "That is one of the reasons why a boy should have a room, a trunk and all the equipment with which to take care of his things. That is not the only reason he should have a separate room, but that alone is enough."[29]

Kirtley also tried to masculinize the teen bedroom by minimizing its association with interior design and other so-called domestic pursuits. This was accomplished by encouraging mothers to adopt decoration schemes that would appeal to the masculine sensibilities of their sons. "Dainty bed-spreads" were characterized as unnecessary luxuries, while rugs and carpets were to be included only "under strict regulations" because "it is hard to make them harmonize with boys." Instead, mothers were told to decorate their children's rooms with items that reflected accepted notions of masculinity, including athletic equipment, weaponry, and flags. Similarly troubled by the feminine thrust behind most discussions of room décor, William Byron Forbush addressed this issue by focusing on semantics rather than concrete issues of design. "One good plan, especially for winter time," he argued, "is to let the boys 'fix up' their rooms on Sunday. I say 'fix up' rather than 'clean up' for obvious reasons." Though he was loath to explain his choice of phrasing here, it is clear that Forbush sought to downplay the homemaking aspect of room maintenance and re-brand it as a form of home repair. Forbush no doubt agreed with Kirtley's rather forceful assertion that a boy's room "is no parlor, it is a den."[30]

Despite Kirtley's and Forbush's best efforts to masculinize the teen bedroom during the early decades of the twentieth century, the child development community faced an even greater obstacle in addressing the problem of social class. As Leta Hollingworth acknowledged in the late 1920s, separate bedrooms were not feasible for most teenagers because only "well-to-do" families could afford such a setup. John Watson, however, felt that this wasn't necessarily a bad thing because it would somehow lower birthrates among poorer families. "No mother has a right to have a child who cannot give it a room to itself for the first two years of infancy," he argued. "When our homes come to realize that the child has a right to a separate room and adequate psychological care, there will not be nearly so many children born. Not more babies, but better brought up babies will be our slogan." The suggestion here is obvious: the absence of separate bedrooms in the home was a reflection of the worthiness of parents and their ability to raise children properly. While wealthier parents could use the separate bedroom as a sign of affluence and an expression of loyalty to modern parenting ideas, poorer or larger families could not hope to keep up with the Joneses. Though Watson's explicitly classist argument was rarely evoked by his peers in the child development community, his veiled attacks on lower- and working-class families continued to inform discussions of teen bedroom culture during the interwar years and beyond. As historian Peter Stearns notes, many observers felt that shared beds and bedrooms simply "smacked of poverty—a successful family could surely afford more bedrooms, or at least a bunk bed."[31]

Nonetheless, child development experts were quick to offer alternatives that could supposedly encourage autonomy without requiring parents to invest in a new house or costly home renovations. For some experts, this meant simply creating an autonomous space within a preexisting room. "A corner of the family room is better than nothing," James Kirtley argued in 1912, "provided that corner is recognized as his own property at certain important times." "Where a separate room cannot be given to the adolescent," Leta Hollingworth added in 1928, "autonomy may be approximated by assigning at least an 'own' chest of drawers, or a corner of the room, where the self and its belongings are entrenched against the complete invasion of privacy." For best results, however, many experts suggested that entire rooms be appropriated, particularly low traffic spaces where privacy could be easily accommodated. William McKeever, for instance, urged rural mothers to create lightly decorated, inexpensive "attic chambers" for their children, while William Byron Forbush pointed to basements, attics, as well as backyard sheds and shacks as acceptable surrogates.[32]

Though Hollingworth and her peers should be applauded for trying to include poorer and larger families in discussions of teen bedroom culture, their ideas may have stigmatized working-class parents and others who could not embrace the "own room" concept. By placing such an intense emphasis on the supposed benefits of separate sleeping quarters, many of these experts suggested that children who most needed separate bedrooms—poorer adolescents who lived in overcrowded homes—were being denied an important tool in bringing the maturation process to a proper conclusion. Regrettably, the living arrangements of less affluent families were sometimes regarded with pity and condescension. "Unhappily," a child-rearing expert acknowledged at the turn of the century, "arrangements are often such that several children have to occupy sleeping rooms together. The better way, and one which ought to be pursued in every case where possible, is for each child to have a room, however small, to himself." Lost on many child-rearing experts was the fact that much of the advice that was being offered to poorer families was not very practical. After all, many of these alternate designs still required a surplus of household space—including unused sheds, habitable basements, and attics—that many families simply didn't have or couldn't afford.[33]

By the 1930s, of course, these types of issues were no longer restricted to working-class families. Indeed, the Depression years represent an interesting era for both teen bedroom culture and the child development profession as a whole. As Watson's influence waned and Freud's climbed, child-rearing experts continued to place emphasis on freeing teens from parental control. Edmund Conklin, a professor of psychology at Indiana University, suggested in 1935 that it was quite normal for teens to abandon parental guidance—"the day of idolization of parents has passed"—and seek inspiration, instead, from "extra-familial sources," including friends, teachers, and athletes. This type of behavior, he continued, represented nothing more than "a phase of that progressive emancipation from parental domination which is a part of normal adolescent development."

Lawrence Averill, a child guidance expert and follower of Freud, similarly recognized "the psychological necessity for the younger generation to face its problems and make its way without needless parental restrictions," while also encouraging "sympathetic but unobtrusive parental concern and oversight." Meanwhile, Ada Hart Arlitt, a child care expert from the University of Cincinnati, decided to tap into the political temper of the times and associate overzealous parenting with the rise of fascism. "So much are some children dominated," she explained in 1938, "that they even use the words and phrases and imitate the voice of the dominant parent. All of this might be permissible under a dictatorship, but in a democracy all children must be trained to be independent citizens." Parenting, she concluded, should be about creating a healthy citizenry that is both respectful and wary of authority: "Constant checks on behavior generate obstinacy and a general attitude of resistance toward authority which interferes in all directions."[34]

Privacy, too, continued to play a prominent role in child development expertise during the 1930s. Though adolescents were often characterized as being slaves to a herd mentality, Edmund Conklin claimed that that "there is also to be observed the contrasting craving for solitude. Youth has periods of longing to be alone, to be away from people and social activities of every sort, to be alone, to meditate." The spiritual or philosophical implications of privacy continued to have an impact on child development strategies, but oftentimes the typical Depression-era teen was portrayed as nothing more than a moody loner. "He will break engagements without bothering to telephone," Ada Hart Arlitt warned. "If asked where he has been, he will refuse to tell, though he may merely have been taking a walk alone. . . . It is all part of psychological weaning, and this weaning must occur if the adolescent is to become a mature adult." E. DeAlton Partridge, a professor of education at New Jersey State Teacher's College, concurred, suggesting that adolescent withdrawal was "a fairly common method of adjustment," particularly among troubled youngsters "who find competition too keen, or whose parents demand too much, or who are unattractive."[35]

Despite this, the teen bedroom all but disappeared from child development literature during the 1930s. In *Understanding and Guiding the Adolescent Child* (1938), Katherine Whiteside Taylor proved to be one of the few experts still willing to counsel parents on the merits of separate bedrooms. The tone of her advice, however, was hardly persuasive, as she devoted exactly two sentences to this once important topic. "When it is at all possible," she explained, "the adolescent should have a room to himself. His need for privacy is undoubtedly greater than that of younger children." Of course, the disappearance of the teen bedroom in child development literature is fairly easy to explain, as the economic turmoil brought about by the Great Depression rendered these types of living arrangements all the more elusive. In many respects, it would have been considered bad form for child development experts to insist on these types of sleeping arrangements in an age marked by home foreclosures, mass unemployment, and crowded living conditions. As sociologist Ruth Shonle Cavan pointed out in her study of Depression-era Chicago families, parents and children from nearly all backgrounds "saw much more of each other than formerly and found themselves cooped up in a small space. There was little privacy, and friction increased." The Depression, in other words, ensured that separate bedrooms for children of all ages remained low on the list of priorities for many families.[36]

Although child-rearing experts were less likely to champion the "own room" concept during the Depression, it would be a mistake to assume that separate bedrooms disappeared altogether. In fact, there is evidence to suggest that the idea of giving teens rooms of their own had become surprisingly popular. In 1932 members of the White House Conference on Child Health and Protection undertook a study that sought to examine the day-to-day lives of American adolescents. Part of the project addressed the domestic space of teens, featuring a survey in which 7,513 boys and girls from across the country were asked to report on their sleeping arrangements. The study's findings suggested that 32.7 percent of those surveyed claimed to have a room all to themselves. Perhaps not surprisingly, race and ethnicity (and, by extension, class) seems to have played a role in determining which teens were more likely to have rooms of their own. So-called "white" teens, for example, were most likely to enjoy these types of arrangements, as adolescents of German descent (39.9 percent) and white youths in small cities (38.8 percent) and urban centers (36.7 percent) topped the list. Although these numbers reinforce the notion that separate bedrooms were more popular among privileged, urban-dwelling whites, evidence emerged to suggest that the separate bedroom ideal was starting to catch on in communities that hadn't taken part in this custom during the nineteenth century. For instance, an impressive number of urban blacks (32.6 percent), rural whites (31.3 percent), Mexicans (30.1 percent), Russian Jews (29.4 percent), Italians (20.1 percent), and rural blacks (19.4 percent) enjoyed rooms of their own as well. These numbers certainly pale in comparison to those found after the Second World War, but it is important to note that they were tabulated during the worst economic crisis the country had ever seen. It perhaps goes without saying that the percentage of teens with rooms of their own may have been slightly higher had this research been concluded during the boom times of the 1920s.[37]

Regrettably, the White House Conference study is only so useful in terms of measuring the teen bedroom's popularity. It didn't take into account class or gender; nor did its creators bother to explain their methodology. It is hard to assess, for instance, the extent to which poorer families embraced this ideal and nearly impossible to discern whether girls were more likely to have rooms of their own than boys. Regardless, the fact that nearly one-third of the teens in this survey had an "own room" during the 1930s should be seen as a harbinger of things to come, a telling indication of how changes in housing and family life that had originated during the nineteenth century were gaining momentum during the early decades of the twentieth century. Child-rearing experts may not have been able to take sole credit for this trend, but they could rest assured in knowing that they had chosen a winning horse, expressing support for a once exclusive custom that would become normative in subsequent decades. Youngsters such as Margaret Mitchell, the soon-to-be-famous author of *Gone with the Wind* (1936), could take solace in knowing that an army of child development experts agreed with her claim that the teen bedroom should be treated as a "sanctuary," a safe space in which adolescent development could unfold in an orderly manner.[38]

Child development experts may have picked a winning horse, but it is important to ask how well some of their claims hold up to scrutiny. One aspect of their findings that leaves them open to criticism is their inability to produce concrete evidence to back up their claims regarding the so-called developmental benefits of separate bedrooms. Child development texts rarely ever included much in the way of statistical analysis, nor did they offer firsthand accounts from parents or teens. Leta Hollingworth, for instance, claimed to have used hundreds of surveys and questionnaires during the course of researching her seminal book on adolescence, yet at no point did she cite them in order to reinforce her argument that the teen bedroom had become a "site of developmental significance." Child development experts seem to have used scientific authority as a means of reinforcing the separate bedroom ideal, but without actually subjecting their ideas and theories to any amount of scientific rigor or analysis. The consensus that formed among the child development community, in short, represented a leap of faith, a scientifically unfounded belief that separate bedrooms could play a significant role in transforming America's teens into productive citizens.[39]

In many respects, child development expertise provides us with a valuable yet imperfect snapshot of teen bedroom culture during the early twentieth century. There is no doubt that the bedroom had become an incredibly important space among many teens, but its influence on the maturation process and parent-child relations is much more varied and complex than many child development experts would care to admit. Accounts of ragtime star Eubie Blake's bedroom, for instance, suggest that the "own room" concept created just as many problems for parents as it supposedly solved. In 1902 Blake began sneaking out of his bedroom window when he was just fifteen years old in order to play music for the patrons of a notorious Baltimore brothel, earning three dollars a week for his services. "He always stopped by Rabb Walker's pool room on his way home to return the long pants he borrowed for twenty-five cents," a writer from *Ebony Jr.* explained in a 1981 article on the renowned musician. "The rest of the money went into hiding under his bedroom carpet." Unable to spend his earnings due to fears that it would arouse the suspicion of his parents, Blake watched as the "bundle under the carpet kept growing bigger." His secret was eventually revealed soon after he was caught returning home late at night by a God-fearing neighbour. By then, however, the lump under his carpet had swelled to nearly $100—a princely sum that managed to impress even his parents. Although many child development experts suggested that the teen bedroom could be used to contain older children within the home and keep them out of trouble, Blake's experiences suggest that it could hide ill-gotten wealth and allow teens to escape from the family home while their parents slumbered.[40]

One aspect of teen bedroom culture that child development experts were wise to focus on was the extent to which teenagers used their sleeping quarters to address serious personal and emotional turmoil. Though legendary actor Marlon Brando noted in his memoirs that some of his "best memories" of growing up during the 1930s involved gazing at the "moonlight cascading through the window of my bedroom late at night," he acknowledged that the room he presided over as an adolescent played host to some rather dark fantasies, many of which helped him deal with the grief, humiliation, and anger associated with his mother's worsening alcoholism. "For a time in Santa Ana," he remarked, "I had a fantasy that the important people in my life were all dead and were only pretending to be alive. I lay in bed for hours, sweating and looking up at the ceiling, convinced I was the only one in the world who was still alive." At times, however, Brando's behavior skirted the line between harmless venting and serious acts of transgression. In keeping with the somewhat intense public persona he cultivated as an actor during the 1950s and 1960s, Brando engaged in some violent behavior in his bedroom that is difficult to cast in a particularly positive light. "I once knocked down one of my sisters after she came into my bedroom while I was asleep, shook me and told me dinner was ready," he confided. "I was so startled that I got

Figure 2 A recent photo of Ati Gropius's room that illustrates the teen bedroom's value as an educational tool. Ati's study desk was designed by her father, Walter Gropius, one of the founders of the Bauhaus style of architecture. Courtesy of Historic New England.

up, walked across the room and punched her, and was bewildered and contrite afterward."[41]

Firsthand accounts also suggest that child development experts were right to characterize the bedroom as a popular site for teen socializing. Ati Gropius's bedroom during the 1930s, for instance, was designed by her father, famed Bauhaus architect Walter Gropius, with an eye toward accommodating both her educational needs and her penchant for entertaining friends. Though economic considerations kept Walter from indulging Ati's requests for a sand-covered floor and a glass ceiling—both of which apparently reflected the teen girl's interest in stargazing and her love of nature—he made sure to build an exterior spiral staircase that ran directly up to his daughter's balcony. According to Peter Gittleman, an architect and onetime curator of the Gropius house, the wrought-iron exterior staircase was built at the request of Ati, who "asked for a way that her friends might visit without having to meet her parents and the maid." Her parents approved of this arrangement for practical reasons, expressing appreciation that they "wouldn't be disturbed by the children going in and out, and their dirt would be kicked off on the way up and not brought into the house." Not all forms of teen socializing, however, were so wholesome. Famed Hollywood producer Robert Evans was probably not the first—nor the last—teen to have entertained girls in his bedroom. "Whenever my parents left town," he explained, recalling an encounter from the early 1940s, "I would sneak girls into the apartment. My parents were vacationing in Boca Raton, Florida. One night, after spending hours with a girl in my bedroom, she asked if she could borrow a comb, brush, and lipstick. She didn't want to look like a tramp, which she was, walking past the doorman." Although it is difficult to assess how prevalent this type of behavior was, Evans's experiences suggest that child development experts should have focused less attention on the masturbatory habits of teens and greater attention on some of the more social forms of sexual expression that took place in the teen bedroom.[42]

The child development community's willingness to associate the teen bedroom with occupational goals also bore a kernel of truth. If advertisements and popular media accounts are any guide, some teenagers (mainly boys) seem to have used their rooms to learn a host of occupational skills. During the Great Depression, R. W. Francis, a contributor to *Boys' Life*, reported on Cecil Keesling, a sixteen-year-old from California who began publishing scouting-related magazines in his bedroom when he was twelve. Keesling's efforts were presented as a tale of pluck and perseverance, as the first magazine the young boy published "was printed with some old type and a broken-down press a San Jose resident loaned Keesling." Impressed by their son's efforts, Cecil's parents allowed him to turn his room into a publishing house, even though they were kept awake "many a night" due to the constant "grinding noise." Corporate interests, too, took note of this trend and occasionally used it as a selling point for their various products and services. During the Second World War, for instance, General

Electric ran an ad campaign for war bonds in which it was noted that William C. White, an engineer in charge of GE's electronics laboratory, first developed an interest in circuitry in his bedroom after creating "an electric circuit devised to set off fire crackers around the house and yard by pressing a button on his bedroom window sill." A few months later, another GE advertisement discussed Winton Padnode, a plastics researcher whose interest in chemistry took shape "in his bedroom workshop." It would be rash to suggest that these types of stories reveal a firm causal relationship between teen bedroom culture and the occupational goals of children, but they do illustrate the extent to which the teen bedroom hosted an assortment of hobbies and intellectual pursuits, some of which could, on occasion, translate into rewarding careers.[43]

Although one could argue that actress Mary Astor's occupational goals were shaped in her room, many of her experiences call into question some of the child development community's more optimistic assessments of teen bedroom culture. Born in Illinois in 1906, Mary, an only child, was given a room of her own at the age of ten. Though she had been content to while away the time "in the attic or in the fields or in the ravine or at the creek" during the first ten years of her life, Mary's new bedroom helped spark an interest in acting as she approached adolescence. "Ceiling and walls were plastered with photographs cut out of movie magazines," she recalled in her memoirs. "No longer did I dream of the farm with its brook and trees and flowers; now I dreamed of being an actress, clothed in satins and ermine, and draped in orchids." As luck would have it, one of the magazines she used as a source of decorative material held a beauty contest every month, which Mary promptly entered and won. After hearing the good news, Mary's father sold the family's belongings and moved his wife and child to Chicago and then New York in hopes of getting Mary work as an actress. In 1920 the fourteen-year-old girl caught the eye of actress Lillian Gish and director D. W. Griffiths during a casting call in Manhattan. By 1923, shortly before her seventeenth birthday, Mary had signed a $500-a-week contract and was starring in films alongside Clark Gable. She used the money she earned to buy an apartment for her family in Long Island, a fully furnished luxury suite with a room of her own that was done up in her favorite colors: "orchid and green."[44]

Unfortunately, this was one of the last times Mary would have any pleasant associations with her bedroom. Her father, who had always been stern and overbearing, became even more so as her star rose and her bank account expanded. His attempts to dominate his daughter oftentimes extended into her bedroom. "If I said, 'Why can't I close my bedroom door, just so I can read and think quietly?' he would counter with self-righteous resentment," she explained. "'What are you doing that you don't want us to know about?' he would say. 'Or maybe your own mother and father disturb you. Perhaps we should just pack up and move out. Maybe you'd rather we just moved off the face of the earth.'" Mary's situation was made even worse by an affair with actor John Barrymore, a man who was both married and twenty-four years her senior. Separated by several thousand miles—Barrymore lived in Los Angeles when the affair began—Mary spent a great deal of time in her room, pining for the dashing actor. "I languished in moodiness and melancholy, in my longing for Jack," she explained, referring to Barrymore by his nickname. "After Mother and Daddy had gone to bed, I would sit in the embrasure of my window, my knees hugged up to my chin, and look out at the stars and wish we were like the lovers in *Peter Ibbetson* [a Broadway play Barrymore had starred in], who by 'dreaming true' could find each other when they slept and travel all over the world together." The decision to move into a new home in the Hollywood Hills in 1925 led to even more anxiety and confusion. Though Mary was pleased with the bathroom suite and balcony in her new room, her parents reasserted control over their only child, providing her with a weekly allowance of $5, despite the fact that she was earning well over $2,500 a week as an actress. Rather than confront her parents, however, Mary simply retreated into her palatial bedroom, much like Marlon Brando would do several years later and a few counties over. "It was easier to escape into the solitude of my room—I was permitted to close the door now—and read, or work a little at learning to write on the typewriter," she lamented. "I even tried my hand at writing a short story. Or I just sat on the balcony and dreamed at the moon, living in the time when my love would return to me."[45]

In the end, however, Barrymore ended the relationship shortly after Mary moved to California, sending the young starlet into an emotional tailspin that once again played itself out in her bedroom. "Fatigue was becoming chronic," she recalled. "I was crying a great deal at night after I went to bed." Frustrated and angry, Mary pledged to escape from her parents' clutches if her father felt the need to comment on her recently dissolved relationship. Mary's father soon obliged her by delivering a "fifteen-minute peroration" on her personal failings. So, like Eubie Blake approximately twenty-three years earlier, Mary waited for her parents to go to sleep so that she could escape from the family home via the balcony. "Taking the cord from my robe," she explained, "I tied one end to the small cypress that had grown just a little higher than the railing of the balcony. I grasped the case and the cord, and swung out. The tree bent to lower me easily to the ground, and I walked away from home." Mary checked into a small hotel on Hollywood Boulevard shortly after two in the morning. One week later, after negotiating greater financial and emotional independence from her parents, Mary was back at home. In the end, she would only gain true independence from her parents three years later, in 1928, when she married director Kenneth Hawkes and bought a house of her own. Contrary to what many child development experts were arguing at the time, Mary's room didn't offer a respite from parental domination, but rather enhanced the means by which her father could assert control over his only child. Mary's room, in short, was little more than a luxuriously appointed prison cell.[46]

* * *

Though child-rearing experts often failed to provide solid proof that the teen bedroom was a *necessary* feature of the maturation process, an argument can be made that their claims complemented and, at times, reflected the lived realities of many families. The teen bedroom acted as an escape from (and a means of dealing with) emotional problems, a flash point of parent-child conflict, an isolated space in which to engage in various sex acts (social and solitary), a place to hide secrets from other family members, a conduit to the outside world, a site for self-improvement, and perhaps even a crucial element in shaping one's future occupation. Regardless of the validity of some of the arguments posed by child development experts—and there is much evidence to suggest that their views on teen bedroom culture were one-dimensional and flawed—their proselytizing efforts should be acknowledged as a contributing factor in enhancing the prestige and popularity of autonomous teen bedrooms during the twentieth century. Their ideas made it difficult for parents to ignore something as rudimentary as where their teenage offspring would sleep, study, and, increasingly, engage in acts of consumption and leisure. And as we will see in the next chapter, ideas on child development would eventually bleed into discussions of room décor, bringing about the merger of scientific expertise and powerful market forces.

THREE

Give a Room a Little Personality—Yours!

It is interesting to note how the personality of the occupant is revealed by the furnishings of a girl's room; what pictures she chooses to put on her dresser or table; what books she keeps near at hand; what colors she uses in even the simplest scarfs or draperies, in what order the whole is kept.

GRACE LOUCKS ELLIOTT, *UNDERSTANDING THE ADOLESCENT GIRL* (1930)

Child development experts were not alone in taking notice of the teen bedroom during the late nineteenth and early twentieth centuries; home décor experts, too, realized that a child's sleeping quarters could (and should) be subjected to their unique brand of expertise. Offering suggestions in a wide array of popular newspapers and magazines—the vast majority of which were underwritten by companies that produced bedroom-oriented consumer items—home décor experts played a vital role in introducing youngsters to the purported pleasures of consumerism by acting as mediators between affluent families who had the money to spend on nonessential consumer goods and the various business interests who were eager to bring their products to a wider audience. That this particular brand of consumerism was focused on a space that was removed from some of the more public expressions of youth-oriented spending is especially noteworthy. Unlike the amusement parks and roller rinks that catered to youth during the late-Victorian era, the teen bedroom managed to encourage consumer activities in the safety and comfort of the family home, thereby allowing teenagers to flex their ever-growing spending powers without, in effect, scaring their parents witless.

Décor experts often supported their claims by couching their advice in the language of child development. Although parental needs were emphasized throughout much of the nineteenth and early twentieth centuries, a much more child-friendly approach emerged during the interwar years. Room design came to be seen as an integral part of the maturation process, offering teens the opportunity to express themselves in a creative manner, craft a unique identity, and free themselves from parental dictates. As a result, teen décor choices were often portrayed as playing a key role in allowing teens to make the successful transition from dependent child to independent adult, an outcome that most (if not all) parents were more than willing to accommodate.

* * *

As several scholars have noted, the economic power of youth grew immeasurably during the late nineteenth and early twentieth centuries. Historian William Leach, for instance, claims that business interests had begun "constructing a separate child world, independent of the adult world and competitive with it as a source of profit" by as early as the 1880s. The effects of this trend were far reaching, as market forces began shaping the material culture of youth—the "things" with which teenagers surrounded themselves—in novel ways. This trend had an especially profound effect on the teen bedroom, transforming the average teen suite into a space in which an increasing collection of clothing, furniture, toys, games, and books could be stored and enjoyed. Though it would be rash to suggest that nineteenth-century bedrooms didn't house a similar collection of household items (think back to the desk Elizabeth Payson received as a gift from her mother in chapter 1), mass-produced, store-bought items were simply much more prevalent during the late-Victorian era as the younger generation assumed greater agency in the market place. Nowhere is this better illustrated than in the lengths to which décor experts and their allies in the business community went in order to provide teens with the tools necessary to decorate their rooms. Their attempts to woo both teen consumers and their parents suggest that the democratization of teen bedroom culture during the twentieth century was often shaped by powerful market forces.[1]

As a discrete area of expertise, teen bedroom design was slow to evolve during much of the nineteenth century due to the persistence of Victorian notions regarding the appropriateness of discussing private spaces in an overwhelmingly public forum. In fact, *Godey's Lady's Magazine*, *Ladies'*

Home Journal, and other popular magazines tended to concentrate on parlors and dining rooms rather than bedrooms. And on those rare occasions when bedrooms were addressed, greater emphasis was placed on master bedrooms and servant's quarters. Although advice on how to decorate children's bedrooms began to appear more frequently during the latter decades of the nineteenth century, much of the expertise being offered was marked by brevity and—above all else—stressed practical concerns, as design experts usually urged parents to purchase furnishings and other accessories that could be cleaned easily and were capable of withstanding youthful tomfoolery.[2]

Bedroom-oriented advice became more common during the interwar years when Victorian reticence began to give way to more frank, social-scientific perspectives. Historian Gwendolyn Wright, for instance, claims that the master bedroom became a focus of attention in women's magazines in the 1920s due to "the new freedom to discuss women's sexual needs and methods of contraception." Nonetheless, specific advice pertaining to bedrooms occupied by teenagers was still rare during this time because the concept of adolescence had not yet been fully embraced by the culture at large. Though G. Stanley Hall's works on the subject created a sensation during the early 1900s, the idea of adolescence as a stage of the life cycle distinct from childhood and adulthood was slow to take root before the Second World War—particularly among rural families, the urban working-class, and other Americans who couldn't afford to keep their children in a dependent state for an extended period of time. The teen bedroom most certainly existed in a physical sense, but not in a linguistic one, with design experts offering audiences advice in which bedrooms for "little boys," "little girls," and "a boy in his teens" were often discussed in the same breath. Even in those rare instances when a distinction by age was made, the criteria was often ill formed and vague by today's standards. Henrietta Murdock, a décor expert for the *Ladies' Home Journal*, argued as late as 1946 that a room for an eight-year-old boy would suffice until he was sixteen, whereupon a separate design "for a boy 16 to 21" was to be utilized. Suffice to say that these types of design strategies would be seen as both woefully out of date and ignorant of the growing "separateness" of teens and teen culture during the years following the Second World War.[3]

Another trend that characterized teen room design during the early twentieth century was the belief that the decoration process should be overseen by adults, and especially mothers. Though there is evidence to suggest that middle-class children were allowed to decorate their nurseries and playrooms with collages and other homemade decorative items during the years following the Civil War, bedroom décor, according to historian Karin Calvert, was usually defined by "an artificial code of childishness devised and implemented by adults." A child's room was, first and foremost, a reflection of his or her mother's taste, an extension of the aesthetic qualities of the master bedroom. Emphasis was placed on "fascinating color schemes" as well as "color and comfort," while words and phrases culled from self-help literature—for example, *enchantment* and *harmonious*—were thrown around in an attempt to stress how a properly designed room could act as a means of "developing good taste" and cultivating "a deep interest in, and an appreciation of, a gracious mode of life." On the surface, then, much of the advice being offered was conceived with an eye toward replicating a uniquely middle-class aesthetic that occasionally served an instructional role. "Surround children with harmonious colors," urged a design expert from the *Olean Evening Times* in 1928, "and they will learn to appreciate beauty, and to apply it, in later life, to everyday problems."[4]

Not all home décor experts, however, believed that children should be shut out of the decoration process. During the years leading up to the First World War, a slim minority believed that the younger set should play a role in both creating and implementing design strategies. The *Christian Science Monitor* was particularly prescient in this regard. "There is a time in the life of nearly all young people when they come as it were into their own," one of its experts claimed in 1911. "At last they are considered old enough and of sufficient importance to be given a room to themselves, and are even allowed a voice in the matter of furnishings." The author went on to draw a connection between room décor and developmental goals, suggesting that giving "a child a free hand in his or her own room" and encouraging his or her "desire for creative work" was an "effective way of planting a seed that will bear rich fruit in later years." In 1913 another contributor to the *Christian Science Monitor* suggested that the child "should be allowed to exercise his individual taste unhampered" when deciding on appropriate wall hangings. Given free rein to decorate his walls according to his own tastes, "Dick," the fictional youth whose room was being redone, would most certainly populate his room with an assortment of "trash," including swords, guns, flags, and pictures that probably would not "measure up to your standard of fine art." Ultimately, though, parents were encouraged to "let him have what he wants" in order to develop the boy's character and establish a sense of self.[5]

Aside from these efforts, child-oriented advice was slow to catch on during the early parts of the interwar years. Lip service was paid to questions of youthful autonomy and independence, but it was rare to see advice that actually encouraged these concepts in practice. Even the *Christian Science Monitor* refused to fully disavow parent-centric approaches. In 1930, one of its columnists claimed that a child's bedroom should enhance "the individuality of the owner," facilitate "the expression of his own tastes and needs and activities," and afford "him free opportunity for his own pursuits, without disturbance, and without disturbing others." This emphasis on individualism and self-discovery was seriously undermined, however, by the fact that the expert who penned the article proceeded to dictate nearly every aspect of the child's bedroom, including wall hangings, furnishings, and even the books that would end up on the child's shelves. In many respects, the continued presence of advice like this reflected both the persistence of traditional child-rearing strategies as well as the relatively weak economic standing of children immediately preceding the Second World War. Without sufficient personal wealth and autonomy at their disposal, teenagers could not be expected to take control of their room in anything but a superficial manner. As a result, décor experts often provided advice that sought to impose individuality on children rather than encourage it directly. "You will find here," one expert explained as late as 1944, "ideas which you can adopt to your own rugged individualists."[6]

Parent-centric approaches to home décor only began to fall out of favor during the years leading up to the Second World War. Here we see growing acceptance of the idea that teens deserved much greater input in decorating their bedrooms—in both theory and in practice—as well as their emergence as a distinct demographic that deserved to be talked to rather than talked about. Though total control over room design was rarely granted to teens during this period, many décor exports began to see that autonomy and individualism could not be forced on youngsters, but rather was something that children had to encounter firsthand. Fathers and mothers may have had ideas on how, in an ideal world, their offspring should decorate their rooms, but the interwar years were a period in which calls for autonomy and independence were the norm among middle- and working-class youths, acting as a dress rehearsal of sorts for the generational conflicts that would emerge during the 1950s, 1960s, and beyond. Parents, in short, were finding that they were slowly being stripped of the right to determine the basic appearance of their teenagers' bedrooms.[7]

This shift toward child-centered design strategies was also hastened by the changes taking place within the child development community. As noted earlier, child development experts came to regard the teen bedroom as a valuable developmental space because it helped encourage introspection, self-reliance, and independence from various forms of parental authority. During the interwar years, home décor experts began offering their own unique spin on these ideas, oftentimes suggesting that room design—by encouraging self-expression and self-governance—was also a key component of the maturation process. A properly designed boy's room, a décor expert from *Ladies Home Journal* argued in 1930, "is in some respects more important than some other rooms in the house, because it is here that much of his time is spent in studying, reading, or just fooling around with his possessions, and the background of his room plays a most important part in his development and character building." A well-maintained girl's room, one expert from *House & Garden* added during the 1940s, will act as a "haven when your young daughter wants to get away from it all, a quiet retreat for her daydreams," and a "study, play area, harbor for collections, refuge from the family and sometimes as a place to entertain friends besides." The lifeguard approach to parenting had finally found its analog in the world of home décor, as parents were now expected to merely stand on the sidelines and offer a nonintrusive form of guidance to their children.[8]

The advice offered by Emily Post during the 1930s illustrates the growing popularity of child-centered approaches and their reliance on various child development theories. Though Post is most known for her somewhat stuffy Victorian views on etiquette, her décor strategies were greatly influenced by cutting-edge child development experts such as Sigmund Freud and Havelock Ellis. Indeed, her best-selling book, *The Personality of a House* (1935), offered a host of design strategies that were often framed in the language of child development. "Children invariably become interested in what they take a part in making," Post argued. "A room done for them and given to them is not as developing to their initiative, or to their taste, as is one that they themselves design." Parents were more than welcome to choose appropriate objet d'art and furnishings for their child's room, but Post insisted that developmental progress was often stifled when the preferences of children are ignored. "A child's room should be as pretty as possible," she warned, "but must not be hampering to freedom. In other words—should a choice be necessary—freedom is of first importance, and beauty second. Normal development is checked—sometimes even deformed—by the continuous pressure of restraint." Post reinforced her views by applauding her own parents' decision to grant her sole decorating privileges in her bedroom when she was all of ten years old. Though she recalled a sense of "bewildered disappointment" when the end results did not match her expectations, Post chalked up her initial forays into room design as an invaluable learning experience, recognizing that self-empowerment was much more important than aesthetic outcomes. "It had been my own taste and my own choice," she declared, "and that was that!"[9]

Post's peers were more than willing to offer like-minded views on room design during the Great Depression, despite the fact that spending on nonessential goods was down throughout most of the 1930s. In the spring of 1937, Martha Davis, a design expert from the *Christian Science Monitor*, wrote a series of articles encouraging adolescents to take command of the design process in a bold manner. One article, for instance, dealt with a thirteen-year-old named Paul, who, together with his parents, decided to redecorate his room in a manner that satisfied both parties. Though larger concerns such as shelving and furniture were provided by his parents, Paul was given free rein to decide on the "little details," the knickknacks and other belongings that defined him as an individual. The end result was a unique, aviation-themed room filled with Indian rugs and maps, while a manly "muzzle-loading shotgun" given to him by his grandfather was "given a place of honor over the bed." The author refrained from commenting on the aesthetic qualities of the room itself, but she did suggest, like Post, that Paul's offbeat design choices were worth encouraging because they allowed him to express himself as an individual. "It doesn't make any difference what a boy is interested in," Davis suggested. "Let that be the dominating note of his room. If he likes to collect shells and rocks, then see that he has sufficient and attractive cases or shelves to house them. If he's interested in scouting or sailoring, then introduce Indian or ship accessories."[10]

Less than a month later, Davis introduced her readers to another teen, a seventeen-year-old named Bob, who transformed his bedroom into a social center where he and his friends could "come in and sprawl around without getting the bedspread mussed up." Once again, Davis pointed to the virtues of a collaborative effort, applauding the fact that Bob redesigned his room with the help of a friend, his friend's father, and his aunt Harriet, who was kind enough to sew new slipcovers for a ratty old chair. Bob's efforts were unique because some of the more feminine forms of expertise were downplayed in favor of a much more masculine approach. Though Aunt Harriet's slipcovers were no doubt a much appreciated addition to Bob's new room, Davis treated the young boy's efforts as a construction project rather than an experiment in home décor. Bob not only decided on the knickknacks and wall coverings in the room, but he also—with the help of his friend's father, a carpenter—designed and built a bed that doubled as a couch, as well as a dresser that would house all his clothes. The end result, according to Davis, was a triumph of manly self-expression, a bold declaration of Bob's ownership of his immediate surroundings: "When Bob's books had been installed, his pictures and trophies hung on the wall, and two braided rugs laid on the floor, it was a room for any boy to be proud of, particularly if he had helped to do it himself."[11]

Even *Ladies' Home Journal*, a beacon of conservatism, encouraged American youth to take control of their personal space during the 1930s and 1940s. "Get busy on your bedroom," one writer demanded of her male readers. "Test your skill. A little ingenuity and a lot of Idaho pine and it's all yours." Yet another of its writers told teen girls to do the same in their bedrooms. "Do your room in your pet color," the author implored. "Why not? This room is yours, personal!" Indeed, as the Second World War drew to a close, it was rare to find a mainstream decoration expert who still defended parent-centered approaches to room design. "In decoration and colors experts are getting away from the idea that everything must seem cute to adult visitors," a contributor to the *New York Times* argued in 1945. "Decorators now favor the child's-eye view." In the case of Ann Hatfield, an interior designer from New York, parental oversight was abandoned altogether when the time came to decorate her twelve-year-old son's room. Hatfield was so confident in her son's judgment, in fact, that she allowed him to fill an entire wall of his room with ads for Winchester rifles. "While the result did not meet with her unqualified approval as a decorator," the author of the piece commented, "as a mother she believed it was important for her son to try out his own ideas."[12]

As the décor choices of Ann Hatfield's son suggest, encouraging children to decorate their rooms with pinups and other ephemera represented one of the most popular expressions of child-centered décor expertise. Mass produced and inexpensive, this type of material offered teens the perfect opportunity to decorate their bedrooms in a manner that complemented their own sensibilities. Moreover, the somewhat impermanent nature of pinups allowed teens to express themselves in a flexible manner. A thirteen-year-old interested in geography, for instance, could dissect copies of *National Geographic* in hopes of tracking down the perfect wall hanging for his or her room, while that same teen, a few years later, could simply replace that material with images from *Popular Mechanics* should his or her interests shift to, say, science and engineering. Publishers were certainly aware of this trend and often went out of their way to make sure that the content they provided was likely to find its way into the rooms of young boys and girls. In March 1938, for instance, *Boys' Life* published a letter from Hans Classet of Astoria, Long Island, thanking the editors for providing him with décor material. "I think you ought to have more covers like that January cover," Hans wrote, "as the pictures are left suitable for framing." The editors subsequently used Hans's letter as an opportunity to announce a significant policy change, one that illustrated the give-and-take that emerged between business interests and teen consumers. "So many fellows said they wanted to use *Boys' Life* cover paintings for framing, to be hung on den and bedroom walls, that we have adopted this new arrangement to continue indefinitely."[13]

Meanwhile, other media outlets offered tips on how ephemera could be repurposed in creative ways. As early as 1912, for example, *Boys' Life* offered advice on how a strip of cardboard and some paper fasteners could transform a collection of postcards into a handsome wall hanging. "Here is yet another way in which you can give your club-room, or even your own bedroom, a homely and 'comfortable' look," the article began. "Most of you receive a number of picture postcards, even if you do not collect them. Why not hang some up in your room instead of placing them all in an album?" In 1930 *Popular Mechanics* similarly suggested that a little wood and mucilage could be used to turn prized photographs into "vases, tops for laundry bags, trinket holders, door stops and bedroom lamps." The author of the article even suggested that mastering this simple little craft could be economically beneficial, adding that "there is real money in these attractive statuettes if you care to turn merchant."[14]

Many décor experts, however, insisted that parents ought to play a sizable role in determining both the content of the wall hangings and where they would be hung. In many instances, youngster were expected to adopt a middlebrow aesthetic, opting for images that were both educational and tasteful. Emily Post urged children to hang "good pictures" on their bedroom walls, including "prints of value" or "home-framed illustrations cut from good magazines," while yet another design expert spoke of populating the room of a teenage boy with "lovely Italian primitives, woodcuts, photographs of mountains and other things especially dear to this individual boy's heart." Parents were similarly encouraged to limit pinups to bulletin boards and mirrors. Whereas many of today's teens have free rein to arrange visual material wherever they can find space, youngsters during the interwar years were told to limit their expression to parts of their room where thumbtacks and unforgiving adhesives could do little damage.[15]

Despite their attempts to preserve a middle-class aesthetic in the teen bedroom, parents and décor experts alike found that the younger generation was looking more and more toward popular culture—particularly, advertisements and other forms of promotional material churned out by the entertainment industry—to add flair to their personal space. Child development experts took special notice of this trend, suggesting that hero worship among adolescents often led teens to hang pictures of famous entertainers and athletes on their bedroom walls. Ada Hart Arlitt, for instance, characterized the adolescent stage as a period in which "the girl raves about heroes in motion pictures. She clips out every picture of a motion-picture star that can be found in magazines and pins them up around her room." Teen boys also seemed to appreciate the value of decorating their walls with pinups. Hugh Hefner, for one, admitted to decorating his bedroom with risqué pinups from *Esquire* while growing up in Chicago during the late 1930s. However, as Hefner's experiences illustrate, pinups shouldn't always be seen as an expression of hero worship, but rather a means of satisfying more primal urges.[16]

The preferred subject matter of wall hangings and pinups may have been in a state of flux during the interwar years, but one trend remained constant: most of the formal designs being offered by design experts continued to reflect deeply entrenched ideas on sex and gender. While it is true that rooms for boys and girls often shared a number of common features—study areas, furnishings that could accommodate visitors, and dedicated areas on the walls for pinups and photographs—the overall aesthetic was usually shaped by the sex of its occupant. Girls' rooms, as one expert explained shortly before the First World War, should be "dainty," "pretty," "bright," and "cheery." This could be accomplished by sticking to so-called feminine color schemes (pink and sky blue were especially popular), frilly fabrics, and period furniture. Like the parlors and master bedrooms many middle-class mothers presided over, girls' rooms were expected to be decorated in a manner that reinforced their future roles as wives and mothers. Woman's rights activist Louise Creighton suggested as much in *The Art of Living and Other Addresses to Girls* (1909):

> Girls probably have not much to say with regard to the furnishing of a house, at least until they have one of their own, but they can begin with their own rooms. These they can do much to make beautiful in their own way, by keeping them tidy, and by not allowing them to be filled with collections of rubbish, meaningless ornaments, and faded photographs.

Norman Richardson made similar suggestions in *The Religious Education of Adolescents* (1918). A "room alone gives opportunity for the expression of many artistic and decorative phases without such violent readjustment of the rest of the house furnishing," he argued, "or such evident lack of appreciation on the part of the family." The bedroom was thus seen as a rehearsal space of sorts, a miniaturized version of the girl's future home that allowed her to hone her matronly skills without disturbing other members of the family.[17]

Boys' rooms were similarly constrained by prevailing ideas on gender, as many plans featured typically masculine themes involving exploration and adventurousness. Military and naval motifs were especially popular, as were designs that emphasized one's athletic prowess. Above all else, boys' rooms were expected to project strength and masculinity while avoiding the more delicate motifs favored by their sisters and mothers. "Plain, substantial furnishings, best described as 'mannish,' are the kind that should be chosen," a writer from the *Christian Science Monitor* declared in 1913. "Beribboned, beruffled trifles that would make a strong appeal to his sister's taste should be avoided. He will probably have none of them." At times, décor experts even took to referring to the boy's room as a "den" or "headquarters," designations that hinted at the boy's future role as breadwinner and head of household. Referring to a boy's room as a "den," after all, was an obvious nod to the father's place of refuge within the home, while "headquarters" suggests that the boy could look forward to years of employment in either a corporate or military setting. In many respects, then, home décor experts reinforced the claims of child development experts who argued that the bedroom could play a decisive role in shaping one's future occupation.[18]

Many home décor experts were similarly adamant in thinking that teen boys were being denied the privilege of presiding over rooms of their own, oftentimes accusing parents of treating the average boy's bedroom as an afterthought. In 1927 Seymour Bullock, a writer from *The Rotarian*, decried this trend in no uncertain terms:

> In the first place the "Boy in the House" should be given his own room. Not a room away off in the attic, some two-by-four dark cubby hole into which the boy is ashamed to invite his friends, but the sunniest, brightest, cheeriest, and homiest room in the whole house, with plenty of shelves for his models of air and water-craft, and a closet where he can put his "shinny sticks" and fish pole and space on the wall for his trophies and a nook for his own radio set to which he may listen when nobody else wants to tune it in.

Some experts believed that the best way to counter this trend was to stress the links between room design and the love of family and home. Schuyler White, a contributor to *Ladies' Home Journal*, argued in the late 1920s that encouraging the young man of the house to take room décor seriously would help introduce him "during his most formative period [to] the very elements which tend to make him sensitive to the benefits and pleasures of home life." Some experts even suggested that being mindful of one's room could improve a boy's chances of finding a wife. One design guru from the 1930s counseled, "Since every man is going to be asked some time whether green wallpaper with apple blossom sprays or a Colonial design looks better in the living room, or whether he would prefer modernistic or Directoire furniture in his bedroom, it's a wise mother who instills some of the fundamentals of interior decorating in her boys." The decorating process was thus regarded as a means of reinforcing the family unit. Without it, some experts seemed to suggest, the joys of family life were at risk of being ignored and cast aside.[19]

* * *

The importance of home décor expertise in shaping teen bedroom culture during the years leading up to the Second World War cannot be underestimated. Home décor experts, in concert with a host of eager retailers and manufacturers, believed that the teen bedroom ought to be subject to the same consumer-driven philosophies that had been gathering momentum in American society since the late nineteenth century. Buoyed by ideas on child development that emphasized the importance of fostering independence and autonomy among the younger set, home décor experts came to regard bedroom-oriented acts of consumption as an integral part of the maturation process. An improperly designed bedroom, they argued, was something more than a mere eyesore; it was an obstacle to proper developmental growth, a means of thwarting the maturation process. As an added bonus, décor experts also claimed that parents who granted their sons and daughters greater powers to decorate their rooms would help keep teens off the streets by creating a safe alternative to movie theaters, roller rinks, and other leisure venues found outside the home.

The irony, of course, is that these same experts, by urging teens to take command of basic room design, ultimately undermined their own attempts to capitalize on the ever-expanding youth market. Whether they were aware of it or not, décor experts were offering advice on room design that, when taken to its logical conclusion, ended up subverting their authority in a rather profound manner. Child-centered strategies—though they found occasional expression in teen room design during the nineteenth century—were often held in check by virtue of the fact that parents (particularly mothers) were given near-total power to decorate the rooms of their children. Once parental prerogative was challenged, however, the younger generation was essentially left to its own devices—which, as we will see in a later chapter, often resulted in a firm rejection of top-down décor advice. In other words, décor experts who rallied around child-centered design strategies during the first half of the twentieth century made it much more difficult for their peers during the last half of the twentieth century to secure the loyalty of teens at a time when the spending power of youth was reaching its apex.

FOUR

The Sign Reads 'Keep Out'

I met kids who lived in shacks, but they almost all had their own bedrooms.
ADRIENNE SALINGER, PHOTOGRAPHER (2010)

In 1944 Alice Grayson published a collection of letters gathered during her time as an advice columnist at *Calling All Girls*, a teen magazine that flourished briefly during the early 1940s and later reemerged as *Young Miss* in the 1960s. Several of these letters addressed teen demands for privacy and autonomy in their rooms, as Grayson's readers expressed concern that their parents and siblings were not respecting their personal space in an appropriate manner. Bert from New Jersey complained that her mother often used her room to store various items of clothing. "My room is on the main floor," she explained, "my mother and father sleep upstairs and my mother insists on keeping some of her clothes in my closet and using my whole bureau for some of her things. . . . I think that a girl's room should be her own private room." Another girl from New York lodged similar complaints. "I think my mother is very mean," she wrote. "I have a key to my bedroom and I value it very much. But my mother lets my sisters in my room, against my will when I want to do something I consider very important." Though Grayson was quick to acknowledge that "separation is often salutary," her advice to both girls tended to favor the needs of other family members. For the girl whose mother insisted on storing clothes in her bedroom, Grayson suggested that she swallow her pride and allow her mother some degree of access to her room. "I'm sorry about having to keep some of my clothes in your closet," Grayson imagined the girl's mother saying.

"Let's see if we can work things out so that I won't have to use your room so much." The girl from New York, meanwhile, was instructed to be more open to the curiosity of her younger siblings. "Some adolescents," Grayson explained, "have found it helpful to permit the younger children in the family to come into their rooms at stated times and to allow them to handle some of their prized and cherished possessions."[1]

This somewhat porous vision of teen space was seriously challenged in subsequent decades. By the 1960s and 1970s in particular, the parent-centered approach to teen space that had found expression in the nineteenth and early twentieth centuries gave way to an aggressive child-centered model that was predicated upon increasingly rigid defenses of adolescent privacy and autonomy. Reinforced materially by the sustained economic growth of the Cold War era, the expansion of the teen demographic, and the continued rise of a robust, consumption-heavy youth culture, the child-centered teen bedroom was treated as a sacrosanct space that was ostensibly off limits to parents, siblings, and any other unwanted visitors. Teens who were victims of arbitrary searches and heavy-handed forms of parental surveillance could rest assured in knowing that they had friends in high places—academia, the professions, and the media, among others—who believed that privacy in one's bedroom was a "right" well worth defending. "Is yours the room with a view—of everyone prying, not only into your personal possessions but into your romantic and social and emotional life as well?" one columnist from *Seventeen* asked in 1960. "If your answer is yes, you're a member of what may be the largest loosely organized society in the United States: The Teen-Age Army of Soldiers in Search of a Sign. The sign reads Keep Out."[2]

Material Conditions

What started out as an exclusive custom among urban-dwelling, middle-class girls from the Northeast during the early nineteenth century became something much more ubiquitous during the last half of the twentieth century. Indeed, various studies found that a majority of teens during the Eisenhower, Kennedy, and Johnson administrations were either sleeping in their own rooms or would jump at the opportunity to do so. In 1960, for instance, advertising executive Eugene Gilbert found that 77 percent of teenagers expressed support for the "own room" concept, the vast majority of which cited privacy as the "paramount reason." In 1964, moreover, the *Christian Science Monitor* claimed that 65 percent of American teenagers had already been granted this privilege. These numbers would continue to rise as the twentieth century drew to a close. By the 1990s psychologists Reed Larson and Maryse Richards reported that 73 percent of ninth graders had their own rooms, while Penn State's Division of Student Affairs claimed that 82 percent of freshman presided over rooms of their own in the three years before attending university. Although there are dangers in taking these types of statistics at face value, one could argue that the last half of the twentieth represented something of a coming-out party for supporters of the separate bedroom ideal.[3]

The growing popularity of autonomous teen bedrooms was not limited solely to affluent families either. Poorer teens—though they were perhaps less likely to have rooms of their own—took part in teen bedroom culture to an extent not seen in previous decades. Anthony Bernier, a native of Los Angeles who lived with his mother and two younger sisters in a one-bedroom converted duplex during the late 1960s and early 1970s, was just one teenager who managed to take part in the "own room" custom, despite less-than-ideal economic conditions. The Bernier family did not enjoy much in the way of privacy in their somewhat cramped quarters. All three children shared a bedroom—the girls had a bunk bed and Anthony slept on a trundle bed—while Anthony's mother, a waitress at a coffee shop, "slept on the pullout couch in the living room." In 1970, however, Anthony was told by his mother that he would be getting a "Big Surprise" for his twelfth birthday. He briefly toyed with the idea that he was getting a pony, but in reality Anthony's mother had been conspiring with the landlord, Chuck, to turn a small porch/laundry room next to the kitchen into a separate bedroom for her oldest child.[4]

Sometime in April or May of 1970, Anthony's mother moved all of her son's belongings into the now completed bedroom while he was attending church with his neighbors. To say that he was appreciative of her efforts would be somewhat of an understatement. "The furnishings and drapes and engineer's lantern are describable," he notes. "They are simply artifacts of material culture. But the emotional landscape that tiny laundry porch . . . opened up inside that twelve-year old boy is, and remains, *in*describable. My bedroom was the best birthday gift I've ever received. The best gift I've ever received, period." Over the course of the next few years, Anthony went out of his way to establish sovereignty in his new bedroom. This was accomplished by hanging "proprietary warning signs" on the outside of his bedroom door, featuring phrases such as "Keep out!," "Knock first and enter only after receiving permission!," and "Property of Anthony, The Great!" Though its existence was dependent in large part on the generosity and ingenuity of his mother and landlord, Anthony's bedroom was personalized in such a way as to announce to other members of the family exactly who its rightful owner was.[5]

While Bernier's experiences with teen bedroom culture illustrate how working-class families managed to take part in the separate bedroom ideal during the postwar years, the experiences of Leslie, a resident of Nampa, Idaho, during the 1980s, suggest that it was not unheard of for teens who resided even lower on the socioeconomic ladder to have rooms of their own. Like Bernier, Leslie had multiple siblings (three sisters) and was raised by a single mother. Her family, however, "lived from welfare check to welfare check," and the bedroom she occupied "was in government housing in a fairly insular, mostly white enclave of very poor people." Nonetheless, Leslie was given a room of her own when she was just eleven years old, occupying "a tiny third bedroom at the top of the stairs" until she was fourteen. Shortly thereafter, her older sister moved out, allowing Leslie the opportunity to move into the "biggest of the girls' rooms in our apartment." Besides providing her with a space in which to indulge her love of writing—"I spent most of my time in my room, reading and (literally) penning poetry and novels"—Leslie's room acted as a safe and secure place in which "a fat, nerdy, queer introvert" could deal with the pressures of adolescence. "My room was my retreat," she notes, "my cave, my safe haven in a frequently hostile, size-ist, homophobic, sexist world. I spent most of my teenage years in my bedroom, reading, writing, and doing homework. Occasionally I invited people into my haven, but most of my time I spent alone."[6]

Given the growing popularity of separate bedrooms among both middle- and working-class families, it should come as no surprise to find that the reputation of shared bedrooms continued to decline during the postwar years. Sharing a room with one or more siblings was regarded by many observers as a necessary evil rather than as a perfectly acceptable mode of living. In an age of plenty, these types of arrangements were seen, at best, as an embarrassing sign of poverty or, at worst, as a source of pathology. Indeed, August Hollingshead, a sociologist at Yale University during the 1940s and 1950s, continued to propagate the idea—common during much of the Victorian era—that shared bedrooms led to sexual depravity. Lower-class teenage girls, he argued in 1949, were being rendered "filthy minded," "dirty," and "full of sex" due to their experiences with shared sleeping arrangements. "Their homes are small, and privacy is almost non-existent," he claimed. "Families are large, and both boys and girls often sleep in the same room." And if sexual perversion weren't bad enough, some experts even claimed that the manger-born Son of God himself was no fan of shared sleeping quarters. Evangelical parenting expert Audrey Williamson insisted during the 1950s that shared bedrooms were inappropriate for Christian youth because siblings were bound to interfere with prayers and other forms of private devotion. "It is highly desirable," Williamson argued, "that your youth should have a place which is his alone, for the time being, where he can meet the Saviour at some hour during the day."[7]

Shared bedrooms were also accused of creating unnecessary stress and tension in the home. "Young people are at an age during their high school years when it is something more than a status symbol to have their own room," parenting expert Rupert Hoover claimed during the early 1960s. "When this is impossible because of limitations of space and financial resources to provide space, we can assume that the family crises will be intensified for the teen-ager and his parents." Joan Jenkins offered similar arguments a few years later, this time from a decidedly feminine perspective: "The daily aggravation of stumbling over somebody else's paraphernalia can't be beat for frazzling the nerve ends. Of course, you can shut yourself away from your sister's clutter if you have a room of your own, but when you share a room with someone who's careless, you've got trouble." To avoid these kinds of conflicts, parents were urged to give adolescents access to other spaces in the home. For instance, sex-education expert Bruce Strain suggested that parents might consider creating "a space in the attic, garage or basement for freedom to play." However, if space and/or financial resources were lacking in the first place, the process of transforming another room into a teen retreat may not have been feasible for many families. In fact, some parents found that the culture's intense emphasis on the separate bedroom ideal was a bit stifling. "Our four children share two bedrooms between them," a Texas mother complained to an advice columnist during the late 1960s. "One one-child mother said to me, 'Oh, but your children will have no privacy if they never have a whole room to themselves!' If she can find us a five-bedroom house that we can afford, I'll gladly give my children separate bedrooms."[8]

In explaining why the teen bedroom could inspire feelings of both frustration and admiration among so many Americans during the late twentieth century, we must take into account the same economic and demographic factors that helped foster the separate bedroom ideal during the nineteenth and early twentieth centuries. For starters, special emphasis must be placed on the unprecedented economic growth that took place between 1945 and 1973. Besides swelling the ranks of the middle classes and raising the standard of living of many working-class families, the postwar economic boom also had a pronounced effect on the types of dwellings families were able to purchase. With a little help from generous lending policies and government initiatives such as the GI Bill, working-

and middle-class families were in a much better position to become homeowners after the war than they were before. In fact, homeownership rates topped the 50 percent mark for the first time ever in 1950 and continued to rise until 1980, when the census reported that 64.4 percent of homes were owner occupied. Moreover, the homes Americans were moving into were getting larger, providing many families with the excess space necessary to accommodate greater privacy and solitude. In 1950 the average home was 1,100 square feet, with the popular Levittown models averaging 800 square feet; by 1971 the average home had ballooned to 1,520 square feet and would reach 1,710 square feet by 1982. To be sure, many families continued to live in cramped conditions; historian Allan Berube has written about growing up in a tiny mobile home during the 1950s, offering anecdotes about how he and his sister slept in shifts and how he once mistook the kitchen for the washroom and almost urinated in the refrigerator while sleepwalking. But few would argue that the economic gains of the postwar years didn't allow more and more families to purchase homes that could better accommodate the separate bedroom ideal.[9]

While homes continued to get larger, the average family became significantly smaller. Despite a brief period when birthrates rose substantially—the so-called baby boom—family size began a downward trajectory that only began to stabilize during the 1980s. In 1950 the average number of family members was 3.37; by 1984 that number had shrunk to an all-time low of 2.7. Though declining birthrates most certainly contributed to this trend, climbing divorce rates were also a factor. In 1960, for instance, 2.2 out of every 1,000 Americans had been divorced or had their marriage annulled; by 1990 that number had more than doubled, rising to 4.7. Suffice to say that divorce often opened up spaces within the home that could be claimed by privacy-starved teens. Laurel from San Jose, California, learned this lesson firsthand in 1975, when her parents' marriage ended and she was able to claim her father's workshop as a room of her own. "Unlike my former bedroom," she explains, "it was uncarpeted and small, but had a really nice built-in desk/workspace/wall shelf unit, plus a wonderful walk-in closet that had served as my dad's darkroom." It must be noted, however, that the effects of divorce didn't always play out in a uniform manner. Anne, a teen from a Rust Belt city in the Northeast, claims that her parents' divorce during the late 1970s actually brought an end to her experiment with separate bedrooms: "A consequence of my parents' divorce was that my sister and I ended up dividing our time between their new households and had to share bedrooms in both, starting around the time I turned 15 and she turned 13." Although many child-rearing experts might have felt pity for teens who found themselves in this situation, Anne did not seem all that bothered by her new arrangements. "Surprisingly, we didn't mind much, despite having grown up with our own private rooms before that." The only problem with her new quarters, she notes, was "finding private space for making out/sex."[10]

Taken together, all of these factors—increases in the standard of living, expanding home size, and shrinking family size—encouraged the widespread adoption of the separate bedroom ideal during the last half of the twentieth century. However, material and demographic factors do not necessarily explain why the poorest of the poor adopted this custom—why, to refer back to the quotation that introduces this chapter, even shack-dwelling teenagers were known to have rooms of their own. To better understand this phenomenon, cultural factors must be considered—most notably, the continued proliferation and popularization of child development expertise.

Developmental Considerations

As pointed out in chapter 2, professionally trained child development experts dominated discussions of teen bedroom culture during the first four decades of the twentieth century. By the 1950s, 1960s, and 1970s, however, popular commentators such as Ann Landers and Abigail Van Buren had earned reputations as the teen bedroom's biggest cheerleaders, expressing support for this custom in a folksy and accessible manner that their academic counterparts simply couldn't match. Regardless, the ascendency of popular expertise should not be seen as evidence of the decline of formal child development theory, but rather as a sign of its ultimate triumph. Popular advice experts acted as surrogates for their peers in academia during the postwar years—foot soldiers, armed with decades of child development theory, who were capable of reaching audiences that academic or professional experts could only dream of. An excellent example of the symbiotic relationship between formal child development expertise and popular parenting advice was none other than Alice Grayson, the expert whose advice opened this chapter. Grayson, as it turns out, was the nom de plume of Jean Schick Grossman, an academically trained child development expert and director of parent education at the Play Schools Association in New York City during the 1930s and 1940s. Grossman's dual identities stand as a rather unique example of how expertise that originated in an academic setting often seeped into the mainstream. Grossman, the academically trained professional, represented the continuing influence of more professional forms of child development expertise, while Grayson, the Ann Landers prototype, served as a reminder that popular experts—preferably ones with anglicized surnames—would play a vital role in bringing these ideas to the culture at large. In the decades to come, a slew of professionals would follow Grossman's lead and parlay their hard-earned credentials into a career in the advice industry, including Dr. Benjamin Spock and Dr. Joyce Brothers.[11]

This is not to suggest, however, that professionally trained child development experts went silent once the Second World War ended. In fact, it could be argued that their influence reached its peak during the 1940s and 1950s, thanks in part to the growing popularity of psychoanalysis. Freudian thought gained a sizable following among artists and intellectuals during the 1920s and 1930s, but it didn't really achieve widespread popularity until after the war, reaching its zenith in April 1956 when an expressionist rendering of Freud graced the cover of *Time*. The field of adolescent development was greatly affected by this trend, as the psychoanalytic community claimed some of the biggest names in the study of adolescence, including Anna Freud (Sigmund Freud's daughter), Erik Erikson, Helene Deutsch, and Peter Blos—the latter of whom came to be known as "Mr. Adolescence" by his admirers at the *New York Times*. However, the ascendancy of psychoanalysis didn't necessarily bring about major changes to the way experts envisioned the maturation process. Child-rearing experts from a wide variety of theoretical perspectives continued to emphasize concepts that first emerged during the interwar years, including the importance of weakening parent-child bonds and giving teens adequate amounts of personal privacy. Differences arose as to how these processes were to manifest themselves, as well as how parents could best facilitate them; but most child development experts agreed that in order to become healthy, well-adjusted adults, adolescents had to break free from parental (particularly maternal) control and establish their own identity outside the family circle. To subvert this process, many experts agreed, was to risk encouraging a host of negative outcomes—including, as one child-rearing expert explained in the mid-1940s, "ruined marriages" and even "fistic combat" between parent and child.[12]

As a result, the teen bedroom continued to be seen as a key contributor to the emancipation process. Consider, for example, Douglas A. Thom's *Guiding the Adolescent* (1946), a child-rearing text that was distributed across the country by the federal government. In one particularly illuminating passage, Thom used an "increasingly secretive" patient of his named Isabel to illustrate how the teen bedroom could be used to free teenagers from their overbearing mothers. Isabel, he argued, used her bedroom as a means of shielding "her own newly developing personality

Figure 3 This sketch, taken from a 1955 Children's Bureau publication, suggests that the bedroom was an integral part of the maturation process. US Children's Bureau, *The Adolescent in Your Family*, pamphlet (Washington, DC: GPO, 1955), 24.

from the mature and dominating personality of her mother." Whenever her mother came into her room, Isabel "fled to the clothes closet; if her mother was around in the evening when she was studying she locked the door of her room; before leaving the house in the morning she locked her desk lest her mother touch any of the things." Instead of withdrawing from her daughter, however, Isabel's mother continued to invade the young girl's personal space on a regular basis. "She would still come into her bedroom occasionally and sit in a corner hoping to watch Isabel dress and be able to talk things over," Thom noted. "Sometime she made such remarks as this: 'Isabel, you seem to forget that I am your mother. You hide yourself so persistently that I don't believe I know what you look like without your clothes on, and I'm your own mother!'" Ultimately, Thom suggested that Isabel's behavior represented a reasonable attempt to wean herself psychologically from the family. The culprit in this instance, he concluded, was Isabel's mother, whose decision to violate the privacy Isabel enjoyed in her room was described by Thom as "fundamentally selfish" and bound to produce unhappy results.[13]

Arnold Gesell, the eminent Yale psychologist and pediatrician, made similar claims about the role bedrooms played in adolescent development. Though Gesell didn't state in explicit terms that teenagers be given rooms of their own, he did suggest that the simple act of retreating or emerging from one's room was linked to various stages of development. Like many of his peers, Gesell characterized the preteen years as a calm before the storm, a rosy period in which parent-child relations were still on a firm footing. Ten, Eleven and Twelve—Gesell referred to his subjects in aggregate, according to their age—were outgoing and sociable, and still enjoyed their families, which was reflected by his observation that Eleven "spends next to no time in his room." The bedroom, he argued, reflected the extent to which the child was able to disassociate him- or herself from the rest of the family. During early adolescence, the bedroom played a lesser role because the child was still in thrall to the authority of his or her parents and dependent on the family unit for socialization. "He is not an isolationist," Gesell proclaimed, once again referring to the average eleven-year-old. "If he is lucky enough to have a room of his own, he does not retire to it. He gravitates to the family group, as though magnetized by them." By the age of thirteen, however, the average child would start demanding more privacy and solitude within the home. "Thirteen spends quite a lot of time in his room," Gesell observed. "He may plaster his walls with pictures of movie actors or actresses or with pennants. He spends a great deal of time lounging on his bed, reading, listening to his radio, or doing his homework. And he often has his door equipped with lock and chain to ensure privacy, especially from younger siblings." This behavior was in direct contrast with Fourteen, whom Gesell characterized as a much more social creature. No longer requiring solitary pursuits to "enrich the structure of the self," Fourteen "is less interested in decorating his room with pennants" and more likely to engage in "social gatherings" outside the home. Fourteen, in other words, has sworn off some of the more antisocial aspects of the maturation process and become more gregarious and other-directed, thereby rendering his or her bedroom less valuable in a developmental sense. "Some Fourteens, like Thirteens, are apt to spend considerable time in their rooms," Gesell concluded. "But on the whole Fourteen uses their room for sleeping and studying and would prefer to read in the midst of the family group."[14]

Gesell believed that generational conflict and demands for solitude are bound to return when adolescents reach the age of fifteen, with the child's bedroom once again taking center stage in the developmental process. "Some Fifteens obviously withdraw in the household," he explained. "They go directly to their rooms the minute they come in the house, hardly greeting their mothers." Described by Gesell as a "contending isolationist," Fifteen "does a lot of traveling in his fancies, when he withdraws remotely to his room." By the age of sixteen, however, the parent-child relationship once again stabilizes, as the maturation process supposedly draws to a close. Sixteen, Gesell concludes, begins to display "greater self-reliance and deeper self-containedness," thereby rendering the bedroom developmentally insignificant. Sixteen has found just the right balance between personal autonomy and family integration. "He thinks he can handle his own affairs and this is very close to true," Gesell noted. "He doesn't strenuously resist his parents. He only desires that they will go their way and he will go his." He is, Gesell added, "remote from his family in a happy way."[15]

Peter Blos, the famed psychoanalyst, offered a somewhat unique twist on the subject: he not only suggested that the teen bedroom could help further the emancipation process, but he also made the rather astounding claim that it could cure preexisting psychological conditions. In *On Adolescence* (1962), Blos referred to a patient of his named Judy, a friendless teenage girl "disfigured" by acne, who was constantly "possessed by feelings of rage and despair, alternating with remorse and depressed moods." Though Blos admitted that Judy's problems were the result of several factors, he also suggested that some of them could be attributed to the fact that she slept in the living room of her parents' house (and occasionally in their bed) for much of her teen years. Indeed, Blos claimed that Judy's personality underwent several important changes when she was finally given a room of her own during the latter stages of adolescence. While noting the somewhat alienating aspects of Judy's first experiences in her new space—it was reported that she initially felt "condemned to look at the four walls of her room"—Blos claimed that her new arrangements helped enhance the individuation process, weakened parental (particularly, maternal) ties, and forced Judy to face up to her problems as an individual. This simple gesture, he argued, basically freed her from pathology by forcing her to accept "her conflicts as her own . . . beyond resolution by maternal protection and gratification." Judy's bedroom, in short, provided her with some much-needed conflict resolution skills and taught her the virtues of self-reliance, transforming a potential case study in pathology into a developmental success story.[16]

One of the most poetic discussions of the teen bedroom's relationship to the maturation process was crafted in 1968 by Barry Schwartz, a psychology student at the University of Pennsylvania. Schwartz's ideas on teen space were published in an essay in the *American Journal of Sociology* that dealt with the psychological aspects of privacy. Though his approach was quite broad—addressing several issues relating to privacy and its effect on institutions, social groups, and individuals—Schwartz ended his essay by discussing how demands for privacy shaped the parent-child dynamic:

> During infancy the door to self is generally fully open; it closes perhaps halfway as a recognition of self development during childhood, it shuts but is left ajar at prepuberty, and closes entirely—and perhaps even locks—at the pubertal and adolescent stages when meditation, grooming, and body examination become imperative. Parents at this time are often fully denied the spectatorship to which they may feel entitled and are kept at a distance by means of the privacy that a locked door insures.

Here we see Schwartz making the rather Gesellian claim that the bedroom reflects its occupant's developmental progress, offering family members a spatial reminder of how growing up was often predicated on creating distance between parent and child. During infancy, when the child is thought to be most dependent, the bedroom door is wide open in order to allow full parental access. As the development of the child progresses, however, the bedroom door slowly begins to close, culminating in the adolescent stage when autonomy is fully secured via a closed and/or locked door. By framing the issue thusly, Schwartz acknowledged, through a particularly lively metaphor, what many Americans during the late 1960s probably already knew: that the teen bedroom was essentially out of bounds to other members of the family.[17]

Perhaps not surprisingly, teen sexuality remained a hot topic of conversation in discussions of the teen bedroom. Whereas early child development experts were known to obsess over the supposedly negative effects of masturbation, Cold War–era commentators placed greater emphasis on how the teen bedroom allowed adolescents to hide themselves away during the onset of puberty. The appearance of facial hair on males, breasts on females, and the intensification of sexual urges in both sexes was thought to produce in adolescents a self-consciousness about their bodies that could turn even the most gregarious soul inward. According to Urban Fleege, an educational psychologist at Catholic University during the 1940s, the child's fragile ego is basically under attack during puberty. Once "he becomes more aware of the precarious position of his own ego," he claimed, the average teen tends to lock himself away from others and "tighten his own defenses for its protection." Mary and Lawrence Frank made similar claims in *Your Adolescent at Home and in School* (1956), suggesting that it was "not at all unusual for a boy or girl to become extra modest about bathing and dressing." The demands of sexual maturation, they argued, saddled teens with "feelings and impulses" that "separate him from his parents and very often from all adults," resulting in behavior that can only be described as "guarded and secretive." Of course, the teen bedroom was thought to be particularly well-suited for this process, allowing anxiety-ridden teens to feel at ease amidst a sea of bodily change. In the letters section of his popular parenting text *Hide or Seek* (1974), James Dobson, a psychologist who would later become a prominent figure in the Christian Right, rebuked a mother who felt that her teenage daughter's demand that she leave her room while changing her clothes was "silly." On the contrary, he argued, "I would suggest that you honor her requests for privacy. Her sensitivity is probably caused by an awareness that her body is changing, and she is embarrassed by recent developments (or the lack of them). This is likely to be a temporary phase and you should not oppose her in it."[18]

The teen bedroom's value as a space in which grand ideas could be hatched continued to be stressed during the postwar years. "A boy, closing his door to study, may put in only half the evening on his books," a Children's Bureau pamphlet from 1955 declared, "but the half he spends in the clouds may be just as productive. Many great accomplishments have had their beginnings in those flashes by which the future is lit up for expectant boys and girls." Arnold Gesell made similar claims, suggesting that adolescents used their bedroom to enhance their thinking skills through a process of productive meditation. The average thirteen-year-old could be watching TV with the family when all of a sudden "he rises unceremoniously and without a word goes to his room—to cogitate, to ruminate." He is not running away from reality, though: "On the contrary, he probes more deeply into reality by turning things over in his mind. . . . He clarifies and organizes his experiences by inward rehearsals and self-examination." The adolescent essentially enters the bedroom a moody, irrational child and emerges from it with the wit of Voltaire and the reasoning abilities of Descartes. "His inwardizing leads to genuine thinking," Gesell proclaimed. "He takes a new pleasure in rational thought—in stating propositions and raising doubts."[19]

Popular and professional child-rearing experts were unequivocal in believing that the teen bedroom ought to play host to even some of the more irrational forms of teen behavior. For instance, Dick Clark, the amiable host of *American Bandstand,* reminded teenagers in *Your Happiest Years* (1959) that adolescent emotionality often found expression in the comfort of one's own bedroom. The simplest of things could send teenagers "roaring upstairs" to lock themselves in their room, he argued, including a "little brother and his constant jiggling with the radio or television" or an offhand comment from Mom about how "your room isn't as neat as it used to be." Rupert Hoover made similar claims in the early 1960s. "Here is Sara, who is so well-behaved in her childhood years" he described. "Now that she is in her teens, she shouts at her parents in defiance; she refuses to do the simple chores that are not taxing on schedule or playtime; she cries out now and again that she hates her mother and/or father; she slams the door of her room and pouts in solitude." Hoover distinguished himself from Clark, however, by interpreting this type of behavior in developmental terms, suggesting that the best way to address this problem was to simply recognize the "emotional turmoil" of the teen years and give adolescents the space to deal with it on their own terms. Citing the example of a teen boy he had been ministering to, Hoover urged parents to "respect his privacy. A teen-ager may seem to shut us out of his life at times by slamming the door of his room. This is a normal part of the growing up process."[20]

Messy bedrooms, too, were occasionally seen through the prism of child development theory. Although most experts saw messy rooms as a sign of laziness or meaningless rebellion—Dr. Spock, for one, firmly believed that messy rooms were "inexcusable and represent nothing more than 'nose-thumbing' at parents"—a growing number of experts claimed that development was actually being stunted by overly fastidious parents. According to a Children's Bureau pamphlet from the 1950s, parents who insisted on tidy rooms risked undermining their offspring's fragile self-esteem. "When we keep nagging at a girl to keep her room neater," it warned, "we may cancel her elation at having stuck to and carried out school assignments that involved real struggle and determination. Maybe the battle she won is much more important than our prissy emphasis on orderliness." In 1969 a parenting expert from *New York Times Magazine* even argued that messy bedrooms, rather than indicating some sort of moral failing on the teen's behalf, represented a "normal step toward maturity and independence," a welcome and predictable attempt by teens to assert their autonomy. Unfortunately, some observers felt it necessary to adopt a hectoring tone when posing these types of arguments, oftentimes treating traditional-minded parents like idiots or stubborn bitter enders. As syndicated columnist Russell Baker put it during the early 1970s, the question "Why does your room always have to look like a pigpen?" should never be asked because it fails to take into account the role messiness might play in allowing teens to express themselves as individuals. "Anyone so dumb that he has to ask is not worth the attention needed to reply," he exclaimed, "because he could never understand the sensitive person's need for self-expression."[21]

Of course, messy bedrooms may have been tolerated for more pragmatic reasons as well. Ever mindful of the workload of stay-at-home and working mothers—the parenting expert's core audience—some commentators suggested that the teen bedroom could provide adolescents with a space where they could be as messy as they wanted without taxing their mothers' housekeeping abilities. "We live in homes where a glass here and a magazine there can make the small space allotted for 'living' a shambles," Mary and Lawrence Frank argued. "So we tell the adolescent to take up his bed and walk—to the bedroom." Dorothy Baruch offered a similar rationale in *How to Live with Your Teenager* (1953). "I know you like to be messy," declared a hypothetical mother to her hypothetical teenage son. "In your own room, okay. But not in the living room. That's forbidden. I need to have that part of the house clean." Though this strategy could be interpreted as a form of surrender on behalf of parents, a reminder that teens were intrinsically messy and that parents had no hope of reversing this trend, it also illustrates the extent to which the teen bedroom was seen as being separate from other parts of the home. As one design expert from *New York Times Magazine* noted shortly after the end of the Second World War, the teen bedroom should be treated as a "private lair" that "mother closes off hastily when guests are invited to see the rest of the house." Both generations could allegedly benefit from this arrangement: teens were given the opportunity to experiment with various modes of living, while parents, siblings, and visitors were spared the clutter and disorder that that often entailed.[22]

Parenting experts may have also been reluctant to scold teens on the state of their bedrooms because they understood that messiness was a predictable by-product of the various hobbies and extracurricular activities that often took place there. Perhaps not surprisingly, support for many of these hobbies was often influenced by prevailing ideas on gender. Teen boys, for example, were often encouraged to use their rooms to partake in typically masculine activities, most notably physical fitness. One expert confessed that she could not "make clear the difference between a sleeping room and sports museum," while yet another commentator talked about "boys doing push-ups secretly (so they like to think until the plaster falls down) in their rooms." Hobbies that were educational in nature (e.g., making science experiments) or that stressed the accumulation of material goods (e.g., coin collecting) were similarly singled out as popular pastimes for boys. A Children's Bureau pamphlet from 1972 spoke in approving tones of hobby-oriented bedrooms that "bulge with the deserted loves of yesterday and the ambitious plans for today and tomorrow"; it simultaneously warned parents to avoid cleaning it up for fear of interrupting this process of self-discovery. "Don't clean up a thing without the help of your young hobbyist," it cautioned. "Everything you see, including yesterday's clutter, has meaning to him. Gradually he has found out a great deal about himself—what he can do and what he can't; what interests him and what doesn't." James Dobson even played on parental fears of teen drug use to convince a despondent mother to accept her fifteen-year-old son's collection of "caged snakes, wasp nests, plants and insects" in his bedroom. "If he keeps his zoo clean and well managed, then you should let him follow his interests," he argued. "Just remember that at fifteen 'bugs' beat drugs as a hobby!"[23]

Teen girls, meanwhile, were often encouraged to use their rooms to engage in various beauty rituals. This was especially true during the 1940s, 1950s, and 1960s, before second-wave feminism broadened the horizons of the average American girl. Many experts believed that the teen bedroom was an ideal place in which to forge one's personal style, providing girls with "the solitude in which to experiment with new hair styles and try different kinds of make-up." Educational films were especially vocal in this regard. *How to Be Well Groomed* (1949) and *Keeping Clean and Neat* (1956) feature several scenes in which teen girls are taught how to maintain acceptable standards of beauty while perched in front of a bedroom vanity. Indeed, the vanity was seen by many observers as one of the most important pieces of furniture in a teen girl's bedroom, allowing her the opportunity to not only experiment with cosmetics and hairstyles, but also improve her posture and project a more graceful image to the outside world. "Stand in front of a mirror, pull in your chin, keep your spine straight and your shoulders back," popular advice expert Emily Dow instructed in 1960. "See if you can hold the same statuesque pose when you walk away. Pretend you are a fashion model—in the privacy of your own room." For girls whose rooms were equipped for more bookish pursuits, however, the results were not quite so positive. *The Snob* (1958), one of the few educational films from the era to feature a girl's bedroom that was equipped with a desk rather than a vanity, argues that the main character's academic devotion led to her snobby behavior and a lack of friends.[24]

The anti-intellectual arguments found in *The Snob* are noteworthy not because they hold girls to a different standard than boys—this was common practice in the 1950s—but rather because they fail to address just how important educational goals had become after the Second World War. Though experts had long recognized that the teen bedroom could play an important role in the education of youth, this notion took on even greater importance due to the implementation of compulsory education strategies. School attendance began to increase dramatically during the 1930s and 1940s after a coalition of reformers, politicians, educators, and labor groups plucked America's school-age children from the streets and factory floors and pushed them into the classroom. The results of these policies were impressive. In 1900 the census reported that 13 percent of fourteen- to seventeen-year-olds were enrolled in school; by 1940 that number had increased to 73 percent, and would reach 97 percent by 1970. High school graduation rates increased at a similar clip during this period. In 1940, shortly after compulsory education schemes became the norm across the country, 24.5 percent of Americans twenty-five years and over reported having a high school diploma. In 1980, by contrast, 66.5 percent of Americans over the age of twenty-five reported having a high school diploma. College, too, became an increasingly popular option for many teens, particularly in the 1950s and 1960s when the baby boom came of age and Cold War realities—the Soviet Union's development of nuclear weapons in 1949 and its success in launching Sputnik into orbit in 1957—helped push lawmakers to increase investment in postsecondary education. Over the span of forty years, the percentage of Americans age twenty-five and older with a bachelor's degree or more nearly quadrupled, going from 4.6 percent in 1940 to 16.2 percent in 1980. Though not all teens were able to take advantage of these changes, the expansion of secondary education ensured that academics became an enshrined feature of postwar teen culture, as the younger generation faced growing pressure to get good grades, score well on the standardized tests, and be accepted at a reputable college.[25]

As the one area of the home in which scholarly activities were most often situated, the teen bedroom couldn't help but be affected by these changes. During the 1940s, Cornell sociologist Svend Riemer found that more and more families—including a significant number of working-class families—were providing their children with "bedroom-study combinations," separate sleeping spaces that were often defined by their ability to accommodate educational activities. In fact, Riemer suggested that the teen bedroom was often seen by families of modest means as a way of improving their class status by cultivating better academic scores and increasing the child's chances of landing a well-paying job. Though this is certainly a debatable point, Riemer's basic argument was not lost on parenting experts; several commentators, many of whom had little to no background in interior design, gave themselves the task of explaining how to transform even the smallest teen bedroom into a useful study space. Experts talked at length about where to place desks, reading lamps, bookshelves, and other furnishings associated with academic pursuits, while radio use, phone use, and anything else that could interfere with studying was carefully proscribed, using the promise of academic success or the threat of failure as a motivational tool. "You've read and heard the 'quiet room, good light, straight back chair, clean desk' formula often," one expert warned her teen readers in the 1960s. "In spite of this, many of you continue to do your homework flopped on a bed against a Top-Ten background. Some of you even insist that you can't work without this general confusion. You are absolutely and demonstrably wrong."[26]

Suffice to say that poorer and larger families who were unable to give their offspring rooms of their own faced a double bind: not only were experts arguing that shared bedrooms interrupted the maturation process, but now they were claiming that shared bedrooms might adversely affect the child's ability to do well in school and find a well-paying job. In order to remedy this problem, some experts began offering advice on how to create an adequate study space with minimal effort. This included something as simple as placing a desk in a faraway corner, or, as Enid Haupt suggested, hanging a "Please Don't Disturb" sign on the door—"like the ones in hotels"—and attending to one's studies while the rest of the family watched their favorite television program in another room. While perhaps admirable in its attempts to address the needs of less affluent families, this type of advice only reaffirmed the power of middle-class cultural norms by further demonizing the domestic arrangements of those who couldn't live up to this ideal. Poorer teens may have been given greater access to elementary, secondary, and postsecondary education during the Cold War, but the shared bedrooms in which they often studied were still seen as poor facsimiles of the well-appointed, stand-alone suites their more affluent friends enjoyed.[27]

Practical Advice

Lofty ideas on child development were just one part of the equation; practical concerns, too, were often given prominence in discussions of teen bedroom culture during the postwar years. Chief among them was the emergence of the knocking rule—a custom in which family members were encouraged to announce their presence with a gentle rap on the door. Though it is difficult to figure out exactly when this rule became popular, some of the earliest examples seem to have emerged during the Eisenhower administration. Mary and Lawrence Frank, for instance, urged parents in the mid-1950s to "knock at a door before you enter" and "tell the child beforehand when you're going to do some thorough cleaning." In subsequent decades support for the knocking rule seemed to harden, attracting support from some of the biggest names in the advice industry. In 1964 Abigail Van Buren (Dear Abby) declared her support for the knocking rule while fielding a question from a distraught teenage girl whose mother refused to knock before entering her bedroom:

> My mother asked me never to walk into her bedroom without knocking first and I have always respected her wishes. I am 15 and think I should have the same privilege, so I asked her please to knock on my bedroom door before coming in. Now she just bangs on the door once and barges right in and says, 'Does THAT satisfy you?' Then she reminds me that I am living in HER house and she has a right to go into any room she pleases whenever she wishes. What do you think of a mother like mine?

Van Buren's response was unequivocal, as she pointed out that the mother's behavior could lead to family dissolution. "Your mother is wrong and I hope she realizes it and changes her ways soon," she proclaimed, "because that's precisely the kind of maternal action that makes children want to leave home as soon as they become of age."[28]

Van Buren's estranged sister and fellow advice columnist, Ann Landers, was similarly supportive of the knocking rule. In a column from 1962 entitled "Standing Firm on Announcements," Landers took the side of a Michigan mother who opposed her husband's habit of barging into their daughter's room unannounced. "I feel a girl her age should be allowed to have privacy," the mother acknowledged. "He says I'm wrong to encourage such prudishness and that my outlook is unhealthy. When the boys started to grow up I wouldn't dream of going into their rooms without first knocking." Landers agreed, citing pubertal change and the teenage desire to hide themselves as their bodies change as appropriate justifications for giving teens greater privacy in their rooms. Even ultraconservative commentators, many of whom feared the erosion of parental authority at the hands of youth, offered support for the knocking rule. Grace Hechinger, a *New York Times* columnist who devoted much column space to deriding the increased liberties enjoyed by postwar adolescents, suggested in 1964 that parents ought to treat the knocking rule as an etiquette issue, a practical means of ensuring that every family member's right to privacy would be held in high regard. "A child's right to privacy should always be respected," she counseled. "Parents can hardly expect their offspring to knock before entering a room, if they barge into a child's room unannounced."[29]

Nonetheless, many child-rearing experts found that maintaining an entirely consistent view on teen privacy was no easy task. Normally a staunch defender of the inviolability of the teen bedroom, Van Buren addressed a letter in the spring of 1961 from a mother whose fifteen-year-old son kept his bedroom door locked "at all times" and refused to let her do any cleaning there for over a year. "I have to wait until he comes home from school to make his bed so he can go in with me and watch me," the mother complained. "He says he doesn't want anyone monkeying around in his drawers." Van Buren's response managed to both vindicate and undermine the idea of autonomous teen bedrooms in one fell swoop. "All teen-agers like (and deserve) some privacy," she explained, "but your son has gone overboard. It is your duty as the mother of a minor to find out what he is going to such extremes to hide." In 1977 Van Buren offered similar advice to a thirteen-year-old whose mother insisted on opening her mail, quizzing her on where she got all her money, and going through her bedroom whenever she left the house. "Violating one's reasonable privacy at any age breeds disrespect," she began, "but try to see your mother's side of it. Parents are responsible for their underage children, and your mother is apparently a little nervous about you. Continue to give her no reason to mistrust you, and eventually her confidence will grow and her suspicions cease." If Van Buren's somewhat contradictory claims are any guide, it would seem as though the teen bedroom's reputation for impregnability was not always practical or well deserved.[30]

Calls for greater privacy in the bedroom were also shaped by ideas on teen leisure, as parenting experts often lauded the teen bedroom's value as a place to "hang out" with friends. Arnold Gesell, for instance, spoke approvingly of thirteen-year-olds whose bedrooms were "elaborately equipped with food and provisions for entertainment," while Milwaukee social worker Alvena Burnite noticed a similar trend among adolescent girls in *Your Teen-Agers: How to Survive Them* (1952). "Girls," she pointed out, "like to have rooms in which they can entertain their closest teenage classmates. Perhaps they sprawl over the bed, drape themselves on the vanity bench, or lounge on the floor. Let them, it is their private domain." The bedroom's value as a hangout was often predicated on its ability to keep adolescents off the streets and out of trouble. Like their prewar counterparts, Cold War–era parenting experts insisted that there was a relationship between parental willingness to accommodate home-oriented activities and adolescents' desire to entertain themselves in unsupervised public spaces. Oliver Butterfield, a professor of child development at Columbia University during the 1940s, was just one of many commentators to take parents to task for refusing to allow their teen children to bring friends and dates home with them, suggesting that "lack of privacy and consideration for callers is one of the chief reasons why modern young people have turned to the dance floors, the theaters, and highways for most of their courting." During the 1950s, moreover, Mary and Lawrence Frank voiced support for Butterfield's argument by offering parents a stern ultimatum: parents should either provide teenagers with rooms of their own or risk driving them "to less desirable places" such as billiard halls, dance halls, bars, and other unsupervised venues.[31]

Firsthand Accounts

Although there is certainly a danger in assuming that the advice offered by both popular and professional child-rearing experts reflects the lived reality of teen bedroom culture, firsthand accounts suggest that many of their claims bore at least some degree of truth. For instance, anecdotal evidence suggests that parenting experts and teens shared similar views on messy bedrooms, as many teenagers saw a relationship between clutter and long-standing ideas on personal autonomy. Indeed, psychiatrist and popular parenting expert Haim Ginott pointed out that one of his patients saw his messy bedroom in constitutional terms. "My mother has no respect for me," the patient claimed. "She invades my privacy and violates my civil rights. She comes into my room and rearranges my drawers. She can't stand disorder, she says. I wish she'd tidy up her own room and leave mine alone." Identity issues also seemed to inform how teenagers maintained their rooms. Laurel from San Jose, California, justified her "unholy mess" of a bedroom by pointing out its value in bestowing upon her a measure of coolness. "I remember that my oldest cousin, who was my age, hated being in the room because he found it 'oppressive,'" she bragged. "I thought it was cool, though, and that *I* was cool for having created such a statement." Her messy bedroom was seen as something more than a mass of dirty clothes and endless clutter—it was a reflection of her identity, a lens through which she saw herself and her place in the teen pecking order.[32]

Parenting experts were also correct to emphasize the teen bedroom's value in hosting various hobbies and pastimes, some of which helped shape its occupant's future career path. Gary Anderson, a teen who grew up in Axtell, Nebraska, during the mid- to late 1950s, turned his bedroom into a rifle range during his senior year of high school, allowing him the opportunity to practice shooting "for five or six hours an evening when everybody was watching television." According to Arthur Whitman, a writer for *Boys' Life*, Anderson's jury-rigged practice facility may have even contributed to his gold-medal performances in the 1964 and 1968 Summer Olympics. "He did it by tacking some bull's-eyes on one wall of his bedroom," Whitman explained, "standing at the wall opposite and sighting his rifle." In 1964 a writer from *Ebony* claimed that basket-

Figure 4 Douglas Mitchell (seated) and his friends socializing in his attic bedroom, ca. 1960. Courtesy of Dean Quarnstrom.

ball prodigy Cazzie Russell's skills were similarly honed in his bedroom. "Cazzie has been an attention getter ever since his pre high school days when he would awaken his family as early as five in the morning, bouncing a basketball on his bedroom floor." Although Cazzie's mother was wary of his early-morning practice sessions, his father was more forgiving because he was convinced that "something might come of it"—that his son's activities might bear fruit later in life. The journalist who wrote Cazzie's story seemed to agree, as he claimed that the young man's improvised gymnasium provided him with the skills necessary to excel on the court. "The youngster earned varsity status at Carver High School," he noted, "played all three positions and helped the team win the 1962 Chicago public school championships, then guided Carver to the state finals before the team lost to Decatur in the final game by one point."[33]

The teen bedroom also acted as a venue for an array of literary and artistic pursuits. During the late 1950s and early 1960s, Douglas Mitchell could often be found in his attic bedroom in Wilmette, Illinois, perched before his trusty typewriter. "A room like this, with ashtray and typewriter at one's disposal, an eyrie with a bird's-eye view but removed from the humdrum was the ideal place to write," he recalls. "I tried my hand at poetry and a few short stories, but mostly writing letters to friends." Mitchell's growing appreciation of jazz and classical music also led him take up drumming in his bedroom. "I had two drum teachers in those days," he notes, "one for classical percussion technique, the other for jazz. The jazz drum instructor would come to our house to give me lessons, up in my room, of course." Though his tastes in music certainly differed from Mitchell's, Charlie Benante, a founding member of the popular heavy metal group Anthrax, found that his room served a similar purpose during the 1970s. Indeed, his bedroom's transformation into a rehearsal space was hastened when Benante's mother noticed that her son had learned to play "the entire soundtrack to *A Hard Day's Night* on a frying pan." Eager to indulge her son's passion, she bought Charlie a $500 drum set, which he promptly set up in his room on a drum riser of his own making. "And there he sat," a writer from *Spin* explained in 1987, "with a lot of rhythm in him, playing and playing."[34]

There is also little doubt that postwar teens used their rooms to entertain friends on a fairly regular basis. During the height of the Beat era, Douglas Mitchell frequently invited friends over to his third-floor attic bedroom to smoke cigarettes, listen to music, discuss art, read poetry and fiction aloud, and perhaps even engage in some clandestine sex acts. "I have a fairly vivid memory of my girlfriend reading out loud from Henry Miller's *Tropic of Capricorn*," he recalls, "and you can well imagine the bedroom's utility as a site for sexual experimentation." Mitchell's room seems to have bestowed upon his peer group a collective identity that set them apart from those who fell outside of his inner circle. His room was "a magnet for kids who needed a place to test their bohemian know-how and bask in the trappings of hip attitudes, practices, and fulfillments, thus setting them apart from their duller peers"—a place "to segregate oneself from the mundane and unwashed, a place to congregate with like minds." Casey Calloway, a resident of Cumming, Georgia, during the 1980s, recalls using her room as a meeting place as well, albeit under less lofty pretenses: "My bedroom was where we would go to get ready for our nights out, waiting and holding our breath to see if our parents were going to say okay, we could go, then anxiously running into the bedroom to find out what outfits and earrings we were going to wear."[35]

Interestingly enough, Calloway's fondness for entertaining friends was such that she planned and carried out an elaborate clandestine sleepover. It all began when Casey was in middle school and her parents forbade her from spending time with her best friend. Heartbroken, Casey concocted a plan in which her friend would come over during a break in their schooling and spend several nights in her bedroom. "We had this crazy idea that she would come over and stay the week," she recalls, "and we would keep my parents from ever knowing." Casey's friend was smuggled into the home one afternoon while her parents were at work as the young girl pulled out all the stops in order to ensure that her parents didn't stumble upon her ingenious plan.

> Every night when my parents were home, we would stay in my bedroom. I was always in my bedroom anyway, so they didn't think anything of it. I had a walk-in closet and I fixed a place for her to sleep in case my mom came in. My bed was next to the door and my TV was by my bed against the other wall. My friend laid on the floor by my bed, by the TV so she could watch TV. When my mom opened the door, she didn't even know my friend was on the floor because she couldn't see her.

Casey kept her guest well fed by putting extra food on her plate and smuggling it into her room when her parents weren't looking. "To this day," she proudly notes, "I don't think my parents ever found out she stayed a week with me." Obviously, there is a danger in thinking that this type of behavior was commonplace, but it should also serve as a reminder that the privacy teens enjoyed in their rooms could, at times, make it difficult for parents to notice certain types of misbehavior. Although Calloway's parents seemed willing to grant their daughter a fair amount of privacy in her room, one suspects that secret sleepovers did not figure into their decision-making process.[36]

Of course, it takes no great leap of logic to suggest that many teenagers used the privacy they enjoyed in their bedrooms as a means of getting away from the rest of the family. Nancy from Utica, Michigan, for example, claimed that getting a room of her own during the late 1950s and early 1960s was "wonderful" because it gave her a respite from her "annoying" siblings. "[It] gave me sanctuary from my little sisters," she admits. "I had a lot of conflicts with them before I got that room, but was able to mostly ignore them after." Although Laurel from San Jose was "very close" to both her sister and her mother as a teen, she seems to agree with the idea that separate bedrooms may have helped minimize family conflict. "It was a wonderful thing to have a room to myself," she recalls. "My sister and I shared a bedroom at my father's house, where we spent most weekends, and I think if I'd had to share with her full time, I'd have gone out of my mind." Without a room to call her own, Laurel's relationship with her sister would have been tested by a host of issues. "Not only was she five times as messy as I was," she explains, "but she looked for opportunities to expose my weaknesses and embarrass me in front of her friends and mine." There are obviously limits to these types of privacy-oriented arrangements, but parenting experts were probably right to emphasize the "get away from it all" urge as a major selling point of the separate bedroom ideal.[37]

The extent to which parents bought into some of these claims can be discerned by examining their views on the knocking rule. Although it is next to impossible to determine how popular this custom actually was, many parents seem to have been willing to enact some variation of it. For instance, Nancy from Utica recalls that during the late 1950s and early 1960s, her mother "would knock before she came in." Anthony Bernier, meanwhile, notes that his dog Cindy was "the only being who didn't have to knock first" before entering his room. It is important to point out, however, that the knocking rule was only effective when two or more parties were around to give it meaning—an aspect of this custom that was rarely discussed by child-rearing experts. In fact, many types of anti-intrusion measures could be easily ignored once teenagers left either their rooms or the house. Adrienne Salinger found this out the hard way while growing up in Moraga, California, during the 1970s. "I assumed my mother never went in my room because I thought her to be completely disinterested in everything about me," she explains. "Very recently, I realized that she had been through my stuff when I was young—because she made disparaging remarks about my candy bar stash." Salinger's friends also found that the privacy they enjoyed in their rooms was conditional on them establishing a physical presence there. "Most of my friends had complete autonomy in their rooms," Salinger notes. "Or at least they thought so at the time. While they were in their rooms, alone or with friends, they always felt as if it were private. At the same time, it was always emerging that their parents or siblings had violated their privacy when they weren't home—reading their diaries, finding their contraband." Privacy may have been held up as a sacred right when teens were in their rooms, but it could easily be circumvented when no one was around to witness more overt forms of parental intrusion.[38]

To compensate, teens often devised their own strategies for defending their right to privacy, some of which received both tacit and explicit approval from their parents. During the late 1950s and early 1960s, for example, Douglas Mitchell's privacy was preserved in part by a "bell-buzzer" that "could be rung from downstairs when I was needed for meals or other appearances on the ground floor (or for phone calls)," thereby satisfying parental demands for family togetherness without compelling his parents to physically insert themselves into their son's space. During the late 1970s and early 1980s, Laurel from San Jose invested in a deadbolt lock after figuring out that her fourteen-year-old sister enjoyed rummaging through her room. "It was bad enough that she borrowed (and sweated in) my clothes and shoes," she complains, "but she also short-sheeted my bed, sneaked looks at my novel-in-progress and recited the most cringe-worthy parts when I had friends over, and tried to bust in when she knew my boyfriend and I were in my room making out." Although it helped ensure a modicum of privacy while Laurel was entertaining friends, the new lock was virtually "useless" whenever her room was left unattended. "My sister was able to climb out my mother's bathroom window, scuttle over the roof, and get into my room through my window, steal the clothes she wanted, and climb back, all while I was in the shower." Among some teens, moreover, having a lock on the door was a privilege that could be taken away at a moment's notice. Jeff Steele was given permission to put a lock on his bedroom door while attending junior high in Corvalis, Oregon, during the late 1980s. Despite acknowledging that his new lock "felt like ultimate freedom, that much closer to adulthood," Steele's habit of "sneaking out at night to meet friends" ended his experiment in a rather abrupt manner: "Getting caught out late at night by the police my sophomore year meant the end of the lock."[39]

But what about teens who were either unable to afford a deadbolt lock or a buzzer, or whose parents were simply unwilling to let them install these types of devices in their rooms? In instances such as these, it is best not to underestimate the ability of teenagers to find convenient and cost-effective workarounds. Leslie from Nampa, Idaho, had a rather crude yet ingenious method of preserving the sanctity of her room, one that required nothing more than a common household item that most teens probably take for granted. "Privacy was paramount to me as a teenager," she explains. "My room came with no lock on the door, so to discourage unwanted intrusions, I closed the door and stuffed an old steak knife into the doorjamb to prevent the door from opening inward." Once again, it is worth noting that Leslie's makeshift lock was valuable only when she was actually in her bedroom. Since her mother was "so-so about respecting my privacy," Leslie was forced to write her journal entries "in a little bit of code." Although this did little to prevent her privacy from being violated, Leslie's experiment with cryptography prevented her mother from finding out that her first sexual experience was with a girl named "Tanya" rather than a boy named "Tony." To a closeted teenager living in a conservative state during the height of the Reagan era, protecting the privacy she enjoyed in her bedroom was important because it allowed Leslie to engage in a certain amount of sexual experimentation without fear of reprisal.[40]

Unfortunately, supporters of the separate bedroom ideal were not always willing to address some of the more contradictory aspects of teen bedroom culture. Among teenagers who didn't have rooms of their own, or whose experiences with teen room culture were fleeting or inconsistent, much of the literature that addressed this custom must have seemed like wishful thinking. Consider the experiences of Roger, a native of Irving, Texas, who came of age during the late 1960s and early 1970s. The youngest of four children, Roger shared a room with his older brother for the first fifteen years of his life. In 1968, shortly after his brother moved out of the family home, Roger took sole possession of the room they had once shared. His experience with separate bedrooms was short lived, though, as Roger was once again forced into shared accommodations due to economic circumstances. "I had it to myself for a year or two after 1968," he recalls, "but my brother lost his job and had to move back home, and so I never really took charge of it." Roger continued to share a room with his brother until 1973, when the last of his two sisters moved out. After moving into his sister's old room, he soon discovered that it didn't provide much in the way of privacy due to architectural irregularities. "The room was situated between the living room and the bathroom, so it was a transit zone with doors on two sides that could not be locked, meaning that it offered no real privacy." Roger's parents also took in foster children and entertained coreligionists in their home, which prevented him from enjoying any amount of privacy in his room. "Ours was a devoutly religious family, with lots of visitors and foster kids who stayed with us for periods of time," he admits, "so no one ever enjoyed the kind of privacy that a 'teen room' would imply."[41]

Postwar commentators also revealed themselves to be a bit overzealous in terms of how they downplayed the benefits—and exaggerated the dangers—of shared bedrooms. In fact, many postwar teens believed that shared accommodations encouraged a sense of camaraderie and togetherness that separate bedrooms simply could not provide. "When we are busy," one of Eugene Gilbert's interview subjects explained in 1960, "the only time we see each other is when we are in our room. We enjoy each other's company and like to talk." Child-rearing experts, in short, may have underestimated the average teenager's willingness to share his or her personal space with others. Leslie from Nampa, Idaho, for instance, invited one of her sisters into her bedroom on a fairly regular basis. "I consistently invited my younger sister, who was ten years younger than me, into my room," she cheerfully reports. "I adored her then." Parents, too, were occasionally encouraged to spend time within the supposedly sacred confines of the teen bedroom. Thankful for the efforts she went to in order to provide him with a room of his own, Anthony Bernier allowed his mother to nap in his bedroom whenever she returned from a hard day of work. "After a while," he notes, "once my own sense of private space was secure, established, and defended—once I had the opportunity to enact my own spatial aesthetics—I invited my mom to take her after-work naps in my room, away from the higher traffic of the small living room with three kids constantly running in and out." Since Bernier had experience sharing space with other family members, the prospect of temporarily losing access to his own room was taken in stride. "While my mom took those necessary time-outs in the relative afternoon calm and quiet of my room," he recalls, "I would be out playing ball, visiting with the kids down the block in the single mom ghetto in which we lived, or just watching TV."[42]

All of this is to say that many of the arguments presented by supporters of the separate bedroom ideal skirt the line between perceptive and problematic. Once again, very little evidence was presented to prove that adolescent development could be either enhanced by separate bedrooms or undermined by shared bedrooms. In many instances, the relationship between separate bedrooms and positive developmental outcomes continued to be assumed rather than proven. This is not to say, however, that child-rearing experts were wrong to describe the teen bedroom in inherently psychological terms. Many teenagers seemed to have forged an incredibly intense psychological relationship with their rooms, oftentimes noting that their sleeping quarters had a calming and therapeutic effect on them, a way of making them feel safe and valued as individuals. Casey Calloway, for instance, claims that her room, besides acting as a quiet space in which to do homework—"I would pull a stool up to the window sill, put my books on it, open the window enough to feel the breeze blowing my hair, listen to music, and get my homework done"—allowed her ample opportunity to ponder the world around her. "I would catch myself staring out the window, thinking about everything," she recalls. "Once again, in my room I could stare off and get quiet without having to tell anybody what I was thinking."[43]

Tiffany Hauck, a resident of Vancouver, Washington, during the 1980s, had a similarly intense relationship with her bedroom: "I would say my room strongly identified me as a teen. My room was a concrete representation of all my interests—listening to and playing music and watching movies." Tiffany acknowledges, moreover, that the manner in which her family was structured—her only siblings were twin sisters who were six years her senior—helped strengthen the bonds she forged with her bedroom. "Since so many years separated us, I spent a lot of time alone in this room," she notes. "If I wasn't downstairs watching MTV in the living room (the only TV we had that got that channel), I was upstairs in my bedroom." Tiffany's room meant so much to her, in fact, that it continued to inform her views on personal space long after she left adolescence behind.

"Interestingly, wherever I lived after this, I've tried to recreate this room to some extent—usually in the location and proximity of things to one another," she admits. "When I was college-aged and lived in small studio apartments, I set my space up in a similar way, I imagine because it's an environment in which I felt safe." Now married and in her forties, Tiffany hasn't let the memories of her old bedroom fade away. "Even today, I have my own room in our house. The walls here are also covered, though with different things, but my space continues to be a reflection of me—the one place in the house where things aren't 'ours' (mine and my husband's) but 'mine.'"[44]

Adrienne Salinger's bedroom, meanwhile, seemed to have provided her with a means of assessing the various friends and acquaintances who ran in her social circle. A simple glance at the bedroom of a potential love interest, for example, was enough to tell Salinger exactly how "cool" he was, revealing aspects of his persona that his clothes and personal style could not cover up. "A boyfriend from high school had very long hair and wore a red bandanna around his neck," she notes. "When I saw his bedroom, I was amazed. The only things in it were a maple, four-poster bed with a wrinkle-free bedspread and a matching bureau with attached mirror. I thought he'd be cooler." The bedrooms enjoyed by the brothers of one of her friends were conceived along similar lines, acting as forbidden fruit that she and her friend were simply powerless to resist. "We spent entire Friday nights going through their stuff while they were out at parties," Salinger confesses, once again illustrating the limits of teen privacy. "It felt dangerous sitting in their rooms—fingering their guitars and looking up at their Crosby, Stills, Nash and Young posters." These boys, it would seem, were lucky enough to end up on the "cool" side of the ledger—a designation that would have meant the world to almost anyone growing up near San Francisco, the epicenter of cool, during the 1960s and 1970s.[45]

* * *

The expanded popularity of separate bedrooms manifested itself in novel ways during the postwar years. Home sellers in particular were more than willing to publish real estate ads during the 1960s and 1970s that focused special attention on teen bedrooms. "Three bedrooms, plus separate in-law or teen-agers heaven," one homeowner proclaimed in a 1964 edition of the *Oakland Tribune*. "One bedroom with private bath ideal for teen-ager or in-laws," another ad read in a 1968 edition of the *Van Nuys News*. "The bedroom in the lower level could be your teen-ager's delight," a Nebraska seller noted in the summer of 1977. This trend is remarkable because it reaffirms that (a) the teen bedroom's popularity had expanded significantly during the postwar years, and (b) that its popularity was due to something more than an urge among parents to accommodate their privacy-starved children. In an era dominated by youth and characterized by unprecedented levels of wealth, the autonomous teen bedroom assumed a prominent position within the larger narrative of homeownership, serving as a valuable commodity that could attract the attention of home buyers, real estate agents, and other key actors in the housing industry. One could argue, in fact, that the teen bedroom was now acting as both a symbol and a source of wealth.[46]

Humorists, too, took notice of the child-centered nature of the autonomous teen bedroom, oftentimes reinforcing its hegemony by adopting what can only be dubbed an attitude of knowing resignation. The average teenager's sense of entitlement in their rooms and the average parent's blind willingness to accommodate their children's demands were given special attention. In 1970, for instance, a contributor to the *Daily Courier* of Connellsville, Pennsylvania, offered parents some waggish advice that was guaranteed to help widen the generation gap. "I will not respect his privacy," the author began. "When he's out of the house I'll go over his room like an inchworm, looking for evidence of anything he's trying to get away with or keep from me." A list of demands from teens was also presented in comedic terms, including a plea for parents to stop coming into their rooms and asking annoying questions, such as "What's that I smell?," "How can you live in this pigpen?," "Are you going to sleep all week?," and "What's that magazine you just shoved under your mattress?" Martin Ragaway, the cowriter of Abbott and Costello's famous "Who's on First?" routine, adopted a more blunt approach in *How to Get a Teenager to Run Away from Home*, a tongue-in-cheek look at parent-child relations during the Reagan years. Out of the 105 cartoons that made up Ragaway's collection, 27 were predicated on the idea that nothing angers teenagers more than bringing about unwanted change to their bedrooms. This includes calls to "put a TV camera on the ceiling and scan the room every 30 seconds," "draw a moustache on his Farrah Fawcett poster," "burn her John Travolta picture," and "put a lock on the outside of his bedroom door." At times, some humorists went out of their way to convince parents that they had no hope of regaining the authority they had once had in their children's rooms. The autonomous teen bedroom was here to stay, they argued, and any attempts to reverse this trend were doomed to failure. "For your teenager's peace of mind," one contributor to the *Syracuse Herald-Journal* cheekily concluded, "don't ever go into his or her bedroom without permission. For your own peace of mind, don't ever go in there, period."[47]

FIVE

Rooms to a Teen's Tastes

In the Queens brick ranch house Yael shares with her family, everything is neat, everything in its place, until we get to her room. Her room isn't messy, but it's packed, a suburban girl's bedroom in a state of war. On her waterbed, covering the pillows and spilling everywhere, dominating one side of the room, hundreds of stuffed animals pile on top of one another. The wall opposite is covered entirely with Meanstreak backstage passes. Meanstreak and Iron Maiden, Meanstreak and Anthrax, Meanstreak and Motorhead. *SPIN* (1989)

During the 1970s teen-oriented magazines such as *Seventeen* and *Rolling Stone* were among the first to feature advertisements for the "Blow Yourself Up Company," "Photo Poster Incorporated," and "Photo Hang Ups Incorporated"—small backroom enterprises that offered teens the chance to turn pictures of themselves into posters they could hang on their bedroom walls. For anywhere between $2 and $7.50, teens were encouraged to transform their own grinning visages into glossy three-by-four-foot posters with psychedelic colors and personalized messages added for effect. Though there is no evidence to suggest that these posters achieved any amount of popularity, they do act as a reminder of the ways in which room decoration and teen identity were indelibly linked during the latter half of the twentieth century. Other commentators may have encouraged teens to think of wall hangings as a reflection of their emerging personalities, but the companies that offered to "blow up" teens in the back pages of various teen-oriented magazines brought this idea to its logical conclusion in the most literal way possible: by encouraging teenagers to broadcast their flaws and imperfections, their awkward yearbook smiles and intermittent bouts with acne, up on their bedroom walls. The bedroom and the self had effectively merged, and—perhaps more importantly—the end product could be purchased at a relatively low price.[1]

The emergence of "blow up" posters also illustrate the extent to which child-centered design strategies reigned supreme during the latter half of the twentieth century. The parent-centered strategies that prevailed throughout much of the Victorian era were rendered obsolete during the postwar years as new approaches, predicated on exploiting the growing economic power of teens and freeing them from parental dictates, took center stage. Whereas décor experts during the interwar years encouraged parents to simply grant teens a larger role in decorating the teen bedroom, their postwar counterparts were intent on removing parents from the process entirely. The parent-centric, top-down strategies that had dominated during the first four decades of the twentieth century were replaced by direct appeals to teens and a strong do-it-yourself (DIY) ethos, the latter of which threatened to undermine décor experts' authority among the very consumers they sought to influence. It takes no great amount of scholarly insight, after all, to understand that urging teens to take matters into their own hands made it extremely difficult for décor experts to have their own advice taken seriously.

The decline of traditional décor advice is worth noting for another reason: it may have reflected the extent to which teen bedroom culture had expanded its reach beyond the predominantly female and middle-class audiences that had sustained it during the nineteenth and early twentieth centuries. Unlike some of the more formal, middle-class décor strategies that were common before the Second World War—the vast majority of which involved the purchase of expensive items and were shaped by rigid ideas on gender—the DIY approach was restricted only by the imaginations of the teenagers who embraced it. Teenagers would continue to decorate their rooms in a traditional manner, but the pressure to do so was reduced somewhat by the emergence of newer, more flexible strategies that were inspired by the youth counterculture of the 1960s and 1970s and emphasized found items, spontaneity, and creative disorder. Teen bedrooms were no longer seen as youthful variations of the master bedroom or parlor, as their owners were much more likely to take hold of the decoration process in a manner that earlier generations of teens were unaccustomed to.

Teen Uniqueness and the Economics of Room Décor Advice

Children's bedrooms during the nineteenth and early twentieth centuries were not always segregated according to age, as many observers suggested that a room belonging to a preteen was basically no different from the room of a teenager. This line of thinking effectively disappeared by the 1950s and 1960s, when most mainstream experts began to see the teen bedroom as a wholly separate entity. Explaining why this came to be is, admittedly, a tricky proposition, although any explanation must include the growing influence of social science in shaping the way Americans understood adolescents and their place in society. The idea of adolescence as a discrete stage of the life cycle was basically invented by the social scientific establishment during the first half of the twentieth century; in effect, scholars with backgrounds in psychology (G. Stanley Hall), sociology (Talcott Parsons), and anthropology (Margaret Mead) provided the intellectual basis for the emergence of teenagers as a distinct group by choosing to study them as a distinct group. Similarly, the advent of compulsory education schemes, which were heavily influenced by social scientific ways of thinking, also played a role in creating a separate teen identity. Most private and public schools during the postwar years were structured in such a way as to differentiate adolescents from their younger counterparts: preadolescents were sent off to elementary schools where they would be educated alongside other prepubescent children, while adolescents were marched off to junior high or high school, where the vast majority of their peers were either postpubescent or just about to enter into a state of sexual maturity. Gone were the days when six-year-olds were taught alongside thirteen-year-olds in a one-room schoolhouse; the education system that emerged in the 1930s and 1940s breathed life into the concept of adolescence by acknowledging that older children had different needs than their younger counterparts and deserved to be treated accordingly.[2]

Teen "separateness" was also shaped by the growing economic powers of teenagers and, of course, the various business interests that courted them. Although the business community had been targeting youth since at least the 1880s, the empowerment of the teen consumer reached its zenith after the Second World War, when the teen set's discretionary spending powers spiked considerably. In 1944, for instance, *Time* reported that the average teen had approximately $2.41 in spending money per week at his or her disposal; by contrast, that same teen had almost four times that amount ($8.96) in 1956. By the end of the decade, advertising expert Eugene Gilbert claimed that the average teenager was earning approximately $10 per week—two-thirds of which came from allowance, the rest from part-time work. When coupled with positive demographic trends—Cold War–era teens were simply more plentiful than their prewar counterparts—these statistics explain why, to quote Grace Palladino, the teen market was seen as "an advertiser's dream" during the postwar years, one of the few consumer groups with both "the free time and disposable income to support an affluent life of leisure." Teenagers had become an unemployed leisure class, a unique group of consumers whose collective and individual identity rested upon the agency they enjoyed within the marketplace.[3]

All this is to say that the emergence of the teen bedroom as a unique and exclusive space within the home depended in large part on the culture's willingness to embrace the idea that teenagers themselves were a unique and exclusive group of people. This trend was reinforced by décor experts in interesting ways. For starters, they often acted as liaisons between teenagers and the advertisers, manufacturers, and retailers who sought to exploit the teen market's expanding economic powers. Décor experts couldn't force teenagers to spend their money on any specific goods and services, but their expertise was tailored in such a way as to create a dialogue between the younger generation and the very same businesspeople who saw teenagers in singular terms. This helps explain why décor experts offered advice that was much more age specific during the postwar years, as most commentators promoted the idea that a room meant for a seven-year-old would no longer suffice for a seventeen-year-old. Although many experts were firm in their belief that younger children "should be allowed positive participation in furnishing his own room" and that they not be subjected to "decorative ideas conceived and imposed on him by grown-ups," teenagers, it was generally agreed, were to have near-total control over their surroundings, no matter how ungainly the end result may be. "Mother better resign herself," a décor expert from the *New York Times* warned her readers. "The color will be too bright, possibly the wrong hue, and streaked in execution, but Independence Day will have arrived and the children's room will have started to fade away."[4]

Child-centered design strategies also began to take hold among décor experts who catered to African American audiences. During the interwar years, separate bedrooms were rarely, if ever, discussed by the black press, acting as a reminder that economics—in tandem with the often impoverishing effects of institutionalized racism and segregation—limited the separate bedroom ideal to privileged members of society. By the late 1950s and early 1960s, however, the teen bedroom became a topic of discussion in several prominent black newspapers, a phenomenon that reflected both the expansion of the black middle class and the growing popularity of the separate bedroom ideal among groups that had once been excluded from this custom. Indeed, much of the advice offered in African American sources would have seemed quite familiar to the white, middle-class audiences that tended to read *Ladies' Home Journal* or *House & Garden*. The teen bedroom was characterized as a "personal suite" where teens could hide themselves away from the rest of the family, with one expert from the *Chicago Defender* describing it as a "symbol of his status as an individual." Many in the black press similarly argued that African American teens be given the task of decorating their rooms on their own terms. One expert from the *Atlanta World*, for example, suggested that teens use the free time given to them during summer vacation to redesign their own room according to their own wishes, if only because this was the one space within the home "where much time is spent reading, relaxing, listening to the radio, TV or hi-fi."[5]

African American design experts did, however, have differing views on how to manage the issue of shared bedrooms. Though much of their advice reflected ideas that had been bandied about for decades—one observer, for instance, suggested that parents could "avoid discord by giving each his own chest, dresser, closet, and desk" and by purchasing "paneled screens or bookshelf room dividers"—African American experts sometimes veered significantly from the mainstream in addressing this issue. One of the most unorthodox suggestions involved an expert from the *Chicago Defender* who counseled families on how to deal with the arrival of a new baby. Recognizing that the problem of providing space for a baby "can be acute," the expert argued that the infant should share a room with an older brother or sister whose closet could be easily transformed into a makeshift nursery. Suffice to say that this type of advice was verboten among most white, middle-class experts, many of whom subscribed to the notion—argued forcefully by John Watson and his followers during the 1920s and 1930s—that shared bedrooms were a source of pathology. This is not to say that African American design experts ignored major trends in child development, but rather that they may have been more sensitive to the need for practical alternatives. As a segment of the population that was more likely to suffer from the throes of poverty, African American families may have been willing to forsake the separate bedroom ideal in favor of strategies that might have seemed unorthodox, or even unseemly, to middle-class, white observers.[6]

Nonetheless, most décor experts, regardless of the race or ethnicity of their target audience, were paid to publish thinly veiled advertisements for bedroom-oriented consumer goods. Design experts were no doubt passionate about providing readers with useful, cost-effective advice, but the economics of the magazine and newspaper industry was such that the line between editorial content and advertising essentially disappeared. The *New York Times*, for example, regularly used their columns to promote Seneca textiles and stuffed animals from Altman's department stores, while the *Christian Science Monitor* claimed that teen girls could "feel like Cinderella" by stocking their bedroom with furnishings from Lane Company, Thomasville, and American of Martinsville. African American media outlets were not above engaging in this kind of behavior either. In 1975 the *Atlanta World* published a brief column on teen room design that mentioned products from no fewer than four companies, including an early incarnation of Stanley (the power tool company), Imperial Wallpaper, Restonic Corporation, and Spring Mills. One of the most blatant examples of cross-promotion, however, emerged during the 1950s in a recurring advice column by Howard Seifer, a home décor expert whose suggestions were often colored by the fact that he owned a furniture store in suburban Chicago called Seifer's of Park Forest. Perhaps not surprisingly, many of the items that could supposedly afford teen boys "an early opportunity to learn the art of gracious hospitality" were readily available at his own store at affordable prices.[7]

Although most newspapers and home décor magazines adopted variations on this business model, teen-oriented magazines undoubtedly perfected it. *Co-ed*, for instance, offered readers reams of decorating advice in which name brand products were mentioned on a frequent basis, most notably in a recurring column called "Room Service." Perhaps cognizant that much of its audience came from home economics students—*Co-ed* was published by Scholastic, one of the largest suppliers of magazines and books to the American public school system—the editors of *Co-ed* were careful to distinguish editorial content from advertisements by including a list of recommended products at the back of the magazine; companies no doubt paid to have their products mentioned in *Co-ed*, but the articles themselves rarely featured direct mention of any brand-name items. *Seventeen*, on the other hand, had no such policy. In fact, one would be hard pressed to find a *Seventeen* article published between 1944 and 1990 that does not embrace a wholly synergistic approach to design expertise. The most striking example of this is a monthly column written during the early 1960s called "This I Like" by Barbara Broyhill. If the name sounds familiar, it should: Ms. Broyhill was the owner of Broyhill Furniture, one of the largest manufacturers of home furnishings in the world. Like Mr. Seifer, her counterpart in Chicago, Broyhill always ended her column by pointing her audience toward her company's own line of bedroom-oriented furnishings and accessories.[8]

Décor experts also paid significant attention to how bedroom-oriented consumer choices made as a teen could go on to shape consumption habits in adulthood. In 1957, for instance, a design expert from Ohio suggested that brand loyalty among teen girls was often formed in their bedrooms and would continue to affect their buying decisions well after they were married. The teen bedroom was worth keeping an eye on, the author of the piece suggested, because teen girls were aware that their bedroom furnishings could "be used at home now and later in homes of their own." Similar claims were made by Marilyn Hoffman, the chief design expert at the *Christian Science Monitor*. In 1964 she pointed out that 59 percent of American teenagers had redecorated their room in the past year and that three out of four teenage girls were inclined to redecorate their rooms once every two or three years. Hoffman paid special attention to the age at which teen girls were getting married:

> Most companies are trying to accomplish two things at once: design and manufacture furniture which fits the needs and moods of teenagers, while they are living with their parents, but which can also move with them into their own homes after they marry. Since about 600,000 girls of 18 and 19 marry each year, hundreds of them take the furniture from their own rooms as a nucleus of their new homes.

The teen bedroom was thus conceived as something more than a temporary storage space for furniture, linen, bedding, and other mass-produced items; it was seen as a means of creating brand loyalty—of ensuring that teens who bought, say, Broyhill furniture for their bedrooms would continue to buy that brand of furniture long after their teen years had drawn to a close.[9]

The home furnishings industry seems to have taken heed of this trend. In 1951 Lane ran advertisements for chests that drew a strong link between the teen bedroom and the matrimonial home. "Give her a Lane Cedar Chest now—even if she's not engaged," it recommended. "For the sooner she has her Lane, the sooner she can start gathering the beautiful things that will make her future home a happier, more charming place." Other companies quickly followed suit. "To move with ease from your bedroom of today, expand into your newlywed apartment of tomorrow, and flatter every room in your house a few years hence," a 1961 advertisement for Drexel furniture proclaimed. "Just like choosing your sterling pattern, you start with a few Drexel pieces now, gradually add to them as your horizons grow." Bassett, a major manufacturer of bedroom furniture, ran a similar campaign in the early 1970s in which teens were urged to "choose wisely now for later." "Of course your style will change a little when you marry," the advertisement read. "No need to change furniture though. Just put aside the posters, the sneakers, the charming teenage trinkets, and watch your pretty, practical Bassett furniture take on a new glow too."[10]

Department stores were also quick to recognize the money-making possibilities of the teen bedroom. As early as 1948, Carson, Pirie, Scott &

Company, a department store in Chicago, ran a contest for teens to see who could come up with the best bedroom as judged by a panel of prominent interior design journalists. The rules were simple: submissions had to abide by a "down-to-earth" budget of $350 to $425; they had to maximize the efficient use of space; and contestants could not receive any coaching from teachers or parents. At first blush, contests like this should be seen as mere advertising stunts, a means of drumming up business for the stores that sponsored them. The winners of this particular contest, after all, received gift certificates for Carson's that ranged anywhere from $10 for honorable mention to $100 for first place, while the store itself received valuable promotion in both local and national news outlets. However, these contests also acted as a direct form of market research, allowing the owners of the store to figure out that teens wanted a place for "precious collections," bulletin boards that could be used to pin up "important reminders and souvenirs," multiuse furniture for entertaining friends, and several home electronics items. Carson, Pirie, Scott & Company's contest, in sum, provided them with a consumer-validated blueprint that their team of designers could use in order to construct teen-friendly showrooms.[11]

Some of the most famous department stores in America, similarly intrigued by the economic possibilities of the teen bedroom, followed Carson, Pirie, Scott & Company's lead in the coming decades. In 1959 Stern's department store in New York created a "Tween-Timers" section, a showroom aimed specifically at ten- to fifteen-year-old girls. W. & J. Sloane began "thinking young" as early as 1964; Macy's "campaign to get to teenagers where they live" began in 1965; while Bloomingdale's waited until 1966 to offer model rooms to their youthful clientele. Many of these department stores further emulated Carson's by appealing directly to youth in order to determine the products that would be offered to teen consumers. Bloomingdale's, for instance, proudly announced that it had hired four young designers—a twenty-three-year-old, a twenty-seven-year-old, and two twenty-eight-year-olds—to design model rooms for the store, while Stern's often gathered information by asking its female customers what they looked for in an ideal bedroom, which included "a hi-fi, a white television set, a desk, an extra bed for guests, a comfortable chair, floral or striped sheets, a telephone to match the walls and a bulletin board." The managers of the store then used this data to concoct a two-tiered design plan that was expected to capture the interests of both contemporary- and traditional-minded teens. For the teen with more conservative tastes, Stern's offered a frilly, feminine room that wouldn't have been out of place in the late-Victorian era. The contemporary model, in contrast, featured

Figure 5 An advertisement for a furniture store in Lincoln, Nebraska, that uses teen uniqueness as a selling point. Gold's advertisement, *Sunday Journal and Star*, June 19, 1966, 9A.

modernist furnishings and well-appointed study spaces that could accommodate various educational pursuits.[12]

Besides selling a raft of home décor products to teens, department stores also tried to sell them expertise. As a prominent symbol of middle- and upper-class consumption patterns for much of the nineteenth and twentieth centuries, department stores were particularly well suited to cast themselves as arbiters of taste on matters pertaining to fashion and home design. Teens found this out firsthand during the 1960s when a host of department stores began offering seminars and courses on how to decorate and furnish their bedrooms in a tasteful manner. In the fall of 1961, for example, Stern's announced that it was offering a six-week room décor course for teens that cost $2.50 per student. A few years later, in 1965, Macy's announced the creation of a similar course, sponsored by *Co-ed* magazine, that featured advice from its own professional design experts, tours of the store, and lectures by home economics teachers that addressed "Macy's home furnishings operations." Although the course's value in creating loyalty to the Macy's brand wasn't mentioned as a selling point in the media, one can only assume that marketing issues were taken into consideration by the people who actually created the course. Most of the stores that hosted these courses, after all, made a point of letting students know that the products necessary to decorate their rooms could be found just a short walk down the hall from where these classes were actually being held.[13]

By the late 1960s and early 1970s, department stores were just one of many retail outlets to offer bedroom-related products and expertise. Sears advertised Bonnet canopy beds that promised to make teen girls "feel like a princess with its curving lines and white finish with lacy gold-color trim," while smaller mom-and-pop establishments, such as Prange's Budget Store in Appleton, Wisconsin, offered "Teen Mundo" furnishings that promised teen boys and girls years of "worry-free use." Some stores even dedicated their entire operations to the bedrooms of children and teens. In 1967 Marilyn Hoffman reported on the emergence of a Manhattan store called Second Bedroom. Owned by interior designers Donald Ross and Marvin Sochet, Second Bedroom offered furnishings from seventeen manufacturers, free in-home consultation, and advice on how to arrange furniture and broadloom properly. "Here, under one roof," Hoffman explained, "the child and his parents can select an entire room, including area rugs, bedspreads, curtains, and accessories." Though the store's modus operandi indulged parental concerns to a certain degree—especially, one assumes, when the bedrooms of younger children were involved—the owners were quick to point out that the child's needs were given top priority, as all twenty-three of their showrooms were described as "literally quivering with youth." Both of the owners, moreover, claimed that "young people were more aware of style and design than anyone gave them credit for," with one of the proprietors telling Hoffman that he preferred dealing exclusively with younger customers because they were unequivocal about their likes and dislikes. "It would be infinitely easier for us here to deal only with children and teen-agers," he explained. "It's parents who quibble and are indecisive." Young customers, he continued, either "like things, or they don't, and they are quick to say which. They can scent out their personal preferences like a bird dog."[14]

Child Development

While décor experts may have paid significant attention to the various business interests that often underwrote their advice, it is also worth noting that ideas on child development continued to shape experts' arguments in interesting ways. Like their peers during the early decades of the twentieth century, many postwar décor experts believed that granting teens near-total control over the design process could help ensure that the transition from childhood to adulthood went off without a hitch. Parents were still encouraged to offer helpful advice when their teenage sons and daughters sought to change the look of their rooms, but they were forbidden to interfere with their children's decisions lest they disrupt their developmental progress. "Be generous about getting out the family sewing machine and helping whip up the new bedspreads, curtains, or vanity ruffles," one expert from the *Christian Science Monitor* advised in 1967. "But, for heaven's sake, don't interfere, or insist on other schemes. Awareness of décor is part of growing up." Indeed, the emphasis many décor experts placed on teen autonomy was often reflected in the terminology used to describe the teen bedroom, much of which emphasized the distance this space created between its owner and the rest of the family. During the 1950s and 1960s, for example, teen bedrooms were often portrayed as "teen retreats" or "teenage havens"—spaces that were part of the home in a structural sense, yet divorced from it in an emotional one. "A teenager's room is no longer simply a bedroom but a home in which to start living one's own life apart from the family," Cynthia Kellogg, a design expert from the *New York Times*, explained in 1960. "In it, the young person entertains, studies, listens to records, perhaps even watches television or uses a private telephone. To provide for all these activities the room must be furnished almost like a one-room apartment." Of course, it perhaps goes without saying that treating the average teen's sleeping quarters as an "apartment" rather than a "bedroom" made it all the more difficult for parents to establish any sort of ownership claims on this unique space.[15]

Identity formation also figured prominently in postwar décor advice, with many experts suggesting that the teen bedroom acted as an uncomplicated reflection of its occupant's emerging personality. This view was especially popular in teen-oriented publications such as *Seventeen*. As one of their contributors explained in 1951:

> Every girl in the world wants a small place that is completely her own. Some nook or corner, perhaps, which will wholly belong to her; a place bright and cheerful enough to depict *her* personality and *her* interests, and yet private enough to work at a diary or poetry. This special portion of the big, wide world is the pride of a girl's life—for it is, in a way, a record of what the woman was and is and will be. . . . Here, is the corner of the house which signifies You-as-a-Person, You-as-an-Individual.

Enid Haupt, an editor at *Seventeen*, carried this idea one step further in a spin-off book entitled *The Seventeen Book of Young Living* (1957):

> As your personality grows you will want your own room to reflect these new developments. Just as you style yourself in clothes, you will want your surroundings to reflect your personality. Decorating a bedroom or a home allows a display that is truly creative. It is often only after long speculation that you can decide your choices, for in this *you* make a statement!

One décor expert from *Seventeen* even suggested that the teen bedroom be decorated in a way that matched its occupant's physical traits. "Maybe your eyes are blue and your hair is gold and you never till this minute realized you could double for Veronica Lake if you moved your part just a little farther to the side," she began. "If that's the case why not visualize yourself in a room which harmonizes flame and pale gold with just a touch of cornflower." Like the photo "blow ups" mentioned earlier, these types of strategies regarded the emotional and physical characteristics of teenagers as fodder for personalizing their rooms. The self and the physical space it occupied were effectively merged into one.[16]

Co-ed, a competitor of *Seventeen*, was similarly taken with the idea of using one's inner world as inspiration when decorating one's outer world. "Let your mind wander," one of its experts recommended in March 1974, and then "express these kinds of feelings when you think of decorating your room." The average teen was expected to trust his or her instincts, to turn his or her "mood at the moment" into a pleasing décor scheme that no one else could claim ownership to. At times, this intensely personal approach to teen room design led some advice columnists at *Co-ed* to suggest that teenagers ignore the advice of even their closest friends. "Sharing ideas with friends is fun," one expert observed in 1975, "but certain things have to be done on your own. Your room is your own special world, and it should be fixed up to suit you, not your friends." Teens were basically told that taking full control of the décor process not only helped distinguish their personal space from other rooms in the house, but also offered them a powerful means of self-realization and identity production. To decorate one's bedroom according to one's own wishes was seen in somewhat heroic terms, as a means of rising above the herd. "Personalities often seem alike. But, in reality, each is distinctive . . . one of a kind," a writer for *Seventeen* opined in 1960, "What better place to assert your individuality than your own room, your own home?"[17]

Though traditional designs based on hobbies, sports, and other so-called "wholesome" activities were being touted well into the latter half of the twentieth century, a new emphasis on "sophistication" and "worldliness" also emerged during the postwar years. This is worth noting because it illustrates the extent to which décor experts equated teen bedroom design with becoming an adult. If design strategies during the first half of the twentieth century were defined by "an artificial code of childishness devised and implemented by adults," it can be safely said that postwar strategies were often defined by a code of "adultishness," by the idea that teenagers should be seen as young adults rather than old children. As a result, some observers saw the teen bedroom in strikingly adult terms, describing it as a hip apartment—"a perfect teenage den," to quote one expert from the early 1960s, that could be "tailored to a fifteen-year-old bachelor's taste." Some experts even likened the teen bedroom to the most modern (and urban) of living spaces: the studio apartment. "The favored decor for a young modern's room is crisply tailored and grown up," a columnist from Sheboygan, Wisconsin, explained. "It minimizes the bedroom and emphasizes a studio look which makes the teener feel she's gained a sitting room plus the necessary sleeping space." This emphasis on " grown-up" décor strategies was undoubtedly a by-product of the sweeping social and cultural changes of the 1960s and 1970s, when teens and young adults alike began demanding rights—the right to vote, greater sexual freedom, and the right to determine their own educational and occupational paths—that had previously been denied them. In fact, one could argue that the home décor community's emphasis on "sophistication" was a response to these calls for change, an attempt to indulge the teen set's desire to be taken seriously. Although most of these "sophisticated" room plans were formulated with both sexes in mind, one can't help but think that the teen bedroom was seen by some as an *Esquire* or *Playboy* reader's dream space, a sophisticated little realm where a suave, Heffner-esque figure—martini in hand and smooth jazz playing in the background—would feel right at home.[18]

Regrettably, few décor experts were willing to acknowledge the contradictions that arose whenever their advice referred to ideas on child development. This was perhaps best illustrated in 1982, when Sheila Eby, the *New York Times*' resident home décor expert, introduced her audience to twelve-year-old Sydney Silver and her fifteen-year-old sister, Samantha. Given carte blanche to decorate their rooms however they'd like, both girls came up with some interesting, albeit unorthodox, designs. "Recently Sydney Silver, aged 12, decided that she did not care to sleep on a bed," Eby began. "She dragged a discarded refrigerator box into her bedroom, turned it on its side and slipped her old camp sleeping bag into it. Cutting windows in the cardboard and suspending a reading light overhead, she created a cozy if quirky room within a room." Samantha, meanwhile, dismantled her four-poster canopy bed and chose to sleep, as the author put it, "on a mattress and box spring plunked on the floor." Their parents were none too impressed with their daughters' rooms—the father thought they looked "like crash pads"—but decided to look the other way. Eby suggested that this was a wise decision, if only because censuring teens for their design choices would hinder their development. According to a psychologist Eby consulted in the course of writing her article, although younger children "are perfectly happy with whatever organization their parents give their rooms," by the time they turn eleven or twelve, they "start breaking away from their parents and begin developing their own identities." The girls' offbeat decoration schemes were thus regarded as a sign of impending maturity, a demand for greater independence from parents. "A child should feel comfortable in his or her bedroom," yet another of Eby's psychologist experts was quoted as saying. "As long as the house isn't being damaged, walls aren't being broke down and bugs aren't festering, the bedroom should be the teen's domain."[19]

The arguments posed by Eby and her team of psychologists raise an interesting question that few of her peers were willing to address: if parents are essentially powerless to resist their offspring's bizarre choices in room décor, how can décor experts expect their own advice to be taken seriously? Although Eby may not have known it at the time, her arguments constituted a fairly serious threat to the livelihood of anyone whose job description involves providing teenagers with advice on how to decorate their rooms. Granting teens almost unlimited autonomy to decorate their bedrooms as they saw fit may have jibed well with mainstream views on child development, but it also revealed just how tenuous the average décor expert's claims to authority really were. Indeed, the only claim they could make with any authority is that they had little in the way of authority.

Formal Décor Expertise in a Do-It-Yourself Age

Many of the magazines that had been providing middle-class audiences with advice on how to decorate the teen bedroom since the early decades of the twentieth century were no longer so keen on courting teenage consumers during the latter stages of the Cold War. Teen-oriented magazines continued to devote column space to room décor, but publications such as *Ladies' Home Journal* and *House & Garden* all but gave up on the teen bedroom by the 1960s and 1970s, opting instead to concentrate on younger children whose dependent status legitimized greater parental input. In explaining why this happened, we must consider at least two factors. Firstly, it could be argued that décor experts were victims of their own success. Since the early decades of the twentieth century, décor experts were intent on stripping decorating powers away from parents and giving it to children, thereby mimicking the general thrust of larger child-rearing trends. And, of course, this is exactly what happened during the last half of the twentieth century. The boy mentioned in chapter 3 who plastered his walls with advertisements for Winchester rifles may have been a trailblazer back in the 1940s, but by the 1960s his ideas on room design were quotidian. The child-centered approach had emerged victorious, as design experts and parents were seemingly thrust to the sidelines, victims of their own unwavering belief in the idea that room design was a job best suited for teens.

Secondly, an argument could be made that design experts were done in by the emergence of the youth counterculture during the late 1950s and early 1960s. Though many Cold War–era commentators felt comfortable portraying the teen bedroom as a hip studio apartment or a bachelor's paradise, the idea of teens consulting the pages of *Good Housekeeping* or *Better Homes & Gardens* to consume this kind of advice may have seemed absurd to members of the younger generation, particularly those who embraced some of the more oppositional stances associated with the counterculture. This problem was further compounded by experts who insisted on offering somewhat tone-deaf design strategies to their readers. In 1971, for instance, an expert from the *Chicago Defender* suggested that teens furnish their rooms with a "yippy Yertle the Turtle" table, a Dr. Seuss–themed item that was geared toward a much younger audience. Perhaps not surprisingly, this type of advice led some experts to call out their peers for offering design strategies that were simply much too traditional and conservative for contemporary teens. "If left to their own ideas," one interior designer explained in 1970, "not every young girl will do a sweet pink-and-white bedroom. Many prefer bold, clashing colors, huge graphics, offbeat furniture and more than one patterned fabric." Forward-thinking décor experts were adamant in their belief that the ordered, meticulously planned strategies of yesteryear were being abandoned in favor of designs that emphasized spontaneity and eclecticism—qualities that magazines such as *Ladies Home Journal* were simply not well suited to provide.[20]

Nonetheless, many experts did their best to adapt to changing conditions, offering advice that eschewed formality in favor of a much more youthful approach. Of course, the magazines that dealt directly with teens—for example, *Seventeen* and *Co-ed*—were best suited to meet this demand, providing advice that at least hinted at teen calls for vibrancy and spontaneity. In 1960, for example, *Seventeen* was encouraging teens to place a host of "offbeat accessories" on their walls, including fans, old jewelry, seashells, "an exotic abacus from the Orient," painted glove stretchers, and antique rug beaters. In the coming decades, its team of experts urged teens to put wallpaper on their portable phonographs, pepper their walls with glow-in-the-dark stick-on stars, and use markers to draw decorative designs on their bedding and furnishings. *Co-ed* offered similar advice to its readers, urging teens during the 1970s to track down unique furnishings at garage sales, church bazaars, and flea markets; construct chairs out of old towels; decorate windows with seashells; brighten up lampshades, pillowcases, and curtains with yarn; and adopt an array of musical instruments, "unusual hats," and beaded jewelry as wall hangings.[21]

Oftentimes, however, the design community's attempts to remain relevant to teen audiences involved twinning their ideas with larger trends in youth culture. In 1960, for instance, *Seventeen* offered its readers a beatnik-styled room "where the only square is your chessboard." The "Way-Out Room," as the author of the pieced dubbed it, was meant to appeal to teen readers who appreciated the romantic individualism of the Beat generation, but the end result was undermined by a somewhat superficial understanding of Beat culture. Indeed, many of the anticorporate ideals associated with the Beat movement were undercut by the author's insistence that the "Way-Out Room" be populated with items from some big-name manufacturers that weren't Beat friendly in the least, including Lane, Armstrong, General Electric, and Smith-Corona. During the mid-1980s, moreover, *Seventeen* tried to capitalize on the popularity of the New Wave movement by instructing teens on how to "punk out" their bedroom with "new wave linens" and futuristic metal storage units. "First there was new wave music. Then came new wave fashions and hairstyles," the article began. "And now, the newest wave of them all—new wave bedrooms!" Once again, unorthodox design strategies were encouraged, albeit in a somewhat strained and contradictory manner. Although teens were encouraged to use "graffiti scribble pens" to add flair to their room and use old pillowcases to cover up exposed storage space, most of the room's so-called offbeat touches—the pink "fifties-style" radio, a cube-shaped cassette player, and a "black and red narrow-as-an-arrow lamp"—were all mass-produced, store-bought items. Youthful self-expression, as it turns out, was to be as safe and as prepackaged as any other consumer item sold during the waning years of the Cold War.[22]

Newspaper columnists, too, continued to woo teen audiences by emphasizing "offbeat" designs in their columns. One Chicago-area expert offered advice on how to build shelving out of bricks and old planks, build furniture out of discarded doors, and craft pillows out of corduroy or fake fur. An expert from the *Syracuse Herald-Journal* similarly told readers in the early 1980s that a "lively teenage environment" could be brought about by using an old basketball hoop as a nightstand or by making one's own wallpaper out of long stretches of paper and poster paint. Perhaps the strangest attempt to indulge teen sensibilities, however, came from an Ohio newspaper that offered ecology-loving teenagers advice on how to make a bed frame out of tree branches. "For a teen-ager's bedroom," the columnist explained, "small trees, with branches trimmed down, can serve as unusual posts. Posts then are secured via screws to two-by-fours, which act as connecting rails. Let the posts grow white and shiny. Prime and paint with high-gloss paint." If anything, this type of advice represents just how far room décor expertise had fallen since the early decades of the twentieth century. Whereas earlier design experts were proactive and authoritative in their columns, commentators during the 1960s, 1970s, and 1980s adopted a largely reactive approach—one that depended heavily on their own, oftentimes bizarre, interpretation of various trends in youth culture. How else, after all, would one describe an ecologically themed design strategy that required teens to cut down and paint trees?[23]

The DIY Approach in Practice

While décor experts were trying to avoid being tripped up by the vagaries of youth culture, many teens were experimenting with their own ideas on room design, a good portion of which emphasized a somewhat chaotic brand of self-expression. Experts who characterized teen room décor as being "offbeat" or "weird" had plenty of reason to do so once countercultural sensibilities began to establish a firm presence in the teen bedroom. *Co-ed*'s "Room Revival" contest, for example, offers proof that traditional design strategies were slowly being replaced by more unconventional approaches. Admittedly, many of the designs in the first contest (held in 1974) were fairly traditional; the winning entry was as frilly and feminine as any late-Victorian bedroom. Regardless, several entries were influenced heavily by a DIY ethos that ran counter to traditional ideas on room décor. Melanee Florian, a junior high student from Plantsville, Connecticut, submitted an ecology-themed room that featured tin-can wall art, a night table and chair made from old barrels, and curtains that were made out of soda-can tabs. Kandice Maas, a teen from Hebron, North Dakota, submitted a design with a chaotic zigzag wall mural and a homemade tube chair—a hand-crafted, snake-like item that lay coiled at the foot of her bed. The 1975 contest saw more of the same. The winning design, submitted by sixteen-year-old Kimberley Peterson from Little Rock, Arkansas, included shelving that was made out of soda pop cases, a shelf for plants that was made out of an old stepladder, and walls that were painted an electric shade of yellow. Sarah Ann Sly of Tonawanda, New York, in lieu of an actual rug, stenciled one on the floor of her room, while Tammy Evans of Austin, Colorado, painted a constellation of polka dots on her bedroom floor. Ruth Elming of Lafayette, Indiana, meanwhile, populated her room with an odd assortment of abandoned furniture. "Some people might say I've furnished my room with junk. I prefer to call it furniture-with-a-history," she proudly explained.[24]

Nonetheless, as some of the entries in the "Room Revival" contest illustrate, business interests continued to play a role in teen room design. Decorating the teen bedroom may have been regarded as the ultimate act of youthful self-expression, but in reality the business community was still guiding the process in both overt and subtle ways. Notwithstanding the fact that powerful corporate entities such as 3M and DuPont sponsored the "Room Revival" contest, it is interesting to note that most of the winning contestants used soda tabs and other common consumer items to add color to their room. This trend wasn't limited to *Co-ed* readers, nor did it stop at the odd Pepsi or Coke can. In 1977 Georgia Dullea, a reporter for the *New York Times*, reported on teens who had taken to decorating their rooms with empty beer cans, despite parental warnings about their bedrooms smelling "like a barroom." Although this was a relatively minor fad during the already fad-crazy 1970s, Dullea also pointed out that the Beer Can Collectors of America had nearly twelve thousand members as of 1977, 65 percent of whom were students. One boy, the article noted, had over 450 beer cans in his room, while fifteen-year-old Susan Haenel told the reporter that she simply liked "the look of the shiny, gaudy beer cans on the wall." For other teens, meanwhile, empty booze bottles and pop cans could be put to more practical uses. Tiffany Hauck, for instance, used "an empty bottle of Mad Dog 20/20," a potent fortified wine, as a change jar and "an empty RC can" as a makeshift ashtray.[25]

The most popular decorative items among postwar teens, however, continued to be pinups and other images culled from the world of entertainment. These items were coveted for a wide variety of reasons. Some teens saw them as a form of wish fulfillment, a reflection of their dreams and aspirations. In *'Twixt* (1983), a book-length examination of teenagers and the various fads they embraced during the postwar years, journalists Jack Levin and Ernie Anastos discussed a young girl from North Carolina named Donna whose obsession with the star of *Zorba the Greek* (1964) manifested itself on the walls of her room. "I was crazy for Tony Quinn," she declares. "My room was filled with movie magazines. I cut out the pictures and put them on the wall or mirror." In explaining her choices, Donna claimed that Quinn's image was featured prominently in her room because "it was part of dreaming about the future, and who you'd someday marry." Hero worship, too, no doubt motivated teens to decorate their rooms with an assortment of pinups. The walls of Anthony Bernier's bedroom, for instance, featured the April 1973 *Sport Illustrated* cover of Muhammad Ali and "pennants and images of my sports heroes, the California Angels' Hall of Fame–bound pitcher, Nolan Ryan, and their seemingly always underachieving shortstop, Jim Fregosi." Other teens, meanwhile, may have opted for pinups and posters due to more practical concerns. Anne, a teen from a Rust Belt city in the Northeast, ended up "plastering" the walls of the room she shared with her sister "with flyers for local punk bands, which we stole from telephone poles, and set lists and posters of punk bands, which we got from friends of ours who worked at local radio stations and record stores." It perhaps goes without saying that these types of wall hangings provided both girls with an opportunity to forge a personal style and express their pop culture preferences in a relatively inexpensive manner.[26]

There is also evidence to suggest that some of the pinups favored by teens were tied up with the sexual urges of their owners, acting as fantasy objects among boys and girls who had already entered puberty or were on the verge of pubescence. In 1969, for instance, a woman from California wrote to the editors of *Playboy* explaining that many a "bunny" had ended up on walls of her twelve-year-old son's bedroom. This didn't concern her much, she argued, because her son's décor choices were simply a natural by-product of his growing interest in sex. "A while back," she wrote, "my 12-year-old son began removing the Playmate foldouts from my husband's Playboy and hanging them on the wall of his room. Since this seemed perfectly natural at his age, I wasn't disturbed." Approximately twenty years later, Oregon teen Jeff Steele was given approval to hang similarly racy material on his bedroom wall. "I liked classic rock and had mostly posters of Led Zeppelin and the Doors," he explains, "but nothing really raunchy until my mom finally gave in to my pleas and bought me a poster of a young woman seated on a wicker chair, wearing only a towel and baring her breasts, from the adult section of the novelty store at the mall. Her poster bore no name, but I would recognize it anywhere." Though it is safe to say that most parents would have resisted such a permissive approach to room décor, the use of erotica serves to remind us that the middlebrow aesthetic that was popular during earlier eras of American history had been supplanted by a much cruder, pop culture–inspired model that oftentimes reflected many of the culture wars that arose during the late twentieth century.[27]

Perhaps not surprisingly, the prominence given to pinups during the postwar years attracted attention from the business community in ways that hadn't been seen during the interwar years. Inspired by the growing popularity of Warhol-era pop art, psychedelic concert flyers, protest posters, and other homespun visual material associated with the counterculture, poster manufacturers began expanding their operations during the 1960s and 1970s, selling their wares in department stores, record stores, and the back pages of youth-oriented magazines. For a relatively small amount of money—the first issue of *Rolling Stone* in 1967 featured an ad for a store out of Mill Valley, California, whose posters cost between $1.50 and $2—teens could easily get their hands on, say, a reproduction of Pink Floyd's iconic *Dark Side of the Moon* album cover, a pop art rendering of Che Guevara, or an assortment of well-coiffed teen heartthrobs. Costs were kept low due to the fact that the poster industry, as the *New York Times* noted in 1980, was basically "an appendage of the entertainment industry." Since much of their content consisted of already established stars, poster manufacturers did not have to spend significant amounts on advertising and promotion. This allowed them to sell their posters to retailers for anywhere between 85 cents and $1, who would in turn sell them to the general public for $2.00-$2.50.[28]

The most successful of these manufacturers was Pro Arts, an Ohio-based company founded in 1967 by Mike and Ted Trikilis, two Kent State dropouts who had previously owned an art gallery called Green House Gas. Though they initially focused on selling antiwar posters, the Trikilis brothers became famous for one particular item: the Farrah Fawcett swimsuit poster. Estimated to have sold over five million copies (at approximately $2 apiece) between 1976 and 1980, the decision to mass produce posters of Fawcett was actually a direct response to teens and young adults who used photos from popular magazines to decorate their bedrooms. As *People* magazine reported in 1996, the idea for the poster came about when a college student approached Ted Trikilis on his farm and suggested that he "ought to make a poster of Farrah Fawcett-Majors" because "the guys at my dorm buy magazines just to clip out her picture." Trikilis's response not only helped propel Fawcett to fame, but it also convinced others in the business community that selling posters to teens could be an incredibly lucrative venture. The Trikilis brothers were reported to have made $1 million dollars in 1976 due to that one poster alone, and the clout they accrued was such that it allowed Pro Arts to strike a deal with retail giant Kmart, thereby expanding the sale of posters into the mainstream shopping centers of Middle America. The similarly successful release in 1978 of a poster featuring a bikini-clad Cheryl Tiegs allowed Pro Arts to establish a presence in the bedrooms of millions of American teens in a manner that few other companies could match.[29]

Pro Arts was not alone, however, in fulfilling teen demand for cheap and colorful decoration material. Western Graphics Corporation of Eugene, Oregon; C.C. Sales of Chicago, Illinois; Dargis Associates Inc. of Columbia, Maryland; and Adstat-Adprint Company of Los Angeles, California, were just a few companies responsible for producing some of the most well-known posters of the period. Adstat-Adprint, for example, sold the infamous 1978 poster of Bo Derek (which sold 1.2 million copies by 1980), while other companies raked in profits producing images of John Travolta, Cheryl Ladd, Loni Anderson—even the Muppets. Teenagers, it seems, were eager to purchase a vast array of posters that reflected their taste in pop culture, their intellectual interests, and their political views. During the mid-1970s, for instance, Francis Barany, a sixteen-year-old New Yorker, decorated his room with "framed prints of physicians throughout the ages," while twelve-year-old Ricky Gordon, one of the subjects of Donald Katz's *Home Fires* (1992), had posters of Jefferson Airplane and a "day-glo Hasidic rabbi" on the walls of his room. By 1980 the *New York Times* estimated that the poster industry was selling between $100 million and $200 million worth of merchandise per year, the vast of majority of which ended up hanging in the rooms of American youth. As Jeff Steele notes, some teens took more care preserving their posters than the walls of their bedrooms. "I used push pins to hang them," he recalls, "being careful to re-use the same holes in the corners so as not to overly damage the posters themselves, though I didn't give the same regard to the walls, resulting in tiny holes throughout my bedroom."[30]

The pinup/poster craze was also significant because it helped popularize the collage method—a somewhat chaotic approach to room décor in which almost every part of the bedroom ends up covered with posters, pinups, and other found/purchased objects. Though collage was used in children's rooms during the nineteenth century, its boundaries were carefully proscribed by parents, as earlier generations of teens were told to limit their efforts to doors, bulletin boards, mirrors, and other designated areas. "Most of our mothers won't allow us to hang just anything on the wall," Linda Baxter, a twelve-year-old New Yorker, explained in a *New York Times* article from 1959. "So the pin-up board is the center for all our treasures—programs, snapshots, banners and a lot of other junk." By the 1970s and 1980s, however, a much more scattershot approach emerged, as self-expression was expected to extend its reach to all corners of the teen bedroom. An early example of this trend can be found in a documentary entitled *Teddy* (1971), an in-depth look at an African American teen and his thoughts on growing up in Watts, a predominantly poor and black neighborhood of Los Angeles. The walls of Teddy's room feature an assortment of posters, pinups, and found objects, many of which represented his radical political leanings. This includes an army helmet with "power to the people" and "kill pig" written on it; an antiabortion poster produced by the Nation of Islam; African art posters; and cutouts of Che Guevara and Martin Luther King. While Freddy's décor choices served as expressions of his deeply held political beliefs, other teenagers had more practical concerns in mind when adopting the collage approach. During the 1980s, for instance, Tiffany Hauck used collage to both express her love for various pop and rock acts as well as cover up "the god-awful pink and green flowery wallpaper" her "arty mother" had put up years earlier when her younger sister occupied the room. Although Hauck came from a solidly middle-class background, her decision to cover up a poorly painted room with a sprawling mass of pinups and posters was surely mimicked by poorer teens whose own rooms may have been found wanting due to shabby paint jobs and everyday wear and tear.[31]

It is important to note, however, that not all teenagers were reliant on ephemera from the world of popular culture to personalize their rooms. In fact, one aspect of teen bedroom culture that shouldn't be minimized is the tendency toward diversity in room décor, as many teens understood that they didn't necessarily require mass-produced pinups and other forms of inexpensive promotional material to add flair to their personal space. During the early 1960s, Nancy from Utica, Michigan, adopted an arts-and-crafts approach to room décor, creating her own wall hangings "by covering cardboard with fabric that matched the bedspread, and then gluing on pictures of these faces with big eyes." She explains, "That was it. I didn't do any other decorating, and I wasn't one to hang posters." Douglas Mitchell, meanwhile, decorated his attic bedroom with his own "large-scale abstract expressionist paintings," some of which ended up hanging in his friends' rooms. At one point, Douglas's reputation for producing quality art was such that both he and his bedroom drew praise from his high school art teacher on a local radio show. "I was astonished to hear my room described by the art teacher as a veritable aesthetic fortress," he remarks, "as an eyrie on high that housed a young man determined to try his hand in all the arts." Like Nancy from Utica, Mitchell adopted a purist's approach to room décor, one that was almost entirely the product of his own imagination and artistic talent.[32]

The Pros and Cons of DIY Design Strategies

Although the popularity of the DIY approach was based in part on its intense emphasis on personal autonomy and self-expression, one could argue that its democratic nature—the extent to which it allowed teens from nearly all socioeconomic backgrounds to take part in the decoration process—also played an important role. Earlier forms of home décor expertise certainly made claims of affordability and practicality, but most of these plans skewed toward the affluent, featuring a host of expensive

Figs 6 & 7 Tiffany Hauck's bedroom in Vancouver, Washington, during the 1980s—these are excellent examples of the collage approach to room décor. Courtesy of Tiffany Hauck.

furnishings and accessories that were out of the reach of poorer families. By downplaying the importance of large, costly furnishings and emphasizing personal expression through found objects and inexpensive store-bought items, the DIY approach allowed teenagers from even the poorest of backgrounds to take an active part in the decoration process.

Consider, for example, the décor choices of Leslie from Nampa, Idaho, during the 1980s. Leslie's room housed several "homemade treasures," including "a wooden sign with the words 'Foxy Leslie' carved into it," a "really, really bad book stand I'd carved in a woodworking class in junior high," and a "hand-carved gavel my father had made for me to use as Honored Queen in Job's Daughters," a Masonic organization for young girls. The walls of her room were decorated in a similar manner, incorporating an eclectic mix of sacred and profane items, including a "typed list of the ten commandments" and a *Little Mermaid* poster. Leslie, who would later identify as queer, claims that the rest of her wall space "exploded with heterosexual overcompensation," featuring magazine cutouts of "hot boy actors" and store-bought posters of Patrick Swayze and a semipopular 1980s hair band by the name of White Lion. Despite living in subsidized housing and subsisting on Idaho's not-so-generous welfare system, Leslie's décor choices serve to remind us that the DIY approach was open to rich and poor teens alike. All that was needed to decorate one's room was some tape or thumbtacks, a stack of entertainment magazines, an empty beer can or two, and some unwanted furniture.[33]

The DIY approach seems to have also allowed teens to sidestep prevailing gender norms. As historian Elizabeth Collins Cromley argues, traditional ideas on gender cast a huge shadow over home décor expertise during the early decades of the twentieth century:

> All this advice assigns predictable signs of gender to those presumed individuals. All girls should have ruffled dressing tables; all boys need to decorate their rooms with baseball bats. Young men all need to declare their individuality through "frisky" pictures of bulldogs; all mothers' rooms must express nurturance. It seems that the bedroom's décor shapes its occupant into correct gender roles, rather than that the occupant expresses individual taste in shaping the bedroom.

Conversely, the DIY approach provided a much more flexible take on the ways in which gender informed room design. Traditional views on gender continued to shape room design in a somewhat predictable manner during the Cold War; one furniture store, a mere three years after American troops withdrew from Vietnam, tried to appeal to teenage boys by offering bedroom furnishings that featured "a military flair," while a Syracuse-area expert declared in 1983 that girls opted for "ruffles and lace" just as much as boys went for "rugged, heavy pine furniture in the early American country mode." But the emergence of the DIY approach ensured that the overall aesthetic was limited only by the imagination of its occupant. Teen girls could still decorate their rooms with all sorts of frilly, feminine items, if they so desired, or they could ignore those types of strategies altogether by pinning several hundred beer cans to their bedroom wall. The DIY approach, in short, provided teens with a flexibility that more formal, traditional approaches were unable to match.[34]

The DIY approach was also flexible in another way: it allowed teens to quickly alter their room décor whenever the desire for change struck. For some teens, the desire to redecorate their rooms was strangely intense. Casey Calloway, for instance, claims to have changed the layout of her room approximately "every three months," producing within her something akin to a state of euphoria—"a crazy excitement," as she dubs it. Although the desire for change struck Laurel a little less often, she does admit to crafting three separate designs while attending high school and college in Northern California during the late 1970s and early 1980s. The first design, implemented when she was thirteen years old, featured a bedspread with a Van Gogh print on the front, "lots of rainbows and mobiles," and "a *Star Wars* poster or two." The second design, established when she was fourteen, replaced the rainbows and mobiles with rock-oriented wall hangings, including "Van Halen and Aerosmith album covers" and store-bought rock posters. When money was scarce, Laurel also used one of the most iconic rock magazines of the postwar years to create a collage effect on her bedroom walls. "A friend's brother sometimes gave me old copies of Rolling Stone magazine," she explains, "and I'd use pretty much all the photos from the magazine to cover the white space between my scanty collection of legitimate posters till there wasn't any white space left." The third and final version of her room, drawn up when she was seventeen years old, reflected her "renewed interest in school" and the sensibilities of someone who was on the verge of becoming an adult. "I took down the posters and magazine clippings, painted the walls a ubiquitous Navajo White, and"—like Douglas Mitchell several years earlier—"hung the modest collection of halfway decent artwork I'd done at school." Lending credence to the notion that teen identity was often tied up with one's choice of décor, Laurel's decision to employ a DIY approach allowed her to update her bedroom in such a way as to match her changing views on school, pop culture, and life in general.[35]

The idea that girls were more likely to take an active part in teen bedroom culture than boys was also challenged by the emergence of the DIY ethos. By the 1960s and 1970s, these types of arguments had, by and large, disappeared from the discourse, even though some of the most popular sources of design expertise continued to be heavily tilted toward a female audience. The DIY approach may have contributed to this process by allowing teen boys to decorate their rooms on their own terms and avoid the feminine trappings found in most other forms of interior design offerings. According to Ruth Gilkey, a design expert for the *Oakland Tribune* during the 1960s, the DIY approach was well suited to the temperament of boys because they had "been collecting and hanging up posters, stop signs and labels on bedroom walls for years, generations before adults suddenly got around to pop art." Gilkey, in fact, encouraged teen girls to continue consulting with their mothers when redoing their rooms, even though their male counterparts were being told to go it alone. In defending this somewhat strange double standard, she suggested that "boys have better instinct for choosing what is right for them and what is current than adults have." Though her rationale is admittedly quite confusing, Gilkey's views reflect the extent to which some décor experts counted on teen girls to continue consuming formal design expertise, while abandoning any hope of attracting a sizeable male audience. Boys, so the argument went, were essentially on their own when it came time to decorate their bedrooms.[36]

Despite some of the positive changes associated with the DIY approach, its larger impact on teen bedroom culture cannot be fully grasped by concentrating solely on ideas of empowerment and teen agency. Indeed, using the phrase *do-it-yourself* to describe contemporary design strategies is somewhat problematic due to the simple fact that powerful market forces continued to shape room décor in a profound manner. Business interests were well aware of the DIY trend and quite often used it to establish a promotional presence in the teen bedroom, a phenomenon that was noted as early as 1961 when Charles Brown, a contributor to the *Annals of the American Academy of Political and Social Science*, pointed out that the entertainment industry had teamed up with various teen magazines in order to distribute promotional material to teenage audiences. This trend would only intensify in subsequent decades, as teen spending power increased and consumer-oriented ways of thinking established a much firmer presence in American culture. During the 1970s, for instance, Anthony Bernier decorated his room with "cutout logos of the corporations to which boys my age aspired—Adidas, Levis, even Milton Bradley," as well as a "plastic bag from Waldenbooks" that "was hung as proudly as a small cloth American flag." At one point, executives at General Motors even tried to convince teenagers to pay for the honor of advertising GM products on their bedroom walls. In 1983 the world's largest auto company ran ads in *Seventeen* encouraging teens to pay $3 for a poster of GM's newest concept car. "Park a Dream on Your Bedroom Wall," the ad proclaimed. "This concept car was designed and built for the future by General Motors. You can't see it on the highways yet, but you can see it every single day in your own room." Notwithstanding the fact that posters of automobiles may not have had too much appeal among *Seventeen's* predominantly female audience, this advertisement suggests that corporations—though they may have been generous in providing teens with various types of decorative material—regarded the teen bedroom, first and foremost, as a means of creating brand loyalty and improving their bottom line. Under these circumstances, it is easy to conclude that any décor strategy that relies on purchasing decorative material from one of the world's most powerful corporations probably doesn't really deserve the DIY moniker.[37]

* * *

If there is one bedroom that best illustrates how various design trends shaped teen bedroom culture during the postwar years, it probably belongs to Amelia Eve, a resident of Northern California during the 1970s. Like many teens, Amelia populated her room with an assortment of store-bought posters (a lithograph of Douglas Fairbanks's *Thief of Baghdad*), "teen idol pinups" of Bobby Sherman and the Partridge Family, and ads for her favorite radio station, San Francisco's KSAN. The counterculture, too, played a significant role in her choice of décor. Referring to her sense of style as "hippie chic," Eve claims that she owned Indian-themed cotton bedspreads, an elaborate Indian-themed wicker headboard, and homemade "café curtains of a purple cotton fabric that had a complicated pattern of twisting vines and tiny flowers." Found items also made up part of Amelia's room décor, with her interest in renaissance fairs proving especially fruitful. "My most prized bit of decor came from a renaissance faire (the original one, started in Marin County in the 1970s)," she explains. "There was a half wreath of dried flowers with long ribbon streamers, meant to be worn as a crown, and pinned with it to the wall was a small papier-mâché jester's marotte, also streaming colorful ribbons." She even experimented with collage, covering her closet door "with a massive collage of black-and-white stills from the *That's Entertainment* film anthologies."[38]

Amelia's bedroom also illustrates the extent to which postwar teens had assumed control over the decoration process and the emotional trauma that often came about when teens were denied this right. When Amelia was fourteen years old, her mother and grandmother decided to surprise her by redecorating her room while she was out of town. "We'd been talking about getting some new furniture," she recalls, "and I thought I had expressed clearly to my mom that my vision involved more wicker, maybe painted white, and a bedspread and curtains in fabric that mimicked the floral 'Calico' pattern of Staffordshire china." In other words, Amelia hoped to update the "hippie chic" style she had settled on a few years earlier, not eliminate it altogether. The bedroom she returned to, however, did not reflect this vision at all; Amelia "came home to an ultramodern desk set in chrome, walnut, and black leatherette, and a floor lamp with a space-age domed plastic shade." Though her mother and grandmother acted in a spirit of generosity, Amelia's response suggests that the simple act of decorating one's bedroom could have serious emotional repercussions. "I have seldom been more horrified in my life," she notes. "I cried and cried." In an age when teenagers were expected to decorate their rooms relatively free from parental oversight, this type of response does not seem all that unreasonable, all things considered. In many respects, Amelia's sadness was a predictable by-product of the culture's embrace of child-centered design strategies and the various theories on child development that often reinforced them. Parents who ignored these trends did so at their own peril.[39]

SIX

Go to Your Multimedia Center!

She said her stereo was four-way
And I'd just love it in her room.

FRANK ZAPPA AND THE MOTHERS OF INVENTION, "CAMARILLO BRILLO" (1973)

By the 1970s and 1980s, the decision to banish teenagers to their rooms may have lost some of its appeal as a punishment strategy among parents. This is because many teen bedrooms had become self-contained entertainment centers, housing a vast array of home electronic devices, including stereos, telephones, and, increasingly, televisions, gaming consoles, and personal computers. Under these circumstances, parents who insisted on sending teens to their rooms may have been tilting at windmills. Casey Calloway, a resident of Cumming, Georgia, who came of age in the 1980s, certainly saw it this way. Although she was deprived of various rights and privileges whenever her parents sent her to her room, she admits that her home electronics collection softened the blow somewhat. "While I was grounded, my room was where I stayed," she explains. "Some people would consider their room their jail cell when grounded. I had a small black and white TV at the time and of course a stereo. . . . So, when I was at home, I was in my room, lost in my own world." In other words, since Casey still had access to various home electronics items in her room—"I didn't get grounded from those types of things"—she came to regard being sent to her room as little more than a minor inconvenience.[1]

The proliferation of bedroom-oriented home electronics items inspired mixed reactions among cultural commentators. A writer from *Changing Times* magazine took a lighthearted approach to the subject in 1977, using the technologically well-appointed teen bedroom as a means of poking fun at the purported narcissism of adolescents and their somewhat predictable tastes in consumer goods. "A new product we thought up ought to go big," the writer joked. "It's a refrigerator small enough to fit into a teen-ager's bedroom with a full-length mirror inside the door and a special shelf to hold the phone." For other commentators, however, this phenomenon was indicative of larger social ills. In 1970 Harvard-trained sociologist Philip Slater claimed that home electronics ownership among teens and parents alike represented the triumph of individualism and antisocial behavior over community and social interaction. "Even within the family," he argued, "Americans are unique in their feeling that each member should have a separate room, and even a separate phone, television, and car, when economically possible. We seek more and more privacy, and feel more and more alienated and lonely when we get it." Eight years later, cultural historian Christopher Lasch offered a similar critique in his best-selling book *The Culture of Narcissism* (1978), arguing that the contemporary teen bedroom was emblematic of the bankruptcy of consumer-oriented philosophies in which the pursuit of happiness was reduced to a "narcissistic preoccupation with the self." The advertising industry, he added, "flatters and glorifies youth in the hope of elevating young people to the status of full-fledged consumers in their own right, each with a telephone, a television set, and a hi-fi in his own room."[2]

Despite some of their more apocalyptic claims, critics like Lasch and Slater were essentially correct in characterizing the technology-filled teen bedroom as a challenge to various types of family-oriented leisure activities. Some home electronics items, to be sure, were more popular than others; but all of them, at varying times during the twentieth century, helped reaffirm the separateness of the teen bedroom by concentrating youth-oriented leisure activities in a part of the home that was ostensibly off limits to parents and siblings. The teen bedroom was thus transformed into a powerful leisure space that would eventually challenge, if not displace, the family room as the preferred site in which teenagers and their peers could entertain themselves. This is not to say that parents had nothing to gain by encouraging this trend. On the contrary, many parents—some of whom presided over technologically well-appointed bedrooms of their own—were told that these types of items could contain America's increasingly mobile youth within the home. Indeed, many home electronic products were marketed as home-based alternatives to leisure activities that could also be enjoyed in the public sphere. Commentators such as Lasch and Slater may not have liked the way home electronics helped fragment family leisure activities, but allowing teens to listen to music or play video games in their bedrooms was seen by other observers as a means of countering the allure of the video arcade and other public spaces where teenagers could supposedly run riot.

The process of integrating teenagers into the consumer electronics market was not, however, carried out in an especially speedy manner. Many home electronics items took years—even decades—to be fully accessible by adults, much less teenagers. Despite being invented in the 1870s, the telephone, for instance, only found its way into the majority of American homes in 1946, when the census noted that 51.4 percent of American households reported having access to phone technology. Even electricity, one of the most crucial features of any modern home, was only made available to vast swaths of the American countryside in the 1930s and 1940s, when Franklin D. Roosevelt made rural electrification a top priority of his New Deal programs. In other words, the hype generated by technological innovation has often been tempered by factors that prohibit its widespread acceptance, including a lack of appropriate infrastructure, bureaucratic indifference, and access issues related to race, class, and gender. The participation of youth in the home electronics market was no different, especially in the early parts of the twentieth century when the economic power of teens was in a nascent state. In fact, most of the products that would eventually find their way into the teen bedroom were subject to a trickle-down approach in which technological innovation originated in a corporate setting in order to increase productivity, migrated to the parlor in order to entertain the family, and then ended its journey in privacy-oriented parts of the home. Although this rather sweeping narrative doesn't necessarily apply to all the home electronics items discussed in this chapter—televisions and video game consoles, for example, were regarded as home-oriented consumer goods right from the outset—as a rough sketch it provides a useful means of understanding how the proliferation of home electronics technology was a slow and arduous process, one that often began in the boardroom and ended in the bedroom.[3]

Audio Equipment

The American teenager's love affair with home electronics began with the emergence of one of the most popular and enduring consumer items of the twentieth century: the radio. Invented in the 1890s, wireless transmission was initially used by military and shipping interests as a means of maintaining contact with the mainland while engaging in dangerous maritime activities. However, the radio industry as we know it today, with individual stations broadcasting content underwritten by advertisers, only emerged during the 1920s. Approximately seven thousand radios were in use in the United States by 1921; three years later, that number climbed to five million and would reach ten million shortly before the stock market crash of 1929. By the mid-1930s, the acknowledged Golden Age of radio, nearly two-thirds of American households had at least one radio.[4]

Interestingly enough, radio technology began showing up in the bedrooms of teens well before it went mainstream. Between 1905 and 1921, radio construction was a somewhat popular hobby among middle-class teenage boys who tinkered with homemade radio receivers in their spare time. As historian Susan J. Douglas notes, many families caught their first glimpse of radio technology vis-à-vis teen boys who "built their own stations in their bedrooms, attics, or garages." The parts required to make a receiver were relatively cheap, while easy-to-follow blueprints could be tracked down in various magazines and newspapers. In 1909, for instance, *Popular Mechanics* offered tips on how to build wireless transmitters, citing the story of a seventeen-year-old boy from Brooklyn, New York, who ran "a station entirely of his own making" out of his bedroom. "He has a coil which will receive messages 300 miles," the article explained, "and his apparatus occupies about two-thirds of his bedroom. He is so deeply interested in wireless that he studies his lessons in the evening with a receiver to his ear, listening to whatever messages may be flying through the air." Though vacuum tubes—the most important component of radio receivers—were prohibitively expensive, teen enthusiasts soon figured out that inexpensive crystals could be used to make so-called spark sets. Youthful interest in "spark" radio had a practical appeal because it was often associated with traditionally male occupations such as engineering, while also lending itself to military preparedness. As a result, radio clubs were established in high schools and colleges all across the country during the early 1900s, providing many young boys with the kind of engineering know-how that would prove particularly useful during both World Wars. As *Wireless Age* noted in 1925, "The government is right behind the boy who takes up radio seriously."[5]

The commodification of radio in the 1920s and 1930s greatly changed how teenagers interacted with the medium. No longer expected to build their own sets and broadcast their own material, radio enthusiasts could merely enjoy a wide range of free content, whether it was a sporting event, music, or scripted programming. In many respects, the radio was an ideal source of leisure because it didn't require additional investments in terms of content and components, making it particularly appealing to prewar youth whose access to cash was limited. Though still rather bulky in comparison to contemporary sets, early radio receivers were also seen as an attractive bedroom accessory because they were relatively compact. Coupled with the rise of programming during the 1930s and 1940s that catered specifically to youth—*Little Orphan Annie* (1931) and *The Lone Ranger* (1933) were especially popular—the radio industry began to gain a solid foothold in the bedrooms of children in a manner that manufacturers of other bedroom-oriented items could only envy. The response to this trend, however, was somewhat mixed. While home décor experts were more than willing to offer design plans for youngsters that set aside space for bedside radios, other observers argued that late-night radio use was putting teens at greater risk of developing chronic fatigue and other sleep-related ailments.[6]

Nonetheless, we shouldn't exaggerate the popularity of mass-produced radio receivers during the interwar years. For most teens, bedside radios were a luxury item. A slim minority of youngsters continued to tinker with inexpensive "spark" sets in their spare time, but the receivers they built had neither the range nor the clarity of store-bought units. In order to fully enjoy the latest episode of, say, *The Adventures of Superman* (which debuted in 1938), one needed a name brand receiver, most of which were simply too expensive to be purchased by the average teenage consumer. In 1929, for example, RCA was selling tabletop radios for between $95 and $147, while its biggest competitor, Philco, was selling models for anywhere between $95 and $198. As historian Michael B. Schiffer points out, although early portables "certainly found their way into back bedrooms," solitary radio use was most often limited to well-to-do families who could afford the expense of buying more than one receiver. Radio use among poorer families and the middling sort, by contrast, was usually defined along communal lines, oftentimes taking place in the parlor among other family members rather than alone in one's bedroom.[7]

The production and distribution of radio receivers underwent a series of profound changes after the Second World War, which in turn helped cement radio's status as a must-have bedroom accessory for both working-class and middle-class teens. From a technological standpoint, no invention affected the radio industry more than the development of the transistor. Though transistor technology had been around since at least the 1920s, it was only adopted on a mass scale in the late 1940s. Transistors enabled manufacturers to produce smaller, cheaper radios that were particularly well suited to teenage tastes. Whereas earlier models were somewhat bulky and unwieldy, radios produced after the Second World War were built using transistor-driven amplifiers that shrank the overall size and weight of the unit. According to historian Andre Millard, the average tube radio in the 1930s and 1940s was "the size of an airline carry-on bag" and cost anywhere from $50 to $200. By the time Dwight D. Eisenhower assumed the presidency, however, Sony was selling transistor radios that cost around $10 each and could fit into a shirt pocket. As one columnist from the *New York Times* noted during the 1960s, the development of the transistor helped replace the "monstrous pieces of equipment of the past" with "neat, compact boxes that can be placed almost anywhere."[8]

Teenagers were one of the most avid users of these tiny, inexpensive products, purchasing twelve million transistor radios per year by the mid-1960s. In 1966, moreover, *Newsweek* estimated that 72 percent of girls and 75 percent of boys owned transistor radios. Cheap and mobile, these devices represented a perfect addition to the teen bedroom, allowing teenagers to indulge in programs and music that appealed to their youthful sensibilities. This was especially important during the late 1950s and early 1960s, when rock and roll emerged as the music of choice among America's ever-expanding teenage population. More than any other genre of music, rock and roll helped push demand for radio equipment among youth during the Cold War. Teenagers not only had their own type of music to listen to, but they were also able to enjoy it on their own terms—on their own radios, in their own rooms. And if reception wasn't ideal in the teen bedroom, plenty of enthusiasts were willing to offer advice on how to eliminate the static and white noise that could ruin one's listening experience. Eric Blomberg, a youngster from Wayland, Massachusetts, claimed during the early 1960s that all it took to improve reception was a roll of aluminum foil. "Try various lengths and positions of strips of foil before choosing the best setup," he noted. "I tried two 5-foot strips, at right angles to each other, temporarily taped to two of my bedroom walls." A few radio-obsessed teens were even bold enough to start up their own bedroom radio stations during this time. Popular voice-over actor and radio host Shadoe Stevens did just that during the late 1950s. "He had his own radio show at 11, broadcast from his bedroom in North Dakota," *Spin* reported, "and has inflicted his sense of humor on an ever-growing audience since."[9]

Radio, of course, was not the only type of audio equipment available to modern teens. Invented in the late 1870s by Thomas Edison, the phonograph stands as yet another example of the boardroom-to-bedroom narrative described earlier. The talking machine (as it was initially called) was created as a means of preserving telephone messages, storing information, and dictating memoranda. Though early models were rather cumbersome in their design and plagued by technological issues that affected both the recording and the playback process, it was the phonograph's prohibitive cost that initially kept it from becoming a home-oriented consumer product. For instance, the National Phonograph Company sold a phonograph in 1891 for the rather princely sum of $150, while Edison, who promised to bring "opera into the parlors of working men," offered a model in 1893 that sold for $190. At a time when per capita income was hovering near the $900 mark, these prices did nothing to encourage working men and women—much less teenagers—to purchase a phonograph for use inside the home.[10]

The transformation of the phonograph from a business machine to a home-oriented consumer product began during the late nineteenth and early twentieth centuries. This can be attributed to a number of factors, including improvements in sound quality and the plummeting costs of phonographic equipment. Edison and Columbia sold relatively well-crafted machines for as low as $10 in 1898, enabling both affluent and working-class families to enjoy the wonders of the so-called talking machine on a relatively equal footing. In an effort to win over homemakers who were put off by the rather inelegant designs of the 1880s, manufacturers also began producing phonographs that resembled parlor furniture. Thus, the steel horn that was used as an amplifier on early phonographs was often designed to look like a flower, while more expensive models were sometimes encased in fine oak or mahogany in a bid to both camouflage the phonograph's mechanical components and draw comparisons with another popular parlor item, the piano. In short, manufacturers of the talking machine did everything in their power to make the phonograph, as one historian described it, look as "unphonograph-looking as possible"—an approach that began to bear fruit shortly after the First World War. Whereas only three companies were producing phonographs for the American market in 1912, by 1919 approximately two hundred manufacturers were churning out nearly two million phonographs per year.[11]

Though the laws of probability suggest that some teens were lucky enough to enjoy phonographic sound in their bedroom—famed jazz critic Martin Williams had a phonograph in his bedroom while growing up in Richmond, Virginia, during the 1930s—there is very little evidence to suggest that this was a particularly common experience during the interwar years. In explaining why this was so, one can point to cost and size as key factors. Individual machines continued to get cheaper as the years went by, but enjoyment of the phonograph depended on a constant stream of secondary purchases, including needles and records. Suffice to say that the average teen did not have the means to buy a machine of his or her own, attend to its upkeep, and purchase a seemingly unending supply of new and popular records. Moreover, most of the phonographs produced during this period were simply much too bulky and immobile to be adequately stored in one's bedroom. The earliest version of the Victrola, for instance, stood nearly four feet high and was made of "piano-finished" mahogany. Columbia, meanwhile, offered consumers a host of "massive Gothic chests," while Regent offered a $200 model that was described by one historian as a "hulking monstrosity on Chippendale legs that doubled as a table and a phonograph." The phonograph, in sum, was well suited for the parlor, but simply too expensive and too cumbersome to find a place in the bedrooms of children. "Its size and expense," historian Andre Millard has argued, "limited it to the parlors of the well-to-do middle classes."[12]

This all changed after the Second World War, when technological innovation and steep price reductions brought phonographs to a much larger audience. Once again, transistor technology played an important role in bringing these changes about. Although early record players relied on massive steel horns to amplify the music, the units built after the Second World War used transistor-driven amplifiers that shrank the overall size of the phonograph. Most manufacturers continued to offer larger, more ornate models for the parlor or living room, but teens were offered a slew of inexpensive portable phonographs with youth-oriented names such as Teener, Frolic, and Seventeen. Many of these record players were quite cheap, selling for anywhere between $20 and $50, while Columbia even offered a model to members of its record club for $7.95 in 1959. Though the sound quality was often poor and some models posed a significant shock hazard to their users, the low price and portability of many of these record players seemed a natural fit for many teens. "To the pop-music loving teenager with folding money in his blue jeans," a writer from *Consumer Reports* noted in 1957, "many of these portables may appear to be 'really cool.' They are attractively packaged and easy to tote, weighing from 7 to 15 pounds."[13]

Aided once again by the expanding consumer powers of youth and the emergence of rock and roll music as a dominant cultural force, teen phonograph ownership skyrocketed during the 1950s and 1960s. Indeed, one pollster found in 1966 that 72 percent of girls and 50 percent of boys owned their own phonograph, a disparity that can be best explained by drawing attention to the ways in which gender expectations shaped the leisure pursuits of teens. Unlike transistor radios, phonographs encouraged users to remain inside the home. In an era in which women of all ages were (to borrow a phrase from historian Elaine Tyler May) "homeward bound," the phonograph may have complemented prevailing ideas about gender during the Cold War. Boys undoubtedly listened to records in their bedrooms, but their appreciation of the phonograph was probably affected negatively by its reputation for immobility. Compared to the radio—especially handheld units or the ones found in cars—the phonograph was a rather sedentary form of entertainment that contrasted sharply with prevailing ideas on boy culture and masculinity.[14]

Nonetheless, by the 1970s and 1980s, one would be hard pressed to find an American teenager, male or female, who did not have at least one type of audio equipment in their bedroom, be it a record player, a radio, a cassette deck, or a combination of all three. In fact, several studies claimed that listening to music consistently beat out both television and the cinema as the favorite leisure activity of postwar teens. Popular commentators picked up on this trend, too, oftentimes arguing that the teen bedroom was the venue of choice for music-crazy teenagers. In 1976 child-rearing expert Evelyn Millis Duvall discussed the music-listening habits of teens in developmental terms, suggesting that it was perfectly normal for youngsters to "close themselves in their rooms and turn their record players up to drown out the voices of the family." During the 1980s, moreover, humorist Erma Bombeck accused some of the most popular rock acts of the 1960s and 1970s of creating "music that shook the walls of our teenagers' bedrooms," rendering parents "sterile in the next room."[15]

Although Bombeck was most certainly exaggerating for comedic effect, firsthand accounts tell a similar story, even among teens who resisted the lures of rock and roll. During the late 1950s, Douglas Mitchell's room in Wilmette, Illinois, housed a phonograph and an impressive collection of jazz and classical albums, both of which helped transform his bedroom into a Beat-inspired teen hangout. "The record collection had great utility as a point of destination for my hip high-school friends," he explains, "who would come over to listen to everything from Stefan Wolpe, Pierre Boulez, and the Renaissance master Gesualdo to bebop greats like Hank Mobley, Horace Silver, and Art Blakey." Nancy from Utica, meanwhile, claims to have listened to folk and classical music in her room during the late 1950s and early 1960s. "I liked folk music—the Peter, Paul, and Mary kind—and wasn't really into rock and roll," she confesses. "I had a radio, but Peter, Paul, and Mary weren't on the radio much in Motown. I actually listened to classical music some of the time." Interestingly enough, Nancy also claims that the radio in her bedroom was occasionally used to block out noise from other parts of the house: "Mostly I used the radio to play static—white noise—to drown out the noise my sisters and the TV made. I remember having a really hard time concentrating on my homework because the TV would be playing loud enough for me to follow the dialog."[16]

Douglas and Nancy were, nonetheless, outliers during the postwar years, as most teens used the audio equipment in their rooms to indulge their love of more popular forms of music—most notably rock and roll. For instance, Matt Groening, the creator of *The Simpsons*, explained that much of his time growing up in Oregon during the 1960s was spent listening to rock music in his bedroom. His diary, which was reproduced in his weekly comic strip *Life Is Hell*, is dotted with comments about how his music-listening habits were inextricably tied to the pleasures of having his own bedroom: "Dad took us out for hamburgers for dinner and now I'm on my bed listening to Frank Zappa's *Lumpy Gravy*"; "all I did was lie on the floor listening to the Beatles"; "I'm lying on my bed listening to KINK-FM on my radio." Susan Gordon, a middle-class teenager who came of age in Long Island during the 1960s, told *Esquire* reporter Donald Katz that her boyfriend would often "shut himself in his bedroom with his radio and wait for Jean Shepard to go on the air," while her younger sister Sheila could often be found "weeping" beside the record player in her bedroom. It is also worth noting that one of the highest rated radio shows during the 1960s was called *Cousin Brucie's PillowTalk Club*, which, as its name suggests, was aimed at teens who indulged in music listening just before bed. "Kids used to go to bed with teddy bears; now they go to bed with me," Brucie explained (somewhat sleazily) in a 1966 interview.[17]

Although the types of music enjoyed by teens changed dramatically during the 1970s and 1980s, the teen bedroom's value as a venue for listening to music didn't undergo too many significant changes. While attending high school in Northern California during the 1970s, Amelia Eve grew quite attached to the portable record player she received for her twelfth birthday and her "pretty decent music collection." Her radio also played an important role during her formative years, providing her with an escape from both the pressures of adolescence and the boredom of living in a small town. "I also listened to KSAN-FM radio," she notes, referring to a popular San Francisco rock station. "To me it was an oasis of urbanity that kept me feeling connected to the city while in my small-town teenage limbo." During the 1980s, meanwhile, Tiffany Hauck, a resident of Vancouver, Washington, lent credence to Erma Bombeck's claim that teenagers were hell-bent on foisting their music on other members of the family. Describing her stereo as "the most important thing in my bedroom," Tiffany claims to have "put a record on every morning while I was getting ready for school and blasted it."[18]

Though the advantages of allowing teenagers to turn their bedrooms into makeshift concert halls were no doubt few in number, the proliferation of bedroom-oriented audio equipment wasn't an entirely losing proposition for parents. In fact, many parents may have found solace in knowing that their children didn't need to traipse off to a smoky nightclub in order to listen to some of their favorite performers. In an age when rock concerts were often characterized as sites of rampant drug use, sexual licentiousness, and, in rare cases, death—the Rolling Stones and the Who witnessed the deaths of their fans at concerts in 1969 and 1977—home electronics equipment may have provided parents with peace of mind by allowing teens to enjoy music in a relatively safe environment. One could similarly argue that these devices found favor because they acted as a babysitter of sorts, a means of keeping youngsters distracted during times when parents were unable to give them their full attention. Perhaps more importantly, bedroom-oriented stereo equipment may have also reduced tension in communal areas of the home by allowing other family members to distance themselves from music that was not to their liking. If an appreciative audience for, say, the newest Rolling Stones album couldn't be found in the living room, the teen bedroom certainly provided a more welcoming venue—especially if it was equipped with a reliable pair of headphones.[19]

Telephones

The last of the great nineteenth-century inventions to find its way into the teen bedroom was the telephone. Though it didn't establish as ubiquitous a presence in the teen bedroom as audio equipment did, the telephone enjoyed a similar trajectory in terms of how it transitioned from a business machine into a mass-produced consumer item. Invented in 1875, the telephone was initially limited to businesses, governmental entities, and other organizations that had the capital necessary to adopt this new technology. Some households enjoyed phone service during the latter part of the nineteenth century, but it was usually limited to affluent families. In 1899, some twenty-four years after it was invented, the census reported that there were approximately one million telephones in operation in the United States, which at that time had a population of approximately seventy-four million. The peak year for market saturation in the first four decades of the twentieth century was 1929, when 41.6 percent of households reported having a telephone. The Depression caused these numbers to tumble substantially, as the percentage of families that could afford to own a telephone hovered between 31 and 33 percent for much of the 1930s. Indeed, phone ownership did not rise above the 40 percent mark until well after the attack on Pearl Harbor, when the wartime boom helped bring phone technology to a larger audience. By 1970 the census reported that 90 percent of American households had access to some form of home telephone service.[20]

Although the telephone became a must-have item during the years following the Second World War, the telephone industry soon realized that very few families had more than one telephone in the house. For decades most families were content to rent one receiver from the phone company, granting it a prominent place in the parlor, the kitchen, or some other area in the home where all members of the family could access the technology on an equal footing. During the 1950s, 1960s, and 1970s, however, telephone companies responded to this trend by pointing out the inadequacies of the one-phone-per-home model. "The sad thing about an Only Phone," one service provider suggested in 1970, "is you're always somewhere else when it rings." Purchasing an additional phone was thus presented as an affordable means of ensuring some measure of domestic bliss. Parents were told that an extra receiver in the bedroom would provide "a feeling of security" at night, while also bringing much-need relief to the average housewife who, it was claimed, walked nearly nine miles a day in the course of performing her duties. According to yet another telephone advertisement, a kitchen phone could make housewives happier and more productive by allowing them to converse with friends and relatives without interfering with food preparation and other kitchen-oriented tasks. Additional receivers, in short, were marketed primarily to female consumers, offering "step-saving comfort" for Grandma and increased efficiency for busy homemakers.[21]

Spurred on by the teen population's rising discretionary income, telephone companies soon realized that weaning Americans off the one-phone-per-home model could be hastened by creating a dialogue with youth. Much like their peers in child development circles, representatives from the telephone industry tended to emphasize the importance of privacy in selling their products to teens. An extra phone, one company argued, would be "perfect for teenagers' with-it conversations, the kind they can have only in the privacy of their own bedrooms." In fact, many advertisements from this era seemed to suggest that installing a telephone in the teen bedroom would improve the privacy levels of everyone in the home, allowing teens to talk with their friends free from interruptions while ensuring that parents wouldn't have to worry about the family room being overrun by their garrulous offspring. To quote one writer from the

New York Times, additional telephones were good for providing privacy and convenience to youth while simultaneously "protecting the nervous systems of parents." As an added bonus, this type of privacy could supposedly be attained without threatening the family budget. By 1974 an extra receiver could be rented for as little as $1 per month, which was well within the means of many families. One Ohio provider even suggested that an additional receiver was so cheap, it could be paid for by teens themselves.[22]

Telephone companies also began offering teens a series of products that spoke specifically to youthful sensibilities. The best example of this was the Princess telephone. Designed in 1959, the Princess, as its name suggests, was aimed at teen girls and newly married young women. The standard Princess receiver was offered in several colors so as not to clash with the décor schemes of its female owners, while its illuminated dial could be used as both a night light and as a means of enabling teen girls to make, as one writer from the *Wall Street Journal* pointed out, "late-night phone calls when Mom and Dad were asleep." Once again, privacy and autonomy were mentioned as selling points. "This is the room of a princess," one TV spot from the 1960s declared, "a teenage princess, because she has a personal extension phone for the privacy and personal freedom teenagers want and need." Although several manufacturers began offering imitation models during the 1960s and 1970s, with names like Cinderella, Petite, Starlite, and Contessa, the Princess easily distinguished itself from its competitors, becoming one of the most sought-after bedroom items of the postwar era. The *Wall Street Journal* would later declare that the Princess telephone, alongside Beatles merchandise and the game Twister, was one of the most coveted Christmas items for girls between 1960 and 1980.[23]

Teenagers who were unable to afford additional telephones found other ways of bringing telephone technology to their rooms. The most common method involved something as simple as getting a phone with an extra-long cord. Bill Hendley recalls that his parents adopted this strategy in their Los Angeles–area bungalow during the 1950s and 1960s. "During the latter five years of my teenage years," he claims, "my parents did have the single telephone in our home equipped with a twenty-five-foot mounting cord, which allowed both my sister and me to take the telephone into our bedrooms for private conversations." There were also, however, less scrupulous ways of bringing telephone technology to the teen bedroom. According to Paul Fassbender, a vintage telephone collector from California, some technologically astute teens built their own receivers and tapped into the phone company's lines free of charge. "I disconnected the bell so there was no record of a phone in my bedroom," one of his peers recalls. "I ran my own wire. Then I figured out how to have the phone ring, but

her phone costs so little . . . she pays for it herself!

An extra phone in a teenager's room makes life easier for everyone. It gives the teenager the privacy he or she wants. It gives the family peace and quiet that's almost as welcome. And the cost is so low some teenagers pay for the extension themselves.

For many homes a separate telephone line with its own number is a better idea. The extra cost is small when you consider that it fully frees the family phone and brings added comfort and quiet. Just call the business office.

THE MANSFIELD TELEPHONE COMPANY

Figure 8 This advertisement addresses the extent to which phone companies tried to court teen consumers during the postwar years. Mansfield Telephone Company advertisement, Mansfield *News Journal*, December 1, 1961, 12.

[also how to] make it so the telephone company could not detect it." As with early radio technology, the adoption of bedroom-oriented telephone technology seems to have been aided in part by boys with a technical bent. "I would hook up old phones as I needed, usually two or three at a time," recalls another teen who grew up in El Paso, Texas, during the late 1950s and early 1960s. "In one case, I took a 500 apart and built a telephone in a relay rack panel and mounted it in a rack of other equipment in my 'workshop.'" One phone collector from Shelter Island, New York, even claims that his parents knew and benefited from his attempts to outwit the phone company. "Had to chuckle, though, on who paid for phone in room," he notes. "You guessed it: no charge, like the three other phones I installed in my parents' home!"[24]

As it turns out, Fassbender and his telephone-obsessed friends were engaging in an activity known as "phreaking"—a secretive pastime, dominated by high school and college-aged boys, that first appeared during the 1960s. Often seen as a precursor to computer hacking, phreaking was conceived as something more than just a means of getting free long distance; it was predicated on pranksterism and putting one over on the authorities, ideals that were heavily linked to the emerging youth counterculture. Kevin Mitnick, a "phreak" from Southern California during the 1970s and 1980s, used his knowledge of telephones and the telephone industry to track down the unlisted number of Bruce Springsteen, change the status of his friend's home phone to a pay phone—every time his friend picked up the phone, an operator asked him to deposit ten cents—and set up new phone lines once the telephone company invariably discovered what he was doing and cut off service to the apartment he shared with his mother. As Mitnick's experiences suggest, many in the field of telecommunications came to see "phreaking" as a something more than a mere nuisance. In 1976, for instance, AT&T estimated that the use of "blue boxes"—a popular device among phreaks that could secure free long distance by emitting a series of tones into the receiver—cost the company somewhere between $10 million and $20 million per year. Among its predominantly male fan base, however, phreaking allowed technologically inclined teenagers to satiate their curiosity about an aspect of modern life that most Americans tended to take for granted.[25]

Phreaking, of course, often took place in the teen bedroom. During the early 1980s, Lewis De Payne, a close friend of Kevin Mitnick, set up an illegal telephone line in his bedroom that could support conference calls. De Payne, who also went by the nickname "Roscoe," then posted flyers around Hollywood, offering little more than a phone number and the phrase "UFO CONFERENCE CALL NOW." According to hacking experts

Katie Hafner and John Markoff, De Payne ran his chat line in a business-like manner:

> His world was the telephone, and from his small bedroom in the back he operated his HOBO-UFO conference. His phone rang constantly as people called the line. Roscoe continuously monitored the conference through a speaker phone, which created a constant low level of conversation in the room, and he could pick up his telephone any time and interrupt. Another line attached to an answering machine rang frequently as well. Many of those calls came from giggling teenage girls to whom Roscoe had given his private number.

Despite the dangers of phreaking in one's own home, De Payne was not alone in using his bedroom as a space in which to tinker with various types of telephone technology. In 1990, for example, *2600*, an underground magazine that catered exclusively to phreaks and computer hackers, claimed that phreaking could actually be used to spice up one's room décor. COCOTs—customer-owned coin-operated telephones—were given special attention. "Once obtained," the author of the piece observed, "your options vary. You could take it apart, you could hang it on your bedroom wall, you could hold it for ransom; it's up to you."[26]

As the firsthand experiences of phreaks nicely illustrate, the bedroom telephone—like the radio and phonograph before it—was defined by a unique set of gender norms. Boys most certainly enjoyed phone privileges in their rooms after the Second World War, but discussions of teen telephone use tended to concentrate on its popularity among girls. Of course, the telephone's feminine reputation has a long history, taking shape soon after home units became a popular consumer item in the 1920s. The telephone was frequently linked with gossiping, motherly duties, and bringing greater efficiency to the home, while many female-oriented occupations—for example, secretary, receptionist, and switchboard operator—revolved around familiarity with telephone technology. These ideas continued to find expression during the Cold War era. William Geurts, a vintage telephone enthusiast who grew up in Portland, Oregon, during the late 1960s and early 1970s, claims that the girls in his neighborhood "were more likely to have their own phone than boys." Members of the mainstream media took note of this trend as well. "You've seen that little princess telephone," syndicated columnist Lou Boyd pointed out in 1972, "but have you ever seen a little prince telephone? No. Why is clear. It's the teenage girls, those princesses, who make their marks with that instrument." In an attempt to explain why there was no such thing as a "Prince" phone during the early 1980s, Boyd resorted to stereotypes about the talkative nature of girls, stating that "conversational girls make up a far larger market than the less talkative boys."[27]

The popularity of teen telephones also seemed to be contingent on one's class status. Though it should surprise no one to find that Lyndon Johnson's teenage daughter, Lucy, had a bedroom telephone while her father was vice president, the same cannot be said about teens from less affluent families. Paul Hoffman, a former residential phone installer for Bell during the 1970s, claims that middle-class New Jersey families often requested installations as a means of surprising their children—"almost always teenage girls," he adds—with an early Christmas gift. Conversely, Hoffman claimed that he did not "remember *ever* installing a teenager phone in the low-income areas. Most of those folks were lucky enough or satisfied to have just one phone, often located in an apartment hallway, with a long enough cord to reach both front rooms and a rear bedroom." After moving to California in the late 1970s, however, Hoffman began working in several wealthy neighborhoods and quickly noticed that the demand for bedroom phones skyrocketed among well-to-do teens. "I installed a few teenager phones in the middle class areas, and usually as an extension," he recalls. "But I installed *lots and lots* of them in the more well-to-do La-Mor-Inda area, and there they were almost always on their own (new) number, called ADLs (additional lines)." As a sign of just how popular bedroom phones had become among the super-rich by the latter half of the 1970s, Hoffman notes that "most of the new houses in Moraga [an affluent suburb] had been 'preinstalled' with wires run to bedrooms during construction."[28]

Though teens often saw bedroom telephones as a means of socializing—or, in rare instances, as a business tool (Rawson Stovall, a fourteen-year-old from Texas, installed a phone in his room in 1983 as a response to the popularity of a syndicated column he wrote on the topic of video games)—parents may have appreciated its value in keeping teens off the streets. Some parents understood that allowing teenagers to gab on the phone was much better than allowing them to hold court in the streets. "Look," one father explained to a *New York Times* reporter in 1956, "the kids love to talk. At their age ideas are the fire of life to them. If they're talking on the phone, I know where they are. They're not doing their gabbing on the street corner, where I did twenty years ago, or in bars, where plenty of them end up today." By the 1960s and 1970s, moreover, the telephone industry tried to leverage parental fears of children in the public realm into an excuse to invest in a bedroom phone. A classic example of this was an advertisement for the Princess telephone released during the summer of 1968, a period rife with riots, student protests, and assassinations. "Give an Alone Phone," the final line of the advertisement read, "and maybe your teen-ager will stay home a little more often." It should be noted, however, that bedroom telephones were also capable of encouraging misbehavior, including prank calls and unapproved long distance charges. "My own teenagers had a phone in their room and used it quite often," Bob Peticolas, a vintage telephone collector, notes. "Then when they got a private line of their own, they ran up a $100 LD bill calling 'dial-a-joke' numbers." Admittedly, this a somewhat benign form of teen misbehavior—one that some parents may have preferred to deal with, given the alternatives. After all, Peticolas's children were at least getting into trouble at home rather than on the streets, allowing Bob and his wife an opportunity to address the problem free from public scrutiny.[29]

Unfortunately, it is difficult to determine exactly how many teenagers—boys or girls, rich or poor—had telephones in their bedrooms between 1945 and 1990. The census bureau has been keeping track of ownership numbers since 1920, but their findings don't take into account adolescent participation in the telephone market. Making matters worse is the fact that major telephone companies such as AT&T have been reluctant to release production or rental statistics for many of their products. Having said that, the relatively affordable rates of most receivers and the popularity of teen-oriented telephones such as the Princess suggest that bedroom units were probably enjoyed by a small minority of teenagers. The telephone may not have established as firm a presence in the teen bedroom as audio equipment did, but by the 1970s and 1980s, it was taken for granted that many teens, particularly those who were white, female, and affluent, were hardwired to spend an inordinate amount of time in their rooms talking to their friends on the telephone. In 1970, for instance, syndicated columnist Jim Bishop made light of his fifteen-year-old daughter's "obsession" with her pink Princess telephone. "She lolls on the bed after school talking for hours to girls she has just been with." In 1975 yet another newspaper columnist complained that the growing popularity of bedroom phones might have even been responsible for bringing about a posture crisis among America's teenage population. "The normal teenage position for talking on the phone," he joked, "is either on the stomach on the floor with the feet up on the bed, or on the back of the floor with the feet on a chair, or the head on the floor and the feet and body on the bed, or the body on the bed and the head hanging back over the edge like a murder victim."[30]

For the Gordon family, the subject of Donald Katz's longitudinal study *Home Fires* (1992), bedroom telephones were no laughing matter. During the 1960s and 1970s, the Gordon household featured separate phone lines for parents and children alike. Despite the blithe assurances of the telephone industry that bedroom receivers would minimize family conflict, the Gordons found that separate telephones could, on occasion, drive the family apart. Susan and Lorraine Gordon, for instance, recalled how their father, Sam, once smashed a phone against the wall due to the girls' constant bickering over who would get to use it. For his part, Sam resented the way his daughters used their phones to escape from the family. "Sometimes Sam would watch Susan or Lorraine talking on the telephone, and he'd see that they'd disappeared," Katz wrote. "His daughters escaped to the other end of the line, and it was the sight of them looking so much happier for it that wounded Sam most of all." If the experiences of the Gordon family are any indication, one could argue that bedroom telephones provided teens with a certain amount of autonomy and personal privacy while simultaneously driving a wedge between parent and child.[31]

Television

In *Back to the Future* (1985), Marty McFly travels back in time to the 1950s and meets up with his teenage mother, Lorraine. In one of many scenes highlighting the differences between Marty's 1980s upbringing and his mother's experiences growing up during the Eisenhower era, Marty witnesses the installation of the family's new television:

Marty's mother: Our first television set. Dad just picked it up today. Do you have a television?

Marty: Well, yeah, you know, we have two of 'em.

Marty's uncle: Wow! You must be rich!

Marty's grandmother: Oh, honey, he's just teasing you. Nobody has two television sets.

Although the writers who crafted this scene were going for laughs rather than verisimilitude, their take on the way Americans initially interacted with television technology is actually quite accurate. In 1956 the *Analysts Journal*, a trade publication for investment practitioners, estimated that 90 percent of American families had at least one television set, a trend that was applauded for encouraging family togetherness. "Television itself as a new focus of family interest, the fact that the family is together more, and the creation of a bridge between adults and children," a 1949 study cheerfully reported, "all reflect the possibility of an enlarging role of television in creating new ties between family members." Since multi-set households were not yet common, anyone who wanted to use the family set understood that they might have to enjoy it in the company of others. Programming catered to specific demographics—soap operas, for example, were aired in the afternoon for homemakers, and cartoons were aired for children on Saturday mornings—but the evening or prime-time slot, the most lucrative slot for advertisers, was almost always geared toward the family as a whole.[32]

By the early 1960s, however, the television's reputation as an "electronic hearth," a locus of family activity, was beginning to lose some of its luster. For one thing, more and more families were buying additional sets, which helped balkanize viewing habits by encouraging individual family members to watch television in different parts of the home. Part of this was cost related, as recent models were simply much cheaper than the sets that were being produced during the 1940s and early 1950s. Indeed, Marty McFly's uncle was basically correct in assuming that anyone who owned more than one TV set during the early 1950s was probably wealthy. In 1948 the Gordon family from Long Island, New York, bought their first television at a cost of $300, an imposing sum for even the most affluent households. A basic set in the late 1950s and early 1960s, in contrast, could be purchased for between $170 and $200, while portable sets (or "bedroom sets," as they came to be known) went for even less during the 1970s and 1980s. Moreover, once color televisions hit the market in 1961, many homes kept a "good" color set in the family room while the older model was set up elsewhere. Determining where these older sets were moved to is somewhat problematic, but at least one expert suggested in 1980 that 66 percent of second sets ended up in the parents' bedroom, with the remainder ending up in other parts of the home—including, one can assume, the bedrooms of children. This was the arrangement enjoyed by "Banmar," a contributor to the A.V. Club website who came of age during the late 1970s and early 1980s. "I remember when we had cable only on the color TV in the living room," she recalls, "and then we had black-and-white in the bedrooms."[33]

The emergence of multi-set homes and the rise of youth-oriented programming such as *American Bandstand* may have made it difficult for parents and children to watch television together on a regular basis by the mid- to late 1960s. In 1966, for instance, the *Chicago Defender* reported on recent Neilsen data showing that parent-child togetherness was enjoyed in only 27.5 percent of households during prime time, while the average half-hour and hour-long show was being watched solely by adults 61 percent and 72 percent of the time. Family togetherness wasn't disappearing altogether, but as historian Daniel Boorstin suggested in an article in *Life* in 1971, Americans saw this trend as a threat to family-oriented leisure activities: "And while myriad island audiences gather nightly around their sets, much as cave-dwelling ancestors gathered around the fire, for warmth and safety and a feeling of togetherness, now, with more and more two-TV families, a member of the family can actually withdraw and watch in complete privacy." This type of argument only intensified in the 1970s and 1980s, once inexpensive bedroom sets and satellite/cable television became the norm. According to Marie Winn, a prominent critic of television, the images of family togetherness from the 1950s—"Sis on Mom's lap, Buddy perched on the arm of Dad's chair, Dad with his arm around Mom's shoulder"—had lost their relevance by the time Jimmy Carter assumed the presidency. "Who could have guessed that twenty or so years later Mom would be watching a drama in the kitchen, the kids would be looking at cartoons in their rooms, while Dad would be taking in the ball game in the living room?"[34]

Parents and teens had their own reasons for adding a second or third television set to the family home. The most common rationale involved the idea that additional sets could prevent intergenerational conflict. "Two teen-agers in the same house find it impossible to listen to the same radio," a columnist from the *Panama City News* argued in 1969, "and each would be sure his growth would be stunted if he had to watch the same television programs as his parents. Thus a minimum of two sets is imperative." Jack Lyle, a media studies expert from California, echoed this claim during the early 1970s, but he also pointed out that the decline of intergenerational co-viewing was much more common among families with teenage children. According to Lyle's findings, only 24 percent of Los Angeles–area first graders lived in a home with two or more televisions, compared to an astonishing 61 percent of tenth graders. Lyle concluded that additional television sets were often used as peacemakers, as a means of ensuring that differing tastes in programming could be accommodated without producing tension between teenagers and parents.[35]

Determining exactly when television sets began to find their way into the bedrooms of teens is admittedly difficult, but there is evidence to suggest that this phenomenon began to emerge on a limited basis during the early 1960s. In 1961 child-rearing expert Thelma C. Purtell claimed that at least one million teenagers owned their own television set. Although this represents a mere 5 percent of the total teen population at the time, these numbers suggest that teen television ownership was certainly not unheard of during this time, particularly among affluent families. In 1966, moreover, the *New York Times* reported on a study commissioned by Scholastic that found that 17 percent of teenagers owned their own television sets, a trend that wasn't always limited to wealthy teens. Jorge Olivares, for instance, recounts installing a television in his room when his family moved to Miami from Cuba during the early 1960s. Though Jorge, his older brother Alberto, and his mother came to America with very few personal possessions ("all of our stuff fit in one suitcase"), a "small TV" was purchased and set up in Jorge's and Alberto's shared bedroom. Interestingly enough, the decision to put the television in the children's room was based on language considerations, a form of generational difference that many scholars tended to ignore. "The TV was in our bedroom because only my brother and I would watch it," Jorge explains. "Programs were in English and my mother did not speak English."[36]

Surprisingly enough, bedroom sets were initially cast in a positive light by some child-rearing experts. Dr. Spock claimed that installing a TV in a child's bedroom could go a long way toward preserving the sanity of parents. "If the rest of the family is driven mad by having to watch or listen to a child's programs and if they can afford the expense," he stated in the 1963 edition of his best-selling *Baby and Child Care*, "it's worthwhile to get a set for his room." It should be noted, however, that this particular edition of *Baby and Child Care* was both the first and the last to feature this type of advice. Spock's about-face was probably due to a shift among child-rearing experts on the effects of television on children. During the 1970s and 1980s, in particular, many commentators began to suggest that *where* the television was placed was just as important as the messages it propagated, as critics began encouraging parents to ban televisions outright from the bedrooms of youth. The operative word among many of these critics was *control*, with many experts arguing that having the opportunity to shape the viewing habits of youth was just one aspect of parental authority that needed to be reaffirmed in order to ensure that teenagers make smooth transitions into adulthood. Marie Winn, for one, frequently claimed that bedroom sets were a source of "decontrol," a term of her own invention that pointed to the inability of parents to keep track of their children's viewing habits. "Sometimes parents mention in the course of a conference that kids have a set in their own room," one of Winn's acolytes, a public school principal, explained during the late 1970s. "I'll say, 'For heaven's sake why do you have to give your child his own television set? That decontrols the situation completely.'"[37]

Despite the increasingly frantic advice of Winn and her peers, the demand for bedroom sets continued to grow during the 1970s and 1980s. In 1977 Ann Landers claimed that one of the most popular demands from her teen readers was that she use her column as a bully pulpit to convince parents to replace the television sets in their bedrooms with newer, better models. "Why can't I have a new TV in my bedroom?" she asked, gently mocking her teen readers. "This one is lousy." Some parents, it seems, were more than willing to oblige such demands. Jeff Steele reports that his parents purchased two bedroom sets for him during a two-year period in the late 1980s and early 1990s. "I had a TV in my room as far back as the Christmas after I'd turned thirteen," he recalls, "beginning with a thirteen-inch color set with both VHF and UHF dials, bought used, that croaked before my fourteenth birthday. Its replacement, also a thirteen-inch, this time a new Zenith, proved much more reliable—it still resides in the guest room at my folks' current house." Less affluent teens were also known to have had televisions in their rooms during this time. For example, Leslie from Nampa, Idaho, had a thirteen-inch black-and-white television in her room during the late 1980s, despite the fact that her family resided in government housing and was reliant on social assistance to survive. Leslie's recollections, however, tend to emphasize her television's value as a source of light than as a source of entertainment. "I often dimmed the light in my room," she notes, "illuminated it with light from my thirteen-inch black-and-white television, and wrote page after page of what I would now call paranormal romance."[38]

Regardless of how they were being used, bedroom sets became fixtures in the teen bedroom by the early to mid-1990s. In 1996 Steve Sherman, a research manager for Nickelodeon, pointed out that nearly "53 percent of households with teens reported at least one child bedroom set," while 40 percent of prime-time viewing in homes with children ages twelve to seventeen was reported to have taken place in the bedroom. As a network executive, Sherman admitted that these trends were troubling because it made it difficult for the major broadcasters to come up with accurate ratings data. He also understood, however, that the proliferation of bedroom sets was problematic because these televisions were often "out of bounds of parental supervision."[39]

Gaming Consoles and Personal Computers

Video games represent yet another form of popular entertainment that would establish a firm presence in the average American home during the 1970s and 1980s. In the span of thirteen years, several consoles were made available to consumers, including the Magnavox Odyssey Home Entertainment System (1972), the Atari 2600 (1977), the Intellivision (1979), the ColecoVision, and the Nintendo Entertainment System (1985). This trend had a twofold effect on the teen bedroom: besides further differentiating teen leisure pursuits from those of their parents, it also intensified demands for additional television sets. Like contemporary game consoles, all of the early systems required a color television set for maximum enjoyment. Indeed, several commentators have asserted a causal link between video game ownership and the presence of a television in a child's bedroom. Steve Sherman, for example, noted that 44 percent of households with video games had bedroom sets in the early 1990s, compared to only 18 percent of non–video game households. Among families with teens, those numbers were even higher, with 62 percent of video game households reporting bedroom sets, compared to 32 percent of non–video game households.[40]

Although a 2001 study by consumer electronics magazine *Dealerscope* found that 46 percent of all teen-owned video game platforms were located in the bedroom, determining when this arrangement became commonplace is difficult to ascertain because gaming-related statistics are practically nonexistent before the 1990s. Nonetheless, firsthand accounts suggest that bedroom-oriented gaming was not totally unheard of during the 1980s. Video game journalist Brett Weiss had two consoles in his room when he was growing up. In the summer of 1987, Weiss's brother gave him a Nintendo Entertainment System for his birthday, a new console that would complement his older (and soon to be obsolete) ColecoVision. "I was thrilled with the NES," Weiss explained in *Classic Home Video Games, 1985–1988,* "but still kept my favorite system—the ColecoVision—hooked up to my 19-inch television set, which sat on a desk in my bedroom." Although video games were more popular among boys during the 1980s, some girls were known to have consoles in their rooms as well. Dawn Miller, an African American motivational speaker who grew up in Milwaukee, bragged in her memoirs that her room had all manner of electronic devices, including the much-coveted Atari. By the mid-1980s, moreover, video game manufacturers openly acknowledged in their marketing material that gaming had migrated into the bedrooms of children. The best example of this is an advertisement for a track and field game from 1984 in which HesWare urged youngsters to "challenge the Soviet track team to fifty laps in your bedroom." The makers of the game went on: "So come and give HesGames a try and really experience the thrill of victory or the agony of defeat. Without ever leaving your own bedroom."[41]

HesWare's advertising strategy was something more than an attempt to point out the growing popularity of bedroom-oriented gaming; it was also a conscious effort to disassociate their products with the type of gaming that took place in arcades and other poorly supervised leisure venues. It is worth noting, after all, that several communities basically declared war on arcades during the late 1970s and early 1980s, accusing them of encouraging truancy, drug use, alcohol consumption, and gambling. Indeed, the reputation of these places was such that citizen groups in several municipalities—Arlington Heights, Illinois; Pittsburgh, Pennsylvania; Babylon, New York; Oakland, California; and Mesquite, Texas; among others—passed laws banning minors from visiting arcades during school hours. Meanwhile, other communities waged protracted zoning struggles against entrepreneurs who wanted to open up arcades in residential areas. In 1981, for instance, residents of Lynbrook, Long Island, initiated a campaign against a developer who wanted to start a new gaming parlor in an otherwise quiet, middle-class neighborhood. Existing arcades, opponents argued, "had become hangouts for noisy teen-agers who drink too much beer, leave garbage around and vandalize the property of nearby residents." The games that draw teenagers to arcades, they continued, have an "addictive effect" on the kids who play them and often induce "students to play hooky." According to Kurt Arndy, the deputy mayor of Lynbrook at the time, additional game parlors would only succeed in turning "the village into a honky-tonk."[42]

Games manufacturers were, as a result, faced with a substantial problem: they had a product that could be enjoyed by millions of Americans, but was also tainted by its association with arcades. In addressing this problem, game manufacturers did their best to convince parents that video games were nothing but good, clean family fun. Advertisements for games and game consoles quite often adopted a dual-pronged approach, offering family-friendly copy for Mom and Dad while assuring children—the primary consumers of their products—that these games would be just as colorful and exciting as their arcade counterparts. "Enjoy the adventure, competition, amusement and action of arcade games in your own home," a 1980 Atari ad proclaimed. "Perfect gift for the entire family to enjoy." In addition, some supporters of the gaming community claimed that consoles granted parents the opportunity to exert greater control over their offspring's entertainment options. "If parents are concerned about the environment and the games children play," one columnist from a Pennsylvania newspaper claimed in 1982, "buying a home video game may provide some control. Parents can regulate the time of play, types of games, whom children play with and what goes on." One Chicago-area alderman even suggested that buying a home video game system could kill two birds with one stone by providing youngsters with a compelling reason to stay at home and destroy demand for public-oriented gaming. "One rather clever solution to the problem of video arcades was found by 33-year-old Patrick Huels, a Chicago alderman, who is fighting an uphill battle for legislation to stop the proliferation of coin-operated games in his town," the *Daily Intelligencer* reported in 1983. "He bought his own two children home video games to keep them off the streets."[43]

The rise of home computing produced similar debates during the 1970s and 1980s, as the Apple II (1977), the Commodore PET (1977), Radio Shack's TRS-80 (1977), the Commodore VIC-20 (1980), IBM's PC (1981), the Commodore 64 (1982), and the Macintosh (1984) found their way into the bedrooms of many teenagers. During the late 1970s, for instance, Richard Garriot would often sit in front of the Apple computer in his bedroom until the wee hours of the morning, playing games and writing code. "Once the sun came up," he told Steven Levy, an early chronicler of computer culture, "I'd realize how late it was and crash right there on the spot." Dustin Dykes, a computer security consultant who grew up in California during the 1980s, was similarly enthralled by the advent of bedroom-oriented computing. When he was thirteen years old, his stepmother, a systems administrator who worked extensively with computers, decided that Dykes could benefit from this new technology. Intrigued by the "foreign-sounding language" his mother used while talking to clients on the telephone, Dykes recalls how "one night she brought home a computer that I took to my room and programmed to create Dungeons and Dragons characters and roll my dice for me." For the next few years, Dykes used his bedroom computer to teach himself "how to use a modem for dialing into his stepmom's workplace to play adventure games."[44]

Though Dykes's experiences suggest that computers were often used for gaming purposes, vocational and educational concerns also figured prominently in the rise of bedroom-oriented computing. Personal computers were expected to help develop skills that were useful in an increasingly tech-dependent economy, allowing computer-obsessed teens to learn various programming languages and become acquainted with the ins and outs of networking. Less tech-savvy students, meanwhile, were finding that they required at least a cursory knowledge of how computers worked in order to do well in school. Personal computers were regarded as must-have items among even the most disinterested student, as scores of programs were released during the Reagan years that promised to either impart educational content or provide students with the proper tools to write term papers and complete other types of schoolwork. In fact, WordPerfect and Microsoft Word came to market in the early 1980s, thus ensuring that the typewriter—a mainstay of teen bedroom culture during the 1950s, 1960s, and 1970s—was basically rendered obsolete by the mid-1990s.

Computer literacy did, however, have a dark side. Besides entertaining teens and helping them with their schoolwork, personal computers also inspired fears of unscrupulous hackers who might use their knowledge to exploit weaknesses in other computer networks. One of the earliest instances of computer hacking took place in 1973, when Geof Mulligan, a fifteen-year-old from Palo Alto, California, was hired by Tymshare to hack into their computer system in order to test the company's security measures. "Geof, who took a Fortran course at Stanford and knows Basic and Cobol as well, spends as many as fourteen hours daily at a terminal in the bedroom of his home," *Computerworld* reported. "Tymshare provided him with the terminal at no charge. Geof receives no pay from Tymshare but works 'for the fun of it' and what he learns." Although the hacker subculture welcomed practitioners from nearly all age groups, teenage hackers in particular began to capture the public's imagination in an especially striking manner during the 1980s, especially after the release of *WarGames* (1983), a hugely successful film about a teenager whose bedroom-oriented hacking activities almost bring about a nuclear war. One year later, in an example of reality imitating art, four teenagers from Huntsville, Alabama, had their computer equipment confiscated by the FBI after it was discovered that the young boys had tapped into two computers at NASA's Marshall Space Center. Joe Moorman, one of the teenage hackers, claimed that "it was sort of like 'WarGames.' We used an automatic dialer to print out all the codes until we got the right one." Although the FBI decided not to press charges in this particular case, these types of stories reinforced the teen hacker trope while also illustrating how teen computer use often took place outside the bounds of parental supervision. As Lenora Boorman, one of the hackers' mother, explained, "We weren't really sure what he was doing, typing away at that computer all the time. I guess now we know."[45]

Other teen hacking cases soon followed. In 1985 seven teens from New Jersey were accused of "changing the position of satellites" and accessing computers belonging to Pentagon workers, a credit rating company, and a medical library. The detective who broke the case suggested that these types of crimes could be avoided if only parents would pay greater attention to their sons' computer habits. "Most of the parents do not know that their son is actually doing this," he noted. "They are intimidated by the system and they're just letting their son go on with whatever he's doing. I suggest that parents get more involved with their sons' computers." Less than a year later, seventeen-year-old New Jersey resident Herbert Zinn confessed to hacking into AT&T's computer system. According to computer crime expert Chuck Easttom, "Mr. Zinn, operating under the screen name 'Shadow Hawk,' worked from his bedroom in his parents' house and stole more than 50 computer programs. He was eventually sentenced to nine months in jail."[46]

Zinn's case illustrates the extent to which the bedroom has assumed a prominent role in the hacking subculture. Unfortunately for many hackers, law enforcement officials also took notice of this trend, oftentimes targeting this otherwise sacrosanct space because they knew that much of the evidence necessary to successfully prosecute a case—namely, the computer equipment itself—could often be found in the hacker's bedroom. In 1987, a writer from *2600* took law enforcement officials to task for engaging in heavy-handed tactics during a series of nationwide sweeps, claiming that at least one teen hacker was threatened with violence when government agents stormed into his room. "We also have many questions concerning the methods used," the anonymous writer argued. "A teenager was almost shot by the Secret Service when he reached for a shirt after having been woken up in his room." Though there is little evidence to suggest that such scenarios took place on a regular basis, law enforcement officials were most certainly eager to get into the bedrooms of prominent teen hackers. In December 1980, Kevin Mitnick—who had only recently transitioned from phreaking to computer hacking—received a visit from the FBI shortly after he and a friend breached the network of a company called Bloodstock Research. "I was in my bedroom on the second floor of our condo, online, hacking into the Pacific Telephone switches over a dial-up modem," Mitnick claimed in his memoirs. "Hearing a knock at the front door, I opened my window and called down, 'Who is it?' The answer was one that I would come to have nightmares about: 'Robin Brown, FBI.'" Panicking, Mitnick stashed the computer he was using under the bed, but soon realized that other types of damning evidence were taking up space there as well, including a paper trail that proved he "had been hacking for many hours a week into telephone company computers and switches, as well as a load of computers at private firms." When it became apparent that Agent Brown was not going to search Mitnick's room, the cocky teenager resumed hacking as if nothing had happened. "As soon as he left, I went right back online," he bragged. "I didn't even burn the printouts."[47]

A year later, in 1981, Mitnick found himself the subject of yet another unwanted bedroom search. For months, law enforcement officials suspected that Mitnick and a friend had broken into Pacific Bell's headquarters in order to track down passwords and other information that could be used to access COSMOS (Computer System for Mainframe Operations), a database used by many of the nation's largest telephone companies. Assigned to investigate the COSMOS case was an FBI agent named Ewen, who paid a visit to Mitnick's apartment while the seventeen-year-old was out of the house. Ewen was able to convince Mitnick's mother to let him into her son's bedroom, whereupon the agent found "printouts filled with telephone company information, computer passwords and material from one of the computer centers at the University of California at Los Angeles." Perhaps not surprisingly, Mitnick's activities went unobserved by his mother, as she tried to convince Ewen that her son couldn't have been responsible for the break-in. Dumbfounded by her claims, Ewen asked her, "When is the last time you were in your son's room?" Mitnick's mother responded with, "I don't remember." Thus, Mitnick's mastery of the computer produced a situation in which the FBI knew more about what he was doing in his room than his own mother.[48]

* * *

Up until the 1950s and early 1960s, home entertainment for both children and parents was more or less a communal undertaking. According to journalist Amy Goldwasser, family life during this time was marked by "the single Princess phone in the hallway" and the "solo television set in the living room." Although Goldwasser's memories might be rendered somewhat unreliable by the warping effects of nostalgia, few would argue with the notion that leisure activities became increasingly fragmented during the 1970s and 1980s, oftentimes intensifying trends that first emerged during the early decades of the twentieth century. During the 1910s and 1920s, for example, radios and phonographs made their first appearance in the teen bedroom, followed by telephones, televisions, video game consoles, and computers during the Cold War. Over time, the bedrooms of American youth became hubs of teen-oriented leisure that were often defined by their ability to grant teens greater autonomy within the home. As one journalist from the *New York Times* argued in 1985, home electronics had the potential to turn even the smallest bedroom into a "luxuriously appointed cockpit," a technologically advanced wonderland that offered its occupant near total control over his or her surroundings.[49]

Granting teens greater control over their entertainment options did, however, come at a price, as it no doubt challenged parental authority and family togetherness by undermining parents' ability to determine when and where their children listened to music, watched television, or chatted on the phone. For some dissatisfied parents, the best way to respond to this trend was to get rid of the offending technologies altogether. This is exactly what Geraldine Fox, a therapist and contributor to the *New York Times*, did in 1984. "There is not . . . a television in any bedroom of the house," she stated proudly. "Nor are there telephones in my teen-ager's bedrooms or mine." Like Philip Slater, the Harvard-trained sociologist mentioned earlier, Fox felt that many of the home electronics items that ended up in the bedroom contributed to the sense of "alienation" felt by many contemporary Americans by preventing families from taking part in various shared leisure pursuits. Indeed, what is most striking about Fox's recommended course of action is how it harkened back to an era when home-oriented leisure pursuits were defined by communal values rather than individual needs. Her decision to remove these items from every bedroom in the house had nothing to do with sidestepping the purported evils of rock and roll or the mind-numbing qualities of broadcast television; rather, she hoped to reestablish the importance of spending time with family—an activity that was made that much more difficult when nearly every member of the family could slip away and entertain themselves in the comfort of their own rooms. "I can afford the stereo. I can afford the other television sets, the phones for their bedrooms," Fox declared. "I can't afford the toll they will take on the family, and that's what matters."[50]

SEVEN

Danger!

One of my windows opened just above the garage roof, which I could use as an alternate entrance/exit. I used it to come home late only one time, because my parents' window was right next to it and they could hear me clambering onto the garage roof. Mom told me that they thought I might be a burglar and my (police officer) dad could have shot me.

GREG, TEEN BEDROOM SURVEY PARTICIPANT (2012)

On December 23, 1985, eighteen-year-old Raymond Belknap and twenty-year-old James Vance from Sparks, Nevada, decided to kill themselves in a local playground. Belknap went first, placing a 12-gauge shotgun under his chin and pulling the trigger. He was killed instantly. Vance mimicked Belknap's actions, but succeeded only in blowing off his lower jaw because his friend's blood had made the shotgun too slippery to handle properly. Vance would live in constant pain and undergo numerous facial reconstruction surgeries for much of the next three years, eventually slipping into a coma and dying in 1988. Before he succumbed to his injuries, however, Vance and his parents filed a product liability lawsuit against Judas Priest, a band the two boys were listening to before they shot themselves. The Vance family claimed that subliminal messages on Judas Priest's album *Stained Class* (1978) caused both Belknap's death and Vance's disfigurement.

In 1990 the jury in the case agreed with Judas Priest's lawyer, who argued that it was absurd to think that a musical act would "tell the fans who've been buying all their albums" to "go kill yourselves." Though fans of the First Amendment were pleased to see that a genre of music as maligned as heavy metal could have its day in court, an interesting side note to the story involved the role Ray Belknap's bedroom played in bringing about this tragedy. It is worth pointing out, after all, that the two boys spent six hours in Belknap's bedroom drinking beer, smoking marijuana, and listening to Judas Priest before deciding to kill themselves. "The two dipped a few cans of Budweiser out of a 12-pack in the living room," a reporter from *Spin* noted, "and then locked themselves in Ray's room." In order to prevent any untimely intrusions, Belknap and Vance "shoved a two-by-four under his door to keep it closed," spending the rest of the afternoon drawing up a suicide pact and tracking down a firearm. They would not have to look far, as the illegally modified shotgun that eventually ended Belknap's life was kept in his bedroom. "Ray owned a .22-caliber rifle," the reporter for *Spin* pointed out, "pellet guns, and a 12-gauge shotgun he had sawed off and kept under his bed."[1]

Though the teen bedroom was often seen as having a predominantly beneficial impact on adolescent development after the Second World War, the Judas Priest case suggested that giving teens rooms of their own didn't always guarantee positive outcomes. A strong counter-narrative emerged, reminiscent of the anti-masturbation hysteria of the early 1900s, in which the teen bedroom was once again characterized as a site of danger and pathology. Indeed, postwar teen bedrooms were thought by some to be valuable only insofar as they helped harbor dangerous secrets and provide cover for behavior that wouldn't normally find sanction among parents, legal authorities, and other authority figures. This counter-narrative—which was complemented by the emergence of working mothers and latchkey kids during the 1970s and 1980s—ultimately proved ineffectual in terms of diminishing the popularity of the autonomous teen bedroom, as even its most virulent critics were reluctant to turn back the clock to the days of shared bedrooms and heavy-handed acts of parental surveillance. Nonetheless, it does serve as a powerful reminder that teen bedroom culture had a dark side that attracted public attention during times of crisis and moral panic.

Teen Sex

One of the most pervasive fears associated with the teen bedroom was predicated on the idea that it served as a venue for various types of sexual activity, most notably masturbation. Though there isn't much sense in debating whether postwar teens masturbated more or less than their prewar counterparts, it is safe to say that the emergence of autonomous teen bedrooms transformed the manner in which teenagers dealt with these types of urges, allowing this part of the home to become (alongside the bathroom) one of the most common places in which teens could pleasure themselves. Sociologist Floyd Martinson noted this trend in *The Quality of Adolescent Sexual Experiences* (1974). "Every night I noticed my cousin manipulating his penis," one of his teen interview subjects explained. "When I returned home at the end of the summer, I practiced masturbation in my room. I repeated this every night." Another of his interview subjects admitted that he often "practiced masturbation" and "found it very satisfying," engaging in self-love in his room "most every night." It would seem, then, that lingering feelings of guilt and shame did little to prevent many adolescents from using their bedrooms as a site in which to satisfy their masturbatory urges.[2]

Though alarmist approaches to teen masturbation fell out of favor after the Second World War, it would be a mistake to suggest that masturbation was all of a sudden stripped of its power to create anxiety among older generations of Americans. Postwar views on teen masturbation were shaped by a combination of age-old fears and newer, more permissive strategies that sought to curtail masturbatory activities through less intrusive means. Helen Flanders Dunbar was one of many parenting experts during the 1950s and 1960s who believed that parents who took an unhealthy interest in their adolescent's masturbatory habits risked alienating their children and destroying their appreciation of home. "A sense of privacy and love of home are interfered with," she warned, "when father says, 'Son, what were you doing upstairs in your room all afternoon?'" Nonetheless, Dunbar understood that parents were no doubt suspicious about what their children were doing behind closed doors. "If you say 'I was thinking' or 'I was writing a poem,'" one of her teen subjects claimed, "you have a lurking suspicion in the back of your mind that daddy will think you were masturbating or otherwise going crazy."[3]

Many in the child development community—in lieu of diminishing the amount of privacy teenagers enjoyed in their bedrooms—asked parents to encourage activities and hobbies that would essentially pull teens out of their rooms and into more public venues where acts of self-love were less likely to take place. Alvena Burnite, a popular parenting expert during the 1950s and 1960s, claimed that the masturbatory habits of teen girls could be minimized if parents were to simply provide them with "busy schedules so she will have no time to spend by herself in her room." During the 1980s, moreover, a child-rearing expert from the Jehovah's Witnesses suggested that boys who could not control themselves might consider joining the army. Though the Jehovah's Witnesses have always been a pacifist sect, the author of this piece seemed to suggest that onanism was perhaps a bigger threat than militarism, citing the story of a teen boy, referred to only as C——, who had developed "the habit of self-abuse, usually in the secrecy of his bedroom." "When C—— joined the military," the author stated, "he did not have much privacy. Hence, he seldom resorted to self-abuse, which, incidentally, shows that his past habit was not the result of uncontrollable passion."[4]

As it turns out, members of the Jehovah's Witness sect were one of the few groups—religious or otherwise—to lend qualified support to communal sleeping arrangements. Shared bedrooms were preferable for one simple reason: they subjected youngsters to a form of voluntary surveillance. "Being with others, provided, of course, that they are wholesome persons," a writer from the *Watchtower* argued in 1972, "is a protection for you. If you sleep in a room alone and you find that you seem to feel special stress in this direction at night, you may be able to arrange matters to share a room with another member of your family as a protection." A year later, another expert from the *Watchtower* encouraged teenage readers who struggled with immoral thoughts to "never be a loner, seeking to isolate yourself. So, at nighttime arrange to share a bedroom with other members of the family." Though still quite conservative by contemporary standards, these solutions are worth noting because they placed the onus on teenagers rather than parents to minimize the amount of privacy available to them in their bedrooms. Like their mainstream counterparts, many Jehovah's Witnesses were loath to address the situation by resorting to blatantly authoritarian means, arguing that only adolescents themselves could make the decision to give up their private bedrooms. This illustrates the extent to which traditionalists were unable to counter the growing popularity of the autonomous teen bedroom, regardless of the threats it may have posed to their various moral codes. Restrictions could be set in place and certain rights could be denied there, but even some of the most old-fashioned commentators were unwilling to force teens into shared quarters in hopes of addressing the dangers of excess privacy.[5]

Of course, masturbation wasn't the only type of sexual activity to create worry and fear during the postwar era, as cross-sex and same-sex experimentation also prompted a fair amount of anxiety. Unfortunately, studies of adolescent sexuality were rare before the 1970s, so we can only speculate as to how often the teen bedroom played host to these types of activities when more conservative views on sex predominated. As Robert Evans's experiences during the 1930s illustrate (see chapter 2), even teenagers who came of age before the sexual revolution used their rooms for sex. However, these types of stories either went unreported or were simply shrugged off as signs of criminality and depravity. In 1949, for instance, a teen boy named Ronnie Pitts was accused of murdering his girlfriend's father in Jackson, Mississippi. Though the grisly details of the murder were given plenty of column space during the boy's subsequent trial, journalists tended to key in on the young couple's sex life, which included sexual intercourse "in the girl's bedroom" as well as a risky meet-up "in a riverside park where, with one of her friends present, both he and his young sweetheart posed in the nude." Room-oriented acts of sexual expression were also characterized as being a bit too European for American sensibilities, an example of the permissiveness that supposedly marked parent-child relations in the Old World. Sociologist Lester Kirkendall took note of this phenomenon in the early 1960s, when he compared views on teen sex among residents of the United States and Iceland. Whereas Americans frowned upon sexual experimentation among adolescents, Icelanders oftentimes allowed teenagers to have sex in their own bedrooms. "A boy or girl might invite a member of the other sex to his home and his own bedroom after a party," Kirkendall explained, "a generally accepted practice about which the parents ordinarily are not consulted." When American students were informed of these customs, Kirkendall noted that they "envisioned all kinds of promiscuity and indulgence. One student asked if the illegitimacy rate was high."[6]

Regardless, the role teen bedrooms played in the sex lives of America's teens did receive limited attention from the mainstream media during the 1950s and 1960s, albeit in highly coded terms. The teen bedroom's role as a social center was often used as an obvious jumping-off point, a means of explaining how the privacy associated with the teen bedroom could lead to various sexual encounters. Advice columnists in particular addressed the issue of whether or not a boy and a girl should be allowed to socialize with each other in the teen bedroom. In 1961 Ann Landers received a letter from a sixteen-year-old girl named "Eloise," who thought it perfectly normal to spend time alone in her room with her boyfriend. "Is there anything wrong with a respectable, decent 16-year-old girl entertaining her boy friend in her bedroom with the door closed?" the young girl asked. "I've gone steady with Orrin for over a year, so it isn't as if we hardly know each other." The girl's father, however, did not appreciate the fact that his daughter both closed and locked her bedroom door while entertaining her boyfriend. He then confronted Eloise, who promptly assured him that nothing unseemly was going on in her room. "I've told him a million times that we close the door (and sometimes lock it) because my bratty little sisters keep barging in," the girl added. "Don't you think a girl is entitled to some privacy in her own home?" Landers's response was interesting in that it sided with the girl's parents while trying to preserve her friendly rapport with the younger set. "I *am* on your side," she explained, "and that's why I am telling you to entertain your boy friend in the living room. It's up to your parents to keep the younger kids out of your hair when you have guests. You have a right to insist on it. On *this* I'll back you all the way." Landers may have been trying to have it both ways, but many parents undoubtedly agreed with her advice, especially in light of some of the changes taking place as a result of the so-called sexual revolution. During the 1970s, for instance, Amelia Eve's parents held firm in their belief that their daughter was only allowed to entertain female friends in her room. "Having the bedrooms upstairs also made one teenage social rule easy to define and enforce," she notes. "No opposite-sex friends were ever allowed upstairs."[7]

Even attending to one's studies with members of the opposite sex raised red flags among some parents. In July 1968 Landers received a letter from a sixteen-year-old girl whose father "lost his cool" after discovering her and her boyfriend studying French in her bedroom. Like "Eloise" before her, the girl in this instance claimed that she was forced to lock the door due to "two bratty brothers who will not give us any privacy." Her father's reaction—which caused the young girl to cry, embarrassed her boyfriend, and created tensions with her much more sympathetic mother—was characterized by the teen letter writer as being detrimental to her studies. Landers disagreed with that assessment, claiming once again that the bedroom was no place in which boys and girls should spend time alone. "Your mother may be on your side but I'm with your dad," she stated. "A bedroom is not the proper setting for a 16-year-old girl and her boyfriend for studying—or anything else. It's up to your parents to control your bratty brothers. You should be permitted to have a guest in the living room and your mom and dad should see to it that you have privacy." Some teenagers, however, felt that Landers's arguments were simply much too archaic. In October 1968, a teen girl from Fitchburg, Massachusetts, revisited Landers's earlier advice, teasing the columnist for her "old-fashioned rigidity." If teens want to have sex, the girl argued, they can do it "on beaches, in haystacks, in cars, on back porches, in telephone booths and just about any place you can name." Parents, she continued, were basically throwing out the baby with the bathwater by forbidding teens and friends of the opposite sex to attend to their studies in private. "A girl won't do something in her bedroom that she hasn't already done somewhere else," she noted. "My bedroom happens to be the best place in the house to study because it is quiet, private and has a desk in it." Interestingly enough, Landers seemed to have misremembered her earlier advice, pointing out that the primary issue she had with the other girl's study habits was that "the girl's bedroom door was locked." The teen bedroom in and of itself wasn't to blame, Landers now argued, but rather the privacy afforded by a closed door and a sturdy lock.[8]

Fears of incest continued to inform discussions of the teen bedroom as well. In 1969 Abigail Van Buren received a letter from a mother who wanted the world to know that brothers and sisters shouldn't be alone in the same room together. Citing the problems she had with her own sons and daughters, the mother explained to Van Buren how she went out of her way to establish strict rules in her children's rooms. This included forbidding young girls from visiting their brothers in their rooms during bedtime and restricting opportunities for brothers and sisters to be alone together. "I suppose I could be criticized for watching my 11-year-old daughter so closely," the mother confessed, "but I don't care. She has three teen-aged brothers, and when she and one of them are doing something alone, I make some excuse to call her down to do something else." Impelled by her theory that "sex is sex to a boy until he reaches total manhood, be it his sister or cousin or anybody else," the mother claimed that she would rather be safe than sorry, concluding her letter by noting that she knew "too many young girls who were started down the wrong road by 'loving' relatives." Van Buren cast aside the woman's claims by both offering a subtle defense of sex education for children and pointing out the negative effects of resorting to such heavy-handed surveillance methods. "I hope you are as conscientious about 'enlightening' your children as you are 'policing' them," she warned, "or all your efforts have been for naught."[9]

By the late 1960s and early 1970s, debates about sex and the teen bedroom shifted rather dramatically. The quaint discussions regarding the propriety of allowing boys and girls to study or socialize in their rooms did not go away altogether—syndicated advice columnist Jean Adams addressed this issue in 1972 and 1976—but they were definitely overshadowed by more explicit debates about allowing boyfriends and girlfriends to stay overnight (or in some cases live full time) in their rooms.[10] Teen sex become a particularly hot topic due to growing fears over teen pregnancy and sexually transmitted diseases. Whereas stories of cross-sex and same-sex experimentation in the teen bedroom were hard to come by during the 1940s, 1950s, and even much of the 1960s, a much fuller picture emerged during the 1970s. In a 1972 report on the changing attitudes of teens toward sex, a writer from *Time* introduced his readers to Judy Wilson, a teen who had lost her virginity in her bedroom when she was seventeen years old. "One afternoon it just happened," the girl explained in a matter-of-fact manner. "Then we went downstairs and told my younger sister because we thought she'd be excited. We said, 'Guess what. We just made love.' And she said, 'Oh, wow. How was it?' And we said, 'Fine.' Then we went out on the roof and she took pictures of us." Oftentimes, the issue was broached in an alarmist manner. In *Parents in Pain* (1979), John White referred to a mother who found out that her fifteen-year-old daughter was having sex in her room after stumbling across some private letters and racy photographs while cleaning her bedroom. "I couldn't believe it!" the mother exclaimed. "I sat down in a state of shock for half an hour. Where did she learn all this? . . . I couldn't understand some of the words, but filthy. They talked about all the different kinds of sex they'd had, how smart they were getting at shoplifting, what fools parents and police were."[11]

Participants in Floyd Martinson's 1974 study on adolescent sexuality made similar claims. "At the age of thirteen," one boy noted, "my best friend and I would, during fits of passion, hold hands and stroke our bodies. The immediate experience that comes to mind was one evening we were studying in his room. The conversation turned to girls, and we both became aroused. A little prodding and agreement by both of us soon found us without clothes on his bed." One girl who was interviewed in Robert C. Sorensen's 1973 study of adolescent sexuality even "described how a boy lived in her bedroom for several months," while Leslie from Nampa, Idaho, claims that two of her gay male friends in high school "borrowed [her] bedroom for a tryst" on at least one occasion during the 1980s. This memory came flooding back to her many years later when she "found a used condom stuffed in one of [her] shoes" while cleaning out her closet. By the 1970s and 1980s, then, the teen bedroom was not necessarily a place where sex between teenagers *might* occur, but rather a place where it already was occurring on a fairly regular basis.[12]

Many parents, of course, were disturbed by these trends. In 1972 *Time* conducted an informal poll of ten parents from eight major urban centers, asking them their opinion on "unmarried teen-age lovers who want to share a bedroom." A slim majority of respondents did not approve of this arrangement, offering up several interesting rationales. Some parents, for example, explained their views by taking a "my house, my rules" approach. "I tell my daughter and her boy friend, when you're a guest in my home, we try to make you comfortable," a public relations director from Atlanta, Georgia, stated. "I would appreciate it if you would try to make us comfortable by not sleeping together when you're here.'" A lawyer (also from Atlanta) explained his stance in a much less diplomatic manner, telling the reporter, "It's my house and my kids will behave the way I say they'll behave," while a New York artist summed up his stance by claiming that he did not "think it's my province to run a motel." Some respondents, however, seemed open to the idea. A woman from Washington, DC, claimed that she would allow it, so long as they slept in separate beds with the door ajar, while yet another parent from Albany, New York, expressed disinterest with the whole enterprise: "I have too many hangups of my own to try to regulate that kind of thing." Two respondents even used the containment angle to justify their support for the concept. A housewife from Manhattan said that she and her husband resisted the idea at first, but soon "capitulated" because they were afraid that their daughter and her new boyfriend would end up "running off somewhere." Similarly, a campus police officer at Harvard University, though he initially expressed disapproval of the concept, softened his tone somewhat, declaring, "But what I don't know won't hurt me. If I force things on my kids, I might be forcing them out of the house." The experiences of Anne, a teen from a small Rust Belt city in the Northeast, validated some of these fears. Both she and her "main high school boyfriend" shared rooms while they were dating during the mid- to late 1970s, forcing them to experiment in more public venues. "We got up to some amazing things in Central Park a few times," she notes.[13]

Advice columnists and other child-rearing experts weighed in on this issue as well, revealing a similar diversity of opinion. In May 1972 WCAU, an NBC affiliate in Philadelphia, aired a one-hour television program on parent-child relations entitled *If I Were a Parent*. Hosted by Mike Tuck, a local anchorman, and Betty Hughes, the former First Lady of New Jersey, the show touched on several issues relating to the so-called generation gap. When asked whether a sixteen-year-old should be allowed to spend the night in his bedroom with his girlfriend, Hughes—the more conservative of the two hosts—was emphatic in her opposition. "If they were graduate students, I'd fix separate rooms and hope they'd use them," she exclaimed. "But if they were 16, no! Out!" Tuck, the more youth friendly of the two hosts, stated that he "wouldn't personally object." Ann Landers, meanwhile, continued to side with the Betty Hugheses of the world. In 1972 she wrote a column in which she suggested that parents who even debated these types of scenarios were putting their own marriage at risk. In order to buttress her rather fantastic claims, Landers cited an anecdote about a teenager who asked his parents if his girlfriend could move into his bedroom. "Their 18-year-old son told his parents he wanted them to allow his 17-year-old girlfriend to move into their house," she explained. "Her parents had thrown her out (for reasons he did not care to discuss) and he had a nice big bedroom, so why not?" Although the boy's father vehemently opposed his son's request, his mother claimed that "it would be the 'Christian' thing to do." Then she noted glumly, "Three weeks later, the father moved out." Though Landers was reluctant to explain how she would have addressed the issue—she noted only that teenagers who make these types of requests are often "relieved when the answer is no"—she insisted that parents must put up a united front in order to prevent the teen bedroom from becoming a site of premarital sex.[14]

Given the fact that fears of teen pregnancy and sexually transmitted diseases—including the newly discovered AIDS virus—only intensified during the 1980s, it should come as no surprise to find that the teen bedroom's popularity as a site for teen sexual experimentation continued to inspire heated debate. In 1982, shortly after a *New York Times* editorial lauded a bill before Congress that would make it mandatory for parents to be notified whenever teenagers request contraceptives from federally funded clinics, Leonard Glantz and George Annas, professors at the Boston University School of Public Health, pointed out that it was hypocritical for conservatives who "believe Government should stay out of people's lives" to lend support to a bill that seeks to regulate an "activity that takes place in the bedroom, especially adolescent bedrooms." Glantz and Annas assumed a rather permissive stance on teen sex, using the teen bedroom to make a larger point about the rights of adolescents: "It is time we accept adolescents as human beings and citizens with rights, including the fundamental right to make procreative decisions." However, polling data taken during this period suggests that Glantz and Annas' arguments were perhaps a bit too permissive for most Americans. In 1987 *People*, in concert with New York polling firm Audits and Surveys, polled 1,300 high school students, 1,600 college students, and 500 parents on various issues pertaining to sex. Their findings suggested that 76 percent of parents felt that it was right to forbid a twenty-one-year-old child "to share a bedroom at home with a person of the opposite sex." Of course, it goes without saying that if a twenty-one-year-old could not expect to share his or her room with a member of the opposite sex, then a thirteen-year-old shouldn't even bother broaching the topic. According to many Americans, the teen bedroom was expected to be a sex-free zone.[15]

Drugs and Alcohol

Another contentious issue supporters of the autonomous teen bedroom faced during the postwar years involved substance abuse. By as early as the 1950s, commentators were pointing out that the teen bedroom was fast becoming an important space where drugs could be both consumed and stored. Much of the literature dealing with this issue was, admittedly, quite alarmist. In 1951 *Time* reported on a Chicago father who witnessed a "terrifying tableau" after barging into his son's bedroom one day. "His son, a 15-year-old vocational-school student, was sitting there, one forearm bared, a hypodermic syringe in his hand," the author of the article described. "Another boy was holding a teaspoon over the flame of a cigarette lighter. Both the syringe and the teaspoon contained heroin." The boy eventually confessed to his father that he had been using drugs for a year, buying them off a peddler named "Greasy George." "Once supplied," the author of the article explained, "the boy and his friends would repair to basements or bedrooms, furtively dissolve the powder with water in a spoon and give each other shots." Although these types of scenarios were exceedingly rare, many experts suggested that the dangers of hard drug use were such that parents should trample all over their child's privacy rights. This was the approach taken by Lieutenant Arthur M. Grennan, a police detective in Westchester, New York, during the early 1960s. Fearing that teen girls would turn to "prostitution and shoplifting" and boys would turn to "larceny and assault" to feed their habits, Grennan urged parents to rummage through the various nooks and crannies in the bedroom where drugs could be kept, including books, furniture, shoes, and light switches. "White, powdered heroin and coarser cocaine can be hidden in a room wherever there is space," he warned.[16]

By the mid-1960s and 1970s, however, legal authorities and drug experts began placing greater emphasis on recreational drugs such as marijuana and LSD. Although it is impossible to determine how often the teen bedroom was used to consume these types of drugs, firsthand accounts suggest that it was a common-enough occurrence. When not spending time with her boyfriend in Central Park, Anne did drugs in her friends' bedrooms during the mid- to late 1970s. "Mostly I got stoned while hanging out in my friend Laura's bedroom," she admits. "She was a big stoner who knew esoteric information such as how to carve a pipe out of an apple." On at least one occasion, Anne's drug use took place in the bedroom of a friend whose father was "high up" in the Drug Enforcement Agency. "One afternoon [Laura] and I got so stoned at our friend Jeanne-Marie's house that we all passed out on her bedroom floor while the needle on the record player got stuck in a scratch on the 45 we were listening to, endlessly repeating a phrase from I think it was the Steve Miller Band's song 'Fly Like an Eagle.'" Jeanne-Marie's father stumbled into her room while the three girls were enjoying their drug-induced trance and was, as Anne points out, "extra-horrified" by what he saw.[17]

This was also the era that witnessed the emergence of the cliché in which an unwitting parent—usually the mother—stumbles across a stash of drugs in their son's or daughter's bedroom. A particularly pungent example of this trope can be seen in the opening segment of *Keep Off the Grass* (1969), an educational film that dealt with the alleged horrors of marijuana use. Produced by Sid Davis, a filmmaker whose body of work was consistently alarmist and reactionary, *Keep Off the Grass* opens with a mother entering her son's empty bedroom, where she discovers a stash of marijuana in a cigar box that had been sitting on top of her son's television set. The rest of the film chronicles her son's steep descent into drug addiction, as Davis subjects the film's teenage protagonist to a series of humiliating scenarios, including scenes where he gets mugged by drug addicts and finds out that his best friend is selling pot to schoolchildren. The underlying subtext of the film is made abundantly clear when Davis suggests that detecting (and ending) drug use ought to start at home, requiring nothing more than a parent who is willing to snoop through his or her child's room and personal belongings.[18]

Many parents seemed to have been receptive to the advice being offered by Sid Davis and his peers. In 1969 the *Washington Post* reported on two middle-class parents from suburban Maryland who used their sixteen-year-old son's newfound appreciation for incense, as well as the recent arrest of one of his friends on drug charges, as a pretext to rifle through his room. "I went downstairs and tore the bedroom apart and found a full pill vial that looked like it contained weeds," the boy's mother proclaimed. "It was the middle of the afternoon. His father came home and hauled him out of school." Even parenting experts who had previously argued in favor of limiting parental oversight in the teen bedroom began to change their tune once drug use became a prominent issue. In 1972 Abigail Van Buren received the following letter from a concerned parent:

> You have often stressed the fact that parents should respect the privacy of their teen-aged children with regard to letters, diaries, etc. But now that drugs have become so much a part of our lives, and some are both illegal and dangerous, I wonder if you would comment on respect to privacy in this area. If a parent suspects that his teen-ager is taking drugs, or is involved with drugs in any way, doesn't the parent have an obligation to go to all lengths to find out? And of course when the infringement of privacy is discovered, what is the answer then? Please comment, Abby. There are a lot of worried parents out here.

Warning her readers that there was "a vast difference between a parent invading his teen-ager's privacy in order to read his mail or diary, and in attempting to learn whether or not his child is involved with drugs," Van Buren stressed that drug use was reason enough to disregard customary approaches to teen privacy. "Involvement with drugs can make the difference between life and death," she argued. "Parents have a right to learn as much as they can, by whatever means possible. God will forgive them. And so will their children, eventually."[19]

One of the most comprehensive defenses of parental snooping can be found in *When It's Your Kid!* (1978), a guide for parents written by Glenn Bair, a Missouri youth counselor. As the title of the book suggests, *When It's Your Kid!* freely acknowledged that parents were justified in taking drastic measures to address teen drug use. "The concern may reach such a point," the author argued, "that they begin to snoop in an off-limits area—such as their teenager's room—in an effort to discover what is going on in his life." Though Bair acknowledged that most parents would end up feeling guilty after taking such precautions, he nonetheless urged parents to go over their child's bedroom with a fine tooth comb, including vigorous inspections of drawers, mattresses, and "any tiny box you can find." Parents were similarly told to expect a certain amount of hostility from their teenage sons or daughters. "Your adolescent will be as uncomfortable as you," Bair claimed, "and will probably be angry: 'What were you doing in my room? You have no right to go through my things.' For the moment you need to dispose of the problem by saying, 'You have a right to be angry with me for being in your room, but *we* have a problem.'" From Bair's perspective, though, removing drugs from the home and getting the child into treatment was worth a little awkwardness. "At this point," he continued, "the problem of drug use has greater priority than invasion of privacy. If you intervene in a helpful and honest way, the problem about his room and privacy eventually will be resolved."[20]

Calls for Bair's brand of parental snooping only intensified in the 1980s, shortly after Ronald Reagan's War on Drugs began to seep into the public consciousness. Indeed, the amount of literature aimed at teen drug use was simply overwhelming during this period. Nonprofit organizations, parenting experts, and medical authorities often singled out the teen bedroom as an important battleground in the War on Drugs, transforming once-trusting parents into unpaid members of the Drug Enforcement Agency. Among the many experts who discussed the teen bedroom's role in the War on Drugs during the Reagan era, perhaps none was as thorough as Dick Schaefer, an addiction counselor from North Dakota. His book on teen substance abuse, entitled *Choices and Consequences* (1987), featured scores of entries in which the teen bedroom figures prominently. For example, Schaefer asked parents to take note if they smelled pot or found drugs or drug paraphernalia—"papers, pipes, or clips"—in their child's room, while also suggesting that the physical state of a teen's bedroom often reflected its occupant's stage of addiction. Early signs of addiction, he explained, included "coming home and going straight to his or her room," smoking "marijuana in room with window open," and spending "more time in his or her room with the door closed." Compulsive drug use, meanwhile, usually manifested itself in the form of growing carelessness, as Schaefer claimed that habitual drug use left teens so high that they were simply incapable of hiding their habit. "Isn't aware of self as high, so memory and judgment are impaired," he tersely noted. "Uses more recklessly; leaves pipes and drugs in bedroom without hiding them." These types of arguments were meant to convince parents that, although they might find it difficult to catch their sons or daughters using drugs outside the home, any attempts to consume or store drugs in the bedroom would not be so easy to cover up.[21]

The manner in which teenage children guarded the sanctity of their rooms could also be interpreted as a sign of drug use. The simple act of "placing the room off-limits to family," addiction expert Jason Baron pointed out in 1984, was enough to convince one mother and father that their son had begun abusing drugs. "He locked his room whenever he was at home and refused to let his parents in," Baron stated. "Eventually his parents discovered his use of marijuana. They found rolling papers and marijuana pipes hidden in his room and in the garage." This idea was so prevalent during the 1980s that one teen drug abuse text devoted an entire chapter—entitled "Overbearing Protection of Room and Other Personal Possessions"—to the relationship between secrecy and drug use. "Certainly, teens have a right to privacy," the authors were careful to explain. "It's when a child doesn't want you in his/her room—under any circumstance—that may be cause for concern." Such arguments were often based on a somewhat paranoid form of circular logic, as it was assumed that teenagers who vehemently opposed having their privacy violated were not trying to defend their personal autonomy, but rather cover up their own drug use. As Dick Schaefer noted, the teen who protested too much was simply engaging in a "power play" of sorts, one that sought to defuse claims of drug use by, in effect, changing the topic.[22]

The extent to which parents and teens responded to these types of strategies is difficult to measure. For starters, some liberal-minded parents actually encouraged their sons or daughters to experiment with marijuana in their rooms because they feared that other intoxicants, particularly alcohol, were simply much more harmful. Betty Watson, a resident of Pleasantville, New York, was open to the idea of allowing her daughter and her friends to smoke pot in her daughter's bedroom. "They were very quiet," the elder Watson told a reporter from the *Washington Post* in 1977. "I thought how well-behaved, in contrast to the rowdies on beer and liquor." Other commentators argued that many teens, far from being upset over having their privacy violated, were capable of understanding that parental intrusions would benefit them in the long run. In *Getting Tough on Gateway Drugs* (1985), Robert DuPont noted that one of his interview subjects, a teen boy named "Jim," rationalized his parents' intrusions by claiming that the privacy he enjoyed in and out of the home was contingent on his own behavior. "My drug use . . . made me a liar," the young boy explained, "and it made my parents into narcotics agents right in our own house. They could never believe me, and they always searched my room and my clothes, looking for drugs. They used to listen to all my telephone conversations and give my friends the 'third degree.' The only way I could change all that was to stop using drugs."[23]

Though Jim's rationalizations were probably not unheard of during the postwar era, it is doubtful that many teenagers took these intrusions lying down. Adrienne Salinger, for instance, claims that her friends became adept at sidestepping their parents' efforts at snooping while growing up in Northern California during the 1970s. Instead of getting angry that their rooms had been violated, her friends responded by getting "more creative about hiding their drugs." Enterprising members of the business community proved willing participants in this struggle as well, offering teen consumers a host of items that could help restore a measure of privacy inside the teen bedroom. "Decoy" soda cans with screw-off bottoms could be found in head shops and in ads at the back of music magazines, while furniture manufacturers were not above marketing beds to teens that featured hidden shelves and "behind the headboard" storage. Even *Archie* comics—one of the most wholesome examples of teen-oriented popular culture during the postwar era—ran advertisements for a small book-shaped safe that promised to "camouflage your valuables," offering its owner a combination lock that "only you can open." The teen bedroom, in other words, featured all manner of secret hiding places where drugs and other forbidden items could be stored away for safekeeping.[24]

Ultimately, many of these debates on drug use tended to revolve around the idea of how the privacy afforded to teens in their rooms could aid adolescent development without simultaneously endangering it. A tricky balancing act was required—one in which a healthy amount of personal autonomy was granted in most instances, but could be withdrawn if drugs entered the equation. For some conservative-minded experts, however, this issue was emblematic of the wider culture's blithe acceptance of the rights of teens, many of which came at the expense of traditional ideas on parental authority. For instance, one child-rearing expert from the Jehovah's Witnesses used the issue of teen drug use as a pretext for criticizing the lack of parental authority in the teen bedroom in an article in *Awake!* from 1980, entitled "Courts Undermine Parents":

> When a California mother found marijuana in her 17-year-old son's bedroom, she gave it to Los Angeles police, who came to the house. The boy's father gave them permission to search his son's room, and they found nine more bags of the drug. But the California Supreme Court, later upheld by the U.S. Supreme Court, ruled that the warrantless search was illegal, and the evidence could not be used against the apparent dope dealer. California's Attorney General commented that "parents will in many cases be legally precluded from preventing their children from engaging in criminal activity within the family home."

Though the author of the piece was essentially attacking the courts for undermining parental authority in the home, it is interesting to note how the teen bedroom played a central role in bringing this issue to the fore. Rather than pointing out that the warrantless search may have been unconstitutional, the author complained that parents could no longer tend to their children in a proper manner—and legal authorities could no longer be aggressive in prosecuting the War on Drugs—if teens continued to enjoy inviolable privacy rights in the home. The teen bedroom was deemed problematic because it could be used to store a host of illegal drugs and because it represented the culture's supposedly unconditional acceptance of many of the seismic social and cultural changes of the postwar years. The teen bedroom was thus characterized as a space in which the culture wars of the 1960s and 1970s continued to find expression, with law and order and family values supposedly taking a backseat to individual freedoms and the demands of youth.[25]

Alcohol use was also singled out as a particularly dangerous activity within the bedrooms of America's teens. Indeed, one could argue that alcohol's status as a legal consumer product rendered it a much more immediate threat than, say, cocaine or heroin. Whereas illicit drugs could only be tracked down on the black market at an inflated price, the average teenager could send an older friend or relative to the nearest corner store in order to pick up any number of alcoholic beverages. Moreover, alcohol could easily be stashed under a bed or at the bottom of a clothes hamper, while its consumption could be brought about in a much less conspicuous manner than, say, marijuana or other drugs that needed to be burned or cooked prior to ingestion. All that was required was a closed door and perhaps some soft drinks or fruit juice to transform the adolescent bedroom into a teenage speakeasy. In *Did I Have a Good Time?* (1982), Marion Howard spoke of a girl whose bedroom closet acted as a makeshift bar throughout much of her adolescence. Hiding her booze "was such a farce," the girl explained, because her parents rarely ever entered her bedroom. "She made it clear she never wanted her new father to come into her room," Howard noted, "and he never did." Other teenagers had to adopt more surreptitious methods in order to keep their drinking habits a secret. During the late 1970s and early 1980s, Laurel from San Jose, California, stored various types of alcohol in a secret compartment in her desk: "When I had any contraband to hide, I made use of a secret niche behind the drawer compartment of my built in desk." In 1984 a sixteen-year-old girl from Minnesota similarly bragged to journalist Howard Spanogle that she had "a bottle of lime vodka hidden in my bedroom that I occasionally drink from when I need it." Though the young girl claimed that she didn't imbibe on a daily basis, she did note that it was "a comfort to know that it is there if the pressures of life get too hard and I need to escape for a while."[26]

The advice offered to parents who were concerned about their offspring's drinking habits was similar to the advice being offered on teen drug use. In 1971 the Washington State Department of Health released a pamphlet for parents entitled *Teenage Drinking: A Stepping Stone to Other Drug Usage?* that was reproduced in newspapers all across the Pacific Northwest. According to the public health experts who authored the pamphlet, one of the most important warning signs parents should take note of was a "sudden disinterest in family life," a form of voluntary isolation from parents and siblings that manifested itself both inside and outside the home. "The teenager is remaining away from home and returning late at night without being able to offer a logical explanation," the pamphlet explained. "If at home he or she seeks solace in remaining away from family activity by staying in the bedroom for hours." Parents were also told to look out for physical evidence of alcohol abuse, including empty bottles and the smell of alcohol on their child's breath. Charles Carroll's 1985 study of teen substance abuse included a questionnaire in which parents were asked whether they had found "bottles" in the bedroom and other spaces around the home. Vigilance was necessary, he noted, because many of the parents he consulted have found alcohol "under mattresses" or "in stereo speakers." Jerry Hull, an evangelical parenting expert, even addressed the dangers of teen alcohol consumption by channeling the ideas of G. Stanley Hall, suggesting that teen bedrooms be situated as close to the master suite as possible in an effort to facilitate greater amounts of parental surveillance. "Proximity is crucial," he pointed out. "Even though the bedroom is the teen's domain, situate it close to your bedroom so that family ties can be celebrated often." Hull admitted making a "critical mistake" in 1981, when he bought a home with a bedroom in the basement for his son Tim, a bedroom on the main floor for his daughter Karen, and a bedroom on the upper level for him and his wife. "Our separate 'turfs' were too far away and too distinct," he noted.[27]

Mental Illness and Suicide

The teen bedroom also came under increased scrutiny due to its purported role in encouraging antisocial behavior and other psychological problems. As noted in an earlier chapter, many child-rearing experts believed that solitude could be of great benefit to developing teenagers, a means of providing teens with the space in which to ponder the various problems they encountered during adolescence. Famed B-movie actress Pam Grier, for example, responded to the death of her fiancé in Vietnam during the early 1970s by holing herself up in her bedroom. "The first young man I was ever in love with," she told *Ebony* in 1976. "He was just my life. When he died, I must have stayed in my bedroom for a week and just cried." Grier's suffering no doubt created concern among her immediate family, but her mourning process eventually drew to a close, and the young girl emerged from her bedroom showing no obvious signs of pathology. Other teenagers were not so lucky. Child psychologist Richard Vandenbergh discussed the psychological dangers of the teen bedroom in a 1963 article on loneliness in *Psychiatric Quarterly*, citing the case of a sixteen-year-old patient of Chinese ancestry who expressed his cultural isolation by locking himself up in his own room and engaging in "bizarre behavior" there, including "sleeping under his bed and preparing his own meals of starvation proportions in his room, while refusing to eat in the dining room." This type of excessive withdrawal was thought to be an indicator of pathology that parents and acquaintances were well advised to take note of. Teenagers might temporarily withdraw to their rooms in order to deal with the day-to-day stresses of adolescence, but their antisocial ways were expected to subside in a timely manner. As sociologist Evelyn Millis Duvall warned parents in the mid-1970s, "All young people have a need for occasional intervals of isolation. They all desire seclusion at times to work through their problems and come to terms with themselves. But when a young person's withdrawal from normal social and family life goes on for an extended period of time, it is a sign of real distress."[28]

The most troubling aspect of this kind of behavior was its purported association with suicide. Though the vast majority of studies that addressed teen suicide after the Second World War rarely took into account where most suicide attempts were carried out, anecdotal evidence suggests that many teens both planned and carried out their attempts at self-destruction in the privacy of their own bedrooms. In 1959 *Jet* reported that a thirteen-year-old San Francisco boy named Sammy Wilson Jr. shot himself to death after being "ordered to his bedroom because he had made a face at his mother and sassed her." In 1961 psychiatrists Henry Scheer, Paul Kay, and Morris Brozovsky similarly referred to the case of "Carol," an adolescent girl who tried to kill herself when she was fifteen years old. Carol displayed many signs of trouble well before her suicide attempt, including promiscuity and truancy. Nonetheless, the authors of the article focused on one particular incident in which she locked herself in her bedroom and refused to come out for an extended period of time. Carol's desire to shut herself away from the outside world was such that "the police had to be called to get her out" of her bedroom. According to Scheer, Kay, and Brozovsky, this type of behavior was a sure sign that something was seriously wrong with Carol and that a psychiatric intervention was needed.[29]

The teen bedroom's association with suicide would reach its peak during the late 1970s and 1980s, when the media, medical authorities, and government agencies began characterizing rising youth suicide rates as an epidemic that required immediate action. In 1985, the federal government released a report, based on the findings of a Congressional subcommittee, in which it was argued that suicidal behavior could be detected by taking note of how teenagers managed their personal belongings. "Teenagers who are planning to commit suicide," the report stated, "might 'clean house' by giving away favorite possessions, cleaning their rooms, or throwing things away." The report also gave the issue a human face by focusing on the experiences of Heidi Bilodeau, a teenager who had tried suicide numerous times by either slashing her wrists or overdosing on pills. Bilodeau's testimony made clear that thoughts of suicide often found expression in her bedroom. "I stayed in my room most of the time writing dirge, which is depressive poetry," she told the committee, "and planning that day when I would take those pills and never again feel the pain of war in my soul." Thankfully, Bilodeau found the help she needed in order to overcome her problems. However, as several experts on suicide pointed out, many teens were not so lucky. In *Suicide Intervention in the Schools* (1989), educator Scott Poland cited the case of a teen known only as "R" who decided to poison himself in his room. "He found a bottle of aspirin and took all the pills that were in it," Poland noted. "He gulped them down with whiskey and fell asleep in his room." In that same year, psychologist Rene Diekstra published a book on suicide prevention in which a teenager (referred to only as "B") hung himself in his bedroom after being criticized by his father. "B got up calmly and left the table, said goodbye to his friends and went to his room," Diekstra explained. "He was later found dead, hanging from the ventilator in the ceiling."[30]

Although most commentators were reluctant to single out the teen bedroom as a root cause of adolescent suicide, its presence in several case studies did little to weaken its association with pathology. The privacy associated with the teen bedroom was seen as both an aid and an obstacle to proper adolescent development. Parents were expected to offer their children the seclusion needed to encourage self-reliance, self-expression, and personal autonomy, while making sure that the cultivation of self didn't lead to pathological thoughts and behavior. The fears of antisocial behavior and suicide were never seen as good-enough excuses to justify denying teens a room of their own, but it may have been enough to make parents take pause and consider its potentially dangerous effect on adolescent mental health.[31]

Forbidden Forms of Popular Culture

The teen bedroom has long been criticized for allowing teens to hide books, magazines, and music that might alienate adult sensibilities. This type of behavior was not unique to the postwar years, as nineteenth-century youths, including Teddy Roosevelt (see chapter 1), were known to read trashy dime novels in their rooms. The postwar years, however, saw such fears intensify due to the growing consumer power of teenagers and the related growth of cultural products that were aimed specifically at teens. In the 1940s and 1950s, for instance, psychiatrists, educators, and legislators across the country waged war on comic books, claiming that they contributed to rising juvenile delinquency rates. Frederick Wertham, a psychiatry professor from Johns Hopkins University during the 1950s and 1960s, argued that comics were nothing more than how-to guides for budding young criminals. "The average parent has no idea that every imaginable crime is described in detail in comic books," he stated in a *Ladies' Home Journal* article from 1953. "That is their main stock in trade. If one were to set out to teach children how to steal, rob, lie, cheat, assault, and break into candy stores, no more insistent method could be devised."[32]

Although the war on comic books eventually died down by the early 1960s, producers of erotica continued to be singled out by reformers. The fact that public discussions of sex and sexuality were becoming both more common and more contentious by mid-century only inflamed matters. After all, this was the era of Alfred Kinsey, Masters and Johnson, and Hugh Hefner, all of whom shocked traditional-minded critics by bringing Americans' sexual proclivities into various public forums. By the early to mid-1950s, politicians and religious leaders responded to these trends by waging war against so-called smut, taking aim at any magazine shops or mail-order publishing outfits that dared to distribute such salacious material. The teen bedroom would play a small yet vital role in this struggle. In 1952, for instance, the mother of a seventeen-year-old Detroit boy who was charged with murdering a gas station attendant claimed that her son was corrupted by so-called "girlie" magazines. "He got quite fanatic about them," his mother explained. "He started buying magazines with pictures of women with almost no clothes on. He started pinning the pictures up on his wall." In June 1959 Alfred C. Roller, a reporter for the *Daily Reporter* in Dover, Ohio, told of a more quotidian run-in with erotica. "Johnny, a 15-year-old honor student," the story began, "spent long hours cracking the books. It was no surprise to his father to see his son's bedroom light on late into the night. Recently Johnny's father walked in on him unexpectedly and he got the surprise of his life. Instead of reading his French book, Johnny was looking at photos more pornographic than the most obscene French postcards." Roller went on to suggest that Johnny, like his counterpart in Detroit, was at risk of engaging in criminal behavior should his fascination with smut continue. This point was hammered home by transitioning—in the very next paragraph, no less—to the story of an "innocent looking crew cut teenager" who had recently been jailed for "raping a 14-year-old girl" after reading "a book that gave full details of sex attacks by a gang of hoodlums."[33]

Not all discussions of smut were marked by fears of criminality and moral degeneration. Though it would be a mistake to assume that child-rearing experts had become a collection of pleasure-oriented hedonists since the days of Hall and his Victorian-minded peers, some commentators advocated remarkably permissive approaches to the types of reading material that was often found in teen bedrooms. In 1952 Alvena Burnite urged mothers to simply laugh it off when confronted with the presence of salacious literature in their child's room:

"Gadzooks! What is this?" you say, as you drag a battered magazine out from under the mattress of someone's bed. Don't hit the ceiling, just sit down and have a good

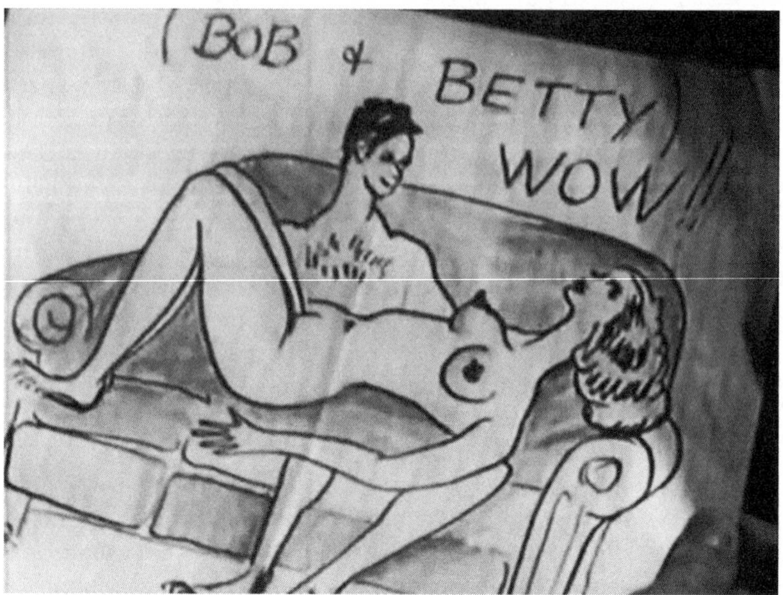

Figure 9 This still was taken from a 1953 sex education film. Bob, a sixteen-year-old boy, manages to produce his own form of erotica, which his mother stumbles across while snooping through his room. *Social-Sex Attitudes in Adolescence* (Toronto: Crawley Films, 1953).

laugh. You know why? Maybe it didn't happen to you, but nine chances out of ten it did. Can you remember a similar incident when you were growing up? Your mother probably almost fainted when she found one of those pulps dealing with love and confessions stowed away in your room.

A few years later, Mary and Lawrence Frank offered similarly liberal advice, telling parents to turn the other cheek when adolescents tell "smutty" jokes in their rooms or keep "a stack of 'sexy' pictures" in their bureau drawers. Although this type of advice was certainly not condoned by most child-rearing experts, its very existence suggests that mainstream views on teen sexuality during the 1950s were not as monolithic as one would presume. Some forms of erotica were given sanction by experts due the fact that the adolescent stage was associated with the sexual awakening of teens, which in turn resulted in a certain amount of curiosity that could be safely explored by, say, flipping through an issue of *Playboy* or even *National Geographic*. The alternative, as most parents were probably aware, is that teens might satisfy their curiosity outside the home in the company of other hormonally driven teenagers. Given a choice in the matter, many parents may have preferred that their sons or daughters see a naked person in a magazine rather than at a strip club or an adult theater.[34]

During the 1960s and 1970s, debates over smut weakened in intensity, even though the porn industry began offering consumers much more explicit products (some of which managed to break into the mainstream; *Deep Throat* and *The Devil in Miss Jones* were nos. 5 and 11 respectively at the box office in key cities in 1973).[35] To be sure, parents were wary of the presence of smut in the teen bedroom, but many experts continued to suggest that a deft touch was needed. In February 1963, for instance, Abigail Van Buren addressed the concerns of a mother who was worried about her son's newfound love of "girlie" magazines. "My 15-year-old son," the boy's mother explained, "seems to be obsessed with those smutty girlie magazines (pictures of women) and I can't do anything about it. I have found them hidden under his mattress, in his closet, and almost everywhere I look. I keep throwing them away, but he keeps buying more. Is this typical of a normal 15-year-old boy's behavior, or is he headed for trouble?" Van Buren pointed out that looking at pornography was a "normal" by-product of adolescent curiosity, while also explaining that this boy's curiosity appeared to be "insatiable" and required some form of adult intervention. However, Van Buren did not encourage her reader to confiscate her son's reading material, but instead insisted that a male adult—preferably the boy's father—make himself available in order to address the boy's curiosity. Somehow this course of action was expected to stave off the so-called "damaging" effects of being preoccupied with sex.[36]

Even experts who agreed that erotica ought to be rooted out of the teen bedroom felt that it should be done in such a way as to avoid undermining the adolescent's fragile ego. Parents who found smut "in their child's schoolbag or in his room," one *New York Times* columnist opined in the spring of 1968, should be as direct as possible with the child. Instead of acting in a punitive manner, parents were told to opt for "friendly questioning" and refrain from judging their offspring. Other experts, meanwhile, replicated the more permissive approaches advocated by Alvena Burnite and the Franks, arguing that erotica didn't need to be taken out of the room at all. In early 1977—the same year in which she told a teen girl to not get too upset whenever her mother rifled through her bedroom—Abigail Van Buren received a letter from a mother who had confiscated a "girlie magazine" from her sixteen-year-old son's bedroom. Confused as to what her options were in dealing with this problem, the mother asked Van Buren how she should confront her son. Suffice to say that Van Buren's response differed dramatically from the suggestions she offered during the early 1960s. "Return the magazine," she stated bluntly. "Even a

16-year-old is entitled to some privacy. . . . If he becomes preoccupied with 'girlie magazines,' a talk is in order. If not, get over your unearned guilt, and don't add to his."[37]

The conservative resurgence of the 1980s failed to produce significant changes to the ways in which parents were expected to address the presence of erotic material in the teen bedroom. This is somewhat surprising given the fact that President Reagan's Attorney General Edwin Meese produced a damning report on the effects of pornography on juvenile delinquency, crime rates, and moral values. Whereas an earlier study, commissioned in 1969 by Lyndon Johnson, found that there was "no evidence to date that exposure to explicit sexual materials plays a significant role in the causation of delinquent or criminal behavior among youths or adults," Meese's study claimed that pornography was a "medical and public health problem" that "encourages patterns of social behavior which have adverse health consequences," such as higher "rates of illegitimacy, teenage pregnancy, abortion, and sexually transmitted diseases." Appealing to his evangelical base, Reagan made clear that his administration would resist the changes wrought by the sexual revolutions of the 1960s and 1970s.[38]

Nonetheless, Reagan's war on porn, unlike his War on Drugs, didn't catch on to any significant extent. Most mainstream child-rearing experts, though they were certainly uncomfortable with pornography, were unlikely to recommend that parents put themselves on a war footing in order to cleanse the home of filth. Consider, for example, a letter received by Bobby Simpson, a teenage advice columnist for the *Boston Herald* during the 1980s, from a confused mother who claimed that she found a *Playboy* in her fifteen-year-old son's room:

> The fact that my son is reading these magazines distresses me, because I feel a boy his age should not be looking at pictures of nude women in suggestive poses. My first reaction was to show the magazine to my husband, but then I realized that he would immediately hand out a harsh punishment to our son. Then I decided to speak with my son about what I found without my husband being present, but because of the situation I wouldn't know what to say. I put the magazine back underneath the bed because until I worked out my plan of action I did not want my son to know I had spotted it.

In many respects, Bobby's response to this "worried mother" was not that different from the advice being offered by Abigail Van Buren years earlier. He not only encouraged the woman to avoid punishing her son, but he also warned her not to confiscate the offensive material. "Everyone has different views on sex," the young man noted, "but I think you are making too much of this situation. It is quite common for adolescents to look at *Playboy*. But if you feel that it is inappropriate for your son, tell him so. You may feel uncomfortable in doing this, but this is the only way for you to get your feelings across to him."[39]

Obviously, many parents would have found it difficult to adopt such a permissive approach to pornography. And yet there is evidence to suggest that these types of responses were something more than mere fantasies concocted by the mainstream media. While growing up in Corvallis, Oregon, in the late 1980s, Jeff Steele stumbled across a box of *Playboys* in the garage, which he later concluded was left for him intentionally by his father. He hid the stash in various nooks and crannies in his room, and even added some more-risqué material—"a *Oui* and a *Hustler* or two"—in subsequent months. One day, shortly after returning from a sledding trip with his friends, his mother informed him that she had cleaned his room, offering him "a look that said she'd found the stash." However, when Steele returned to his room, he found that "the stash was intact." His mother's response was indicative of the culture's paradoxical views on masturbation, the erotic material that often hastened it, and the teen bedroom's role in facilitating both. Though she tacitly admitted that she wasn't happy with her son's reading material, she was reluctant to confiscate it and devise a punishment that could deter such behavior in the future.[40]

Since "sex" and "drugs" have already received significant attention in this chapter, it only makes sense to discuss their partner in crime: rock and roll. The emergence of rock and roll music during the mid- to late 1950s produced a host of anxieties among parents, educators, and others who felt that this new genre of music was, as one husband and wife team argued in the late 1950s, undermining "old fashioned, tried-and-true goals," including "home, family, scholarship, work, [and] respectability." Debates over rock music were often most intense among evangelicals, as their leaders frequently accused rock musicians of numerous transgressions. Bob Larsen, a former rock musician turned evangelical preacher, claimed in the late 1960s that rock and roll was creating a "national state of neurosis in America," blaming the new genre of music and its teenage followers for the "rise of civil disorders and the hippie movement," flirtation with "communist and new left" political philosophies, and renegade sexual behavior, including the "secretion of body hormones." Indeed, these types of arguments were so prevalent during the postwar period that some teens were forced to use their rooms as a clandestine venue in which to indulge their love of rock music. During the 1970s, for instance, famed soul singer Terence Trent D'Arby used to hide a transistor radio in his bedroom in order to listen to pop and country music, both of which were frowned upon by his father, a strict Baptist preacher.[41]

The fears that Elvis Presley's gyrating hips and the Rolling Stone's shaggy haircuts may have inspired among parents during the 1950s, 1960s, and 1970s seem almost quaint when compared to the hysteria witnessed during the 1980s over heavy metal, a new, more aggressive subgenre of rock and roll that emerged in the North of England during the late 1960s and early 1970s. Though the imagery and themes associated with heavy metal are varied and complex, conservative parents—again, evangelicals were at the forefront—came to see this new genre as an attack on Christianity and civil society. In 1985, for example, former 1950s teen idol Pat Boone claimed that top-selling heavy metal acts such as Iron Maiden, Black Sabbath, and Judas Priest were "into sado-masochism, incest, rape, murder, suicide, drugs and the occult." Boone, a born-again Christian, echoed the sentiments of many in the evangelical community who took umbrage with the genre's fascination with the occult and Satanic imagery. This type of fearmongering was often shrugged off as the ramblings of the lunatic fringe, but heavy metal music would come under attack in the mainstream media on a fairly regular basis throughout much of the 1980s, oftentimes in the wake of some particularly heinous act of teen violence. On several occasions, moreover, the teen bedroom would be dragged into these debates due to the fact that this is where heavy metal and other controversial genres of music were often consumed.[42]

The Judas Priest case discussed earlier was certainly one of the more high-profile attempts to indict heavy metal as a genre of music, but it wasn't the only one. In January 1988 Tommy Sullivan, a fourteen-year-old boy from New Jersey, stabbed his mother to death with a Boy Scout knife, set fire to her remains, and then slit his own throat in his neighbor's backyard. In the months leading up to the murder-suicide, Tommy had apparently developed an interest in both heavy metal and the occult, an aspect of the case that investigators and the media latched on to in order to explain the boys' terrible actions. Tommy's bedroom was given a prominent spot in the narrative the media presented to the general public. It was pointed out that Tommy's bedroom was filled with books on the occult and witchcraft and that the walls of his room were decorated with posters of prominent heavy metal acts. "Inside Tommy's room, there were more such books, along with a collection of crude satanic drawings and diagrams," a writer for *Spin* described a few months after the murders. "On the wall was a small bedside crucifix that was dwarfed by his poster of Ozzy Osbourne and a maniacally grinning Alice Cooper." As sociologist Jeffrey Victor noted, Tommy's murderous scheme was actually concocted in his bedroom, as the young boy forged "a kind of compact with the devil" while his parents and younger brother went about their daily routines. "I believe that evil will arise and conquer the love of God," a letter that was later found in his room explained. "If this pact is to your approval, sign below."[43]

Tommy also used his bedroom as a means of withdrawing from his family for extended periods of time, which, as was noted earlier, was seen as an indicator that he may have been suffering from serious psychological problems. Once again, Sullivan's fascination with heavy metal music was thought to have played a major role in creating distance between Tommy and the rest of his family. "After saving for what seemed like ages," the reporter for *Spin* claimed, "he purchased a $1000 stereo system and began to spend his days in his room listening to a growing collection of heavy metal records." The boy's parents, Tom and Bettyanne, were unaware that their son—inspired by the grim theatrics of heavy metal music and the occult—was using his bedroom to plot their murders. A detective assigned to the case even suggested that "Tommy could have been sacrificing elephants in his room and the parents wouldn't have known about it." If there is a lesson to be learned from Sullivan's case, it's that the privacy afforded to Tommy in his bedroom drove a wedge between the young boy and the rest of his family and made it easier for him to enjoy controversial forms of popular culture that were associated with criminality and pathology. The boy's bedroom, not to put too fine a point on it, was thought to be a source of danger that ultimately determined the fate of the entire Sullivan family in a most unfortunate way.[44]

These types of stories were commonplace during the 1980s. In December 1987 three teenage boys, Pete Roland, Ron Clements, and Jim Hardy, smashed their friend's head in with a baseball bat before dumping the body in a cistern outside of Carl Junction, Missouri. The teens later told the police that the murder was the result of two factors: their desire to find out what it was like to kill someone and their loyalty to Satan. Once again, the teen bedroom was portrayed as a space in which this type of pathological behavior was nurtured. Tamara Jones, a journalist from the *Los Angeles Times*, claimed that Ron Clements's mother searched her son's "bizarre room" a few months before the murder and was disturbed by what she found: "Ghastly heavy metal posters were plastered across every spare inch of wall space. Black cloth covered the windows. A stuffed wolf's head hung from the ceiling." Ron's mother also found her son's journal in his room, which featured "graphic depictions of violence and sexual fantasies." She was so shaken up by her son's musings that she took the journal to the local police department, where an officer urged her to immediately get her son into treatment. The counselors she consulted, however, weren't worried about the contents of Ron's journal, using decades-old ideas on teen privacy and child development to assuage her fears. "The counselors reassured Diana that Ron was just going through a normal adolescent phase," Jones noted. "She should be glad he could get his aggressions out on paper. And she should stay out of his room. Privacy is very important to teen-agers."[45]

Pete Roland's room was similarly characterized as the product of a disturbed mind. It was reported that his mother searched his room and found several "crude weapons," including "broken glass" and "a stick with nails poking out," as well as a Satanic bible. Like Ron Clements, Pete also loved heavy metal music, particularly thrash—a faster, more aggressive subgenre of metal that emerged during the 1980s. The décor in Pete's room reflected both his fascination with thrash metal and the violence and ugliness that was supposedly brewing deep in his soul. "The posters on Pete's wall were hideous," Tamara Jones explained, "like the album covers in his record collection. One showed a singer drinking blood from a human skull." Years later, Pete's mother admitted that the amount of time her son spent in his room should have been seen as an early indicator of trouble. "He didn't want to be around us," she told a prominent evangelical preacher. "I remember mostly when I would come home and fix dinner, he would come home, go to his room, and when my husband and I were through eating and had left the kitchen, then Pete would come in and eat. Then he would go back to his room. He really avoided us." Though Jim Hardy's room was not subjected to as much scrutiny as Ron's and Pete's rooms were, the media pointed out that it did play host to some unusual and violent behavior. When Jim was thirteen, his father, James Sr., confronted the boy about smoking marijuana and "popping pills." Enraged by the accusation, Jim "smashed a baseball bat into his bedroom door with such force that chunks of wood flew into the hall and hit his retreating father." Similarly, friends of all three boys remembered sitting in Jim's room watching him "drive screws through a Barbie doll's head, then burn the plastic face and wish out loud that it was human." The three boys also used Jim's room to fantasize about setting an old woman on fire. "They thought I was joking, but in my mind, that was exactly what I wanted to do," Jim later admitted.[46]

Predictably, parents were told to address the problems associated with heavy metal music and the occult by keeping an eye on their offspring's bedrooms. In 1985, for instance, a reporter for *U.S. News & World Report* claimed that there was a direct link between heavy metal music, its expression in the teen bedroom, and the overall health of the family unit.

"Up go Black Sabbath, Motley Crue and Iron Maiden rock posters on bedroom walls," he warned parents. "Styles shift to dramatic clothing and haircuts. School grades slip. A sweet nature turns irritable." In order to reverse these trends, the reporter recommended that parents consult with Darlyne Pettinicchio, a tough-love advocate and cofounder of the Back in Control Training Center in Fullerton, California. Pettinicchio urged parents to "depunk or demetal" teenagers immediately. "Take down the posters," she advised. "Take away the black clothes. They'll get upset, but you have to give clear, direct commands." Similar arguments were expressed by members of law enforcement. In 1988 Robert Simandl, a veteran of the Chicago Police Department and self-described expert on "occult behavior," presided over a series of seminars that informed parents, educators, and police organizations on how to recognize and prevent occult-related crimes. His only advice to parents was to "check their kids' bedrooms" whenever they noticed that their children were acting strangely. "Besides occult literature, tarot (fortune-telling) cards, certain heavy-metal rock albums, candles, posters of mythological beings and martial-arts weaponry," Simandl stated, "warning signs that suggest a need for professional help include ceremonial knives, diaries of rituals written in blood (known as a 'Book of Shadows') and a 'contract' with Satan to commit suicide."[47]

* * *

Many of the anecdotes discussed in this chapter serve to remind us that the postwar teen bedroom was capable of producing a great deal of fear and anxiety among certain segments of the population. While the bedrooms that emerged in the nineteenth and early twentieth centuries accommodated a significant amount of parental control and surveillance, the bedrooms that emerged in the 1960s, 1970s, and 1980s were seen by some observers as parent-free zones where teens could run riot. Indeed, as Adrienne Salinger notes in *In My Room* (1995), the postwar teen bedroom excelled at hiding various forms of teen misbehavior. For instance, one of Salinger's friends from high school hid all of her forbidden possessions in her bedroom, including "the ID bracelet from her boyfriend who worked at the 76 station and who used to be in jail, a hash pipe collection, birth control pills, [and] the *I Ching*." Though parental authority wasn't banished entirely, it is safe to say that the walls of the teen bedroom had become much less permeable in the last half of the twentieth century, establishing firmer boundaries between the private lives of adolescents and their parents and siblings. According to some observers, this was nothing more than a recipe for disaster, a means of ensuring that teenagers enter into adulthood without benefiting from the wisdom and guidance of their elders. One of the ways to reverse this trend—and reverse the perceived decline of parental authority as a whole—was to reassert parental control over the teen bedroom, to adopt a "law and order" strategy that, like so many law-and-order strategies before it, was more likely to be implemented during times of crisis. Well-behaved teens, after all, weren't gracious enough to offer their parents a firm reason to snoop through their rooms. On the other hand, teenagers who dabbled in drugs or alcohol, collected pornography, or engaged in other unacceptable activities were strong candidates to have their rooms reopened to the parental gaze.[48]

EIGHT

Just Like Brian Wilson Did . . .

"Did you really spend four years in bed?"

"Yes, I did."

"What did you do?"

"I stayed in my bedroom and snorted cocaine."

INTERVIEW WITH BRIAN WILSON IN THE *NEWARK ADVOCATE* (1976)

If it were possible to sum up the postwar teen bedroom by referring to a single figure from the world of popular culture, one would be hard pressed to find a better candidate than Brian Wilson, the legendary founder of the Beach Boys. For starters, Wilson and his neighbor, Gary Usher, wrote perhaps the most iconic song about the teen bedroom: the Beach Boys' 1963 hit "In My Room." An ethereal little ditty, "In My Room" presents a familiar image of the bedroom as a safe haven teenagers could flee to in order to escape from the rigors of adolescence. Described as "a world where I can go and tell my secrets to," the teen bedroom was also celebrated as a space where teens could "lock out" all their "worries" and "fears." Ultimately, the lyrics of "In My Room" reveal the bittersweet nature of teen bedroom culture, emphasizing both the feelings of loneliness teens might encounter in their rooms as well as its therapeutic value in allowing them to confront their fears: "Now it's dark and I'm alone, but I won't be afraid," the Beach Boys coo in the final verse. The phrase "in my room" is then repeated, mantra-like, seven times before the song fades into nothingness.[1]

"In My Room" was inspired by Wilson's own experiences with teen bedroom culture while growing up in Southern

California during the late 1950s and early 1960s. Though he shared a room with his brothers Carl and Dennis throughout much of his early childhood—allowing them to practice the multipart vocal harmonies that became an integral part of the Beach Boys' sound in subsequent years—Brian was given his own bedroom in 1958, when Murry Wilson, Brian's authoritarian father and band manager, gave the sixteen-year-old songwriter permission to convert the family's music room into his own personal bedroom/songwriting space. "I slept right next to the piano," Wilson noted in his memoirs. "I could play until I dropped, then roll straight into bed. It was a comforting setup during a directionless period." An awkward boy who was terrorized by his father—at one point, he was forced by his father to defecate on a folded newspaper in the middle of the kitchen floor—Brian saw his bedroom as a means of dealing with the violence and dysfunction that often marked the Wilson household. "I had a room, and I thought of it as my kingdom," he told an interviewer during the 1980s. "And I wrote that song, very definitely, that you're not afraid when you're in your room. It's absolutely true." Gary Usher was similarly struck by the importance his fellow songwriter placed on his room, noting in an interview before his death in 1990 that "Brian was always saying that his room was his whole world."[2]

Wilson's somewhat intense relationship with his bedroom continued well into adulthood, manifesting itself in a particularly telling manner during the 1970s when he suffered a much-publicized nervous breakdown. Wilson had been living in a somewhat reclusive manner since he stopped touring with the Beach Boys in the mid-1960s. By 1973, however, he began spending nearly every hour of every day in his room. "I went up to my bedroom, undressed, climbed into my enormous four-poster bed, pulled up the covers, stared at the intricate carved angels on the headboard, and stayed there, more or less, for the next two and a half years, from summer 1973 to late 1975." Wilson later claimed that this behavior continued into the early 1980s, as he often used his room to abuse drugs, eat junk food, and watch television. "Basically, I did about 10 years on and off of bedroom scenes," he told an interviewer in 1995. "In my bedroom, all the time. Under the sheets." Although Wilson was no longer a teenager when his mental health began to deteriorate, the bedroom he presided over as an adult seems to have been regarded in much the same way as the bedroom he presided over as a teen. Haunted by drug addiction and schizophrenia, Wilson felt that his bedroom was one of the few places in which he truly felt safe. "I had withdrawn into a private world," he explained, "and showed absolutely no interest in leaving it."[3]

What follows is a brief examination of the teen bedroom as it was understood by members of the cultural community, including select artists from the worlds of literature, music, film, and television. Like Brian Wilson, many of these artists offered highly personalized takes on teen bedroom culture that both reinforced and undermined preexisting ideas on the separate bedroom ideal. The postwar teen bedroom was often seen as a bundle of contradictions, acting as a safe haven or a muse for some, a prison for others. As with their peers in the business community and child development, few artists offered a sustained critique of teen bedroom culture. They understood that the teen bedroom could be a problematic space, but the custom of providing older children with rooms of their own was rarely ever called into question.

Popular Music

The fact that teen bedroom culture occasionally found expression within the world of popular music should surprise no one. As noted earlier, the proliferation of cheap audio equipment during the postwar years transformed the teen bedroom into an important spot in which to listen to rock and roll, hip-hop, heavy metal, or any other genre of popular music that struck the fancy of America's youth. Indeed, by the 1980s music reviewers occasionally used the teen bedroom as a means of measuring the resonance of a particular song or album among teenagers and college-age youth. Karen Tucker, a writer for *Spin*, declared in 1989 that the Goo Goo Dolls' second album *Jed* is "[what] you listen to when you barricade your bedroom door and fly spastically around the room with a guitar made of air." One year later, Jonathan Bernstein and Steven Daly (also from *Spin*) declared that Depeche Mode's seventh album, *Violator*, was ideal for teenage girls whose gloomy sensibilities often found expression in their rooms. "Throughout the country," they wrote, "when bedroom doors slammed shut in unison, when faces were buried in pillows to muffle the sobs, when you could find a partner for that suicide pact, there was only one soundtrack to mirror the pain."[4]

The teen bedroom's reputation for inducing feelings of loneliness and alienation was not entirely undeserved. While experts in child psychology and interior design applauded its ability to rationalize the young, many of the LPs and 45s spun by teenagers on portable phonographs during the 1950s and 1960s told quite a different story. Connie Francis, for one, seems to have made an entire career out of putting the pain of teenage love to music, oftentimes using the bedroom as an important setting. In her 1959 song "Among My Souvenirs," Francis paints a vivid portrait of a young girl dealing with lost love in the privacy of her own room:

Some letters tied in blue, a photograph or two
I see a rose from you among my souvenirs
A few more tokens rest within my treasure chest
And though they do their best to give me consolation
I count them all apart and as the teardrops start
I find a broken heart among my souvenirs.

Francis would return to this theme in her 1963 song, "If My Pillow Could Talk":

If my pillow could talk,
It would tell you 'bout my sleepless nights
Tell you 'bout the rivers I cried
Ever since you said good-bye

If Francis's lyrics are any guide, then, the drama and heightened emotionally that was often associated with adolescence had the potential to transform the teen bedroom into a rather dark and depressing place.[5]

Francis's views on the teen bedroom can be interpreted as both an attempt to empathize with her predominantly teenage (and female) fan base and a reflection of her own experiences with teen bedroom culture. Though she lived with her overprotective parents until she was well into her twenties, Francis was given a room of her own as a five-year-old, shortly after her parents moved from an apartment in Brooklyn to a semidetached home across the river in Newark, New Jersey. Decorated by her mother in a fairly traditional manner, the bedroom Francis occupied during her preteen teen years seem to have played a positive role in her budding singing career. "I loved our house," she noted in her memoirs. "I especially loved my very own bedroom painted pink with its Early American maple furniture. Mommy even took an old table and, with thumbtacks, covered it with a pretty pink eyelet skirt; above it hung a mirror—a great big mirror I could practice in front of." As a teenager, shortly after her singing career began to take off, Francis started using her room as an office in which to respond to fan mail. "At the end of my second year on TV, nearly 75 letters poured in a week, completely overwhelming my parents and me," she wrote in an advice book for teens. "Every night I used to climb into bed, read by the light of a little frilly pink table lamp, and answer every single letter myself. I really did."[6]

By the time Francis was in her late teens, however, her bedroom was transformed into a site of generational conflict. Frustrated by her parents' controlling ways, Francis began writing a diary, which she dubbed her "secret confessor." Her parents often read the young girl's diary while she was out of the house, which led her to engage in various acts of subterfuge. "Every night of the week I'd furtively conceal The Daring, Deadly Diary in a different location," she explained. "On Mondays, it went under the bed; Tuesdays, it was under my slips in the drawer; Wednesdays, under the shoes in the closet . . ." When this failed to keep her parents at bay, Francis even taught herself shorthand in order to disguise the content of her diary entries. "My mom snooped so much that it wasn't long before she had my whole game plan down pat. So for a while there, I even had to relinquish Diary Rights; that is, until I sent away for the *Gregg Book of Shorthand*. It was purely and simply a case of survival." After five weeks of instruction, Francis "mastered shorthand," allowing her to "hide the truth" about her so-called "decadent" life.[7]

Francis also struggled with romantic problems in her bedroom. At one point, her father—an overbearing man who was suspicious of any boy who so much as talked to his talented young daughter—refused to let her go to the prom. Devastated, Francis decided to protest her father's decision by holding a prom of her own in her bedroom. "On prom night, I got to wear my pretty new gown, although no one I knew saw me in it," Francis relates in her memoirs. "I even had my hair and nails done by my girl friend, Connie. I locked myself in my room and wore my gown all that night. I played my 45s and pretended to hold Stevie Cohen [her former prom date] as we danced the night away to 'Moments to Remember' and 'Pretend You're Happy When You're Blue'—a 'perfect' song for the 'perfect' evening." A few years later, after her father pulled a gun on her boyfriend Bobby Darin, Francis once again used her bedroom as a means of protesting her father's heavy-handed ways, buying black-and-white-striped wallpaper for her room, which she later admitted was a conscious attempt to protest the rather confining relationship she had with her parents. Like Mary Astor in the 1920s (see chapter 2), Connie Francis came to see her bedroom as a prison. "I chose black just in case my parents were curious about what kind of mood I was in. Yup! Black paper with teeny white stripes, which reminded me of jail. Why not? It was a fitting touch, wasn't it, for my dismal new bedroom in our dismal new house?"[8]

Bedroom-oriented melancholia was not limited solely to young girls. In 1961 Faron Young released "Hello Walls," a chart-topping song written by Willie Nelson, that describes how a young man deals with heartbreak by talking to the only friend he has—the walls of his bedroom:

Hello, walls
How'd things go for you today?
Don't you miss her,

Since she up and walked away?
And I'll bet you dread to spend
Another lonely night with me
Lonely walls, I'll keep you company.

In a later verse, the lyrics establish a poetic link between the protagonist's psychological state and his immediate surroundings, as parts of the boy's room actually begin to take on characteristics of its occupant's fragile emotional state:

Hello, window
Well I see that you're still here
Aren't you lonely,
Since our darlin' disappeared?
Well, look here, is that a teardrop
In the corner of your pane?
Now, don't you try to tell me that it's rain.

As with Francis's weepy odes to teenage love, Nelson's song paints a dark and irrational portrait of teen bedroom culture, one that contrasts sharply with the largely optimistic assessments offered by child development and home décor experts. Indeed, judging by some of the other songs that were released in the late 1950s and early 1960s—for example, "Tears on My Pillow" by Little Anthony and the Imperials, and "Tossin' and Turnin'" by Bobby Lewis—parents from that era could perhaps be forgiven for thinking that the separate bedroom ideal was more likely to produce the next William Blake rather than the next Voltaire.[9]

The emergence of punk as a subgenre of rock and roll during the 1970s and 1980s helped cement the teen bedroom's association with youthful alienation and generational discord. This isn't particularly surprising, as punk's aesthetic—much like the teen bedroom itself—was often defined in opposition to parents and other forms of authority. One of the most striking examples of this phenomenon is "Institutionalized," a song released in 1983 by Suicidal Tendencies that offers a sympathetic examination of one teen's attempts to deal with a host of personal problems. The first verse is presented as a monologue, as the song's protagonist, Mike, explains that his day-to-day activities "just [don't] work out the way I wanted to," resulting in feelings of frustration and confusion. Mike just wants to be left alone so that he can figure these things out for himself, but his parents misinterpret his difficulties as a sign of mental illness and insist that he seek professional help—that he "get away" and "talk about it." Mike's resistance to this idea is expressed in the chorus, when the tempo of the song reaches a fever pitch and the singer explains that his parents are, in fact, suggesting that he be shipped off to a mental institution that would "brainwash" him and strip him of his personal autonomy:

So you're gonna be institutionalized
You'll come out brainwashed with bloodshot eyes
You won't have any say
They'll brainwash you until you see their way.

The first verse, then, reiterates a common trope in teen-oriented popular culture: the idea that parents are simply incapable of understanding their teenage offspring. According to Dee Dee Ramone, the bassist for legendary punk act the Ramones, this approach suited Suicidal Tendencies' core audience well. "They sing about someone's mother coming into some kid's bedroom and accusing him of being on drugs," he told *Spin* in January 1986, "and the kid wants to be left alone. And the parents accuse him of being crazy. They sing about the frustrations of being young."[10]

The second verse builds on this idea by moving the narrative into Mike's bedroom, using it as a means of amplifying the growing divide between teens and their parents. "I was in my room and I was just like staring at the wall thinking about everything," Mike explains. "But then again I was thinking about nothing." His mother then enters his bedroom, leading to a comical exchange that is worth reproducing in full:

And then my mom came in and I didn't even know she was there
She called my name and I didn't even hear it
And then she started screaming: MIKE! MIKE!
And I go: What, what's the matter?
And she goes: What's the matter with you?
I go: There's nothing wrong, mom.
And she goes: Don't tell me that, you're on drugs!
And I go: No mom, I'm not on drugs. I'm okay, I was just thinking you know, why don't you get me a Pepsi.
And she goes: NO, you're on drugs!
I go: Mom, I'm okay. I'm just thinking.
She goes: No you're not thinking, you're on drugs! Normal people don't act that way!
I go: Mom, just give me a Pepsi, please.
All I want is a Pepsi, and she wouldn't give it to me
All I wanted was a Pepsi, just one Pepsi, and she wouldn't give it to me.
Just a Pepsi.

After a reprise of the chorus, the third and final verse offers another bedroom scene in which Mike's parents, fearing that he's "gonna hurt somebody" or hurt himself, inform him that "it would be in your interest if we put you somewhere where you could get the help that you need." Their decision sets the young boy off, as Mike places the blame for his behavior firmly on his parents:

Wait, what are you talking about, we decided?
My best interest? How can you know what my best interest is?
How can you say what my best interest is? What are you trying to say, I'm crazy?
When I went to your schools, I went to your churches,
I went to your institutional learning facilities? So how can you say I'm crazy?

What started off as one teen's attempt to be alone in his room in order to sort out some personal problems (and perhaps enjoy a Pepsi) eventually ends with an indictment of both the boy's parents and the various institutions that tried to socialize him. His rant proves futile in the end, however, as the lyrics suggest that Mike is eventually sent away to have his brain fixed. He takes it all in stride, informing the listener that "it doesn't matter, I'll probably get hit by a car anyway."[11]

It is also worth noting that a video for "Institutionalized" was made in 1984, receiving extensive airplay on MTV and bringing Suicidal Tendencies to a much wider audience. In many respects, the visual narrative touches on similar themes as the lyrics, but with a twist: though Mike's bedroom—decorated with Suicidal Tendencies posters and equipped with a cassette player and a portable television set—is still portrayed as a site of teen rumination and generational conflict, it is also characterized as having a distinct carceral function. During the second verse, when Mike's mother bursts into his room and accuses him of being on drugs, his father is seen transforming his son's bedroom into a cell in an insane asylum. He attaches wrought-iron bars to the bedroom windows, adds padding to the walls, installs a toilet, and removes the shade from the overhead light in order, one presumes, to recreate the harsh lighting found in prisons and hospitals. As the second verse ends, the lead singer is shown sitting in his newly decorated room/cell in a straightjacket. He eventually gains his freedom, however, when the other members of the band tear the bars off his window with a car. A more complex narrative thus emerged when "Institutionalized" was presented in visual terms, allowing the teen bedroom to be seen as both a site of personal autonomy and a parent-made prison.[12]

Film

The world of cinema does not have an equivalent of "In My Room," a signature film that focuses on some of the more unique features of teen bedroom culture. Nonetheless, given the growing economic power of youth during the postwar years and the spate of films that claimed to speak to teen sensibilities in its wake, teen bedroom culture did find expression in a few notable releases, including *Gidget* (1959), the big-screen adaptation of the novel of the same name. Although much of the film takes place on the beaches of Southern California, the opening scene is set in sixteen-year-old Gidget's bedroom, as the eponymous heroine is being berated by her friend Patti for refusing to find a boyfriend. In terms of its basic décor, Gidget's room is much more conservative than some of the teen bedrooms that would emerge during the late 1960s, 1970s, and 1980s. In fact, her bedroom is defined in large part by the same gendered design strategies that would eventually fall out of favor in the coming decades, featuring a pastel color scheme—an accent wall behind her bed is painted light blue, and her bedding is light pink—flowery wallpaper and borders, and frilly curtains. Unlike many cultural representations of the teen bedroom during this period, however, Gidget's room comes equipped with both a vanity *and* a study desk, the presence of which confirms a key aspect of the young girl's identity. A blond and athletic girl who should have no problem finding a boyfriend, Gidget is simply much too bookish for her own good, spending great amounts of time studying or playing her cello in her bedroom. "The kid's studied up on about everything but sex," her friend Patti complains. Gidget's room is thus set up as a means of both reinforcing and repudiating traditional gender expectations; it may be decorated in a stereotypically feminine manner, but it also reveals Gidget's preference for books over boys.[13]

Gidget eventually heeds Patti's advice and heads to the beach for some much-needed socializing. Here she discovers the allure of surfing and a boy named Moondoggie, an experienced surfer who takes a liking to Gidget. Regarded earlier in the film as a source of Gidget's problems in finding a boyfriend, the young girl's room is eventually recast as a means of addressing her issues with the opposite sex. Gidget and her mother not only exchange dating advice in her room, but she even starts using her bedroom as a practice space in which to hone her surfing skills. One particularly clever scene shows Gidget standing on a surfboard with a shimmering blue sky behind her. As the camera slowly pulls out, the viewer soon realizes that Gidget is standing on a surfboard atop her bed, that the blue sky is, in fact, the accent wall in her bedroom, and that her friend B.L. has been given the task of shaking the bed in order to simulate real waves. This strategy, Gidget boldly declares, will allow her to become "the best female surfer in California," thereby winning the admiration of Moondoggie and his friends. Realizing, however, that mastering the art of surfing is not enough to attract the attention of the average American boy, Gidget also uses her bedroom to perform various exercises in hopes of increasing her breast size. Once again B.L. is enlisted to help Gidget in her efforts at self-improvement, standing by with a stopwatch and keeping time as her blonde friend holds her arms in front of her chest and flexes her pectoral muscles every two seconds. Though Gidget eventually complains that these exercises will "take forever to add even an inch," her efforts suggest that the teen bedroom allows teens to attend to issues of both mind and body.[14]

Although Gidget's world was about as white-bread as it gets, the 1960s and 1970s witnessed the release of films in which groups that had often been excluded from teen bedroom culture—particularly African Americans and working-class immigrants—were given a more prominent voice. Chief among them was *Cooley High* (1975), a coming-of-age story that focuses on two African American teenagers, Leroy "Preach" Jackson and Richard "Cochise" Morris, who are trying to figure out what to do with their lives while growing up on the South Side of Chicago during the mid-1960s. The portrayal of teen bedrooms in *Cooley High* is unique for two reasons: it serves as a reminder that race and social class often determine the types of bedrooms teenagers preside over, while also examining teen bedroom culture from an African American perspective. Richard, the poorer of the two main characters, does not have a room of his own; his family is simply too large, the apartment they live in too small to accommodate such an arrangement. An early scene, set in the kitchen of the Morris home, suggests that Richard probably sleeps on a trundle bed in the living room. As a result, at least one of his attempts to seduce a woman is shown as taking place in another friend's apartment. Like many American teens, Richard's experience with the teen bedroom was defined in large part by absence and want. His friend Leroy, however, does have a room of his own, albeit one that looks more like a boardinghouse than a stereotypical middle-class teen bedroom. Leroy's room features very little in the way of personalization—the only objects on the wall are a calendar and a hammered copper portrait of dog—and it is furnished with nothing more than a bed and a lamp. Regardless, Leroy's bedroom occasionally plays host to some sexual experimentation. Near the end of the film, Leroy brings a girl up to his room while his mother is at work. Soon thereafter he is interrupted by his two sisters, who stumble into his room while he and his girlfriend are getting dressed. Leroy's frenzied response suggests that

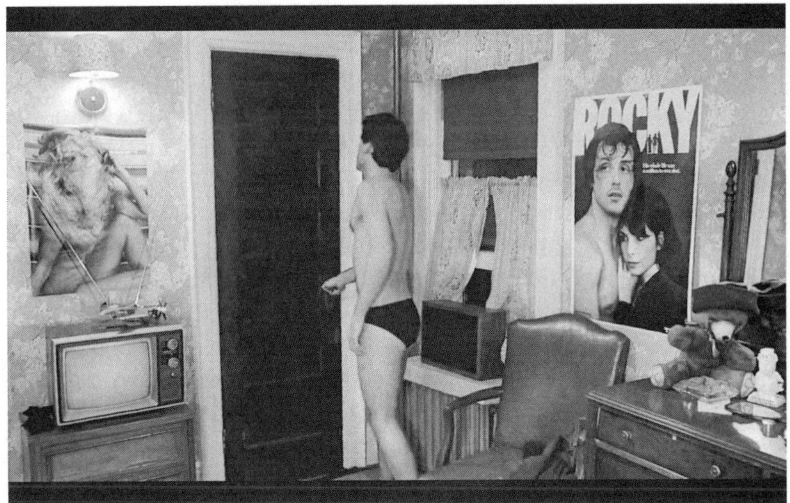

Figure 10 Tony Manero's bedroom in *Saturday Night Fever*. The famed Farrah Fawcett poster can be seen on the far left, above the television. Tony's vanity, which he often uses to prepare himself for a night of dancing, is on the far right. *Saturday Night Fever*, directed by John Badham (1977; Los Angeles: Warner Brothers, 2007), DVD.

although his room is dingy and sparsely decorated, he still considers it an important personal space that is subject to rules of his own design. "Damn it," he screams as his two sisters stand dumbstruck in the doorway, "now, didn't I tell you not to come into my room before you knock!" Though Leroy's room may not have lived up to the standards set by middle-class tastemakers, it was still expected to provide him with a measure of autonomy and privacy that his friend Richard was simply unable to experience.[15]

For an intriguing glimpse into the bedroom of a fictional working-class immigrant teen, one need look no further than one of the top-grossing films of the 1970s: *Saturday Night Fever* (1977). Best known for its wildly successful soundtrack and lavish dance sequences, *Saturday Night Fever* also comments on the struggles that emerge between first generation immigrants and their native-born offspring. The Manero family lives in a working-class Italian neighborhood in Brooklyn. Three generations of Maneros occupy the same tiny apartment, but Tony Manero (John Travolta's character) has a room of his own. Sure, the wallpaper and trim are dull and grimy, and the furnishings consist of little more than a bed and a dresser, but Tony's room is nonetheless highly personalized, featuring a crucifix and posters of Bruce Lee, Wonder Woman, Sylvester Stallone, and Al Pacino hanging on the wall. Though his Italian-born parents and grandparents might appreciate Tony's decision to decorate his room with the Savior and photos of two of the most respected Italian American actors in the country, at least one of his wall hangings ends up creating tension between Tony and his traditional-minded parents. While scolding his son for spending so much time in the dance clubs, Tony's father notices the iconic Farrah Fawcett poster hanging on Tony's wall. The look on his father's face, coupled with a close-up shot of Ms. Fawcett's erect nipples, suggests that Tony's father does not appreciate how the hyper-sexualized world his son enjoys in the dance club has found expression within the family home.[16]

Tony's love of dance, a major source of conflict between he and his parents, is also tied to his bedroom, as his activities there are shown as having a profound influence on his performance on the dance floor. He practices dance moves in front of his mirror while also engaging in various grooming rituals inside his room. And, of course, it goes without saying that Tony's wardrobe—the tight pants, the thick-heeled shoes, and the flashy, wide-collared shirts—are stored in his room and assessed in front of his bedroom mirror. Tony's room, in sum, is to the dance club as the bullpen is to a starting pitcher in baseball, providing the young man with a space in which to prepare for the long night ahead. And yet, despite the various freedoms Tony enjoys in his room, his working-class status ensures that he can never take those freedoms for granted. At the end of the first act, Tony's older brother, Frank, returns home after leaving the priesthood. Of course, this means that Tony no longer has a room of own—a situation that is addressed when Tony offers to let Frank "sleep in my room." What in many circumstances may have been regarded as an inconvenience is quickly shown to be a chance for the two brothers to reconnect and bond. Tony and Frank engage in a heart-to-heart conversation in which Frank explains why he left the church. Frank eventually rewards his brother's generosity shortly before moving into his new apartment by leaving Tony a gift in his room. His storyline achieves closure in front of the bedroom mirror, as Tony tries on Frank's now useless frock, drawing a direct comparison with an earlier scene in which Tony is shown dressing up for a night at the dance club. The religious path is bound to lose out in this instance, however, as Tony grabs the back of the frock and pulls it up around his neck like a hangman's noose. Dancing, not God, is Tony's all-abiding passion.[17]

During the 1980s, just as the disco music that had helped make *Saturday Night Fever* a hit was going into steep decline, a new genre of film emerged. Though teen sex comedies are often held in low regard due to the release of such critically panned films as *Porky's* (1981) and *Revenge of the Nerds* (1984), the one entry in the genre whose reputation has actually improved in the years since its release is *Fast Times at Ridgemont High* (1982), Amy Heckerling's film about the day-to-day lives of several California teenagers. During the course of its ninety-minute running time, *Fast Times at Ridgemont High* offers the viewer a peek into the bedrooms of two female and two male characters. The first appearance of the teen bedroom comes relatively early in the film, when Mike Damone, the local ticket scalper, is shown entertaining one of his friends in his room. Damone's room is an excellent example of the DIY ethos in action, featuring a host of found objects that have been repurposed into interesting decorative items. The headboard of his bed is in actuality a door from a late-model automobile, while an old baby buggy has been transformed into a fully stocked wet bar. Though the walls of his room are smothered with an assortment of store-bought posters, he has also added color to his walls courtesy of a stop sign and a "Caution Men Working" sign. In terms of home electronics items, Damone's bedroom is as well stocked as his bar, featuring a telephone, a color television set, and an expensive stereo system. Damone's room, in short, is ideal for numerous teen-oriented activities. He not only dishes out dating advice to his friend Mark "Rat" Ratner in his room, but he also uses it as a space in which to conduct business, using his telephone to take ticket orders from his largely teenage clientele.[18]

Mike Damone's room stands in stark contrast to the room of Stacy Hamilton, a fifteen-year-old sophomore who constantly frets over her inability to find a boyfriend. Stacy's room is used as a means of juxtaposing her emerging interest in boys with the childhood she is essentially leaving behind. Her room is girlie in appearance, featuring frilly bedding and curtains, floral print wallpaper, and a preponderance of pink and other pastel colors. Moreover, her room first shows up in a scene in which her mother tucks her in and wishes her a goodnight, a nightly ritual that is usually reserved for younger children. Once her mother exits the room, however, Stacy emerges fully clothed from her bed, props open a window, and escapes from her bedroom in order to go on a date with a twenty-six-year-old stereo salesman who deflowers her in a baseball dugout. Although her first sexual experience requires that she flee from her bedroom, Stacy, in a later scene, brings Mark Ratner—the same boy who had sought dating advice from Mike Damone—back to her room in an attempt to seduce him while her parents are away for the weekend. A somewhat nerdy and insecure boy, Mark is caught off guard by Stacy's forthrightness and decides to leave before any clothing is removed. Despite her best efforts, Stacy's attempts to purge her bedroom of any last vestiges of childhood innocence ends in failure.[19]

Mark's decision to resist Stacy's advances leads to the third appearance of the teen bedroom. Upset that she was unable to seduce Mark, Stacy seeks advice from her friend Linda, a sexually experienced senior who teaches Stacy the ins and outs of dating, including how to perform oral sex on a boy. Just as Mike Damone did earlier in the film, Linda uses her room to dole out dating advice to Stacy. This is accomplished as the two girls apply skin cream to their faces while sitting in front of Linda's rather expansive vanity. Once again, the female version of the teen bedroom is shown as a space in which to engage in various beauty rituals. This point is made abundantly clear by a study desk in Linda's room that, rather than being covered in school textbooks, binders, and other educational accoutrements, is covered with various beauty products that don't fit on her already overflowing vanity. Beauty rituals, not books, are granted prominence in Linda's room.[20]

As the final bedroom to make an appearance in *Fast Times at Ridgemont High* nicely illustrates, however, boy-crazy teenage girls were not the only ones guilty of downplaying the teen bedroom's educational function. Jeff Spicoli is Ridgemont High's resident burnout, a surfer dude who spends much of the film fraying the nerves of his history teacher, Mr. Hand. Spicoli's room reflects the character's aspirations and laid-back attitude in several important ways. A wood-paneled monstrosity decorated primarily with surfing posters and pinups of naked women, Spicoli's room acts as a venue in which to smoke marijuana, talk on the telephone with friends, and fantasize about becoming a world-class surfer whose exploits garner him an interview on ABC's *Wide World of Sports*. The privacy he enjoys in his bedroom is safeguarded in part by insisting that family members knock on the door before entering his room. "Get out of here, Curtis," Spicoli warns his younger brother late in the film. "I don't hear you unless you knock." Although Curtis promptly backs out of the room and closes the door, Spicoli's demand backfires on him when the next person to enter the room isn't his brother, but rather Mr. Hand, Spicoli's long-suffering high school history teacher. Thus begins one of the cleverest scenes in the entire film, one in which Spicoli's bedroom is transformed into a learning space.[21]

Knowing full well that Spicoli is planning on attending the graduation dance later that evening, Mr. Hand informs him that the two of them will instead carry on a conversation about American history in Spicoli's room in order to make up for the estimated eight hours of time he has wasted in Mr. Hand's classroom over the course of the previous eight months. "Now I have the unique pleasure of squaring our account," Mr. Hand proudly declares while taking a seat next to Spicoli's bed. "Tonight, you and I are going to talk in great detail about the Davis Agreement, all the associated treaties, and the American Revolution in particular. If you can just turn to page forty-seven of *Land of Truth and Liberty*." The joke, of course, is that Spicoli and his teacher end up engaging in a rather animated conversation about history in his room, even though much of it is phrased in the unique vernacular of a stoned surfer dude. "What Jefferson was saying," Spicoli explains, "was, 'Hey, you know, we left this England place because it was bogus, so if we don't get some cool rules ourselves, pronto, we'll just be bogus too.'" The scene ends on a happy note, as Mr. Hand—satisfied that Spicoli is familiar with at least some aspects of American history—agrees to let his student go to the graduation dance. The bond between teacher and student is only slightly undercut by the scornful look that emerges on Mr. Hand's face when he finally notices all the naked pictures hanging on the walls of Spicoli's room.[22]

In 1981, shortly before *Fast Times at Ridgemont High* began racking up impressive box-office numbers, a more serious (some might say alarmist) take on teen bedroom culture found its way into movie theaters in the form of *Endless Love*. Starring Brooke Shields as a fifteen-year-old girl named Jade Butterfield who falls in love with a seventeen-year-old high school senior named David, *Endless Love* relies on a well-worn plot device to create drama: the conflict that arises whenever parents attempt to undermine their offspring's romantic relationships. In telling Jade and David's story, the writers of *Endless Love* use the teen bedroom to comment on the limits of so-called liberal parenting methods. Jade's father and mother—Hugh and Ann, a general practitioner and an author—live a bohemian lifestyle, openly engaging in recreational drug use and alcohol consumption alongside their children. Though a bohemian lifestyle often entails a more open approach to sexuality, Jade's father grows concerned when he finds out that David begins sleeping overnight in Jade's room. The first sign of trouble occurs when Hugh spots a partially nude David in Jade's room shortly before heading to bed. David, of course, is worried about the consequences of being seen by her father, but Jade—who bids her father goodnight while wearing nothing but a towel—tries to assuage his fears by stating, "Oh, come on. They're always claiming they're so open-minded. I mean, this is my room. They can't say anything." Jade's nonchalance is shown to be incredibly misguided, however, as Hugh quickly informs his wife that he "just caught them bare-assed up in her room." Ann, the more liberal of the two, tries to settle her husband down by reminding him that "you didn't raise her to be a hypocrite." Reminded by his wife that they had always taught their children to be "open about sex," Hugh points out that this situation is bound to affect Jade's performance in school as well as her sleeping habits. "When is she going to study?" he asks nervously. "When is she going to sleep?"[23]

Despite his reservations, Hugh lets the issue slide for the time being. Nonetheless, his permissive approach is soon tested when he catches his daughter stealing a sleeping pill from his office after a steamy night of sex with David. "You bring your goddamn boyfriend over here," he screams, "you keep everybody else awake. I'm fed up with this. . . . I will not have this family torn apart. David cannot stay here." Jade responds by accusing her father of treating her like a child and, perhaps most importantly, by making an ownership claim on her own bedroom. "Yes, he can," she sputters. "It is my room. We are not a couple of little kids." Curiously enough, Hugh does not challenge his daughter's ownership claim, but instead points out that David's motives are less than honorable. "He doesn't give a damn about you. All he cares about is his own satisfaction. I don't want him in your room! I don't want him in this house!" Jade's father wins out in the end, as both he and Jade's mother agree that David will not be allowed to visit for thirty days so that both teens can study for their final exams. Hugh explains the situation to David in the laneway in front of the house, abandoning his liberal ideals by making it seem as though his decision was based on more practical matters. "This thing's gotten totally out of control," Hugh explains while making repairs to a Volkswagen Beetle, a symbol of Hugh's countercultural leanings. "We made a mistake giving you too much freedom around here. Now Jade's falling behind in her schoolwork, she can't sleep at night."[24]

In the end, *Endless Love* offers its audience a somewhat strange yet familiar take on teen bedroom culture. On the one hand, David's and Jade's bedrooms are sometimes portrayed in relatively benign ways, acting as spaces in which both teens could study and listen to music. On the other hand, it is hard to deny that the main characters' fates are not determined—or at least set in motion—by the young couple's decision to use Jade's bedroom for sex. By the end of the film, Hugh and Ann are divorced, Ann attempts to seduce David, Jade is nearly raped by David, Hugh dies after being run over by a taxicab while chasing David, and David is sentenced to life in prison after being found responsible for Hugh's death. The Butterfield family has essentially fallen apart and all manner of calamity has descended on its members. Indeed, the moral of the story appears to be that liberal parents should be wary of allowing their teenage offspring to hold opposite-sex sleepovers in their bedrooms.[25]

Literature

Some of the alarmist ideas found in films such as *Endless Love* also showed up in more literary forms. Writers of so-called cautionary literature—

works of fiction and nonfiction that touch on sensational themes in order to warn youngsters about the dangers of, say, drug use or premarital sex—were especially fond of using the teen bedroom as a setting for various forms of self-destructive behavior. One of the most controversial examples of the genre is *Go Ask Alice* (1971), a book about an anonymous fifteen-year-old girl whose life spirals out of control after becoming involved with drugs. Though the author of *Go Ask Alice* is officially listed as "Anonymous," the book's editor, Beatrice Sparks, a former child psychologist, is most often cited as the person responsible for coming up with the basic narrative. For years, *Go Ask Alice* was advertised as nonfiction, as Sparks and her publisher claimed that the story was culled from the diary entries of an actual teenage girl who went through many of the experiences described in the book. Though this claim has since been proven false—or at least questioned to the point where the book is no longer listed as nonfiction—the faux-diary approach offers the reader an interesting look at how at least one author/child psychologist envisioned the teen bedroom during the 1960s and 1970s.

Sparks's narrative frequently emphasizes how important the young girl's bedroom is to both her well-being and her basic identity. For instance, shortly before her life is turned upside down by illicit drug use, the teen narrator expresses concern that an upcoming move to a new home might have serious consequences on her mental state. She regards the bedroom she is leaving behind as an indelible part of her developing personality, a unique space that defines her sense of self in numerous ways. "I've lived in this room all my fifteen years, all my 5530 days," she writes. "I've laughed and cried and moaned and muttered in this room. I've loved people and things and hated them. It's been a big part of my life, of me. Will we ever be the same when we're closed in by other walls? Will we think other thoughts and have different emotions?" The girl expresses a similarly heartfelt take on her room after falling headlong into the drug scene and moving to San Francisco with a friend from high school. "Anyone who has desperately needed to come home knows what a tremendous feeling it is to be lying in his own bed," she declares after returning home. "My pillow! My mattress! My old silver hand mirror." This emphasis on personal possessions also reemerges near the end of the book, when the girl is released from a mental institution after a classmate has slipped some acid into a bowl of chocolate-covered peanuts. "I'm doing what I love most," the girl elatedly reports, "just enjoying myself in my own lovely room with my books and all my personal possessions. I just can't decide what to do first, go play my lovely piano or stay here and curl up with a lovely book or take a nap. I think the nap is going to win."[26]

Although *Go Ask Alice* was designed to scare teens away from illegal drugs, its author seems to have ignored much of the antidrug literature that situates drug use in the teen bedroom. The main character is briefly dependent on sleeping pills after a pregnancy scare, but for the most part her drug use takes place outside the family home—usually at house parties, the apartment of an older boy she dates, or on the streets. Nonetheless, the protagonist's self-destructive behavior does find expression in her bedroom when she experiences a particularly intense acid flashback several months after going clean. While relaxing in bed one night, the young girl's "mind got all mixed up" as her room was suddenly transformed into a "smoky" head shop. "I was the highest person in the world," she explains, "and I was looking down at everyone and the whole world was in strange angles and shadows." Following the sort of logic found only in one's dreams, the girl's flashback then turns into "some kind of underground movie," featuring naked girls who were "dancing around, making love to statues." She then found herself back on the street panhandling and "shouting at tourists" before being "smothered" by "a glare of revolving lights and beacons." "Everything was going round," she continues. "I was a shooting star, a comet piercing the firmament, blazing through the sky." When the flashback finally ends, the young girl is lying naked on the floor next to her bed. Sparks uses the girl's experience to highlight the dangers of drug use, suggesting that teens who are no longer using could be the victims of sudden psychological trauma, even in the comfort of their own rooms. "I was just lying on my bed, planning my mother's birthday," the shaken-up teen notes in her diary, "listening to records and bham!"[27]

In so many cautionary tales, the teen protagonist ends up in a bad state by the end of the narrative. *Go Ask Alice* is no different in this regard. Despite finally kicking her drug habit, mending her relationship with her parents, and finding a new boyfriend who loves her unconditionally and new friends who don't use drugs, the young girl ends up dead. The epilogue notes only that

> The subject of this book died three weeks after her decision not to keep another diary. Her parents came from a movie and found her dead. They called the police and the hospital but there was nothing anyone could do. Was it an accidental overdose? A premeditated overdose? No one knows, and in some ways the question isn't important. What must be of concern is that she died, and that she was only one of thousands of drug deaths that year.

Sparks doesn't inform the reader exactly where the girl's last breath was expelled, but the flashback scene from earlier in the book clearly illustrates that the purported horrors of drug use can show up at any time and in one of the most private and personal spaces of all: the teen bedroom.[28]

In 1978 Sparks followed *Go Ask Alice* with an equally alarmist book about teen suicide, *Jay's Journal*. Supposedly based on the experiences of a sixteen-year-old Mormon boy from Alden Grove, Utah, who killed himself in 1971, *Jay's Journal* outdoes Sparks's previous work in reaffirming the importance of the teen bedroom in defining its teenage protagonist and shaping his experiences with family and friends. Early on in the narrative, Jay writes about how he has been sent to his room for injuring his brother after catching him snooping through his bedroom. "Being grounded is really the shits," he explains in his journal. "I've been imprisoned for a week and I've read and studied and drawn till I'm about to go stir-crazy, all because I punched Kendall out for getting in my room and messing up my stuff." Indeed, Jay's relationship with his parents was so tumultuous—at one point he notes that "my clothes, my hair, my teeth, my room, everything sets them off"—that he often finds himself imprisoned in his bedroom for a wide variety of offenses, the most serious of which involves theft of narcotics. "Sentenced to my room again," Jay complains in one entry, all because he dared to steal drugs from his dad's pharmacy and pass them on to his girlfriend, Debbie.[29]

The teen bedroom's potential for danger is discussed at length in *Jay's Journal*. In one particularly melodramatic scene, Debbie uses a wholesome family dinner as an opportunity to try to tempt Jay into having sex in his room. "Today Debbie came to our house for dinner. Everybody was really neat to her. It made me feel guilty as hell, because all the time they were telling her how nice she looked and how sweet she was and stuff, she was trying to get me to take her down to my bedroom." Jay's room also helps hasten his growing interest in the occult, a hobby that Sparks—perhaps channeling the growing fears of devil worship and witchcraft that emerged during the late 1970s and early 1980s—ties to the boy's eventual suicide. "One after another I have intrusions of unwanted family in my room," Jay writes in his journal. "My auwa nightly rituals are the only thing that make me feel better, and the strange sounds of the ancient expressions as they gurgle out of my throat." On one occasion, Jay escapes out of his bedroom window in order to attend an occult ritual, and his friend Tina even uses his room as a means of smuggling various occult-related accoutrement into the family home. "I heard a soft tapping on my bedroom window and opened it as fast as I could," Jay explains. "There was a little package but Tina had gone. I ran out the front door, she had disappeared into the shadows." Tina, as it turns out, is somewhat of an expert in keeping her interest in the occult secret; her room is described as being equipped with a "beautiful little chest" that features a "secret compartment": "The whole back comes out and one sees that actually the drawers in the front are dummies, only go half way through. In this secret part, she's got an Ouija board, a crystal ball, little jars of herbs, lots of Cosmic Consciousness and Rosicrucian stuff about the mastery of life, and of course all the Astral junk." Sparks seems to suggest that some of the more shadowy spaces found within the teen bedroom—and the various items found therein—can play a role in teen suicide.[30]

Literary critiques of teen bedroom culture weren't always lacking in nuance and subtlety. Indeed, one of the most astute discussions of the teen bedroom was published in *Seventeen*, a publication that could usually be counted on to tout the merits of teen bedroom culture in an uncritical manner. In August 1972 *Seventeen* published a short story by future Pulitzer Prize winner E. Annie Proulx entitled "The Ugly Room." Ralla, the protagonist in Proulx's tale, lives in Opal Corners, a fictional mountain town in rural America. Her family is poor, and the house they live in is run down. "The house was narrow and also unpainted," Proulx describes in the early going. "Many clapboards were loose, cardboard was taped over a broken window upstairs. Out back were skeletons of an old barn, several out-buildings and dead rusted bodies of old cars, some of them dating back to the thirties." Ralla is friends with Audris, an affluent girl who has all the good things in life: beautiful hair, lots of clothes, a car, and of course, a beautiful bedroom. The way Proulx describes it, one would be forgiven for thinking that Audris's room came straight out of the pages of *Seventeen*:

> Audris had a white fur rug on the floor. The bed was red enamel and there were special red and white striped sheets. She had a tiny little television set and a stereo tape deck. She had floor-to-ceiling walnut shelves supported on stainless steel poles. She had a bay window and a window seat. She had a dressing table and two walk-in closets. She had a special couch that converted into a bed for any one of the many friends that stayed overnight with her. She had her own phone in her room and it was red too. Ralla never tired of hearing Audris describe this room.

Ever the good friend, Audris gives Ralla "a stack of House and Hearth and Handsome Homes magazines," which she studies "greedily." "The magazines," Proulx notes, "said it was only a matter of labor and paint to transform the dingiest room into a jewel box." Ralla's mother, however, is skeptical of the experts' claims. "That girl shouldn't of give you these magazines," she scolds her daughter. "You already want too many things. You set yourself up too high. This room you are so crazy about is never going to happen."[31]

Proulx uses dramatic irony to great effect in "The Ugly Room," thus ensuring that the reader is aware of aspects of the story that its characters don't know about. Ralla's enthusiasm is presented to the reader in a rather pathetic manner, as Proulx makes clear from the outset that the young girl's plans were doomed to failure:

> Ralla did not see the reality of her room. A single narrow window overlooked the backyard trash heap. The walls, made of old lumpy, damp plaster, were covered with more lumpy layers of wallpaper. The top one was a pattern of enormous purple feathers on a pale green, watery background. In many places faded pink roses peeped forth from an earlier paper. The floor was rough and splintered, covered in the center with worn linoleum in a sad shade of brown. The ceiling was a crazy quilt of odd-sized rectangles, a bunch of leftovers Daniel Cavendish had got for nothing somewhere. A closet without a door gaped like a toothless mouth. Ralla's furniture was sparse: a narrow bed with badly sagging springs, and a huge oak veneer bureau contorted with curves and bulges. Most of the original knobs had been replaced with empty spools, and the veneer on one side bulged out in a sinister way, as though a great toad lay hidden underneath. The two pieces of furniture were awkward, and ill-mated companions, but Ralla's enchanted eyes did not realize the impossibility of redoing this room.

Ralla eventually comes to acknowledge that her mother's warnings are basically correct, but unfortunately this realization only comes about after Audris and her two friends, Dodie and Barbie, come over to assess Ralla's efforts. Only then does Ralla see that the new layer of paint was unable to cover up the old wallpaper, which "had softened and wrinkled and dried in tortured relief maps"; that the woodwork "had swelled and burst forth with knots and grainy ridges"; and that the newly painted furniture was "now the awkward color of moldy bread." In fact, the view from Ralla's bedroom window tells the reader everything he or she needs to know about the young girl's attempt to replicate the rooms of her affluent friends. "And through the narrow window," Proulx sourly notes, "the ugly heap of junk in the yard below proclaimed that here was a room, a house and a property so worn-out and neglected that no renovation short of bulldozers and fire could ever change it." The story ends with a suitably devastating one-liner, as Ralla says to her friends, "Come on, girls, I'll see you down to your car."[32]

Proulx's dark take on teen bedroom culture is important to note for several reasons. For starters, "The Ugly Room" is guilty of biting the hand that feeds. Though Proulx's story calls out the type of home décor magazines that were ostensibly aimed at older, married women, it should also be seen as a broadside attack on the magazine in which it was published, as well as other publications that offered teens advice on how to spruce up their rooms. At the heart of Proulx's narrative is the idea that social class invariably limits the extent to which certain American teens are able to live up to the consumer ethos that defined many aspects of teen bedroom culture. Proulx argues that Ralla's renovation efforts are nothing more than a doomed attempt to transcend her lower-class roots, and that teen bedroom culture is a luxury that only more affluent adolescents can afford to indulge in. This point is driven home when Ralla reflects back on the advice her mother gave her earlier in the narrative. "What she had mistaken for apathy in her mother was, rather, a proud refusal to lament about life," Proulx explains. "Perhaps her mother found a measure of satisfaction in the people she knew and loved." Though her advice is presented in a somewhat cold and impersonal manner, Ralla's mother understands that relationships with friends and family define a person, not material concerns such as having a fancy bedroom. Only by having her dreams dashed does Ralla come to realize the futility of "masquerading as a disenfranchised princess."[33]

Whereas the teen bedroom is portrayed as an elusive ideal in Proulx's short story, Vladimir Nabokov regards it as a site of forbidden lust and perversity in *Lolita* (1958), the Russian émigré's darkly funny look at Eisenhower's America. A stickler for detail, Nabokov makes a point of discussing some of the more mundane aspects of teen bedroom culture. For instance, Lolita uses her bedroom to vent her anger and frustration (an idea that found regular expression among child development experts and advice columnists). "That Tuesday, Lo had her dinner in her room," Humbert Humbert, the novel's troubled protagonist, observes soon after moving in with Lolita and her mother, Charlotte. "She had been crying after a routine row with her mother and, as had happened on former occasions, had not wished me to see her swollen eyes." Lolita, of course, endures many more arguments with her mother as the narrative moves forward. This is due to the fact that Charlotte falls in love with Humbert and grows jealous of the attention her daughter receives from the middle-age literature professor. At one point, Charlotte's vindictiveness is even directed toward her twelve-year-old daughter's bedroom. While vacationing near a "dazzling lake," Charlotte explains to Humbert that she dreams of hiring a "real trained servant maid" who would tend to their every need. When Humbert notes that there is "no room" in her current home for a live-in servant, Charlotte explains that "we would put her in Lo's room" and send her daughter off to boarding school. Lolita's mother essentially conflates her daughter's bedroom with Lolita herself, as the room and the girl are described in similar terms. "I intended to make a guestroom of that hole anyway," she notes coolly. "It's the coldest and the meanest in the whole house."[34]

Nabokov also provides his readers with a compelling physical description of Lolita's bedroom. In keeping with the era in which *Lolita* was written—the early 1950s—Nabokov points out that Lolita's bed is "littered with comics." The basic décor in her room, meanwhile, is of the do-it-yourself variety, as the walls featured a smattering of pinups, including a full-color advertisement for "Drome" cigarettes, a "crooner's mug," "the lashes of a movie actress," and "a full page ad ripped out of a slick magazine" in which a husband is seen handing a breakfast tray to his wife while wearing a handsome bathrobe. Humbert notices that the young girl has drawn a "jocose arrow" and written "H.H." next to the husband with the breakfast tray. Though Humbert's reliability as a narrator can't always be trusted, one suspects that the young girl's choice of room décor is used in this particular instance as a means of describing the early contours of Humbert's and Lolita's unseemly relationship. Nabokov doesn't clarify whether the young girl's decision to deface the pinup is an attempt at mockery or a means of illustrating the depths of her infatuation with Humbert—his use of the word "jocose" could apply to either interpretation—but the Russian-born author's expertise in matters of teen room décor was no accident. According to Jane Grayson, a specialist in Russian literature, Nabokov performed an exceptional amount of research on postwar teens before sitting down to write *Lolita*. This involved listening to the "idiom and slang" of his son Dmitri and a colleague's daughter, reading up on "adolescent abnormality and sexual perversion," and flipping through the pages of several teen-oriented magazines, including *American Girl*, the *Best in Teen Tales*, and *Calling All Girls*. The teen bedroom, it would seem, was yet another aspect of postwar American culture that was deemed ripe for satire in the pages of *Lolita*.[35]

Anyone familiar with Nabokov's masterpiece knows that Lolita's room begins to take on a much more sinister aura, its role in the forbidden relationship between the young girl and Humbert becoming much more pronounced as the narrative unfolds. Humbert's relationship with Lolita is mediated in part by monetary considerations, as he often gives the girl money in exchange for kisses and caresses. A "cruel negotiator," Lolita offers prices that range from three pennies to three nickels per day, with a "fancy embrace"—Nabokov does not explain what this actually entails—costing the harried academic somewhere between $3 and $4 apiece. However, before Lolita can fritter away her earnings on "some item of juvenile amusement," she makes sure to hide her money in her bedroom (much like the young Eubie Blake did while growing up in Baltimore in the 1890s;

see chapter 2). Humbert's losses are temporary, though, as he would often "burgle her room and scrutinize torn papers in the wastebasket with the painted roses, and look under the pillow of the virginal bed I had just made myself." On one such occasion he finds $8 in a book ("fittingly—Treasure Island"), while a "hole in the wall behind Whistler's Mother" once "yielded as much as twenty-four dollars and some change." Lolita eventually catches on to Humbert's activities and finds "a safer hoarding place" that Humbert "never discovered." By the end of the book, shortly after Lolita's rape and murder allegations are finally aired, Humber demands that the young girl "go upstairs and show me all her hiding spaces." In explaining his demands, Humbert informs the reader that he isn't afraid that Lolita would ruin him per se, but rather "that she might accumulate sufficient cash to run away." Nabokov's use of irony here is both dense and overwhelming: Lolita's bedroom is a prison of sorts, one that allows her to store the money that might eventually facilitate her escape—money that was given to her by her captor in exchange for sexual services, many of which were performed in her bedroom.[36]

Television

Teenagers have figured prominently on the so-called small screen since network television began to replace radio as the most popular form of entertainment in the United States in the years immediately following the Second World War. In the late 1940s, for instance, several popular programs featuring teen characters caught the imagination of television audiences, including *The Aldrich Family*, *The Goldbergs*, and *The Life of Riley*. During the 1950s, moreover, iconic programs such as *The Adventures of Ozzie and Harriet*, *Make Room for Daddy*, *Father Knows Best*, and *The Donna Reed Show* capitalized on the country's growing fascination with teenagers by giving teen characters more prominent roles in the various wholesome family narratives that were being beamed into millions of homes on a weekly basis. Although the teen bedroom often acted as a setting in individual episodes of early television—the third episode of *The Life of Riley*, entitled "Egbert's Chemistry Set," features a scene in which thirteen-year-old Chester Jr. claims to have invented the yo-yo in his room—it didn't serve as a particularly important plot device during the early years of network television. Oftentimes, it helped illuminate the extent to which gender norms influenced basic set design during this period, as bedrooms belonging to male television characters usually featured desks for studying and generic sports-related banners hanging on the walls, both of which emphasized traditionally masculine pursuits. Rooms belonging to female characters, meanwhile, were often decorated in a frilly, stereotypically feminine manner, while the desks that usually took up space in the rooms of boys were replaced with vanities and other furnishings that emphasized personal grooming.[37]

By the late 1950s, however, the teen bedroom began to be employed by television writers as a means of creating both dramatic and comedic tension. In 1958 an episode of *Leave It to Beaver*, entitled "Cleaning Up Beaver," commented on how shared bedrooms often encouraged friction between older and younger siblings. The episode begins by establishing thirteen-year-old Wally Beaver's newfound respect for neatness and tidiness—a trend his father, Ward, explains by noting Wally's discovery of girls. "When girls come in the door," Ward says to his wife, June, "dirt goes out the window." By contrast, Wally's younger brother, Theodore (also known as "the Beaver" or just "Beaver"), is portrayed as being quite sloppy, appearing in the front foyer of the Beaver home covered in dirt, his hair unkempt. During dinner, Wally complains that his brother's messiness was driving a wedge between them. "What about the way you keep up our room?" Wally asks his younger brother. "You ought to see it, Dad. I'd be better off living with a pig." Ward, adopting what he dubs a "modern approach" to parenting, agrees with Wally in an attempt to shame Beaver into being more mindful of his older brother's needs. "I'm afraid, Beaver, I have to agree with Wally, though," Ward explains tenderly. "You see, Wally's at the age where he's trying to be neat and clean, both about himself and his room, and, well, you're just not cooperating." Humiliated by his father's remarks, Beaver consults with his similarly messy friend, Larry, while eating lunch at school the next day. Larry claims to have "fixed [his] brother good" after being taunted in a similar manner. "I told my mother I wanted a room for myself," Larry tells Beaver. "If you got your own room, if it gets dirty, you can just close the door. Then there's nobody around to squeal on you."[38]

The next scene begins with Beaver's mother helping him move into the guest room, which is furnished with a hundred-year-old bed and several nineteenth- and early-twentieth-century photographs. He soon makes it his own by populating it with his own unique collection of knickknacks and personal belongings, including (much to his mother's dismay) a jar of dead worms. Shortly before Beaver's mother leaves him to his own devices, the audience gets its first hint that Beaver's new living arrangements might not last long. Beaver inadvertently reveals anxiety about sleeping alone when he asks his mother if she's heard any lions in the neighborhood recently. She says no and then asks if he would like her to leave the light on in the hall. Putting up a brave front, Beaver tells her not to bother and settles into bed for the evening. June then exits Beaver's new room and promptly accuses Ward of turning the kids against each other. In a calm and soothing manner that would emerge again and again over *Leave It to Beaver*'s six seasons, Ward tells his wife that Beaver will rejoin his brother after spending just one night alone in his new room.[39]

Ward's comments prove prophetic. Beaver's attempts to fall asleep are soon thwarted by the scary photos, a man-shaped shadow on the wall (the result of a lamp with a hat placed on top of the shade), and an assortment of stray cats who insist on howling outside his window (Beaver, of course, suspects that they're lions). Beaver reacts by hiding under his blankets, but not before placing a tomahawk under his pillow. Just as the howling outside his window reaches a crescendo, Beaver screams for Wally and runs into his old bedroom. Again, he tries to put on a brave face, downplaying his own fears by asking Wally if he was afraid. "Are you crazy? Why would I be scared?" Wally asks while lying comfortably in bed. "Well, you never slept by yourself before," Beaver responds. "That's scary to some people." Receiving no sympathy from his brother, Beaver starts walking back to his new room, but before he can leave, Wally tells him that "it might be a good idea if you stayed in here." Ecstatic, Beaver jumps into bed with his brother and says, "This is a lot better, isn't it, Wally?" Wally nods and the boys agree to a compromise: Wally will be "a little bit sloppier," while Beaver will be "a little bit neater." June and Ward are then seen checking in on the boys; Ward, with an "I told you so" smirk hanging across his face, remarks that "blood is thicker than dirt." The episode ends with Larry asking Beaver why he no longer has a room of his own. "I couldn't sleep," Beaver explains. "Anyway, my brother got a little lonely all by himself."[40]

"Cleaning Up Beaver" offers a unique take on teen bedroom culture during the 1950s. After all, Wally, the teenage character, makes no attempt to lobby his parents for a room of his own; he most definitely resents living with his "pig" of a brother, but the writers of the episode seem to suggest that this is something Wally could live with. This can probably be explained by noting that Beaver, rather than Wally, is the star of the show, which means that most of the plots for *Leave It to Beaver* are bound to revolve around the younger sibling. The decision to reunite Wally and Beaver in their old bedroom, meanwhile, was probably the result of practical considerations as well as the show's somewhat conservative outlook on family life in 1950s America. In practical terms, it wouldn't make sense to split up the two boys, as their interactions propel much of the humor of the show. Regardless, Beaver's fearful response to sleeping alone suggest that the show's writers were inspired by older ideas on domestic sleeping arrangements, despite the fact that child development and interior design experts had been touting the merits of separate bedrooms since at least the early twentieth century. Indeed, Beaver's fears have a distinct nineteenth-century feel to them, mimicking in many ways the short story from *Aunt Eleanor's Childhood Memories* (1863) discussed in chapter 1. Ultimately, it would seem that childish fears and ideas of family togetherness triumphed over the so-called "modern parenting" methods referred to by Ward Cleaver earlier in the episode. "You have to send them to orthodontists, psychologists," Ward observed sardonically. "They've even got experts to teach children how to play. No self-respecting parent would dream of relying on nature."[41]

The tensions that often arise among siblings who are forced to share a bedroom was once again used as a plot device in the early 1970s, as a teen character from television's first blended family tried to convince his parents that he was simply too old to share a room with his two younger brothers. The character who makes this request is Greg Brady, the eldest son on ABC's hit sitcom *The Brady Bunch*. On February 5, 1971, "Our Son, the Man" made a case both for and against giving teenagers rooms of their own. As the title of the episode suggests, the writers reaffirmed the idea that separate bedrooms are associated with the maturation process. The episode begins with Greg, the family's eldest child, complaining to his mother, Carol, about how his brothers make too much noise in the room they share with him. "Those kids," he tells her, "they have no respect for a man's privacy." He goes on: "A man doesn't want to be pestered by kids. He wants privacy. Mom, I think we have to make some changes around here." Greg then talks to his father, Mike, pleading to have a room of his own. "A man needs privacy," Greg explains. "I never get a free minute to myself." Fortunately for Greg, both of his parents agree that his demands are reasonable and begin making plans to set up a new bedroom in Mike's den. Elated by the news, Greg promises to turn it into "my own pad. My own scene."[42]

Although Mike and Carol Brady's decision to grant their eldest teenage son a room of his own conforms with much of the advice that was being offered by parenting and child development experts during the postwar years, the writers of the show also made sure to comment on an aspect of the separate bedroom ideal that rarely ever drew attention from other mainstream sources. Indeed, one of the most striking parts of "Our Son, the Man" involves a scene in which Mike is forced to explain to Greg's younger brothers, Peter and Bobby, why Greg is moving into a room of his own. Upon hearing the news, the two youngest boys start thinking that Greg's decision proves that he doesn't like them anymore. Mike assuages their fears, however, by once again resorting to ideas on child development. Greg's love for his brothers "has nothing to do with it," he tells the boys. "It's just men need their privacy, that's all." This scene is remarkable not because Mike used developmental arguments to reinforce the value of the teen bedroom, but because it reveals the extent to which child development experts failed to discuss how granting older teens rooms of their own might produce emotional turmoil among their siblings. The writers of *The Brady Bunch* understood that separate bedrooms were not just about the individual teens who were given rooms of their own, but also the siblings they ostensibly left behind.[43]

The room Greg Brady creates for himself—his "great inner sanctum"—is heavily influenced by the hippie subculture that emerged during the mid-1960s, featuring a lava lamp, colorful furnishings, and rock posters. Mike and Carol are initially shocked to see how quickly the den "went from Danish Modern to American Disaster," but ultimately refuse to admonish Greg, using accepted ideas on the importance of encouraging teen autonomy to justify their policy of nonintervention. "Well," Mike begrudgingly admits while surveying his son's new room, "it's what Mr. Greg Brady wanted." Soon, however, Greg's attempts to become a man begin to have a negative effect on the family as a whole. He starts referring to his parents by their first names and excuses himself from taking part in family activities, including a camping trip that had been in the works for several weeks. Soon after an older classmate refuses Greg's request for a date, telling him that she might agree to date him once he's "grown up," Greg realizes that his attempts to cut ties with his family were probably ill advised. He eventually decides to go camping with the family, and the episode ends with Mike Brady back in his den, drawing up plans to build an eight-bedroom house for his family. As with the earlier episode of *Leave It to Beaver*, "Our Son, the Man" ends with a return to more traditional sleeping arrangements.[44]

Though ideas on family togetherness would eventually triumph at the end of "Our Son, the Man," *The Brady Bunch* would end up revisiting this issue in 1973. The final episode of the fourth season, entitled "A Room at the Top," once again sees the Brady family struggling with teen demands for separate bedrooms. The episode begins with Greg and a college-age friend named Hank talking in the family room. Greg, a senior in high school by this point in the series, is eager to hear about his friend's experiences in college. They are soon interrupted by the youngest son, Bobby, who sits down to watch television while Greg and his friend are chatting. They then go up to Greg's room, but are soon interrupted by his other brother, Peter, who wants to read comic books in his bunk bed. Sensing Greg's frustration, Hank asks if he would like to move in with him, an offer

Greg quickly accepts. Before he can start packing, though, Greg decides to run the idea past his father. Besides claiming that living with his two younger brothers is "like a jail sentence," Greg once again tries to convince his father that privacy and maturity go hand in hand. "I really need the privacy," he explains. "A guy my age needs a room of his own. I got Peter and Bobby in my hair all the time." Unfortunately for Greg, Mike isn't swayed by his son's arguments, but promises Greg that he can move out the following year when he goes to college. "In a few short months," Mike jokes, "you'll be paroled for good behavior."[45]

Greg isn't the only member of the Brady family who yearns to preside over a room of his own. In the very next scene, the entire family is shown cleaning out the attic in order to donate some of their belongings to a charity bazaar. While the other members of the family are toting various items downstairs, Marcia, the eldest daughter, asks her mother if she can lay claim to the attic once all the junk is removed. "Could I use it?" she asks. "I really want a room of my own." Marcia, like Greg, claims that the privacy offered by separate bedrooms is developmentally beneficial. "Oh please, Mom," she begs her skeptical mother. "When a girl gets to be my age, she really needs a room of her own." Carol is not convinced by her daughter's claims, and even asks Marcia if she wouldn't "feel all alone up here by yourself?" "But that's the whole point," Marcia retorts. "I'd have privacy." Swayed by her daughter's arguments, Carol agrees to give the attic to Marcia, who soon starts drawing up plans to decorate her room with "posters" and "that big rug we used to have in the den." Unbeknownst to both Carol and Marcia, Greg is having a similar conversation with his dad out in the laneway. Greg points out that giving him the attic would prevent him from moving out of the family home, while also granting greater privacy to his two younger brothers. Predictably, Mike agrees to give the room to Greg.[46]

Once both children start moving their belongings into the attic, Carol and Mike decide that they have to sit Greg and Marcia down in order to figure out who most deserves to have the space. They eventually conclude that age will be the determining factor, offering it to Greg due to the fact that he's the oldest of the Brady children. Marcia is devastated by the news and retreats to her room, teary-eyed. Greg follows Marcia into her bedroom and tries to explain that she'll only have to wait a year to move into the attic. Marcia, however, decides to use age-old ideas on femininity to reinforce her claims to the room. "A girl needs more space," she explains to her brother. "There's never any room in my closet or my drawers. I can't even use my hair dryer when I want to." Marcia drives this point home by claiming that she has already invited six of her closest friends to come over for a slumber party. Ever the nice guy, Greg decides to give the room to Marcia.[47]

Greg and Marcia weren't the only Brady siblings to get caught up in the great debate over which child would gain control of the attic bedroom, as the younger children once again received significant consideration from the writers of the show. Jan and Cindy, Marcia's younger sisters, are heartbroken by their sister's decision to move upstairs, even though Marcia cheers them up by promising both girls that they can come up and visit whenever they want. The younger boys, meanwhile, go through a range of emotions when they find out that one of their siblings would be moving into the attic. When Greg is given the room, Peter and Bobby respond to the news by expressing great joy over their brother's departure. However, their mood quickly sours when Greg gives the room to Marcia. Lamenting the fact that Greg "chickened out" because Marcia used "that mushy girl stuff" to get her way, Peter and Bobby use the distance between Marcia's new bedroom and the telephone to get her to move back to her old room. A friend of theirs named Charlie calls the house three times in order to pose as a friend of Marcia's. Every time he calls, Marcia trudges downstairs from the attic and ends up being greeted by nothing more than a dial tone when she picked up the receiver. The boys' plan eventually falls apart, however, when one of her friends calls up and informs Marcia that she wasn't responsible for the earlier phone calls. Marcia accuses Greg of sabotaging her enjoyment of her new attic suite, but Greg is able to get Peter and Bobby to confess, both of whom rationalize their behavior by explaining that "we just wanted the room to ourselves." Realizing how selfish everyone is acting, Marcia decides to give the attic back to Greg, acknowledging that her parent's age-based plan is the fairest means of settling this dispute. Peace and togetherness return to the Brady family—although not all the children are happy. Before the end credits start to roll, Cindy, the youngest child, is shown writing numbers on a chalkboard. When Alice asks the young girl what she's doing, Cindy explains somberly that she won't be getting a room of her own until "almost the year 2000."[48]

* * *

In 1985 a controversy on the set of the highest-rated program on network television summarized the extent to which artistic expressions of teen bedroom culture were often shaped by pressing, real-life concerns. In August of that year, shortly after filming had ended on the second season of NBC's *The Cosby Show*, newspapers and magazines across the country reported that the star of the show, Bill Cosby, had been told by network censors to remove a sign that had been hung on the bedroom door of his fictional teenage son, Theo. The sign featured only two words: "Abolish Apartheid." This was enough to rattle the censors at NBC, who claimed that the network wanted to avoid endorsing "one side of a two-sided controversy." Cosby would have none of it and decided to stand up to the network for reasons both practical and political. For starters, Cosby was heavily involved in the antiapartheid movement. In fact, a few days after the controversy with NBC was made public, Cosby made headlines by offering Dorothy Boesak and her seven-year-old son, Allen Jr., his "support and love" after her husband, Allan Boesak, a prominent antiapartheid activist, was arrested by South African authorities. However, Cosby also claimed to have resisted NBC's demands due to the importance of establishing a certain amount of verisimilitude in the fictional world of *The Cosby Show*. "There may be two sides to apartheid in Archie Bunker's house," Cosby told entertainment reporter Harry F. Waters, "but it's impossible that the Huxtables would be on any side but one. That sign will stay on that door. And I've told NBC that if they still want it down, or if they try to edit it out, there will be no show." Though one wonders how well Cosby's strategy would have worked had his show not been a ratings hit, network executives knew that they couldn't risk alienating the man who had "lifted NBC from the basement of the Neilson ratings to the No. 1 spot for both regular and rerun seasons." NBC backed down, and the sign remained. In later seasons, a "Free Mandela" poster was even seen hanging in Theo's bedroom.[49]

Cosby's attempts to defeat the censors at NBC illustrate the extent to which cultural expressions of teen bedroom culture are capable of illuminating some rather important social and political issues. For decades, child development experts and members of the business community had been singing the bedroom's praises in terms of its value in socializing American teenagers. Cosby's struggles, however, suggest that the teen bedroom was capable of inspiring heated political debate as well. Though apartheid may have been concocted and enforced approximately ten thousand miles away from the Hollywood studio where *The Cosby Show* was filmed, it is astonishing to note how debates over this brutal and archaic social system intensified greatly in the United States—if only for a brief moment in time—by the decision to decorate a fictional teen character's bedroom with a sign disparaging South Africa's treatment of its black majority. Even in fictional form, the teen bedroom was shown to be something far greater than just a space within the home in which America's teenage population could sleep, study, and amuse itself; Theo's bedroom, in its own little way, played a part in one of greatest social movements of the twentieth century.

Conclusion

One morning when he was 15, Takeshi shut the door to his bedroom, and for the next four years he did not come out. He didn't go to school. He didn't have a job. He didn't have friends. Month after month, he spent 23 hours a day in a room no bigger than a king-size mattress, where he ate dumplings, rice and other leftovers that his mother had cooked, watched TV game shows and listened to Radiohead and Nirvana.

NEW YORK TIMES (2006)

Hikikomori is a Japanese word meaning "social withdrawal." In recent years, it has been used to summarize the experiences of Japanese youths (mainly male) who refuse to leave the family home or socialize with non-family members. Statistics vary, but studies suggest that between 200,000 and 500,000 Japanese teens and young adults can currently be described as *hikikomori*. Though the *hikikomori* phenomenon has been around since the 1980s, experts have been unable to agree on its root causes. Psychiatrists and psychologists regard it as a "cognitive malfunction" or a by-product of other forms of mental illness that can be treated with drugs and therapy. Social scientists, meanwhile, tend to emphasize larger social factors, including shifting family structures and shrinking economic opportunities. One thing these experts agree on, however, is that the bedroom plays an outsized role among Japanese youths who are in the grips of *hikikomori*. According to Alan R. Teo, a professor of psychiatry at the University of California, the average *hikikomori* is a male, middle-class teen who spends "23 hours a day" in his room. "He eats food prepared by his mother who leaves trays outside his bedroom. He sleeps all day, then awakes in the evening to spend his time surfing the internet, chatting on online bulletin boards, reading manga (comic books), and playing video games."[1]

Although no cases of *hikikomori* have been diagnosed in the United States, many American youths have found that their relationship with teen bedroom culture has been similarly shaped by shrinking economic opportunities. Just as the separate bedroom ideal has been revised and adopted to meet the needs of younger children—a 2004 study estimated that 62 percent of children in grades one through five have rooms of their own—young adults who are normally expected to leave home and start a family continue to preside over rooms of their own long after they have graduated from high school. According to a study commissioned by Deutsche Bank in 2014, approximately one-third of Americans between the ages of eighteen and thirty-four currently live with their parents due to record levels of student debt and a sluggish job market. Republican vice presidential candidate Paul Ryan even used this trend as a means of indicting the policies of President Barack Obama during the 2012 general election. "College graduates," he complained, "should not have to live out their 20s in their childhood bedrooms, staring up at fading Obama posters and wondering when they can move out and get going with life." Ryan's comments, though certainly warped by the heated rhetoric of an up-for-grabs presidential campaign, bear a degree of truth insofar as they illustrate the extent to which economic factors continue to shape teen bedroom culture. They also serve to remind us that the autonomous teen bedroom, though it has often been seen as a means of hastening the maturation process, can also act as an embarrassing reminder of the dependency of youth. A seventeen-year-old high school student might be made to feel like more of an adult by presiding over a room of his or her own, but the same cannot be said for a twenty-seven-year-old college graduate who goes to sleep every night in a bedroom that has long outlived its developmental usefulness.[2]

The decision to close this study with a discussion of *hikikomori* in Japan and the "failure to launch" generation in the United States was arrived at in order to underscore two of the most important trends in shaping teen bedroom culture over the past two hundred–plus years.[3] Firstly, *hikikomori* serve to remind us that the autonomous teen bedroom has always been defined by psychological processes—with special emphasis on how we attend to matters of self. Throughout much of the nineteenth century, separate bedrooms were seen as a means of attending to a host of spiritual, emotional, and intellectual matters, as middle-class Protestant girls in particular used this space to forge personal relationships with God, address both pressing and not-so-pressing personal issues, and engage in various literary pursuits. By the late nineteenth and early twentieth centuries, however, a more secular vision of teen bedroom culture emerged—albeit one that continued to emphasize literacy, personal growth, self-reliance, and other pillars of mainstream Protestant thought. Indeed, the growing authority of social scientific ways of thinking reaffirmed preexisting ideas on the autonomous teen bedroom, while also giving them a more universal sheen. God-fearing middle-class urbanites may have been the first demographic to embrace the separate bedroom ideal, but academically trained psychologists, educators, medical doctors, and other experts were on hand to make sure that families from nearly all points on the socioeconomic spectrum understood the developmental benefits of providing teenagers with rooms of their own. Although many of their arguments were tempered by fears of masturbation, drug use, social withdrawal, and other types of troubling behavior, child-rearing experts played an outsized role in convincing families that the "own room" concept was an integral part of the maturation process, a valuable addition to the family home that could supposedly shape one's identity and character in a positive manner.

The economic struggles faced by millennials, meanwhile, remind us that teen bedroom culture has always been tied to larger economic trends. From its inception in the early decades of the nineteenth century, the autonomous teen bedroom was often associated with abundance rather than want, finding expression in the homes of merchants, bureaucrats, professionals, and others who benefited from the emergence of commercial and industrial capitalism. Separate bedrooms were seen as a luxury item that only a select few families were able to enjoy during much of the nineteenth century. The expansion of the American economy during the latter stages of the Victorian era, the 1920s, and the years immediately following the Second World War ensured that the separate bedroom ideal would eventually transcend its middle-class origins and take root among groups that had once been excluded from this custom, including farmers, African Americans, and working-class immigrants, among others. Being able to provide your teenage offspring with bedrooms that were fitted with all manner of consumer items was a sign that your family had made it, that at least one small part of the American dream had been attained. Recent generations, however, have seen this notion turned on its ear. Instead of highlighting one's ability to succeed within modern economic structures, the contemporary teen bedroom just as often underscores the weaknesses of a system that is seemingly incapable of integrating youth within the prevailing economic order. Among many Americans, the teen bedroom has become an all-too-familiar sign of economic failure.

The news isn't all bad, though. In fact, the autonomous teen bedroom continues to enjoy a largely positive reputation, and has even started to be seen as a historical curiosity of sorts. In 2004 through 2005, for instance, "Teen Chicago," an exhibit at the Chicago Museum of History, argued that the teen bedroom was (and continues to be) an important psychological space that has helped youngsters achieve a measure of self-realization. The contents and arrangement of the teenage bedroom, the curators of the exhibit argued, often exposed "individual character and uniqueness" and allowed adolescents "to express who they are and are becoming, as individuals and family members. More than storage for the ever-growing number of teen products, teen bedrooms have evolved from sleeping rooms into sanctuaries of self-expression." Ari Fulton, a high school student who lent her expertise to the exhibit, explained that this notion was something more than a fantasy drawn up by museum curators. "My own bedroom is my own private island away from the world," she described in a pamphlet promoting the yearlong exhibit. "It's the only place where I can chill out from homework, adolescent drama, and parents. It's a reflection of my identity, decorated to show my own personal style."[4]

The autonomous teen bedroom continues to draw attention from the entertainment industry as well, as several television programs have used it as a somewhat predictable means of dramatizing parent-child conflict. In a one-week period during October 2004, the plots of two television shows—ABC's *Desperate Housewives* and CBS's *Clubhouse*—centered around two teenage characters whose parents removed their bedroom doors as a disciplinary measure. Marc Cherry, the creator of *Desperate Housewives*, explained that the script for his show was based on the account of a friend during the 1970s whose door was removed soon after his parents found marijuana in his room. Screenwriter Sheila Lawrence, meanwhile, explained that the script for *Clubhouse* was inspired by her parents, who often threatened to remove her bedroom door when she was a teen during the 1980s. Whereas earlier generations of parents might have punished their children by sending them to their room, the creators of both of these shows suggest that contemporary parents prefer to use the popularity of teen bedrooms against their offspring by, in effect, rendering their personal space less private, less exclusive. Privacy, Lawrence claimed, was "the most horrifying thing for a teenager to lose."[5]

Old anxieties continue to shape teen bedroom culture, especially when fears of drug use emerge. In 1998 *U.S. News & World Report* ran a story on Russ Ebersole, the owner of Detector Dogs against Drugs and Explosives (DDADE), a Virginia company that "provides narcotics and fire-arms sweeps for schools, businesses, and private homes." Along with Texas-based Interquest Group and California-based Kontraband Interdiction and Detection Services, DDADE offered to "give the once-over to a teen's bedroom or a factory floor, sniffing out everything from marijuana to vials of methadone." According to DDADE's owner, parental peace of mind should always trump the rights and liberties of America's teens, despite the concerns of parenting experts such as Micki Levin, a child psychologist for the American Civil Liberties Union, who believed that these types of intrusive strategies do more harm than good. "Obviously, privacy is being violated," Levin complained when informed of DDADE's services. "It makes a difficult problem even worse."[6]

In 1999 the Columbine massacre raised similar fears about the purported links between teen bedroom culture and lawlessness. Though the shootings were carried out in the halls of a publicly funded high school, the arsenal used during the massacre was assembled and stored in the bedroom of Eric Harris. Fireworks were dissected on his bed in order to secure much-needed gunpowder for their raid; bomb-making equipment was kept in the drawers of his desk; pipe bombs were stored behind his CD collection; and a receipt from a local gun store was hidden in a CD case. Eric's bedroom also acted as a studio in which numerous confessional videos were made. One railed against a police officer named "Walsh" who had arrested the boys a year earlier for breaking into a van, while yet another showcased "all the illegal shit" the two boys had collected—all the weapons, Harris noted, that "you will find on my body in April." As journalist Dave Cullen explained, a search of Eric's room after the massacre produced several items that would cause any right-thinking American to recoil in horror: the police "found a sawed-off shotgun barrel on a bookshelf, unspent ammunition on the bed, fingertips cut off gloves on the floor, and fireworks and bomb materials on the desk, the dresser, the windowsill, and the wall." As inspiration, Eric also kept in his room a photocopied quote from Heinrich Himmler in which the infamous SS leader claimed, "Whether or not 10,000 Russian women collapse from exhaustion while digging a tank ditch interests me only in so far as the tank ditch is completed for Germany."[7]

Mere days after the attacks took place, members of the Baby Boomers HeadQuarters website claimed that the privacy associated with teen bedroom culture may have encouraged Dylan Klebold and Eric Harris's antisocial behavior, with several contributors expressing shock that the teens' parents were incapable of noticing that their own children were making bombs and hoarding weapons right under their noses. One contributor suggested that the best way to ensure that another Columbine doesn't take place is to "know what's in their room"—adding, "there is no such thing as privacy for a 14-year old-when Mom helps to keep it clean." The suggestion here is simple: parents who grant teens too much privacy in their bedrooms risk producing a generation of disturbed children. This idea was reinforced in 2006 with the release of *Super Columbine Massacre RPG*, a video game that offers players the opportunity to walk around in one of the killer's shoes. Aside from employing "photographs of Klebold and Harris" and "excerpts from their written rantings" in the basic narrative, the game begins—where else?—in the bedroom of Eric Harris.[8]

Even some of the more thoughtful perspectives on the Columbine shootings tended to confirm many of the fears associated with teen bedroom culture. Gus Van Sant's film *Elephant*, a controversial retelling of the massacre that won the Palme d'Or and Best Director prize at Cannes in 2003, offered art-house audiences a take on teen bedroom culture that managed to both confirm and undermine many of the views cited above. For all its flaws, *Elephant* presents a rather subtle, complicated view of the massacre and the motivations of its teen participants. Indeed, Van Sant courted controversy by refusing to cast judgment on the event itself, offering instead a naturalistic "day in the life" account of the tragedy. His portrayal of the teen bedroom is similarly complex, as Van Sant characterized it as both a parent-free zone that provided the two boys with the privacy necessary to plan the attack as well as a therapeutic space that served to humanize the teen killers. Not only was the teen bedroom used as a site for homosexual experimentation between the two boys, but it also played host to a riveting scene in which one of the characters, Alex, plays a Beethoven sonata while his coconspirator plays a first-person-shooter video game on his laptop. Though the video game reference is an obvious nod to the commonly held view that this type of entertainment is a source of teen violence, Van Sant seems to suggest—like many of the commentators and experts cited throughout this study—that the teen bedroom was capable of nurturing both creativity and pathology.[9]

While it is safe to say that the contemporary teen bedroom continues to be defined by decades-old ideas on child development and consumption, the one area in which this part of the home has witnessed seismic change involves the extent to which new technologies have erased the boundaries between the public and private sphere. Since the days of Hall and Hollingworth, child-rearing experts have argued that the teen bedroom could help parents contain teenagers within the home. The development and proliferation of home computing and the Internet, however, has eroded the underlying strength of this narrative. Instead of acting as a line of defense between its teen owners and the outside world, Internet-equipped bedrooms allow the outside world to breech these defenses on a fairly regular basis. Social networking websites, instant messaging programs, and webcam technology allow complete strangers to establish a spectral presence within the teen bedroom, oftentimes without securing any type of parental consent. The distance between home and street has thus shrunk considerably, in both a physical and a psychological sense, as the Internet has rendered the walls of the teen bedroom much more porous.

In 2005 the *New York Times* published a cautionary tale about the so-called dangers of the "connected" bedroom, presenting its readers with a "dark coming-of-age story" that sought to explain the "collateral effect of recent technological advances." At the center of this narrative was Justin Barry, a teenager from California who bought a webcam for his bedroom computer in 2000 in a bid to connect with other teenagers. Soon thereafter, Justin was being propositioned by a spate of older men who promised to pay him "$50 to sit bare-chested in front of his Webcam for three minutes" and $100 to sit in his underwear. According to Kurt Eichenwald, the author of the piece, these types of activities have become increasingly common in recent years. "Minors, often under the online tutelage of adults, are opening for-pay pornography sites featuring their own images sent onto the Internet by inexpensive Webcams. And they perform from the privacy of home, while parents are nearby, beyond their children's closed bedroom doors." By the time Justin stopped performing cam shows in his room in 2005, he had amassed a client list of over 1,500 people and, one can assume, a marked expansion of his savings account. When asked to explain why she agreed to let her son have this type of computer equipment in his bedroom, Justin's mother made reference to age-old ideas on teen creativity and occupational wish fulfillment. "The Webcam," Eichenwald explained, "was just another device that would improve her son's computer skills, and maybe even help him on his Web site development business."[10]

Internet technology is also having a pronounced effect on teen identity formation, an aspect of the maturation process that the teen bedroom has long played an important role in shaping. Although the teen bedroom will continue to be defined by the vast array of posters, pinups, trinkets, and other found, purchased, or handmade items that supposedly reflect the emerging identity of its occupant, it is safe to say that social networking websites such as Facebook, Twitter, Instagram, and Google Plus—in concert with the proliferation of smartphone technology—have brought the identity-formation process into much more public venues. Is it too much of a stretch, for instance, to suggest that the average teen pays just as much attention to what's on his or her Facebook wall as to what's on the walls of his or her bedroom? Is the selfie not just a more streamlined version of the "blow up" wall hangings that were once advertised in the back pages of *Rolling Stone* and *Seventeen*? The difference is one of scale. After all, the urge among teens to project their image in a virtual setting is fraught with dangers that aren't necessarily found in more private spaces. It perhaps goes without saying that there is a huge difference between hanging an embarrassing photo on a bedroom wall, where only a handful of people will ever see it, and posting it on a social networking site where thousands—even millions—of people can download it, critique it, and even alter it with digital editing software. Indeed, one could argue that the privacy and opportunities for self-expression that teens enjoy in their bedroom have taken on even greater importance in the age of social media and the rather withering brand of criticism and harassment it often engenders.

The proliferation of the Internet and other new technologies reaffirms that the autonomous teen bedroom remains a contested space that is defined by narratives of salvation and perdition. One wonders, however, if it is not the teen bedroom's contradictory character that best explains its basic appeal. Its resonance within American culture might just stem from its ability to be all things to all people. Liberal-minded parents, on the one hand, can take pleasure in the notion that it represents a supposedly progressive and humane way of raising children, an affirmation of the belief that individuals are essentially good and capable of making the right decisions without being swayed by unseemly methods of coercion. For conservative-minded parents, on the other hand, the teen bedroom projects an almost frontier-like view of the child-rearing process, offering a space that is defined by its purported ability to encourage self-reliance, self-sufficiency, and other character traits the Right has often claimed as its own in recent decades. Parents of all persuasions, meanwhile, might appreciate the teen bedroom because it offers a reassuring myth of safety, a general belief that teens can entertain themselves and their peers without straying too far from the sanctity of home. Of course, this narrative, too, is riddled with contradictions, as parents must accept teen withdrawal and a general weakening of the togetherness ideal as an unavoidable by-product of the teen bedroom's continuing popularity.

Teenagers, meanwhile, enjoy a similarly complex relationship with teen bedroom culture. Although the autonomous teen bedroom offers adolescents a space in which they can participate fully in the world of consumer culture, the fact that many of these activities are marketed in the context of identity formation is problematic. According to many décor experts, for instance, purchasing bedroom-oriented decorative items is a good way of creating an authentic adolescent identity marked by spontaneity and individuality. But is it really all that spontaneous or individualistic to base one's identity on store-bought posters, home furnishings, and other mass-produced items? If anything, this approach to teen room décor emphasizes conformity and sameness rather than individualism and authenticity. "The décor differs wildly," Adrienne Salinger explains when asked about the teen bedrooms she photographed during the early 1990s, "but there is a consistency in what teenagers surround themselves with. Girls tend to have more cosmetics and beauty 'information.' Boys tend to have more sports stuff. They all have Chapstick in their rooms. Funny."[11]

In a similar vein, it is worth noting that the idea of the teen bedroom as a fortress, a castle, or some other space defined by seclusion or impregnability is not altogether accurate. Contemporary teens may enjoy a more expansive type of privacy in their rooms than earlier generations of children did, but it is important to remember that other members of the family are never more than a few steps away. "I agree that teenagers are probably expected to use their rooms to identify their own identity as separate from their parents," Salinger notes, "but I don't know how free anyone is to form a separate identity until they leave home." One suspects that Mary Astor, the tormented actress whose bedroom was turned into a prison of sorts by her controlling father (see chapter 2), would no doubt agree with this sentiment were she alive today.[12]

Notes

INTRODUCTION

Epigraph: Casey Calloway, e-mail to author, December 3, 2013. Emphasis hers.

1. Sonia Livingstone, *Young People and New Media* (London: Sage, 2002), 155. The literature on teen bedroom culture isn't especially vast, but scholars have been examining this topic since at least the 1970s. See Angela McRobbie and Jenny Garber, "Girls and Subcultures," in *Resistance through Rituals*, ed. Stuart Hall and Tony Jefferson (London: Hutchinson, 1976), 209–22; Marcel Danesi, *Cool* (Toronto: Univ. of Toronto Press, 1994), 54–55; Jeanne Steele and Jane Brown, "Adolescent Room Culture," *Journal of Youth and Adolescence* 24 (October 1995): 551–76; Jeffrey Arnett, "Adolescents' Uses of Media for Self-Socialization," *Journal of Youth and Adolescence* 24 (October 1995): 519–33; Kandy James, "I Just Gotta Have My Own Space!," *Journal of Leisure Research* 33 (January 2001): 71–90; Claudia Mitchell and Jacqueline Reid-Walsh, *Researching Children's Popular Culture* (London: Routledge, 2002), ch. 4.
2. Jane Hunter, *How Young Ladies Became Girls* (New Haven, CT: Yale UP, 2002), 95; Sally McMurry, *Families and Farmhouses in Nineteenth-Century America* (New York: Oxford UP, 1988), 196. See also Gwendolyn Wright, *Building the Dream* (New York: Pantheon, 1981), 111–12.
3. The medicalization of female teen bodies is discussed in Joan Brumberg, *The Body Project* (New York: Random House, 1997), ch. 2. The medicalization of female adolescence as a whole is discussed in Rachel Devlin, *Relative Intimacy* (Chapel Hill: Univ. of NC Press, 2005), passim.
4. The rise of public amusements and their importance to late-Victorian youth culture is noted in Kathy Peiss, *Cheap*

Amusements (Philadelphia: Temple UP, 1986), passim; Sarah Chinn, *Inventing Modern Adolescence* (New Brunswick, NJ: Rutgers UP, 2009), passim.

5. The domestic containment of women is noted in Elaine Tyler May, *Homeward Bound* (New York: Basic, 1999), passim. The bedroom's value among latchkey kids is discussed in Deborah Belle, *The After-School Lives of Children* (Mahwah, NJ: Erlbaum, 1999), 94, 105, 113, 151.
6. Beach Boys, "In My Room," from the album *Surfer Girl*, lyrics and music by Brian Wilson and Gary Usher, Capitol, 1963.
7. The rise of egalitarian parenting strategies is discussed in Linda Kerber, "The Republican Mother," *American Quarterly* 28 (Summer, 1976): 187–205; Mary Beth Norton, *Liberty's Daughters* (Ithaca, NY: Cornell UP, 1980), passim; Steven Mintz and Susan Kellogg, *Domestic Revolutions* (New York: Free Press, 1988), ch. 6; Ann Hulbert, *Raising America* (New York: Knopf, 2003), ch. 1.
8. Michel Foucault, *Discipline and Punish*, trans. Alan Sheridan (New York: Vintage, 1995), 209.
9. Christine Hunter, *Ranches, Rowhouses, and Railroad Flats* (New York: Norton, 1999), 61. Privacy-oriented housing is also discussed in McMurray, *Families and Farmhouses*, 199–203; G. Wright, *Building the Dream*, 96, 111–12; Clifford Clark, *The American Family Home* (Chapel Hill: Univ. of NC Press, 1986), 35–42, 172–83; S. J. Kleinberg, "Gendered Space," in *Domestic Space*, ed. Inga Bryden and Janet Floyd (New York: St. Martin's, 1999), 142–61.
10. Steven Mintz, *Huck's Raft* (Cambridge, MA: Harvard UP, 2004), 343–44.
11. Jean Piaget and Barbel Inhelder, *The Growth of Logical Thinking from Childhood to Adolescence* (New York: Basic, 1958), 335–37. Physiological and cultural definitions of adolescence are discussed in Robert Winch, *The Modern Family* (New York: Holt, 1963), 418–22.
12. Helen Flanders Dunbar, *Your Preteenager's Mind and Body* (New York: Hawthorn, 1962), 15.

CHAPTER ONE

Epigraph: Herman Melville, *Moby Dick* (New York: Penguin, 1972), 108.

1. Anna Stanton, *My Autobiography* (Des Moines, IA: Bishard, 1908), 19–20.
2. John Gough, *An Autobiography* (Boston: self-published, 1845), 16; Upton Sinclair, *The Autobiography of Upton Sinclair* (New York: Harcourt, Brace, 1962), 3–4, 10. The lack of privacy in early American homes is also discussed in Gwendolyn Wright, *Building the Dream* (New York: Pantheon, 1981), chs. 1–5; John Demos, *A Little Commonwealth* (New York: Oxford UP, 2000), ch. 1.
3. Serge Chermayeff and Christopher Alexander, *Community and Privacy* (Garden City, NJ: Doubleday, 1963), 215.
4. Dolores Hayden, *The Grand Domestic Revolution* (Cambridge, MA: MIT Press, 1989), 26; Clifford Clark, *The American Family Home* (Chapel Hill: Univ. of NC Press, 1986), 38. For more on the emergence of privacy-oriented homes, see Mary Ryan, *The Cradle of the Middle Class* (New York: Cambridge UP,

1981), ch. 4; Kenneth Jackson, *Crabgrass Frontier* (New York: Oxford UP, 1985), 47–48; Stephanie Coontz, *The Social Origins of Private Life* (New York: Verso, 1988), 259–63.

5. Declining birthrates are noted in Daniel Scott Smith, "Family Limitation, Sexual Control, and Domestic Feminism in Victorian America," *Feminist Studies* 1 (Winter/Spring 1973): 44. The relationship between wealth, family size, and the separate bedroom ideal is noted in Sally McMurry, *Families and Farmhouses in Nineteenth-Century America* (New York: Oxford UP, 1988), 200; Peter Stearns et al., "Children's Sleep," *Journal of Social History* 30 (Winter 1996): 360; Peter Ward, *A History of Domestic Space* (Vancouver: Univ. of BC Press, 1999), 82–83.
6. Viviana Zelizer, *Pricing the Priceless Child* (New York: Basic, 1985), 3.
7. Sheltered childhood is discussed further in Steven Mintz, *Huck's Raft* (Cambridge, MA: Harvard UP, 2004), ch. 4; Howard Chudacoff, *Children at Play* (New York: NYU Press, 2007), ch. 2.
8. The common school system is discussed in Carl Kaestle, *Pillars of the Republic* (New York: Hill and Wang, 1983), chs. 4 and 8; William Reese, *America's Public Schools* (Baltimore: Johns Hopkins UP, 2011), ch. 1.
9. Henry Adams, *The Education of Henry Adams* (Boston: Houghton Mifflin, 1971), 7–8, 11.
10. William Mavor, *The Catechism of Health* (New York: Wood, 1819), 42. The popularity of separate bedrooms among builders and housing reformers is discussed in Clark, *American Family Home*, 35.
11. O. S. Fowler, *A Home for All* (New York: Fowler and Wells, 1854), 63–64.
12. Lydia Maria Child, *The Mother's Book* (Boston: Carter, 1831), 153.
13. Benjamin Hallowell, *Autobiography of Benjamin Hallowell* (Philadelphia: Friends, 1884), 11; Samuel Goodrich, *Recollections of a Lifetime* (New York: Miller, Orton, 1856), 432. For more on the practical and emotional benefits of shared beds and bedrooms, see Carroll Smith-Rosenberg, "The Female World of Love and Ritual," *Signs* 1 (Autumn 1975): 1–29; E. Anthony Rotundo, "Romantic Friendship," *Journal of Social History* 23 (Autumn 1989): 1–25; Stearns et al., "Children's Sleep," 357–58.
14. E. M. Bruce, *Aunt Eleanor's Childhood Memories* (Boston: R. A. Ballou, 1863), 11, 15–17, 20.
15. Ibid., 34, 46.
16. Hallowell, *Autobiography*, 11; William Nowlin, *The Bark Covered House*, ed. Milo Quaife (Chicago: Lakeside, 1937), 114. Sharing a room with other family members, despite living in a house with an unoccupied guest room, remained popular after the Civil War. Sinclair Lewis, for instance, enjoyed similar arrangements while growing up in Minnesota during the 1890s. See Richard Lingeman, *Sinclair Lewis* (New York: Random House, 2002), 5; Merritt Ierley, *Open House* (New York: Henry Holt, 1999), 157–59.
17. Sarah Connell Ayer, *Diary of Sarah Connell Ayer* (Portland, ME: Lefavor-Tower, 1910), 104, 149–50.

18. Mary Gove Nichols, *Mary Lyndon* (New York: Stringer & Townsend, 1855), 21, 27, 51.
19. Ibid., 30–31.
20. Elizabeth Prentiss, *Stepping Heavenward* (New York: Randolph, 1880), 12, 18–19, 70. The bedroom's value in encouraging literary pursuits is also noted in Sara Pryor, *My Day* (New York: Macmillan, 1909), 70.
21. Prentiss, *Stepping Heavenward*, 16, 65.
22. Ibid., 30, 60, 70.
23. Julia Ward Howe, *Reminiscences* (New York: Houghton Mifflin, 1899), 45, 62–63. The bedroom's value among evangelicals is also discussed in Jane Hunter, *How Young Ladies Became Girls* (New Haven, CT: Yale UP, 2002), 94–98.
24. Louisa May Alcott, *Louisa May Alcott* (Boston: Roberts, 1889), 45–47.
25. Ibid., 24.
26. Ibid., 47–48.
27. Ibid., 63.
28. Thomas Wentworth Higginson, *Cheerful Yesterdays* (New York: Houghton Mifflin, 1898), 24; William Foulke, *A Hoosier Autobiography* (New York: Oxford UP, 1922), 7. Fears of male masturbation are discussed in G. J. Barker Benfield, *The Horrors of the Half-Known Life* (New York: Routledge, 2000), ch. 14. The public nature of nineteenth-century boys' culture is discussed in E. Anthony Rotundo, "Boy Culture," in *The Children's Culture Reader*, ed. Henry Jenkins (New York: NYU Press, 1998), 337–62.
29. A. D. Rockwell, *Rambling Recollections* (New York: Hoeber, 1920), 31–32.
30. Eliza Ripley, *Social Life in Old New Orleans* (New York: Appleton, 1907), 103–4.
31. John Allen Wood, *The Autobiography of John Allen Wood* (Chicago: Christian Witness, 1904), 7.
32. John Braly, *Memory Pictures* (Los Angeles: Neuner, 1912), 107–8.
33. Richard Smith, *Twigs for Nests* (London: Nisbet, 1866), 18; L. Emmett Holt, *The Care and Feeding of Children* (New York: Appleton, 1894), 63.
34. Phyllis Browne, *Common-Sense Housekeeping* (New York: Cassell, 1877), 164–65.
35. Resurgam, "A Plea for City Children," *Mother's Nursery Guide*, February 1893, 94–95.
36. Decreasing birthrates, the average size of farmhouses, and support for separate bedrooms in progressive farm magazines are discussed in McMurry, *Families and Farmhouses*, 7, 196–97, 199–200.
37. Penelope Franklin, ed., *Private Pages* (New York: Ballantine, 1986), 152; Theodore Roosevelt, *Theodore Roosevelt* (New York: Scribner, 1922), 13, 15.
38. Roosevelt, *Theodore Roosevelt*, 14. See also *The Roosevelts: An Intimate History*, episode 1, "Get Action," aired on PBS on September 14, 2014.
39. Harlow Gale, "A Typical Adolescent Religious Experience," *Journal of Adolescence* 1 (1900): 19–20.
40. Mary Ellen Chase, *The White Gate* (New York: Norton, 1954), 179.
41. Ibid., 181, 183.
42. Ibid., 183–85.

43. Ibid., 185. Fears of sleeping alone are also discussed in Mabel Loomis Todd Papers, journal entry, Friday, November 11, 1877, Yale University Library and Archives; H. Clay Trumbull, *Hints on Child Training* (Philadelphia: Wattles, 1891), 235.
44. Home ownership statistics can be found in US Department of Commerce, *Historical Statistics of the United States, Colonial Times to 1970* (Washington: GPO, 1975), 646; Eric Monkkonen, *America Becomes Urban* (Berkeley: Univ. of CA Press, 1988), 200. For information on home ownership rates among African Americans and immigrant families, see Steven Mintz, "Sources of Variability in Rates of Black Home Ownership in 1900," *Phylon* 44 (1983): 312–31; Carolyn Kirk and Gordon Kirk, "The Impact of the City on Home Ownership: A Comparison of Immigrants and Native Whites at the Turn of the Century," *Journal of Urban History* 7 (August 1981): 471–98. Wright's quote can be found in G. Wright, *Building the Dream*, 111–12.
45. The decline of boarding is discussed more fully in Mark Peel, "On the Margins," *Journal of American History* 72 (March 1986): 813–15; Richard Harris, "The End Justified the Means," *Journal of Social History* 26 (Winter 1992): 331. The decline of live-in servants is discussed in Linda Martin and Kerry Segrave, *The Servant Problem* (Jefferson, NC: McFarland, 1985), vi; Faye Dudden, *Serving Women* (Middletown, CT: Wesleyan UP, 1983), 209–10; Daniel Sutherland, *Americans and Their Servants* (Baton Rouge: LSU Press, 1981), 183–99.
46. Mary Blake, *Twenty-Six Hours a Day* (Boston: Lothrop, 1883), 169. The decentralizing effects of central heating are discussed in Andree Brooks, "Huddling Concept of Past Revived," *NYT*, January 24, 1982, CN1. For more on the lack of utilities in working-class neighborhoods, see Roger Simon, "Housing and Services in an Immigrant Neighborhood," *Journal of Urban History* 2 (August 1976): 450; Kirk and Kirk, "The Impact of the City on Home Ownership," 473.
47. Lucy Larcom, *A New England Girlhood* (New York: Houghton Mifflin, 1889), 39, 158.

CHAPTER TWO

Epigraph: H. Addington Bruce, "It's the Room That Makes the Child," *Mother's Magazine*, April 1917, 327.

1. The shift away from moral/religious precepts toward medical/social scientific precepts is discussed in Peter Stearns, *Anxious Parents* (New York: NYU Press, 2003), 18–21.
2. Hall's thoughts on separate beds and separate rooms can be found in G. Stanley Hall, *Adolescence* (New York: Appleton, 1904), 1: 468. Hall discusses girls' bedrooms and boarding school bedrooms in G. Stanley Hall, *Youth* (1906; repr., New York: Arno, 1972), 310–11; G. S. Hall, *Adolescence*, 2: 637–38.
3. G. S. Hall, *Adolescence*, 1: 468. Hall's war on masturbation is outlined in R. P. Neuman, "Masturbation, Madness, and the Modern Concepts of Childhood and Adolescence," *Journal of Social History* 8 (Spring 1975): 14–16.

4. Louis Starr, *The Adolescent Period* (Philadelphia: Blakiston, 1915), 185–86, 189. Intrusive anti-masturbation strategies were ubiquitous during the early twentieth century. See B. S. Talmey, *Genesis* (New York: Practitioners, 1910), 133; Winfield Hall, *The Biology, Physiology, and Sociology of Reproduction* (Chicago: Wynnewood, 1913), 84–90; Albert Moll, *The Sexual Life of the Child* (New York: Macmillan, 1912), 311–12; Franklin Johnson, "The Problems of Boyhood," *Biblical World* 43 (April 1914): 262; Maurice Bigelow, *Sex Education* (New York: Macmillan, 1916), 141; John Meagher, *A Study of Masturbation and Its Reputed Sequelae* (New York: Wood, 1924), 56, 58; Maurice Bigelow, *Adolescence* (New York: Funk & Wagnalls, 1924), 41–42, 143; Winfield Hall, *From Youth into Manhood* (New York: Association, 1925), 57, 101–4.
5. G. S. Hall, *Youth*, 310–11.
6. G. S. Hall, *Adolescence*, 1: 315; G. S. Hall, *Youth*, 207; Leslie Paris, *Children's Nature* (New York: NYU Press, 2008), 28.
7. G. S. Hall, *Adolescence*, 1: 315; G. S. Hall, *Youth*, 208. For a more thorough explanation of Hall's recapitulation theory, see Gail Bederman, *Manliness and Civilization* (Chicago: Univ. of Chicago Press, 1995), ch. 3. Support for Hall's ideas can be found in Ernest Abbott, *On the Training of Parents* (New York: Houghton Mifflin, 1908), 83; Hanford Burr, *Studies in Adolescent Boyhood* (Springfield, MA: Seminar, 1910), 7, 13–16, 20; Margaret Slattery, *The Girl in Her Teens* (Philadelphia: Sunday School, 1910), 30–33; Cyril Andrews, *An Introduction to the Study of Adolescent Education* (New York: Rebman, 1912), 63, 80–81, 90–91, 118, 122; Nathaniel Fowler, *The Boy* (New York: Moffat Yard, 1912), 62–63; Harry Bartow, *Our Boy* (Philadelphia: Union, 1913), 91–92; J. W. Slaughter, *The Adolescent* (New York: Macmillan, 1915), 6, 26, 51, 73; G. Walter Fiske, "The Boy's Home Relationships," in *Boy Training*, ed. John Alexander (New York: Association, 1915), 43–44; Newton Riddell, *Child Culture* (Chicago: Riddell, 1915), 91–92; Edwin Puller, *Your Boy and His Training* (New York: Appleton, 1916), 118–20, 123; Norah March, *Towards Racial Health* (New York: Dutton, 1919), 84; Sidonie Gruenberg, *Your Child Today and Tomorrow* (Philadelphia: Lippincott, 1920), 195–96, 201, 204, 209.
8. Esther Buchholz and Rochelle Catton, "Adolescents' Perceptions of Aloneness and Loneliness," *Adolescence* 34 (1999): 203; G. S. Hall, *Adolescence*, 1: 318; G. S. Hall, *Youth*, 223; G. Stanley Hall, *Life and Confessions of a Psychologist* (1923; repr., New York: Arno, 1977), 17. Hall's views on solitude are also discussed in Paola Corsano et al., "Psychological Well-Being in Adolescence," *Adolescence* 41 (Summer 2006): 342–43. For more on the importance of solitude during Hall's day, see William Burdick, "Adolescence," in *Boy Training*, ed. John Alexander (New York: Association, 1915), 16; Joseph Conroy, *Talks to Boys* (St. Louis: Queen's, 1915), 39; Laura Knott, *Vesper Talks to Girls* (New York: Houghton Mifflin, 1916), 60–62.
9. James Kirtley, *That Boy of Yours* (New York: Hodder & Stoughton, 1912), 193; William McKeever, *Farm Boys and Girls* (New York: Macmillan, 1913), 66–67;

Norman Richardson, *The Religious Education of Adolescents* (New York: Abingdon, 1918), 107.

10. For more on the decline of masturbation hysteria during the 1920s and 1930s, see Thomas Laqueur, *Solitary Sex* (New York: Zone, 2003), 52, 359; Jean Stengers and Anne Van Neck, *Masturbation* (New York: Palgrave, 2001), 155.
11. Frederick Tracy, *The Psychology of Adolescence* (New York: Macmillan, 1920), 15; Frankwood Williams, *Adolescence* (New York: Farrar & Rinehart, 1930), 102, 109–10. Support for psychological weaning can also be found in Edmund Conklin, "The Foster Child Fantasy," *American Journal of Psychology* 31 (January 1920): 59–76; Phyllis Blanchard, *The Adolescent Girl* (New York: Moffat, Yard, 1920), 17, 34, 39–40, 52, 54, 88–91; H. Crichton Miller, *The New Psychology and the Teacher* (New York: Selzter, 1922), 40–43, 73–118; H. Crichton Miller, *The New Psychology and the Parent* (New York: Selzter, 1923), 7, 10, 32, 58–74, 77–96; L. A. Pechstein and A. Laura McGregor, *Psychology of the Junior High School Pupil* (New York: Houghton Mifflin, 1924), 62, 140; Smiley Blanton and Margaret Blanton, *Child Guidance* (New York: Century, 1927), 142; Leta Hollingworth, *The Psychology of the Adolescent* (New York: Appleton, 1928), 36–37, 58.
12. Ella Lyman Cabot, *Seven Ages of Childhood* (New York: Houghton Mifflin, 1921), 149–50; Kathleen Jones, *Taming the Troublesome Child* (Cambridge, MA: Harvard UP, 1999), 123. Variations on the lifeguard approach can also be found in Tracy, *Psychology of Adolescence*, 209; E. Leigh Mudge, *The Psychology of Early Adolescence* (New York: Caxton, 1922), 102; Hollingworth, *Psychology of the Adolescent*, 58, 184; Grace Elliot, *Understanding the Adolescent Girl* (New York: Holt, 1930), 46, 121–22.
13. John Watson, *Psychological Care of Infant and Child* (London: Allen & Unwin, 1928), 5–6, 9–10, 103. For more on the mother-blaming phenomenon, see Ann Hulbert, *Raising America* (New York: Knopf, 2003), 71, 112, 147; Molly Ladd-Taylor and Lauri Umansky, introduction to *Bad Mothers*, ed. Molly Ladd-Taylor and Lauri Umansky (New York: NYU Press, 1998), 11–14; Kathleen Jones, "Mother Made Me Do It," in ibid., 101–8; K. Jones, *Troublesome Child*, ch. 7.
14. Sidney Schwab and Borden Veeder, *The Adolescent* (New York: Appleton, 1929), 115, 117–18, 255.
15. Sigmund Freud, "Family Romances," in *The Freud Reader*, ed. Peter Gay (New York: Norton, 1989), 298. This process is also discussed in Sigmund Freud, "The Origin and Development of Psychoanalysis," *American Journal of Psychology* 21 (April 1910): 210; Sigmund Freud, "The Development of the Libido and the Sexual Organizations," in *Introductory Lectures on Psychoanalysis*, ed. Angela Richards, trans. James Strachey (Harmondsworth, UK: Penguin, 1974), 380; Sigmund Freud, "On the Universal Tendency to Debasement in the Sphere of Love," in *The Freud Reader*, ed. Peter Gay, (New York: Norton, 1989), 394–99; Sigmund Freud, *Dora*, ed. Phillip Rieff (New York: Collier, 1963), passim.

16. Eli Zaretsky, *Secrets of the Soul* (New York: Knopf, 2004), 5, 9, 297, 317. For more on psychoanalysis during the interwar years, see Nathan Hale, *The Rise and Crisis of Psychoanalysis in the United States* (New York: Oxford UP, 1995), chs. 1–2.
17. Ralph Pringle, *Adolescence and High-School Problems* (New York: Heath, 1922), 83; Cabot, *Seven Ages of Childhood*, 171–72, 178. Solitude is also emphasized in Gruenberg, *Your Child Today and Tomorrow*, 201; H. C. Miller, *The New Psychology and the Teacher*, 47–60; H. C. Miller, *The New Psychology and the Parent*, 37–47. Mystical interpretations of adolescent solitude can also be found in Edward Yeomans, *Shackled Youth* (Boston: Atlantic, 1921), 121; Hollingworth, *Psychology of the Adolescent*, 159–60, 163; Schwab and Veeder, *The Adolescent*, 67, 162, 167.
18. Sigmund Freud, "Three Essays on the Theory of Sexuality," in *On Sexuality*, ed. Angela Richards, trans. James Strachey (New York: Penguin, 1977), 150–51; Hollingworth, *Psychology of the Adolescent*, 46, 52. Freud's claim regarding weaning and human progress was also echoed in Mudge, *Psychology of Early Adolescence*, 50; Lawrence Averill, *Adolescence* (New York: Houghton Mifflin, 1936), 86.
19. Watson, *Psychological Care of Infant and Child*, 103.
20. Blanton and Blanton, *Child Guidance*, 113, 121–22.
21. Ibid., 72; Gwendolyn Wright, *Building the Dream* (New York: Pantheon, 1981), 128. The link between room sharing and incest was also noted in Douglas Thom, *Child Management* (Washington, DC: GPO, 1925), 20; Peter Stearns et al., "Children's Sleep," *Journal of Social History* 30 (Winter 1996): 359.
22. B. R. Hergenhahn, *An Introduction to the History of Psychology*, 5th ed. (Belmont, CA: Thomson-Wadsworth, 2005), 296.
23. Hollingworth, *Psychology of the Adolescent*, 187–88.
24. Starr, *The Adolescent Period*, 147; W. Hall, *From Youth into Manhood*, 58; Blanchard, *The Adolescent Girl*, 49. For more on the teen bedroom as an exercise room and a place to vent, see Seymour Hicks, *Difficulties* (London: Duckworth, 1924), 271; N. Richardson, *Religious Education*, 107.
25. William Forbush, *The Boy Problem in the Home* (New York: Pilgrim, 1915), 190; Blanton and Blanton, *Child Guidance*, 117. The rise of recreational sex and its relationship to children's bedrooms is discussed in Stearns et al., "Children's Sleep," 359.
26. March, *Towards Racial Health*, 244; McKeever, *Farm Boys and Girls*, 207–8; H. W. Gibson, *Boyology* (New York: Association, 1922), 87–89. Fears of youth in the public realm are discussed in Kathy Peiss, *Cheap Amusements* (Philadelphia: Temple UP, 1986), chs. 3–6; Christine Stansell, "Women, Children, and the Uses of the Streets," *Feminist Studies* 8 (Summer 1982): 309–35; Beth Bailey, *From Front Porch to Back Seat* (Baltimore, MD: Johns Hopkins UP, 1989), 3–6. The idea that encouraging a greater interest in home life could curb the roving instinct of youth can also be discerned in Fiske, "The Boy's Home Relationships," 48–49; Thom, *Child Management*, 34; Sally McMurry, *Families*

and *Farmhouses in Nineteenth-Century America* (New York: Oxford UP, 1988), 203; Lisa Jacobson, "Revitalizing the American Home," *Journal of Social History* 3 (Spring 1997): 581–96.

27. Kirtley, *That Boy of Yours*, 190; Forbush, *The Boy Problem*, 232; Starr, *The Adolescent Period*, 130. For more on the bedroom as a means of containing youth, see N. Richardson, *Religious Education*, 69–70. The link between crowded bedrooms and adolescent misbehavior is also discussed in Moll, *Sexual Life of the Child*, 156, 247–48; Harriet Daniels, *The Girl and Her Chance* (New York: Revell, 1914), 15; K. M. Bridges, "Factors Contributing to Juvenile Delinquency," *Journal of the American Institute of Criminal Law and Criminology* 17 (February 1927): 535, 558; Edith Wood, "The Statistics of Room Congestion," *Journal of the American Statistical Association* 23 (September 1928): 263–64.
28. Michael O'Shea, *The Trend of the Teens* (Chicago: Drake, 1920), 120; Kirtley, *That Boy of Yours*, 190, 192. Similar arguments are posed in Arthur Melville, "Drums of Destiny," *Rotarian*, November 1924, 42; Martha Falconer, "Causes of Delinquency among Girls," *Annals of the American Academy of Political and Social Science* 36 (July 1910): 77.
29. Kirtley, *That Boy of Yours*, 78–79, 191.
30. Ibid., 193; Forbush, *The Boy Problem*, 190.
31. Hollingworth, *Psychology of the Adolescent*, 188; Watson, *Psychological Care of Infant and Child*, 13; Stearns et al., "Children's Sleep," 360.
32. Kirtley, *That Boy of Yours*, 191; Hollingworth, *Psychology of the Adolescent*, 188; McKeever, *Farm Boys and Girls*, 64–65; Forbush, *The Boy Problem*, 232. Similar strategies can be found in Florence Winterburn, *From the Child's Standpoint* (New York: Baker and Taylor, 1899), 191; Blanton and Blanton, *Child Guidance*, 120; Katharine Taylor, *Understanding and Guiding the Adolescent Child* (New York: Grosset & Dunlap, 1938), 122.
33. Winterburn, *Child's Standpoint*, 191.
34. Edmund Conklin, *Principles of Adolescent Psychology* (New York: Holt, 1935), 129–30; Averill, *Adolescence*, 76, 94; Ada Hart Arlitt, *The Adolescent* (New York: Whittlesey, 1938), 68, 86. Similar views on psychological weaning can be found in Winifred Richmond, "Sex Problems of Adolescence," *Journal of Educational Sociology* 8 (February 1935): 336–38; E. B. Reuter, "The Sociology of Adolescence," *American Journal of Sociology* 43 (November 1937): 416, 419, 421; E. DeAlton Partridge, *Social Psychology of Adolescence* (New York: Prentice-Hall, 1939), 192, 338–39; Hedley Dimock, *Rediscovering the Adolescent* (New York: Association, 1937), 141–50; Ira Wile, *Challenge of Adolescence* (New York: Greenberg, 1939), 11, 218–19, 231–32, 240.
35. Conklin, *Principles of Adolescent Psychology*, 9; Arlitt, *The Adolescent*, 115–16; Partridge, *Social Psychology of Adolescence*, 59. For more on the importance of solitude, see Averill, *Adolescence*, 25; Williams, *Adolescence*, 102; Dimock, *Rediscovering the Adolescent*, 259.
36. Taylor, *Understanding and Guiding the Adolescent Child*, 122; Ruth Cavan, *The Family and the Depression* (Freeport, NY: Books for Libraries, 1969), 85–86.

The crowded living conditions of the Depression era are also discussed in Eli Ginzberg, *The Unemployed* (1934; repr., New Brunswick, NJ: Transaction, 2004), 160; Steven Mintz and Susan Kellogg, *Domestic Revolutions* (New York: Free Press, 1988), 136–37.

37. White House Conference on Child Health and Protection, *The Adolescent in the Family* (New York: Appleton-Century, 1934), 180–81.
38. Jane Eskridge, ed., *Before Scarlett* (Columbia: Univ. of SC Press, 2000), xx.
39. Hollingworth, *Psychology of the Adolescent*, 187.
40. Maurice Pollom, "Mouse: That Ragtime Kid," *Ebony Jr.*, February 1981, 29–31. See also Al Rose, *Eubie Blake* (New York: Schirmer, 1979), 19–21.
41. Marlon Brando, *Brando* (New York: Random House, 1994), 21–22, 43.
42. Peter Gittleman, "The Gropius House" (MA thesis, Boston University, 1996), 27; Robert Evans, *The Kid Stays in the Picture* (Beverly Hills, CA: Phoenix, 1994), 14.
43. R. W. Francis, "Lone Scout," *Boys' Life*, January 1931, 40; General Electric advertisement, *Boys' Life*, June 1944, 25; General Electric advertisement, *Boys' Life*, October 1944, 33. For more on the teen bedroom as a site of scientific/technological experimentation, see Edward Bigelow, "On Nature's Trail," *Boys' Life*, January 1918, 21; Herbert Zim, *Science Interests and Activities of Adolescents* (New York: Ethical Culture Schools, 1940), 137, 159; Herbert Yahraes, "Static from the Stars," *Popular Science*, January 1948, 148–54.
44. Mary Astor, *My Story* (Garden City, NJ: Doubleday, 1959), 38, 46, 66–67.
45. Ibid., 78–79, 85–86.
46. Ibid., 93, 96–97.

CHAPTER THREE

Epigraph: Grace Loucks Elliott, *Understanding the Adolescent Girl* (New York: Holt, 1930), 109.

1. William Leach, *Land of Desire* (New York: Vintage, 1993), 38. Youth-oriented consumerism is discussed further in Kathy Peiss, *Cheap Amusements* (Philadelphia: Temple UP, 1986), passim; Miriam Forman-Brunell, *Made to Play House* (New Haven: Yale, 1993), chs. 1–2; Gary Cross, *Kids' Stuff* (New York: Harvard, 1997), ch. 2; Sarah Chinn, *Inventing Modern Adolescence* (New Brunswick, NJ: Rutgers UP, 2009), passim; Kelly Schrum, *Some Wore Bobby Sox* (New York: Palgrave Macmillan, 2004), passim.
2. All the arguments here are discussed in greater detail in Gwendolyn Wright, *Moralism and the Model Home* (Chicago: Univ. of Chicago Press, 1980), 35–36, 39, 159.
3. Gwendolyn Wright, *Building the Dream* (New York: Pantheon, 1981), 209; Henrietta Murdock, "Rooms to Grow In," *LHJ*, April 1946, 193.
4. Karin Calvert, "Children in the House, 1890 to 1930," in *American Home Life*, ed. Jessica Foy and Thomas Schlereth (Boston: Northeastern UP, 1992), 86; Ethel Davis Seal, "The Young Girl's Room," *LHJ*, January 1927, 30; Ethel Davis

Seal, “Boys Like Fine Rooms Too,” *LHJ*, November 1928, 30; Alice Starr, “A Whole New World of Enchantment in Children’s Rooms,” *H&G*, April 1931, 63, 120, 122; Schuyler White, “A Boy’s Red-White-and-Blue Room,” *LHJ*, July 1930, 58; Louise Fillebrown, “Child’s Bedroom,” *Olean Evening Times*, May 7, 1928, 10. The popularity of collages in nurseries and playrooms during the nineteenth century is discussed in Karen Sanchez-Eppler, “Marks of Possession: Methods for an Impossible Subject,” *PMLA* 126 (January 2011): 152.

5. “Young People’s Own Rooms,” *CSM*, August 25, 1911, 6; “Dick’s Own Room as His Den and Headquarters” *CSM*, November 22, 1913, 23.
6. “A Room of His Own,” *CSM*, September 9, 1930, 9; “With the Teens in Mind,” *H&G*, August 1944, 29. Parent-centered advice can also be found in Seal, “The Young Girls Room,” *LHJ*, 185; Seal, “Boys Like Fine Rooms Too,” *LHJ*, 30, 146; Margaret McElroy, “Rooms for Little Boys and Girls,” *H&G*, February 1927, 68–73, 150; “Color Scheme Is Important in the Child’s Bedroom,” *Davenport Democrat and Leader*, April 12, 1929, 6; Maxine Livingston, “A Grown-up Room for the Teens,” *Parents’*, March 1940, 39; Mary Madison, “Children’s Rooms,” *NYTM*, March 19, 1944, SM24.
7. The emergence of a powerful youth demographic during the interwar years has been noted in Paula Fass, *The Damned and the Beautiful* (New York: Oxford UP, 1977), passim; Grace Palladino, *Teenagers* (New York: Basic, 1996), chs. 1–3; Schrum, *Some Wore Bobby Sox*, passim.
8. White, “A Boy’s Red-White-and-Blue Room,” *LHJ*, 58; “With the Teens in Mind,” *H&G*, 29.
9. Emily Post, *The Personality of a House* (New York: Funk & Wagnalls, 1935), 391–92, 401. Freud’s and Ellis’s influence is discussed in G. Wright, *Moralism and the Model Home*, 208.
10. Martha Davis, “Rooms—for and by Boys,” *CSM*, April 7, 1937, 8.
11. Martha Davis, “Rooms—for and by Boys,” *CSM*, May 5, 1937, 9.
12. Henrietta Murdock, “The Right Room for a Good Scout,” *LHJ*, May 1939, 28; Henrietta Murdock, “Yours Personal . . . A Bedroom for a Sub-Deb,” *LHJ*, May 1938, 93; Edith Sonn, “A Room to Grow Up In,” *NYT*, October 7, 1945, 34; Mary Roche, “A Permanent Room for Junior,” *NYTM*, September 18, 1949, SM48.
13. “Along Boys’ Life Trail,” *Boys’ Life*, March 1938, 51.
14. “A Picture Postcard Rack,” *Boys’ Life*, June 1912, 40; Lela Brown, “These Attractive Statuettes Are Easy to Make,” *Popular Mechanics*, May 1930, 836–38.
15. Post, *Personality of a House*, 402; “A Room of His Own,” *CSM*, 9. Post’s genteel approach to wall hangings is also echoed in Louise Creighton, *The Art of Living and Other Addresses to Girls* (New York: Longmans, Green, 1909), 65–66; “Young People’s Own Rooms,” *CSM*, 6; “Dick’s Own Room as His Den and Headquarters,” *CSM*, 23. The importance of bulletin boards in preventing damage to bedroom walls is on full display in “With the Teens in Mind,” *H&G*, 31.
16. Ada Hart Arlitt, *The Adolescent* (New York: Whittlesy, 1938), 102. Heffner’s wall hangings are discussed in Russell Miller, *Bunny* (New York: Holt,

Rinehart and Winston, 1985), 42. Recall, too, that the walls of Mary Astor's bedroom were peppered with pinups from movie magazines. See Mary Astor, *My Story* (Garden City, NJ: Doubleday, 1959), 46.

17. "Young People's Own Rooms," *CSM*, 6; Creighton, *The Art of Living*, 65–66; Norman Richardson, *The Religious Education of Adolescents* (New York: Abingdon, 1918), 70. Similar claims are made in Helen Henley, "Teen-Agers Deserve Special Consideration in New Homes Geared to Family Activities," *CSM*, February 12, 1946, 10.
18. "Dick's Own Room as His Den and Headquarters," *CSM*, 23. Design schemes emphasizing adventure and athletic prowess can be found in Post, *Personality of a House*, 399; "The Right Room for a Good Scout," *LHJ*, 28, 81; "A Room of His Own," *CSM*, 9; "With the Teens in Mind," *H&G*, 29, 31; "Young People's Own Rooms," *CSM*, 6. Boys' rooms are described as dens or headquarters in "Dick's Own Room," *CSM*, 23; "The Right Room," *LHJ*, 28; Davis, "Rooms—For and by Boys," *CSM*, May 5, 1937, 9.
19. Seymour Bullock, "The Boy in the House," *Rotarian*, June 1927, 23; White, "A Boy's Red-White-and-Blue Room," *LHJ*, 58; Davis, "Rooms—For and by Boys," *CSM*, March 10, 1937, 8. The gender gap and the containment angle are also discussed in Seal, "Boys Like Fine Rooms Too," *LHJ*, 30.

CHAPTER FOUR

Epigraph: Adrienne Salinger, e-mail to author, February 28, 2010.

1. Alice Grayson, *Do You Know Your Daughter?* (New York: Appleton, 1944), 164, 166, 182.
2. "Your Secret World," *Seventeen*, September 1960, 95.
3. Eugene Gilbert, "Teen-Agers Want Big Families," *Hammond Times*, January 24, 1960, 23; Marilyn Hoffman, "Teen-Age Décor: It's All for Them," *CSM*, July 1, 1964, 4; Reed Larson and Maryse Richards, *Divergent Realities* (New York: Basic, 1994), 280; Penn State Division of Student Affairs, "Impact of Sharing a Room," February 1998, http://studentaffairs.psu.edu/Assessment/pdf/43.pdf (accessed August 12, 2007).
4. Anthony Bernier, e-mail to author, October 14, 2012.
5. Ibid. Emphasis his.
6. Leslie, e-mail to author, September 10, 2012.
7. August Hollingshead, *Elmstown Youth* (New York: Wiley, 1949), 145; Audrey Williamson, *Your Teen-Ager and You* (Anderson, IN: Warner, 1952), 73–74. The idea that shared bedrooms could lead to sexual precociousness can also be found in Floyd Martinson, *Infant and Child Sexuality* (St. Peter, MN: Book Mark, 1973), 29.
8. Ruper Hoover, *Enjoy Your Teen-Ager* (New York: Abingdon, 1962), 87–8; Joan Jenkins, *A Girl's World* (New York: Hawthorn, 1967), 24; Bruce Strain, *Teen Days* (New York: Appleton, 1946), 122; Paul Popenoe, "Modern Marriage: Domestic Problems," *Port Arthur News*, March 8, 1968, 4. For more on the dif-

ficulties larger and poorer families had in living up to the separate bedroom ideal, see "Youngsters Appreciate Privacy," *Lima News*, April 8, 1957, 14; Louise Saul, "Portrait of a Happy Father of 18," *NYT*, June 15, 1975, NJ68; Donald Katz, *Home Fires* (New York: Asher, 1992), 44, 69. The relationship between shared rooms and family conflict is also discussed in Alvena Burnite, *Your Teen-Agers* (Milwaukee: Bruce, 1952), 96; Mimi Sheraton, "Bird's-eye View of Two in a Room" *Seventeen*, August 1950, 180.

9. Home ownership statistics can be found in US Department of Commerce, *Demographic Trends in the Twentieth Century* (Washington, DC: GPO, 2002), 124–25. Statistics regarding home size can be found in Patricia Leigh Brown, ". . . And a New House Bends to a Family's Needs," *NYT*, September 19, 1996, C10; Steve Brown, "Ever-Bigger House Finally Stops Growing," *Milwaukee Journal Sentinel*, March 30, 2007, http://www.jsonline.com/realestate/29227759.html (accessed June 21, 2007). Berube's experiences are recounted in Allan Berube and Florence Berube, "Sunset Trailer Park," in *White Trash*, ed. Matt Wray and Annalee Newitz (New York: Routledge, 1997), 27.

10. Statistics pertaining to family size can be found in US Census Bureau, *Statistical Abstract of the United States* (Washington, DC: GPO, 1984), 105: 40. Divorce rates are enumerated in US Census Bureau, *Statistical Abstract of the United States* (Washington, DC: GPO, 2011), 131: 65. Laurel's and Anne's experiences were related to the author via e-mail on September 9, 2012.

11. The popularization of psychology during the postwar years is discussed in John Burnham, *How Superstition Won and Science Lost* (New Brunswick, NJ: Rutgers UP, 1987), ch. 2.

12. Henry Fountain, "Peter Blos, a Psychoanalyst of Children, Is Dead at 93," *NYT*, June 19, 1997, D21; Douglas Thom, *Guiding the Adolescent*, 2nd ed. (Washington, DC: GPO, 1946), 62, 81. The importance of psychological weaning and privacy on adolescent development is discussed in Luella Cole and John Morgan, *Psychology of Childhood and Adolescence* (New York: Rinehart, 1947), 205–6, 218–25; Dorothy Baruch, *New Ways in Discipline* (New York: Whittlesey, 1949), 137–141, 269, 275–76; Phyllis Greenacre, *Trauma, Growth, and Personality* (New York: International UP, 1952), 168, 173, 246, 302; Raymond Kuhlen, *The Psychology of Adolescent Development* (New York: Harper & Row, 1952), 552–54, 537–38, 573–74, 581–89; Robert Hess, "The Adolescent," *Review of Educational Research* 30 (February 1960): 10; Peter Blos, "The Second Individuation Process of Adolescence," *Psychoanalytic Study of the Child* 22 (1967): 162–86; Erik Erikson, *Identity, Youth, and Crisis* (New York: Norton, 1968), 156–58, 246–47; Ruth Strang, "The Transition from Childhood to Adolescence," in *Understanding Adolescence*, ed. James Adams (Boston: Allyn and Bacon, 1968), 18, 30–37; Marvin Powell, *The Psychology of Adolescence* (New York: Bobbs-Merrill, 1971), 49–50, 176, 290; Dorothy Rogers, *Adolescence* (Monterey, CA: Brooks/Cole, 1972), 98, 100–101, 103; David Ausubel et al., *Theory and Problems of Adolescent Development* (New York: Grune & Stratton, 1977), 164, 166–67, 181; Shirley Gould, *Teenagers* (New York: Haw-

thorn, 1977), 4, 6, 8–10, 25–26, 47, 50, 54; Michael Bloom, *Adolescent-Parental Separation* (New York: Gardner, 1980), 23–24, 35, 42; Marianne Marschak, *Parent-Child Interaction and Youth Rebellion* (New York: Gardner, 1980), 17, 152. The popularity of psychoanalysis after the Second World War is discussed in Nathan Hale, *The Rise and Crisis of Psychoanalysis in the United States* (New York: Oxford UP, 1995), chs. 14–16; Eli Zaretsky, *Secrets of the Soul* (New York: Knopf, 2004), ch. 11.

13. Thom, *Guiding the Adolescent*, 79–81.
14. Arnold Gesell, *Youth* (New York: Harper & Row, 1956), 90, 139, 152, 175, 189, 202.
15. Ibid., 217–18, 234, 250, 264, 266.
16. Peter Blos, *On Adolescence* (New York: Free Press of Glencoe, 1962), 36, 40, 42. Blos's suggestion that bedrooms can help individualize teens is also addressed in Grace Overton, *Living with Teeners* (Nashville: Broadman, 1950), 32–33; US Children's Bureau, *Your Child from 6 to 12* (Washington, DC: GPO, 1972), 11, 29; Evelyn Duvall, *Parent and Teenager* (Nashville: Broadman, 1976), 42; Carl Malmquist, *Handbook of Adolescence* (New York: Aronson, 1978), 14–15.
17. Barry Schwartz, "The Social Psychology of Privacy," *American Journal of Sociology* 6 (May 1968): 749.
18. Urban Fleege, *Self-Revelation of the Adolescent Boy* (Milwaukee: Bruce, 1948), 172; Mary Frank and Lawrence Frank, *Your Adolescent at Home and in School* (New York: Viking, 1956), 63; James Dobson, *Hide or Seek* (Old Tappan, NJ: Revell, 1974), 128. For more on the links between bodily change, solitude, and the teen bedroom, see Blos, *On Adolescence*, 8–9; Dick Clark, *Your Happiest Years* (New York: Rosho, 1959), 43; Simon Glustrom, *Living with Your Teenager* (New York: Bloch, 1961), 4–5; Ruth Cavan, *The American Family* (New York: Crowell, 1963), 261; Hoover, *Enjoy Your Teen-Ager*, 118; US Children's Bureau, *Moving into Adolescence* (Washington, DC: GPO, 1970), 12–13; James Oraker and Char Meredith, *Almost Grown* (San Francisco: Harper & Row, 1980), 88.
19. US Children's Bureau, *The Adolescent in Your Family* (Washington, DC: GPO, 1955), 33; Gesell, *Youth*, 140–41. For more on the bedroom as a site of introspection, see Natalie Gittelson, "Daydreaming . . . again?," *Seventeen*, February 1950, 72; Hoover, *Enjoy Your Teen-Ager*, 118; Joseph Stone and Joseph Church, *Childhood and Adolescence* (New York: Random House, 1968), 445; Ruth Boyer, *The Happy Adolescent* (Palo Alto, CA: R&E, 1981), 64–67.
20. Clark, *Your Happiest Years*, 42–43; Hoover, *Enjoy Your Teen-Ager*, 16, 118. Similar arguments are made in Lois Pemberton, *The Stork Didn't Bring You* (New York: Hermitage, 1948), 104–5; Emily Dow, *Of Parties and Petticoats* (New York: Barrows, 1960), 35; Henry Maas, "Some Social Class Differences in the Family Systems and Group Relations of Pre and Early Adolescents," *Child Development* 22 (June 1951): 149; Geoffrey Leigh, "Adolescent Involvement in Family Systems," in *Adolescents in Families*, ed. Geoffrey Leigh and Garry Peterson (Cincinnati, OH: South-Western, 1986), 69; Thomas Smith, "Influence in Parent-Adolescent Relationships," in ibid., 146.

21. "Spock on Teens," *Time*, November 16, 1970, 54; US Children's Bureau, *The Adolescent in Your Family*, 38; Rita Kramer, "The State of the Boy, 1969," *NYTM*, March 30, 1969, SM97; Russell Baker, "Surviving Adolescence Can Be an Experience," *Dominion-News*, April 21, 1972, 4A. Parents are also scolded in Ernest Osborne, *Understanding Your Parents* (New York: Association, 1956), 50–51.
22. Frank and Frank, *Your Adolescent at Home and in School*, 191–92; Dorothy Baruch, *How to Live with Your Teenager* (New York: McGraw-Hill, 1953), 107; Mary Roche, "Ideas and Gadgets," *NYTM*, March 17, 1946, SM20. Housekeeping was also taken into consideration in Osborne, *Understanding Your Parents*, 56; Jenkins, *A Girl's World*, 38–39; Haim Ginott, *Between Parent and Teenager* (New York: Macmillan, 1969), 108.
23. Burnite, *Your Teen-Agers*, 98–99; Thelma Purtell, *The Intelligent Parents' Guide to Teen-Agers* (New York: Eriksson, 1961), 20; US Children's Bureau, *Your Child from 6 to 12*, 11; Dobson, *Hide or Seek*, 74. For more on the importance of letting teenage boys use their bedroom as a hobby space, see Helen Burnham et al., *Boys Will Be Men* (New York: Lippincott, 1949), 15–16.
24. Evelyn Duvall, *Today's Teen-Agers* (New York: Association, 1966), 29; *How to be Well Groomed* (Coronet, 1949), Internet Archive, 10:41, https://archive.org/details/HowtoBeW1949 (accessed January 9, 2008); *Keeping Clean and Neat* (Encyclopaedia Britiannica Films, 1956), Internet Archive, 9:58, https://archive.org/details/0348_Keeping_Clean_and_Neat_E00571_02_35_47_00 (accessed January 8, 2008); Dow, *Of Parties and Petticoats*, 83; *The Snob* (Centron, 1958), Internet Archive, 13:23, http://www.archive.org/details/SnobThe1958 (accessed January 8, 2008). The grooming function is also discussed in Stone and Church, *Childhood and Adolescence*, 445; *Social-Sex Attitudes in Adolescence* (Crawley, 1953), Internet Archive, 23:00, http://www.archive.org/details/SocialSe1953 (accessed December 2, 2007).
25. Enrollment statistics and graduation rates can be found in Thomas Snyder, *120 Years of American Education* (Washington, DC: GPO, 1993), 27; Nicole Stoops, *A Half-Century of Learning* (Washington, DC: GPO, 2006), https://www.census.gov/hhes/socdemo/education/data/census/half-century/index.html (accessed January 27, 2006).
26. Svend Riemer, "Sociological Theory of Home Adjustment," *American Sociological Review* 8 (June 1943): 276; Jenkins, *A Girl's World*, 94. Educational benefits are also discussed in Grayson, *Do You Know Your Daughter?*, 166; Svend Riemer, "The Family and Its Home," *Marriage and Family Living* 4 (November 1942): 84; Burnham et al., *Boys Will Be Men*, 15–16; "Simple Room Divider Is Help to Students," *Odessa American*, August 10, 1958, 50; Graham Blaine, *The Parents' Guide to Adolescence* (Boston: Little Brown, 1962), 61–63; "Student's Room Atmosphere May Raise Grades," *Frederick News-Post*, August 19, 1964, 24; "How Can I Improve My Study Habits?," *Awake!*, August 8, 1984, 13, *Watchtower Library 2007*, CD-ROM.
27. Enid Haupt, *The Seventeen Book of Young Living* (New York: McKay, 1957), 28.

28. Frank and Frank, *Your Adolescent at Home and in School*, 172; Abigail Van Buren, "Dear Abby," *Times Recorder*, September 25, 1964, B4.
29. Ann Landers, "Advice from Ann Landers," *Reno Evening Gazette*, May 8, 1962, 9; Grace Hechinger, "Chores—They Still Breed Character," *NYTM*, August 9, 1964, SM50. The knocking rule is also encouraged in Helen Flanders Dunbar, *Your Preteenager's Mind and Body* (New York: Hawthorn, 1962), 89; Ann Landers, *Since You Ask Me* (Englewood Cliffs, NJ: Prentice-Hall, 1961), 151; Duvall, *Parent and Teenager*, 91; Jenkins, *A Girl's World*, 24; Mel Johnson, *How to Live with Your Teenager* (Tempe, AZ: Success, 1970), no pagination; "Are You Teaching Your Children?," *Watchtower*, September 15, 1973, 562, *Watchtower Library 2007*, CD-ROM; Robert Green, "Manners," *NYTM*, March 12, 1978, SM16; Jane Brody, "Personal Health," *NYT*, September 30, 1981, C10.
30. Abigail Van Buren, "Start Monkeying, Mom!," *Morgantown Post*, May 29, 1961, 3; Abigail Van Buren, "Give Mom Reason to Stop Snooping," *Daily Times-News*, March 8, 1977, A5.
31. Gesell, *Youth*, 323; Burnite, *Your Teen-Agers*, 96; Oliver Butterfield, *Love Problems of Adolescence* (New York: Emerson, 1941), 29; Frank and Frank, *Your Adolescent at Home and in School*, 172. For more on the bedroom as a teen social center and containment tool, see Riemer, "Home Adjustment," 278; Grayson, *Do You Know Your Daughter?*, 228; Thom, *Guiding the Adolescent*, 53; Dunbar, *Your Preteenager's Mind and Body*, 85; Marynia Farnham, "Those Teenage Strangers," *Parents' Magazine*, June 1966, 93–94; M. Johnson, *How to Live with Your Teenager*, no pagination; *Making Your Family Life Happy* (New York: Watchtower, 1976), 138–40, *Watchtower Library 2007*, CD-ROM; Duvall, *Parent and Teenager*, 59, 112.
32. Ginott, *Between Parent and Teenager*, 39; Laurel, e-mail to author, September 9, 2012. Emphasis hers.
33. Arthur Whitman, "Gary Anderson: Top Gun at the Olympics," *Boys' Life*, September 1965, 36–37; "Cazzie Russell—Sophomore Cage Phenom," *Ebony*, April 1964, 102. Similar arguments are made in Dick Miles, "King of the Racketeers," *Boys' Life*, January 1966, 28.
34. Douglas Mitchell, e-mail to author, February 1, 2014; John Leland, "My Son the Headbanger," *Spin*, July 1987, 51–52. The bedroom's value as a hobby space is also discussed in Art Sears, "Va. Lad, 12, Lives in Private," *Jet*, June 21, 1962, 52; Robert Schleicher, "Collections," *Boys' Life*, October 1968, 34–38; Earl Paige, "Factory Dist. vs Reps—A Rep Raps on It," *Billboard*, June 15, 1974, 30; "Hobbies Hold Fun and Rewards for Celebrities," *Ebony Jr.*, March 1984, 40.
35. Douglas Mitchell, e-mail to author, February 1, 2014; Casey Calloway, e-mail to author, December 3, 2013.
36. Casey Calloway, e-mail to author, December 3, 2013.
37. Nancy, e-mail to author, September 14, 2012; Laurel, e-mail to author, September 9, 2012.
38. Nancy, e-mail to author, September 14, 2012; Anthony Bernier, e-mail to author, October 14, 2012; Adrienne Salinger, e-mail to author, February 28, 2010.

39. Douglas Mitchell, e-mail to author, February 1, 2014; Laurel, e-mail to author, September 9, 2012; Jeff Steele, e-mail to author, December 9, 2013.
40. Leslie, e-mail to author, September 10, 2012.
41. Roger, e-mail to author, September 10, 2012.
42. E. Gilbert, "Teen-Agers Want Big Families," 23; Leslie, e-mail to author, September 10, 2012; Anthony Bernier, e-mail to author, October 14, 2012.
43. Casey Calloway, e-mail to author, December 3, 2013.
44. Tiffany Hauck, e-mail to author, September 7, 2012.
45. Adrienne Salinger, *In My Room* (San Francisco: Chronicle Books, 1995), preface.
46. Classified ad, *Oakland Tribune*, October 24, 1964, B14; classified ad, *Van Nuys News*, June 2, 1968, 25; classified ad, *Sunday Journal & Star*, June 12, 1977, 7G. See also classified ad, *Oakland Tribune*, July 21, 1962, 16B; classified ad, *Austin News*, November 4, 1964, 17; classified ad, *Reno Evening Gazette*, June 12, 1970, 27; classified ad, *Iowa City Press-Citizen*, April 13, 1973, 11B; classified ad, *Reno Evening Gazette*, June 4, 1975, 31; classified ad, *Reno Evening Gazette*, June 25, 1977, 17; classified ad, *Daily Herald*, January 4, 1979, 69; classified ad, *Frederick News*, February 27, 1982, 32; classified ad, *Post-Standard*, April 18, 1982, F13.
47. "Are You Guilty of Widening the Generation Gap in 1970?," *Daily Courier*, January 3, 1970, 5; Martin Ragaway, *How to Get a Teenager to Run Away from Home* (Los Angeles: Price, 1983), no pagination; "Surviving Your Teenagers," *Syracuse Herald-Journal*, March 5, 1980, 23.

CHAPTER FIVE

Epigraph: Legs McNeil, "Slut Metal," *Spin*, July 1989, 48. Meanstreak is the name of Yael's band.

1. Photo Poster Inc. advertisement, *Seventeen*, June 1972, 170; Photo Hang Ups Inc. advertisement, *Seventeen*, February 1973, 230; Photo Poster advertisement, *Rolling Stone*, June 24, 1971, 54.
2. High school's role in teen culture is discussed in Joseph Kett, *Rites of Passage* (New York: Basic, 1977), 263; Kelly Schrum, *Some Wore Bobby Sox* (New York: Palgrave Macmillan, 2004), 3, 12; Sarah Chinn, *Inventing Modern Adolescence* (New Brunswick, NJ: Rutgers UP, 2009), 65.
3. "Bobby Soxers' Gallup," *Time*, August 13, 1956, 72; Eugene Gilbert, "Why Today's Teenager Seems So Different," *Harper's*, November 1959, 77; Grace Palladino, *Teenagers* (New York: Basic, 1996), xi. The growing economic power of teens is also discussed in Bennet Berger, "Teen-Agers Are an American Invention," *NYTM*, June 13, 1965, SM85, SM87; John Modell, *Into One's Own* (Berkeley: Univ. of CA Press, 1989), ch. 6; Lizabeth Cohen, *A Consumer's Republic* (New York: Knopf, 2003), 318–19.
4. Elizabeth Wooley, "Young Needs Must Be Considered in Designing Children's Room," *CSM*, November 8, 1944, 17; Mary Roche, "A Permanent Room for Junior," *NYTM*, September 18, 1949, SM48.

5. "Upstairs Room Provides Privacy for Busy Teen," *Chicago Defender*, September 14, 1965, 19; "Rooms to a Teen's Taste . . . 'Real Cool' Is the Word for It!," *Chicago Defender*, March 5, 1960, 16; "With the Teenagers," *Atlanta World*, July 11, 1963, 3. See also "Kids Need a Room of Their Own," *Los Angeles Sentinel*, May 2, 1957, C7; Gaile Dugas, "Making the Most of Space," *Chicago Defender*, September 14, 1965, 19; "New Decorating Idea for Teenagers' Room," *Chicago Defender*, September 19, 1966, 18; "Studio Look," *Chicago Defender*, August 12, 1967, 26; "Budget Decorating Can Be Easy, Fun," *Chicago Defender*, 18; "Sunny Studio for Teenagers," *Atlanta World*, May 1, 1975, 5.
6. "Rooms to a Teen's Taste," *Chicago Defender*, 16; Dugas, "Making the Most of Space," *Chicago Defender*, 19. See also "Budget Decorating," *Chicago Defender*, 18.
7. "Fabrics for Teen-Agers," *NYT*, August 19, 1953, 26; Virginia Warren, "The Teen-Age Set Goes for Stuffed Animals in a Big Way," *NYT*, August 11, 1966, 22; Marilyn Hoffman, "Teen-Age Décor: It's All for Them," *CSM*, July 1, 1964, 4; "Sunny Studio," *Atlanta World*, 5; Howard Seifer, "You and Your Home," *Chicago Heights Star*, August 19, 1952, 14.
8. Barbara Broyhill, "This I Like," *Seventeen*, October 1960, 160.
9. Kay Sherwood, "Homemakers-to-Be Buy for Adaptability First," *Lima News*, April 8, 1957, 14; Hoffman, "Teen-Age Décor," *CSM*, 4. Similar claims are made in Rita Reif, "Décor Trade Held Ignorant of Teen-Ager," *NYT*, May 21, 1959, 24; Lisa Hammel, "Voice of Teen-Ager Heard in Market," *NYT*, April 7, 1965, 48.
10. Lane advertisement, *Seventeen*, May 1951, 17; Drexel advertisement, *Seventeen*, September 1961, 174; Bassett advertisement, *Seventeen*, February 1972, 207.
11. Grace Miller, "New Tips on Decorating for Teen-Agers Uncovered During Chicago Store's Contest," *CSM*, April 21, 1948, 10.
12. "Teen-Agers Select Décor for Bedroom," *NYT*, May 23, 1959, 16; "Rooms for Young Shown," *NYT*, February 26, 1964, 24; Lisa Hammel, "Store Woos Teen-Agers with Décor," *NYT*, May 25, 1965, 36; Virginia Lee Warren, "Bloomingdale's Shows 8 Young Model Rooms," *NYT*, April 5, 1966, 31.
13. Hammel, "Store Woos Teen-Agers," *NYT*, 36; "Eight Weeks of Beauty Offered to Teen-Agers," *NYT*, January 6, 1961, 30; "Room Décor Course," *NYT*, August 31, 1963, 30.
14. Sears advertisement, *Frederick News*, April 27, 1978, 50; Prange's Budget Store advertisement, *Post Crescent*, January 23, 1969, A6; Marilyn Hoffman, "A Room of Their Very Own," *CSM*, August 9, 1967, 18. Teen-oriented furniture can also be found in RB Homemaker advertisement, *Oakland Tribune*, January 1, 1972, E3; Fleischman's advertisement, *Syracuse Herald-Journal*, April 15, 1976, 11; Bedrooms Unlimited advertisement, *Chronicle Telegram*, April 27, 1978, C9.
15. Marilyn Hoffman, "Rummaging Parents Design for Teen-Age Life," *CSM*, March 15, 1967, 20; "Rooms to a Teen's Taste," *Chicago Defender*, 16; "Teenage Havens, Boy and Girl," *LHJ*, January 1961, 66; Cynthia Kellogg, "Designs for a Teen-Ager's Castle," *NYTM*, April 10, 1960, SM76. Similar terminology can

be found in "Teen Apartments Above . . . Hobby and Play Space Below," *LHJ*, October 1957, 94; "A Room Becomes a Castle," *News Journal*, August 4, 1968, 5; "High-Tech Makes Fun Functional," *Syracuse Herald-Journal*, April 18, 1980, B5; "The ABCs of Decorating for Kids," *NYT*, October 23, 1983, C16; Denise Salvaggio, "Whose Bedroom Is It, Anyway?," *Syracuse Herald-Journal*, March 16, 1985, B12.

16. Mimi Sheraton, "A Special Place Just for You," *Seventeen*, August 1951, 201; Enid Haupt, *The Seventeen Book of Young Living* (New York: McKay, 1957), 63; Pati Hill, "Home Talent," *Seventeen*, October 1944, 68. Similar arguments are made in Betty Pepis, *Be Your Own Decorator* (New York: Pyramid, 1961), 31; Adrienne Salinger, preface to *In My Room* (San Francisco: Chronicle Books, 1995).
17. "Sensitivity Training: How to Live with Your Room," *Co-ed*, March 1974, 68; "Room Service," *Co-ed*, May 1974, 107; "Room Service," *Co-ed*, October 1975, 7; Broyhill, "This I Like," *Seventeen*, 160. Arguments about how décor choices can help distinguish the teen bedroom from other spaces in the house can also be found in Ray Faulkner and Sarah Faulkner, *Inside Today's Home* (New York: Holt, Rinehart and Winston, 1960), 49.
18. Karin Calvert, "Children in the House, 1890 to 1930," in *American Home Life*, ed. Jessica Foy and Thomas Schlereth (Boston: Northeastern UP, 1992), 86; Kellogg, "A Teen-Ager's Castle," *NYTM*, SM76; "Teen-Agers Crave Their Own Sophisticated Studio," *Sheboygan Press*, March 23, 1963, 10. "Sophisticated" strategies are also offered in Kay Sherwood, "Teen-Agers Get 'Day-Dream' Space at Low Cost," *Lima News*, February 1, 1956, 17; George O'Brien, "Teen-Ager's Domain," *NYT*, November 10, 1963, 82; Marilyn Hoffman, "Rummaging Parents," *CSM*, 20; "New Studio Look in Teen Bedroom," *Indiana Gazette*, July 3, 1967, 8; "Studio Look," *Chicago Defender*, August 12, 1967, 26; "Pets for Your Pad," *Seventeen*, August 1972, 281, 283; "Romantic Surround," *Seventeen*, February 1983, 122.
19. Sheila Eby, "When a Teen-Ager Redecorates, Results Say, 'It's My Own Room'," *NYT*, August 12, 1982, C1, C8.
20. "Kemp Furniture Sets 1972 trend," *Chicago Defender*, June 28, 1971, 17; *Encyclopedia of Interior Design and Decoration*, s.v. "teenagers' rooms."
21. "If It's Pretty, Hang It Up," *Seventeen*, July 1960, 123; "Shopping for Secondhand Furnishings," *Co-ed*, October 1974, 56. See also "You Have the Niftiest Ideas," *Seventeen*, January 1973, 76–77; "Room Service," *Co-ed*, March 1975, 51; "$1 to $10 Decorating Ideas," *Co-ed*, October 1975, 60–63; "Brighten Your Room with Yarn," *Co-ed*, November 1975, 42–43; "Paint a Pillow," *Seventeen*, April 1985, 94; "Make Your Mark," *Seventeen*, May 1985, 185.
22. "The Way-Out Room?," *Seventeen*, October 1960, 116–17, 152; "New Wave Knockouts," *Seventeen*, June 1985, 86–87. Offbeat/DIY approaches can also be found in "Bring Summer into Your Room," *Co-ed*, May 1974, 80–81, 90; "Something Old to Something New," *Co-ed*, October 1974, 60–62, 73; "Room Service," *Co-ed*, May 1977, 50; "Desk-Top Cover-ups," *Seventeen*, March 1983, 152–53.

23. Debra Piot, "Ingenuity and Elbow-Grease Add Up to a Personal Touch," *Daily Herald*, September 23, 1979, sec. 4, p. 1; "High-Tech Makes Fun Functional," *Syracuse Herald-Journal*, B5; Colleen Dishon, "Make Your Own Bed, You Have to Sleep In It," *Lima News*, July 11, 1975, 12.
24. "Room Revival Revisited: Co-ed Picks a Winner," *Co-ed*, April 1974, 62–64, 66, 68; "Room Revival Contest," *Co-ed*, April 1975, 42–46.
25. Georgia Dullea, "All Those Cans of Beer on the Wall Empty," *NYT*, December 19, 1977, 54. Anthony Bernier also decorated his room with empty Coors cans. Anthony Bernier, e-mail to author, October 14, 2012.
26. Jack Levin and Ernie Anastos, *'Twixt* (New York: Watts, 1983), 41; Anthony Bernier, e-mail to author, October 14, 2012; Anne, e-mail to author, September 9, 2012.
27. "Failure to Communicate (letters)," *Playboy*, May 1969, 70; Jeff Steele, e-mail to author, December 9, 2013.
28. East Totem West advertisement, *Rolling Stone*, November 9, 1967, 19; Steve Lohr, "Stars Rise Quickly in Poster Boom," *NYT*, February 2, 1980, 27, 31.
29. "The All-American Model," *Time*, March 6, 1978, 38; "Classic Pin-Ups," *People*, May 6, 1996, 193. Tiegs represents yet another interesting link between DIY pinups and the poster industry, as she was featured on the cover of *Sports Illustrated*'s wildly popular swimsuit issue in 1970, 1975, and 1983.
30. Ted Morgan, "Lord of the Venus Flytrap," *NYT*, March 31, 1974, 19; Donald Katz, *Home Fires* (New York: Asher, 1992), 252; Lohr, "Stars Rise Quickly in Poster Boom," *NYT*, 31; Jeff Steele, e-mail to author, December 9, 2013. For more on the popularity of posters among American teens, see "Posters, Posters, Posters" *Co-ed*, November 1974, 42–43; "Sale of Posters Considered Clue to Day's Temper," *Lima News*, July 16, 1976, 12.
31. "Teen-Agers Select Décor for Bedroom," *NYT*, May 23, 1959, 16; *Teddy*, Extension Media Center, UCLA, 1971, Internet Archive, http://www.archive.org (accessed June 11, 2008); Tiffany Hauck, e-mail to author, September 7, 2012. The use of collage in nineteenth-century children's bedrooms is discussed in Karen Sanchez-Eppler, "Marks of Possession: Methods for an Impossible Subject," *PMLA* 126 (January 2011): 151–59. Contemporary manifestations of the collage method can be found in Salinger, *In My Room*, passim; Jeanne Steele and Jane Brown, "Adolescent Room Culture," *Journal of Youth and Adolescence* 24 (October 1995): 551–76.
32. Nancy, e-mail to author, September 14, 2012; Douglas Mitchell, e-mail to author, February 1, 2014.
33. Leslie, e-mail to author, September 10, 2012.
34. Elizabeth Collins Cromley, "A History of American Beds and Bedrooms, 1890–1930," *Perspectives in Vernacular Architecture* 4 (1991), 183; Bedrooms Unlimited advertisement, *Chronicle Telegram*, April 27, 1978, C9; Emily Butterfield, "How Local Teens Decorate Their Bedrooms," *Syracuse Herald-Journal*, March 16, 1985, B12.

35. Casey Calloway, e-mail to author, December 3, 2013; Laurel, e-mail to author, September 9, 2012.
36. Ruth Gilkey, "A Room of One's Own," *Oakland Tribune*, January 19, 1969, CM7.
37. Charles Brown, "Self-Portrait: The Teen-Type Magazine," *Annals of the American Academy of Political and Social Science* 338 (1961): 18; Anthony Bernier, e-mail to author, October 14, 2012; General Motors advertisement, *Seventeen*, April 1983, 124–25.
38. Amelia Eve, e-mail to author, September 10, 2012.
39. Ibid.

CHAPTER SIX

Epigraph: Frank Zappa and the Mothers of Invention, "Camarillo Brillo," from the album *Over-Nite Sensation*, lyrics and music by Frank Zappa, DiscReet, 1973. The title of this chapter was borrowed from a phrase in Alison Roberts, "TV or No TV Is No Longer a Question: Most Kids' Rooms Have Electronic Entertainment," *Chicago Sun-Times*, February 26, 2006, E01.

1. Casey Calloway, e-mail to author, December 3, 2013.
2. "Notes on These Changing Times," *Changing Times*, July 1977, 2; Philip Slater, *The Pursuit of Loneliness* (Boston: Beacon, 1971), 7; Christopher Lasch, *The Culture of Narcissism* (New York: Norton, 1978), xv–xvi, 74. For more on the ubiquitous presence of home electronics in teen bedrooms, see Judy Mann, "Yesterday's Luxuries Drop in Today's Bucket," *WaPo*, March 7, 1980, B1; Margaret Drabble, "Teen-Age, Good Age," *NYT*, November 4, 1981, A31; Geraldine Fox, "So Much and So Little," *NYT*, December 30, 1984, LI12; Judy Mann, "Children of Disorder, Hear This," *WaPo*, May 10, 1985, B3.
3. Telephone statistics can be found in US Department of Commerce, *Historical Statistics of the United States, Colonial Times to 1970*, (Washington: GPO, 1975), 783–84. For more on rural electrification, see David Nye, *Electrifying America* (Cambridge, MA: MIT Press, 1990), ch. 7. Saturation levels are discussed in Sue Bowden and Avner Offer, "Household Appliances and the Use of Time: The United States and Britain since the 1920s," *Economic History Review* 47 (November 1994): 725–48.
4. Early radio ownership statistics can be found in Paul Schubert, *The Electric Word* (New York: Macmillan, 1928), 212; Christopher Sterling and Michael Keith, *Sounds of Change* (Chapel Hill: Univ. of NC Press, 2008), 14.
5. Susan Douglas, *Listening In* (Minneapolis: Univ. of MN Press, 1999), 59; "Amateur Wireless Installations," *Popular Mechanics*, November 1909, 650; "A Word about the Shut-ins," *Wireless Age*, June 1925, 38. Radio clubs are discussed in Anthony Rudel, *Hello, Everybody!* (New York: Harcourt, 2008), 15, 16, 43–44. For more on the popularity of "spark" sets among young boys, see Schubert, *The Electric Word*, 194; Orrin Dunlap, "The Radio Listening Post," *Boys' Life*, February 1928, 31.
6. Fears of late-night radio listening are discussed in Peter Stearns et al., "Children's Sleep," *Journal of Social History* 30 (Winter 1996): 351. For design plans

that include radios, see Ethel Davis Seal, "Boys Like Fine Rooms Too," *LHJ*, November 1928, 30; Henrietta Murdock, "The Right Room for a Good Scout," *LHJ*, May 1939, 28; "With the Teens in Mind," *H&G*, August 1944, 30.

7. RCA advertisement, *NYT*, January 27, 1929, X16; Philco advertisement, *NYT*, June 25, 1930, 32; Michael Schiffer, *The Portable Radio in American Life* (Tuscon: Univ. of AZ Press, 1991), 154. The communal aspects of radio listening are discussed in Douglas, *Listening In*, 5.
8. Andre Millard, *America on Record* (New York: Cambridge UP, 1995), 218–19; Theodore Strongin, "High Fidelity: Fighting for Its Identity," *NYT*, Sept. 15, 1968, H1.
9. "Pleasures of Possession," *Newsweek*, March 21, 1966, 71; "Hobby Hows," *Boys' Life*, December 1961, 73; Bob Guccione Jr., "Blurvision," *Spin*, October 1986, 95. For more on bedroom radios during the 1960s and 1970s, see Kevin Sweeney, "Radio: And the Booming Next Decade," *Financial Analysts Journal*, March–April 1960, 39–40; Jack Lyle and Heidi Hoffman, "Children's Use of Television and Other Media," in *Television and Social Behavior*, ed. Eli Rubenstein et al. (Washington, DC: GPO, 1972), 153–54.
10. Edison's quote about exposing working men to opera can be found in Millard, *America on Record*, 4. Personal income statistics were taken from US Department of Commerce, *Historical Statistics of the United States, Colonial Times to 1970*, 224. For more on the early uses of phonograph technology, see Oliver Read and Walter Welch, *From Tin Foil to Stereo* (New York: Bobbs-Merrill, 1976), chs. 1–5.
11. The quote about making the phonograph look as "unphonograph-looking as possible" can be found in Roland Gelatt, *The Fabulous Phonograph, 1877–1977* (New York: Macmillan, 1977), 156. Production statistics can be found in Donna Braden, "The Family That Plays Together Stays Together," in Jessica Foy, ed. *American Home Life, 1880–1930* (Boston: Northeastern UP, 1992), 156; Gelatt, *The Fabulous Phonograph*, 208. For more on the phonograph's transformation into a popular consumer item, see Millard, *America on Record*, 49–50,123.
12. Martin Williams's bedroom phonograph is discussed in William Kenney, *Recorded Music in American Life* (New York: Oxford UP, 1999), 20. Descriptions of early parlor phonographs can be found in Gelatt, *The Fabulous Phonograph*, 146, 156, 192. Millard's thoughts on the phonograph's popularity among middle-class families can be found in Millard, *America on Record*, 131. The difficulties teens had in purchasing phonographic equipment are also discussed in Ray Giles, "Making Youth the Bull's-Eye of the Advertising Target," *Printers' Ink*, September 14, 1922, 60.
13. Columbia House advertisement, *Life*, August 31, 1959, 77; "Low Cost Phonographs," *Consumer Reports*, August 1957, 370.
14. "Pleasures," *Newsweek*, 71; Elaine Tyler May, *Homeward Bound* (New York: Basic, 1999), passim. Similar statistics on teen phonograph ownership can be found in "A New $10 Billion Power: The U.S. Teenage Consumer," *Life*, August 31, 1959, 78; Lyle and Hoffman, "Children's Use of Television and Other Media," 153–54.

15. Evelyn Duvall, *Parent and Teenager* (Nashville: Broadman, 1976), 52–53; Erma Bombeck, "Talkin' 'Bout That Generation," *Capital*, September 20, 1989, D6. For more on the popularity of music listening among teens, see Evelyn Banning, "Recreational Interests and Needs of High School Youth," *Recreation* 48 (January 1954): 43; Dwight MacDonald, "A Caste, A Culture, A Market," *New Yorker*, November 29, 1958, 58; George Gallup, "Radio: Teen-Agers' Favorite Medium," *Alton Telegraph*, July 28, 1984, B5.
16. Douglas Mitchell, e-mail to author, February 1, 2014; Nancy, e-mail to author, September 14, 2012.
17. Matt Groening, "Life Is Hell," *Now*, June 1–7, 2000, 26; Matt Groening, "Life Is Hell," *Now*, January 27–February 2, 2000, 24; Matt Groening, "Life Is Hell," *Now*, February 3–9, 2000, 24; Donald Katz, *Home Fires* (New York: Asher, 1992), 126, 180; "The Nubes," *Time*, March 11, 1966, 63. The ritualistic aspects of teen stereo use are also discussed in Douglas, *Listening In*, 5; Rollye Bornstein, "Satellite Nets Help Spread the Clear Channel 'Disease'," *Billboard*, July 31, 1982, 18.
18. Amelia Eve, e-mail to author, September 10, 2012; Tiffany Hauck, e-mail to author, September 7, 2012.
19. For more on the dangers associated with rock concerts, see *Gimme Shelter*, dir. Albert Maysles, David Maysles, and Charlotte Zwerin (1970; Burbank, CA: Warner Home Video, 2008), DVD; *Woodstock*, dir. Michael Wadleigh (1970; Burbank, CA: Warner Home Video, 2001), DVD.
20. US population numbers and phone ownership rates can be found in US Department of Commerce, *Historical Statistics of the United States, Colonial Times to 1970*, 8, 783–84. The early applications of telephone technology are discussed in Claude Fischer, "Touch Someone: The Telephone Industry Discovers Sociability," *Technology and Culture* 29 (January 1988): 32–61.
21. C&P Telephone advertisement, *Frederick Post*, April 21, 1970, A3; New York Telephone advertisement, *NYT*, October 9, 1961, 30; New York Telephone advertisement, *NYT*, January 29, 1964, 12; Michigan Bell Telephone Company advertisement, *Traverse City Record Eagle*, October 11, 1955, 8.
22. New York Telephone advertisement, *NYTM*, June 16, 1968, SM41; Howard Teichmank, "For Whom the Bell Rings—and Rings," *NYTM*, May 15, 1960, SM41. The monthly rate quoted above can be found in Harry Golden, "Only in America," *Chicago Defender*, March 30, 1974, 26. The idea that teens could pay for their own telephones can be found in Mansfield Telephone Company advertisement, *News Journal*, December 1, 1961, 12.
23. Daniel Costello, "Art & Collecting: Plug Into the New Antiques," *WSJ*, April 7, 2000, W9; Princess telephone advertisement, circa late 1960s, http://www.youtube.com/watch?v=XgK2ttxLYeo (accessed February 24, 2009); Cynthia Crossen, "The Evolution of Gift Giving," *WSJ*, November 27, 2000, B1. The Princess telephone's iconic status is also discussed in Frank Rich, "Busy Signals," *NYTM*, December 19, 1993, SM26.
24. Firsthand accounts of bootlegged teen telephones were taken from an informal telephone survey administered for the author by Paul Fassbender,

a vintage telephone collector, in 2009. Fassbender surveyed his colleagues in the Antique Telephone Collectors Association and Telephone Collectors International.

25. Mitnick's exploits are discussed in Kevin Mitnick and William Simon, *Ghosts in the Wires* (New York: Little Brown, 2011), 16, 31–32. AT&T's losses were quoted in Sanford Jacobs, "Blue Boxes Spread from Phone Freaks to the Well-Heeled," *WSJ*, January 29, 1976, 1. For more on the emergence of "phreaking," see Phil Lapsley, *Exploding the Phone* (New York: Grove, 2013), passim.
26. Katie Hafner and John Markoff, *Cyberpunk* (New York: Touchstone, 1995), 30; "An Introduction to COCOTs," in *The Best of 2600*, ed. Emmanuel Goldstein (Indianapolis, IN: Wiley, 2009), 454.
27. Lou Boyd, "Sons-in-Law Get to Top," *Record Eagle*, March 17, 1972, 13; Lou Boyd, "Potpourri," *Paris News*, January 28, 1983, 6. The gendered aspects of telephone technology are discussed in Ellen Lupton, *Mechanical Brides* (Princeton, NJ: Princeton Architectural Press, 1993), 29–41. Geurts's comments came from the same survey cited in note 24.
28. Lucy Baines Johnson's bedroom telephone makes an appearance in "The Texan Sits Tall in the Saddle," *Life*, December 13, 1963, 30–31. Hoffman's recollections came from the survey mentioned in note 24. Emphasis his.
29. Dorothy Barclay, "The Telephoning Teens," *NYT*, May 20, 1956, 245; New York Telephone advertisement, *NYTM*, June 16, 1968, SM41. Peticolas's remarks were culled from the survey mentioned in note 24. Rawson Stovall's bedroom telephone is discussed in Keith Monroe, "He Turned Computer Games to Gold," *Boys' Life*, January 1987, 15.
30. Jim Bishop, "Jim Bishop: Reporter," *Anderson Daily Bulletin*, December 11, 1970, 4; Sam Levenson, "Can an Average Father Rip a Phone Book in Half?," *Journal News*, March 2, 1975, FW4–5. Phone-obsessed teenage girls are also mentioned in Abigail Van Buren, "Dear Abby . . ." *Post-Standard*, December 11, 1959, 10; "Room for Being a Girl," *Seventeen*, June 1960, 94; Dan Halligan, "Girl Has Home Phone Trouble," *Brainerd Daily Dispatch*, March 24, 1961, 12; John Leonard, "Private Lives," *NYT*, April 4, 1979, C14; "Q&A: How Much Time Do You Spend on the Telephone?," *Syracuse Herald-Journal*, January 30, 1982, A8.
31. Katz, *Home Fires*, 102, 106.
32. *Back to the Future*, dir. Robert Zemeckis (1985; Los Angeles, CA: Universal, 2002), DVD; Edgar Greenbaum, "Investing in Electronics," *Analysts Journal*, June 1956, 88; John Riley et al., "Some Observations on the Social Effects of Television," *Public Opinion Quarterly* 13 (Summer 1949): 232. The togetherness argument is also discussed in Lynn Spigel, *Make Room for TV* (Chicago: Univ. of Chicago Press, 1992), 37–50, 183; Ray Barfield, *A Word from Our Viewers* (Westport, CT: Prager, 2008), introduction, chs. 1–4; Cecelia Tichi, *Electronic Hearth* (New York: Oxford, 1991), passim.
33. Katz, *Home Fires*, 37; Noel Murray, "Happy Digital Day!," A.V. Club, June 12, 2009, http://www.avclub.com/articles/happy-digital-day,29136/ (accessed

June 12, 2009). The price quotes for television sets can be found in Hoylan-Huffman advertisement, *Charleston Gazette*, October 20, 1958, 30; Dumont advertisement, *NYT*, November 6, 1960, SM75.

34. "Kind Words for TV," *Chicago Defender*, June 2, 1966, 17; Daniel Boorstin, "Television," *Life*, September 10, 1971, 36; Marie Winn, *The Plug-In Drug* (New York: Viking, 1977), 106. For more on the decline of co-viewing, see Robert Bower, *Television and the Public* (New York: Holt, Rinehart & Winston, 1973), 144–49; Jerry Mander, *Four Arguments for the Elimination of Television* (New York: Morrow, 1978), 133, 168; Lynn Gross and R. Patricia Walsh, "Factors Affecting Parental Control over Children's Television Viewing," *Journal of Broadcasting* 24 (Summer 1980): 412–16; Jack McLeod, "Television and Social Relations," in *Television and Behavior*, ed. David Pearl et al. (Washington, DC: GPO, 1982), 276; Daniel McDonald, "Generational Aspects of Television Coviewing," *Journal of Broadcasting & Electronic Media* 30 (Winter 1986): 80.

35. Hal Boyle, "Curbstone Comments of Pavement Plato," *Panama City News*, April 8, 1969, 4; Jack Lyle, "Television in Daily Life," in *Television and Social Behavior*, ed. John Murray et al. (Washington, DC: GPO, 1972), 4. The relationship between additional television sets and the presence of adolescent children in the home is also discussed in Lyle and Hoffman, "Children's Use of Television," 131, 140; Irene Goodman, "Television's Role in Family Interaction," *Journal of Family Issues* 4 (June 1983): 414; Reed Larson, "Secrets in the Bedroom: Adolescents' Private Use of Media," *Journal of Youth and Adolescence* 24 (October 1995), 539.

36. Thelma Purtell, *The Intelligent Parents' Guide to Teen-Agers* (New York: Eriksson, 1961), 132; Charles and Bonnie Remsberg, "Wooing the Dimply, Pimply," *NYT*, June 5, 1966, 291; Jorge Olivares, e-mail to author, July 27, 2009. Teen television ownership is also mentioned in Leonard Buder, "Parents Warned on Excess Giving," *NYT*, August 15, 1960, 25; "Beautiful Home for Work, Play," *Ebony*, October 1962, 122; Bernard Gladstone, "For More Than One Set," *NYT*, November 25, 1973, 204; Nelson Magombo, "Additional Help Needed for Family," *Los Angeles Sentinel*, November 6, 1975, A2.

37. Benjamin Spock, *Baby and Child Care*, 5th ed. (New York: Pocket, 1963), 395; Winn, *Plug-In Drug*, 185. For more on the negative influence of bedroom sets, see Marie Winn, "Questions Parents Can Ask Themselves about TV," *Danville Register*, May 29, 1977, FW12–13; Nancy Larrick, "Schools Get Tough on TV Addicts," *NYT*, November 13, 1977, EDUC8; "Control Your Television!," *Awake!*, April 22, 1978, 18–19, *Watchtower Library 2007*, CD-ROM; "Fatal TV Influence," *Awake!*, January 8, 1980, 31, *Watchtower Library 2007*, CD-ROM; Leslie Bennetts, "Ways to Control Family Viewing," *NYT*, April 20, 1980, EDU19; Francis Zappone, "Teaching Children How to View TV," *NYT*, May 9, 1982, CN22.

38. Ann Landers, "Some Familiar Teen Dialogue," *Oakland Tribune*, September 18, 1977, 21; Jeff Steele, e-mail to author, December 9, 2013; Leslie, e-mail to author, September 10, 2012.

39. Steve Sherman, "A Set of One's Own: TV Sets in Children's Bedrooms," *Journal of Advertising Research* 36 (November–December 1996): 10–11.
40. Ibid., 10. See also Virginia Linn, "Study Warns against TVs in Teens' Rooms," *Pittsburgh Post-Gazette*, April 9, 2008, C5. Home-based gaming is discussed in Van Burnham, ed., *Supercade* (Cambridge, MA: MIT Press, 2001) passim; Steven Kent, *The Ultimate History of Videogames* (Roseville, CA: Prima, 2001), passim; Ted Friedman, *Electric Dreams* (New York: NYU Press, 2005), 92–112; Leonard Herman, *Phoenix* (Union, NJ: Rolenta, 1994), passim.
41. Todd Thibideaux, "Gaming: The First CE Contact," *Dealerscope*, March 2001, 12; Brett Weiss, *Classic Home Video Games, 1985–1988* (Jefferson, NC: McFarland, 2012), 3; Dawn Miller, *Our Time to Be Blessed* (Bloomington, IN: Xlibris, 2010), e-book, ch. 8; HesGame advertisement, *Boys' Life*, October 1984, 19. Another instance of bedroom-oriented gaming can be found in Danny Evans, *Rage against the Meshugenah* (New York: Penguin, 2009), 161. More recent statistics on the presence of game consoles in teen bedrooms can be found in Kaiser Family Foundation, "Key Facts: Children and Video Games," (Fall 2002), 1, http://www.kff.org (accessed March 4, 2008).
42. The communities that banned minors from arcades during school hours are discussed in Kent, *Ultimate History of Videogames*, 152. The zoning struggles in Lynbrook, Long Island, can be found in Barry Abramson, "Game Parlors Face Curbs," *NYT*, August 9, 1981, LI11. For more on the fears generated by arcades, see Franklin Whitehouse, "Village Zeroes In on Space Invaders," *NYT*, June 15, 1981, B1; Glenn Collins, "Children's Video Games: Who Wins (or Loses)?," *NYT*, August 31, 1981, B4; Debbie Absher, "The Electronic Game Battle: Video Vice or Just Clean Fun?," *Daily Herald*, October 5, 1981, 1, 10; "Drugs Sold at Video Sites," *Post-Standard*, March 16, 1982, D4; "Amusement Arcades No Place for Teens," *Daily Intelligencer*, August 24, 1982, 6; "Whir, Flash, Zap: Game Over," *Mountain Democrat*, January 14, 1983, 24.
43. Sears advertisement, *Daily Herald*, December 3, 1980, 14; David Scott, "Arcade Avocation or Video Vice?," *Daily Intelligencer*, October 24, 1982, C8; Nancy Josephson, "The Video-Game Wars," *Daily Intelligencer*, January 2, 1983, 7, 10. Variations on Huel's arguments can be found in letter to the editor, "Video Games Offer a Lot More Than Fun," *NYT*, January 20, 1982, A26; Lynn Walters, "Video Fever: A Cure for Boredom," *Daily Intelligencer*, February 8, 1982, 1; Betty Debnam, "Arcades for Kids," *Chronicle Telegram*, November 1, 1982, D9; letter to the editor, "Don't Ban Video Games," *Daily Herald*, June 13, 1983, 8.
44. Garriot is cited in Steven Levy, *Hackers* (Cambridge, MA: O'Reilly, 2010), 330. Dykes's experiences are cited in Kevin Mitnick and William Simon, *The Art of Intrusion* (Indianapolis, IN: Wiley, 2005), 124. Bedroom-oriented computing is also discussed in Michael Hemery, *No Permanent Scars* (Columbus, OH: Silenced Press, 2011) 80.
45. "Your Mission, Geof, Crack That Security," *Computerworld*, August 29, 1973, 2; *WarGames*, dir. John Badham (1983; Los Angeles: Twentieth Century Fox, 2000), DVD; "Teen-Agers Tap NASA Computers," *Index-Journal*, July 18, 1984, 14.

46. "Pentagon Says No Security Breached in Computer Case," *Galveston Daily News*, July 18, 1985, 2A; Chuck Easttom, *Computer Crime, Investigation, and the Law* (Boston: Cengage, 2011), 42. For more incidents of teen hacking, see Timothy Harper, "Computer Raiders," *Galveston Daily News*, September 1, 1983, 7B; "FBI Raids Teen Computer Hackers," *Paris News*, October 14, 1983, 12; Max Miller, "Hackers Put 'Byte' on Newsweek Reporter," *Santa Cruz Sentinel*, December 5, 1984, B5; "Sunnyvale, Fremont Youths Face Charges in Computer Hackers Group," *Santa Cruz Sentinel*, March 14, 1986, A16.
47. "The Summer Games of '87," in *The Best of 2600*, ed. Emmanuel Goldstein (New York: Wiley, 2009), 198; Mitnick and Simon, *Ghosts in the Wires*, 37–38.
48. Agent Ewen's sweep of Mitnick's room is described in Hafner and Markoff, *Cyberpunk*, 52–53; Mitnick and Simon, *Ghosts in the Wires*, 46–52.
49. Amy Goldwasser, "Family Politics Shift from TV to Keyboard," *Indiana Gazette*, May 26, 2002, E6; Suzanne Slesin, "New Design for Sight and Sound," *NYT*, June 27, 1985, C1.
50. Fox, "So Much and So Little," *NYT*, LI12.

CHAPTER SEVEN

Epigraph: Greg, e-mail to author, November 29, 2012.

1. Dean Kuipers, "Executioner's Song," *Spin*, November 1990, 66. For more on the Judas Priest case, see James Richardson, "Satanism in the Courts," in *The Satanism Scare*, ed. James Richardson et al. (New York: de Gruyter, 1991), 211–13; Jeffrey Victor, *Satanic Panic* (Chicago: Open Court, 1993), 168–69.
2. Floyd Martinson, *The Quality of Adolescent Sexual Experiences* (St. Peter, MN: Book Mark, 1974), 5, 123. Similar observations are made in Aaron Hass, *Teenage Sexuality* (New York: Macmillan, 1979), 119.
3. Helen Flanders Dunbar, *Your Preteenager's Mind and Body* (New York: Hawthorn, 1962), 84–85.
4. Alvena Burnite, *Your Teen-Agers* (Milwaukee: Bruce, 1952), 131; "Accept God's Help to Overcome Secret Faults," *Watchtower*, April 15, 1985, 17, *Watchtower Library 2007*, CD-ROM. The importance of distraction in minimizing self-love is also discussed in *Social-Sex Attitudes in Adolescence* (1953, Crawley Films).
5. "Why Avoid Self-Abuse?," *Watchtower*, February 1, 1972, 94, *Watchtower Library 2007*, CD-ROM; "Breaking Free of Self-Abuse—Why? How?," *Watchtower*, September 15, 1973, 569, *Watchtower Library 2007*, CD-ROM. See also Watchtower Bible and Tract Society of Pennsylvania, *Your Youth*, 41–43, *Watchtower Library 2007*, CD-ROM.
6. "Youth Faces Life Term," *Reading Eagle*, December 20, 1949, 23; Lester Kirkendall, "Sex and Social Policy," *Clinical Pediatrics* 4 (April 1964): 239.
7. Ann Landers, "Stay in Living Room," *Sunday News and Tribune*, February 5, 1961, 20; Amelia Eve, e-mail to author, September 10, 2012.

8. Ann Landers, "Open Your Heart to the New Kitten," *Salina Journal*, July 14, 1968, 19; Ann Landers, "Why All the Fuss over a Bedroom?," *Youngstown Vindicator*, October 1, 1968, 33.
9. Abigail Van Buren, "Is Mother's Mind Dirty?," *Daily Times-News*, July 15, 1969, 3B.
10. Adams' parent-friendly advice can be found in Jean Adams, "Teen Forum," *Daily Times-News*, March 9, 1972, 27; Jean Adams, "Teen Forum," *Reading Eagle*, August 31, 1976, 19.
11. "Teenage Sex: Letting the Pendulum Swing," *Time*, August 21, 1972, 38; John White, *Parents in Pain* (Westmont, IL: InterVarsity, 1979), 63.
12. Martinson, *Quality of Adolescent Sexual Experiences*, 71; Robert Sorensen, *Adolescent Sexuality in Contemporary America* (Cleveland, OH: World, 1973), 69; Leslie, e-mail to author, September 10, 2012. The teen bedroom is also portrayed as a site of teen sexual experimentation in Alayne Yates, *Sex without Shame* (New York: Morrow, 1978), 219, 221; Hass, *Teenage Sexuality*, 104, 107, 111; Leon Dash, *When Children Want Children* (Champaign, IL: University of Illinois, 1989), 68.
13. "Sex under the Parental Roof: Home Rules," *Time*, August 21, 1972, 36; Anne, e-mail to author, September 9, 2012.
14. "If I Were a Parent . . . [review]" *Variety*, May 17, 1972, 50; Ann Landers, "Sex and the Single Teenager," *Pittsburgh Post-Gazette*, January 12, 1972, 12.
15. Letter to the editor, *NYT*, May 3, 1982, A18; David Van Biema, "What's Gone Wrong with Teen Sex," *People*, April 13, 1987, http://www.people.com/people/archive/article/0,,20096056,00.html (accessed November 18, 2013).
16. "High and Light," *Time*, February 26, 1951, 24; Merrill Folsom, "Westchester Told of Narcotic Peril," *NYT*, April 2, 1960, 25. See also "Pot and Parents," *Time*, August 30, 1968, 44–45; "The Junior Junkie," *Time*, February 16, 1970, 36; Howard Rusk, "An Addict in the Family," *NYT*, April 26, 1970, 66; Linda Greenhouse, "At the Talk Center, They Talk of Drugs," *NYTM*, February 21, 1971, SM68; Bernadine Morris, "When Your Child Is 15, Teetering on the Brink of Maturity," *NYT*, January 12, 1975, 48.
17. Anne, e-mail to author, September 9, 2012.
18. *Keep Off the Grass* (Sid Davis Productions, 1969), 20 min., 40 sec., Internet Archive, http://www.archive.org/details/keep_off_the_grass (accessed September 2, 2008). For some more recent examples of the "finding drugs in the bedroom" trope, see "Surviving Teenagers," *Syracuse Herald-Journal*, March 5, 1980, 23; Bobby Simpson, *Dear Bobby Simpson* (New York: Dell, 1984), 142; Wayne Wooden and Randy Blazak, *Renegade Kids, Suburban Outlaws* (Belmont, CA: Wadsworth, 2001), 79; *I Learned It by Watching You!* (Partnership for a Drug-Free America, 1987), 29 sec.; https://www.youtube.com/watch?v=Y-Elr5K2Vuo (accessed September 11, 2008).
19. Myra MacPherson, "Children, Parents and Pot: 'Basically He's a Good Kid'," *WaPo*, July 8, 1969, D1; Abigail Van Buren, "Dear Abby," *Holland Evening Sentinel*, March 18, 1972, 4.

20. Glenn Bair et al., *When It's Your Kid!* (Kansas City, MO: Lowell, 1978), 46–47, 49.
21. Dick Schaefer, *Choices and Consequences* (Minneapolis, MN: Hazelden, 1987), 38–41, 46. Similar information can be found in Marsha Manatt, *Parents, Peers, and Pot II* (Rockville, MD: GPO, 1983), 19; Robert DuPont, *Getting Tough on Gateway Drugs* (Washington, DC: American Psychiatric, 1985), 90, 231; Kathleen McCoy, *Coping with Teenage Depression* (New York: Penguin, 1985), 150; George Beschner and Alfred Friedman, *Teen Drug Use* (Lexington, MA: Lexington, 1986), 189; Joan Anderson, *Teen Is a Four-Letter Word* (White Hall, VA: Betterway, 1990), 76; Chris Lutes, *What Teenagers Are Saying about Drugs & Alcohol* (Wheaton, IL: Campus Life, 1988), 142–43.
22. Jason Baron, *Kids & Drugs* (New York: Perigree, 1984), 14, 22; Carmella Bartimole and John Bartimole, *Teenage Alcoholism and Substance Abuse* (Hollywood, FL: Fell, 1987), 55; Schaefer, *Choices and Consequences*, 60.
23. Margaret Mason, "Travels in Search of a Self," *WaPo*, July 10, 1977, F4; DuPont, *Getting Tough*, 217.
24. Adrienne Salinger, e-mail to author, February 28, 2010. Decoy pop cans are discussed in Barry Abramson, "Head Shop Sparks Protests in Cedarhurst," *NYT*, February 11, 1979, LI12; Elisabeth Brynner, "New Parental Push against Marijuana," *NYTM*, February 10, 1980, SM10. The bed with "behind the headboard" storage can be found in Scan advertisement, *Daily Herald*, April 20, 1984, 25. The safe disguised as a book can be found in Secret Book Safe advertisement, *Laugh*, November 1974, 10.
25. "Watching the World," *Awake!* April 8, 1980, 30, *Watchtower Library 2007*, CD-ROM.
26. Marion Howard, *Did I Have a Good Time?* (New York: Continuum, 1982), 100; Laurel, e-mail to author, September 9, 2012; Howard Spanogle, ed., *Teenagers Themselves* (New York: Adama, 1984), 140.
27. "What Parents Can Do to Help Teenager Who Drinks," *Daily Chronicle*, January 14, 1971, 6; Charles Carroll, *Drugs in Modern Society* (Dubuque, IA: Brown, 1985), 343; Jerry Hull, *No!* (Kansas City: Beacon Hill, 1989), 62–63. Similar arguments can be found in Kay Strom and Lisa Strom, *Mothers and Daughters Together* (Grand Rapids, MI: Baker, 1988), 63.
28. Louie Robinson, "Pam Grier: More Than Just a Sex Symbol," *Ebony*, June 1976, 36; Richard Vandenbergh, "Loneliness: Its Symptoms, Dynamics, and Therapy," *Psychiatric Quarterly* 37 (July 1963): 468; Evelyn Duvall, *Parent and Teenager* (Nashville: Broadman, 1976), 82. For more on the teen bedroom's association with antisocial behavior, see Mary Kelly, *Starring You* (Chicago: Mentzer-Bush, 1949), 44; James Oraker and Char Meredith, *Almost Grown* (San Francisco: Harper & Row, 1980), 102; "Your Secret World," *Seventeen*, 97, 164; "For Youngsters, the Urge to Be Alone Can Be Normal," *Los Angeles Sentinel*, August 13, 1987, B10.
29. "Boy, 13, Sasses Mom, Rebuked, Kills Self," *Jet*, October 22, 1959, 46; Henry Scheer et al., "Events and Conscious Ideation Leading to Suicidal Behavior in Adolescence," *Psychiatric Quarterly* 35 (July 1961): 512.

30. Subcommittee on Juvenile Justice, *Federal Role in Addressing the Tragedy of Youth Suicide* (Washington, DC: GPO, 1985), 35, 68–69; Scott Poland, *Suicide Intervention in the Schools* (New York: Guilford, 1989), 54; Rene Diekstra, ed., *Suicide and Its Prevention* (Boston: Brill, 1989), 148.
31. For more on the relationship between excess solitude and teen suicide, see Stuart Finch and Elva Poznanski, *Adolescent Suicide* (Springfield, IL: Thomas, 1971), 56; Joy Hoag, "When the Cry for Help Comes," *Seventeen*, March 1973, 154–55; Myron Benton, "Emotional Problems," *Seventeen*, April 1973, 123, 174; "Girl's Farewell Note Answered by Psychiatrist," *Port Arthur News*, November 3, 1977, 11; Arnold Madison, *Suicide and Young People* (New York: Clarion, 1978), 88; Jim Jerome, "Catching Them before Suicide," *NYTM*, January 14, 1979, SM10–11; Nancy Rubin, "Teenage Suicide Reported on the Rise," *NYT*, August 5, 1979, WC1; "Suicide Belt," *Time*, September 1, 1980, 56; "Recognizing Trouble in Teen-Agers," *NYT*, September 30, 1981, C10; "When a Teenager Gets Really Depressed," *Changing Times*, June 1982, 27; Sandra Gardner, "Danger Signals to Watch For," *NYT*, April 10, 1983, NJ17; G. Keith Olson, *Counseling Teenagers* (Loveland, CO: Group, 1984), 46, 368; Glenn Kaup, "Teen-Age Tragedy: Suicide Has Become an Adolescent Health Problem," *Daily Intelligencer*, September 13, 1984, 8; Barbara Hicks, *Youth Suicide* (Bloomington, IN: NES, 1990), 37.
32. Frederic Wertham, "What Parents Don't Know about Comic Books," *LHJ*, November 1953, 215. The fears generated by comic books are discussed in greater detail in Bradford Wright, *Comic Book Nation* (Baltimore, MD: Johns Hopkins, 2001), ch. 4; David Hadju, *The Ten-Cent Plague* (New York: Picador, 2009), passim.
33. "Mother Blames 'Girlie' Books for Son's Troubles," *Bakersfield Californian*, December 9, 1952, 4; Alfred Roller, "Obscene Magazines Corrupt Morals of Our Young People," *Daily Reporter*, June 8, 1959, 1.
34. Burnite, *Your Teen-Agers*, 57; Frank and Frank, *Your Adolescent at Home and in School*, 171–72.
35. The box-office success of *Deep Throat* and *The Devil in Miss Jones* is discussed in Vernon Scott, "Inside Hollywood," *Tyrone Daily Herald*, January 2, 1974, 12.
36. Abigail Van Buren, "Girlie Magazine Fan Needs Talk," *Ogden Standard-Examiner*, February 18, 1963, 5.
37. Rita Kramer, "The Dirty Book Bit," *NYTM*, June 9, 1968, SM102; Abigail Van Buren, "Dear Abby," *Chronicle Telegram*, January 29, 1977, 9.
38. US Commission on Obscenity and Pornography, *The Report of the Commission on Obscenity and Pornography* (New York: Bantam, 1970), 32; United States Attorney General's Commission on Pornography, *Final Report of the Attorney General's Commission on Pornography* (Nashville: Rutledge, 1986), 489.
39. Simpson, *Dear Bobby Simpson*, 30–31.
40. Jeff Steele, e-mail to author, December 9, 2013.
41. Bill Fisher and Florence Fisher, "Is Rock-and-Roll Bad for Teen-Agers?," *Tri-City Herald*, March 23, 1958, 6; Bill Lhotka, "Hippie Song Combos Seen as Threat," *Alton Telegraph*, September 23, 1967, A6; John Leland, "Son of a

Preacher Man," *Spin*, October 1989, 58. Larson's crusade against rock music received extensive coverage in the late 1960s and early 1970s. See "Ex-Rock and Roll Singer at Auditorium Saturday," *Anniston Star*, December 3, 1970, 11A; "Former Rock Performer to Conduct Workshop," *News-Palladium*, May 8, 1974, 7; Jim Eaton, "Ex-Rock Singer Turns to Gospel to Tell about Satanism, Drugs," *Daily Reporter*, September 10, 1974, A9. For a more scholarly look at the backlash against rock and roll, see Linda Martin and Kerry Segrave, *Anti-Rock* (New York: Da Capo, 1993), passim.

42. "Gospel Video," *Tyrone Daily Herald*, August 12, 1985, 4.
43. Ed Kiersh, "Book of Shadows," *Spin*, August 1988, 24; Victor, *Satanic Panic*, 166. The letter describing Sullivan's pact with Satan is discussed in "Devil Worship: Exposing Satan's Underground," *A Geraldo Rivera Special*, NBC, October 25, 1988, http://www.youtube.com/watch?v=EcWbuBPNtPw (accessed March 14, 2013).
44. Kiersh, "Book of Shadows," *Spin*, 24, 68.
45. Tamara Jones, "Satanists' Trail: Dead Pets to a Human Sacrifice," *Los Angeles Times*, October 19–20, 1988, http://articles.latimes.com/1988-10-19/news/mn-3570_1_human-sacrifice (accessed March 12, 2013).
46. Roland's mother is quoted in Sananda, *Satan's Drummers* (Phoenix, AZ: Phoenix, 1995), 133. The remaining quotations in this paragraph can be found in T. Jones, "Satanists' Trail." For more on the purported relationship between heavy metal music, the occult, and teen violence, see Victor, *Satanic Panic*, 330–54.
47. Harold Kennedy, "Expert Advice: Keep Control of Family Fun," *USN&WR*, October 28, 1985, 54; Jon Anderson, "Satanic Crime Police Say the Devil Made Some People Do It," *Chicago Tribune*, April 18, 1988, 3. Similar claims are made in Rick Jones, *Stairway to Hell* (Ontario, CA: Chick, 1988), 199.
48. Adrienne Salinger, preface to *In My Room* (San Francisco: Chronicle Books, 1995).

CHAPTER EIGHT

Epigraph: Tom Shales, "Brian Wilson Proves Monosyllabic," *Newark Advocate*, September 2, 1976, 17. The title of this chapter comes from Barenaked Ladies, "Brian Wilson," from the album *Gordon*, lyrics and music by Steven Page, Reprise/Sire, 1992.

1. Beach Boys, "In My Room," from the album *Surfer Girl*, lyrics and music by Brian Wilson and Gary Usher, Capitol, 1963.
2. Wilson's thoughts on practicing harmonies with his brothers, moving into his new room, and being forced to defecate in the kitchen can be found in Brian Wilson, *Wouldn't It Be Nice* (New York: Harper Collins, 1991), 27, 34, 39. His thoughts on feeling safe in his bedroom can be found in David Leaf, *The Beach Boys* (Philadelphia: Courage, 1985), 48. Usher's comments can be found in Steven Gaines, *Heroes and Villains* (New York: Da Capo, 1995), 74.
3. Wilson, *Wouldn't It Be Nice*, 204, 208; Larry McShane, "Beach Boy Brian Wilson Catches Up with Era," *Paris News*, August 27, 1995, 16.

4. Karen Tucker, review of the Goo Goo Dolls' "Jed", *Spin*, July 1989, 119; Jonathan Bernstein and Steven Daly, "Depeche Mode," *Spin*, December 1990, 42.
5. Connie Francis, "Among My Souvenirs," lyrics and music by Edgar Leslie and Lawrence Wright, released as a single by MGM Records, 1959; Connie Francis, "If My Pillow Could Talk," lyrics and music by Jimmy Steward Jr. and Robert Mosely, released as a single by MGM Records, 1963.
6. Connie Francis, *Who's Sorry Now?* (New York: St. Martin's, 1984), 14; Connie Francis, *For Every Young Heart* (Englewood Cliffs, NJ: Prentice-Hall, 1962), 14.
7. Francis, *Who's Sorry Now?*, 46; Francis, *For Every Young Heart*, 30.
8. Francis, *Who's Sorry Now?*, 61–62, 86. Francis's prison décor is also discussed in Francis, *For Every Young Heart*, 181.
9. Faron Young, "Hello Walls." Lyrics and music by Willie Nelson. Released as a single by Capitol, 1961.
10. Suicidal Tendencies, "Institutionalized," from the album *Suicidal Tendencies*, lyrics and music by Mike Muir and Louiche Mayorga, Frontier, 1983; Legs McNeil, "Punk," *Spin*, January 1986, 53.
11. Suicidal Tendencies, "Institutionalized."
12. The video for "Institutionalized" can be seen in its entirety at http://www.youtube.com/watch?v=LoF_a0-7xVQ (accessed January 8, 2013).
13. *Gidget*, dir. Paul Wendkos (1959; Los Angeles: Sony, 2004), DVD.
14. Ibid.
15. *Cooley High*, dir. Michael Schultz (1975; Los Angeles: MGM, 2000), DVD.
16. *Saturday Night Fever*, dir. John Badham (1977; Los Angeles: Warner Brothers, 2007), DVD.
17. Ibid.
18. *Fast Times at Ridgemont High*, dir. Amy Heckerling (1982; Los Angeles: Universal, 2004), DVD.
19. Ibid.
20. Ibid.
21. Ibid.
22. Ibid.
23. *Endless Love*, dir. Franco Zeffirelli (1981; Los Angeles: Universal, 2014), DVD. Sex in the teen bedroom is treated with a lighter touch in *Parenthood*, dir. Ron Howard (1989; Los Angeles: Universal, 1998), DVD.
24. *Endless Love*, dir. Zeffirelli.
25. Ibid.
26. Anonymous, *Go Ask Alice*, ed. Beatrice Sparks (Englewood Cliffs, NJ: Prentice-Hall, 1971), 90, 149–50.
27. Ibid., 93–94.
28. Ibid., 159.
29. Beatrice Sparks, ed., *Jay's Journal* (New York: Times Books, 1979), 5, 13, 18.
30. Ibid., 15, 39, 95, 103, 115.
31. E. A. Proulx, "The Ugly Room," *Seventeen*, August 1972, 242, 288.
32. Ibid., 290.

33. Ibid.
34. Vladimir Nabokov, *Lolita* (New York: Vintage, 1997), 64, 82–83.
35. Ibid., 69; Jane Grayson, *Vladimir Nabokov* (New York: Penguin, 2001), 99.
36. Nabokov, *Lolita*, 184–85, 205.
37. Irving Brecher, Alan Lipscott, and Reuben Ship, "Egbert's Chemistry Set," *The Life of Riley*, season 1, episode 3, dir. Herbert I. Leeds, aired October 18, 1949 (Cherry Hill, NJ: TGG Direct, 2011), DVD. For an archetypal girl's room during the 1950s, see Ed James and Paul West, "Betty Earns a Formal," *Father Knows Best*, season 2, episode 19, dir. William D. Russell, aired January 18, 1956 (Los Angeles: Shout! Factory, 2008), DVD.
38. Bill Manhoff, "Cleaning Up Beaver," *Leave It to Beaver*, season 1, episode 21, dir. Norman Tokar, aired March 7, 1958 (Los Angeles: Universal, 2005), DVD.
39. Ibid.
40. Ibid.
41. Ibid.
42. Albert E. Lewin, "Our Son, the Man," *The Brady Bunch*, season 2, episode 18, dir. Jack Arnold, aired February 5, 1971 (Los Angeles: Paramount, 2005), DVD.
43. Ibid.
44. Ibid.
45. William Raynor and Myles Wilder, "A Room at the Top," *The Brady Bunch*, season 4, episode 23, dir. Lloyd Schwartz, aired March 23, 1973 (Los Angeles: Paramount, 2005), DVD,
46. Ibid.
47. Ibid.
48. Ibid.
49. "Cosby Takes Anti-apartheid Stand," *Milwaukee Journal*, August 26, 1985, 2; "Bill Cosby Calls Anti-apartheid Leader's Wife," *Daily Sentinel*, August 29, 1985, 1. Theo's "Free Mandela" poster is noted in Ron Krabill, *Starring Mandela and Cosby* (Chicago: Univ. of Chicago Press, 2010), 101. Theo's antiapartheid sign is also briefly discussed in Ronald L. Smith, *The Cosby Book* (New York: S.P.I., 1993), 207; Mark Whitaker, *Cosby* (New York: Simon & Schuster, 2014), 340–41. For more on Bill Cosby's antiapartheid activism, see "Cosby Joining Apartheid Protest," *New York*, September 28, 1987, 14.

CONCLUSION

Epigraph: Maggie Jones, "Shutting," *NYT*, January 15, 2006, F46.

1. Andy Furlong, "The Japanese Hikikomori Phenomenon," *Sociological Review* 56 (2008): 309–12; Alan R. Teo, "A New Form of Social Withdrawal in Japan," *International Journal of Social Psychiatry* 56 (2010): 179.
2. National Sleep Foundation, "2004 Sleep in America Poll," March 1, 2004, 28, http://www. sleepfoundation.org (accessed May 21, 2008); Sam Ro, "A Third of America's 18- to 34-Year-Olds Live with Their Parents," *Business Insider*, June 2, 2014, http://www.businessinsider.com/18-34-years-olds-living-with

-parents-2014-6 (accessed June 3, 2014); Jim Rutenberg, "Rousing G.O.P., Ryan Faults 'Missing' Leadership," *NYT*, August 29, 2012, A1. Deutsche Bank's findings have also been confirmed in US Department of Education, *Educational Longitudinal Study of 2002* (Washington, DC: NCES, 2013), 19.

3. The use of the term *failure to launch* to describe a young adult who still lives with his or her parents comes from *Failure to Launch*, dir. Tom Dey (2006; Los Angeles: Paramount, 2006), DVD.
4. Teen Chicago, "Home," http://www.teenchicago.org/exh_home.asp?page=3 (accessed November 22, 2004; site now discontinued). The Fulton quote was taken from Chicago Historical Society, *Teen Chicago*, 2004.
5. Michael Greppi, "The Insider: When Pilots Collide," *Television Week*, November 1, 2004, 8. The door-removal strategy can also be found in *Freaky Friday*, dir. Mark Waters (2003; Burbank, CA: Buena Vista Pictures, 2003); Norma Safford Vela, "No Talking," *Roseanne*, season 2, episode 12, dir. John Pasquin, aired December 12, 1989 (Beverly Hills: Anchor Bay, 2005), DVD.
6. Brendan Koerner, "Mom, a Dog Is Here Sniffing, Um, Oregano," *USN&WR*, October 5, 1998, 62.
7. Brooks Brown and Rob Merritt, *No Easy Answers* (New York: Lantern, 2002), 205; Dave Cullen, *Columbine* (New York: Twelve, 2009), 68, 266, 275.
8. Baby Boomer Headquarters, "Peanut Gallery," http://www.bbhq.com/cgi-bin/pnutlnch.pl (accessed June 13, 2000); Leonard Pitts Jr., "Unspeakable Tragedy, Unjustifiable Game," *Hays Daily News*, June 7, 2006, A4.
9. *Elephant*, dir. Gus Van Sant (2003; Burbank, CA: Warner Home Video, 2004), DVD.
10. Kurt Eichenwald, "Through His Webcam, a Boy Joins a Sordid Online World," *NYT*, December 19, 2005, A1, A30–31. The dangers of "camming" are also explained in Emily Bazelon, "Defining Bullying Down," *NYT*, March 12, 2013, A23.
11. Adrienne Salinger, e-mail to author, February 28, 2010.
12. Ibid.

Bibliography

I. Primary Sources

Newspaper and periodical articles, songs, films, television episodes, and web pages are cited fully in the notes and are not included in this list of references. General lists of those sources are given below.

Abbott, Ernest. *On the Training of Parents*. New York: Houghton Mifflin, 1908.

Adams, Henry. *The Education of Henry Adams*. Boston: Houghton Mifflin, 1971.

Alcott, Louisa May. *Louisa May Alcott: Her Life, Letters, and Journals*. Edited by Ednah D. Cheney. Boston: Roberts Brothers, 1889.

Anderson, Joan. *Teen Is a Four-Letter Word: A Survival Kit for Parents*. White Hall, VA: Betterway Publications, 1990.

Andrews, Cyril. *An Introduction to the Study of Adolescent Education*. New York: Rebman, 1912.

Anonymous. *Go Ask Alice*. Edited by Beatrice Sparks. Englewood Cliffs, NJ: Prentice-Hall, 1971.

Arlitt, Ada Hart. *The Adolescent*. New York: Whittlesy House, 1938.

Astor, Mary. *My Story: An Autobiography*. Garden City, NY: Doubleday, 1959.

Ausubel, David, et al. *Theory and Problems of Adolescent Development*. New York: Grune & Stratton, 1977.

Averill, Lawrence. *Adolescence: A Study in the Teen Years*. New York: Houghton Mifflin, 1936.

Ayer, Sarah Connell. *Diary of Sarah Connell Ayer*. Portland, ME: Lefavor-Tower, 1910.

Bair, Glenn, et al. *When It's Your Kid! The Crisis of Drugs*. Kansas City: Lowell, 1978.

Banning, Evelyn. "Recreational Interests and Needs of High School Youth." *Recreation* 48 (January 1954): 36–47.

Baron, Jason. *Kids & Drugs: A Parent's Handbook of Drug Abuse, Prevention & Treatment*. New York: Perigree Books, 1984.

Bartimole, Carmella, and John Bartimole. *Teenage Alcoholism and Substance Abuse: Causes, Cures, and Consequences*. Hollywood, FL: Frederick Fell, 1987.

Bartow, Harry. *Our Boy: Six Steps to Manhood*. Philadelphia: Union, 1913.

Baruch, Dorothy. *How to Live with Your Teenager*. New York: McGraw-Hill, 1953.

———. *New Ways in Discipline: You and Your Child Today*. New York: Whittlesey House, 1949.

Berube, Allan, and Florence Berube. "Sunset Trailer Park." In *White Trash: Race and Class in America*, edited by Matt Wray and Annalee Newitz, 15–39. New York: Routledge, 1997.

Beschner, George, and Alfred Friedman. *Teen Drug Use*. Lexington, MA: Lexington Books, 1986.

Bigelow, Maurice. *Adolescence: Educational and Hygienic Problems*. New York: Funk & Wagnalls, 1924.

———. *Sex Education*. New York: Macmillan, 1916.

Blaine, Graham. *The Parent's Guide to Adolescence*. Boston: Little Brown, 1962.

Blake, Mary. *Twenty-Six Hours a Day*. Boston: D. Lothrop, 1883.

Blanchard, Phyllis. *The Adolescent Girl: A Study from the Psychoanalytic Viewpoint*. New York: Moffat, Yard, 1920.

Blanton, Smiley, and Margaret Blanton. *Child Guidance*. New York: Century, 1927.

Bloom, Michael. *Adolescent-Parental Separation*. New York: Gardner, 1980.

Blos, Peter. *On Adolescence: A Psychoanalytic Interpretation*. New York: Free Press of Glencoe, 1962.

———. "The Second Individuation Process of Adolescence." *Psychoanalytic Study of the Child* 22 (1967): 162–86.

Bower, Robert. *Television and the Public*. New York: Holt, Rinehart and Winston, 1973.

Boyer, Ruth. *The Happy Adolescent*. Palo Alto, CA: R&E Research Associates, 1981.

Braly, John. *Memory Pictures: An Autobiography*. Los Angeles: Neuner, 1912.

Brando, Marlon. *Brando: Songs My Mother Taught Me*. New York: Random House, 1994.

Bridges, K. M. Banham. "Factors Contributing to Juvenile Delinquency." *Journal of the American Institute of Criminal Law and Criminology* 17 (February 1927): 531–80.

Brown, Charles. "Self-Portrait: The Teen-Type Magazine." *Annals of the American Academy of Political and Social Science* 338 (1961): 13–21.

Browne, Phyllis. *Common-Sense Housekeeping*. New York: Cassell, Petter & Galpin, 1877.

Bruce, E. M. *Aunt Eleanor's Childhood Memories*. Boston: R. A. Ballou, 1863.

———. *Aunt Eleanor's Childhood Memories*. Boston: R. A. Ballou, 1866.

Burdick, William. "Adolescence." In *Boy Training: An Interpretation of the Principles That Underlie Symmetrical Boy Development*, edited by John Alexander, 11–22. New York: Association Press, 1915.

Burnham, Helen, et al. *Boys Will Be Men*. New York: J. B. Lippincott, 1949.

Burnite, Alvena. *Your Teen-Agers: How to Survive Them*. Milwaukee: Bruce Publishing, 1952.

Burr, Hanford. *Studies in Adolescent Boyhood*. Springfield, MA: Seminar Publishing, 1910.

Butterfield, Oliver. *Love Problems of Adolescence*. New York: Emerson Books, 1941.

Cabot, Ella Lyman. *Seven Ages of Childhood*. New York: Houghton Mifflin, 1921.

Carroll, Charles. *Drugs in Modern Society*. Dubuque, IA: W. C. Brown, 1985.

Cavan, Ruth Shonle. *The American Family*. New York: Crowell, 1963.

———. *The Family and the Depression: A Study of One Hundred Chicago Families*. Freeport, NY: Books for Libraries Press, 1969.

Chase, Mary Ellen. *The White Gate: Adventures in the Imagination of a Child*. New York: W. W. Norton, 1954.

Chermayeff, Serge, and Christopher Alexander. *Community and Privacy: Toward a New Architecture of Humanism*. Garden City, NJ: Doubleday, 1963.

Chicago Historical Society. *Teen Chicago*. 2004.

Child, Lydia Maria. *The Mother's Book*. New York: Carter, Hendee, and Babcock, 1831.

Clark, Dick. *Your Happiest Years*. New York: Rosho, 1959.

Cole, Luella and John Morgan. *Psychology of Childhood and Adolescence*. New York: Rinehart, 1947.

Conklin, Edmund. "The Foster Child Fantasy." *American Journal of Psychology* 31 (January 1920): 59–76.

———. *Principles of Adolescent Psychology*. New York: Henry Holt, 1935.

Conroy, Joseph. *Talks to Boys*. St. Louis: Queen's Press, 1915.

Creighton, Louise. *The Art of Living and Other Addresses to Girls*. New York: Longmans, Green, 1909.

Daniels, Harriet. *The Girl and Her Chance*. New York: Fleming H. Revell, 1914.

Dash, Leon. *When Children Want Children: The Urban Crisis of Teenage Childbearing*. Champaign: University of Illinois Press, 1989.

Diekstra, Rene, ed. *Suicide and Its Prevention: The Role of Attitude and Imitation*. Boston: E. J. Brill, 1989.

Dimock, Hedley. *Rediscovering the Adolescent: A Study of Personality Development in Adolescent Boys*. New York: Association Press, 1937.

Dizik, Allen, ed. *Encyclopedia of Interior Design and Decoration*. Burbank, CA: Stratford House, 1970.

Dobson, James. *Hide or Seek*. Old Tappan, NJ: Fleming H. Revell, 1974.

Dow, Emily. *Of Parties and Petticoats*. New York: M. Barrows, 1960.

Dunbar, Helen Flanders. *Your Preteenager's Mind and Body*. New York: Hawthorn Books, 1962.

DuPont, Robert. *Getting Tough on Gateway Drugs: A Guide for the Family*. Washington, DC: American Psychiatric Press, 1985.

Duvall, Evelyn Millis. *Parent and Teenager: Living and Loving*. Nashville: Broadman, 1976.

———. *Today's Teen-Agers*. New York: Association Press, 1966.

Elliott, Grace Loucks. *Understanding the Adolescent Girl*. New York: Henry Holt, 1930.
Erikson, Erik. *Identity, Youth, and Crisis*. New York: W. W. Norton, 1968.
Evans, Danny. *Rage against the Meshugenah: Why It Takes Balls to Go Nuts*. New York: Penguin, 2009.
Evans, Robert. *The Kid Stays in the Picture*. Beverly Hills, CA: Phoenix Books, 1994.
Falconer, Martha. "Causes of Delinquency among Girls." *Annals of the American Academy of Political and Social Science* 36 (July 1910): 77–79.
Faulkner, Ray, and Sarah Faulkner. *Inside Today's Home*. New York: Holt, Rinehart, and Winston, 1960.
Finch, Stuart, and Elva Poznanski. *Adolescent Suicide*. Springfield, IL: Thomas, 1971.
Fiske, G. Walter. "The Boy's Home Relationships." In *Boy Training: An Interpretation of the Principles That Underlie Symmetrical Boy Development*, edited by John Alexander, 37–54. New York: Association Press, 1915.
Fleege, Urban. *Self-Revelation of the Adolescent Boy*. Milwaukee: Bruce Publishing, 1948.
Forbush, William. *The Boy Problem in the Home*. New York: Pilgrim Press, 1915.
Foulke, William. *A Hoosier Autobiography*. New York: Oxford University Press, 1922.
Fowler, Nathaniel. *The Boy: How to Help Him Succeed*. New York: Moffat, Yard, 1912.
Fowler, O. S. *A Home for All*. New York: Fowler and Wells, 1854.
Francis, Connie. *For Every Young Heart*. Englewood Cliffs, NJ: Prentice-Hall, 1962.
———. *Who's Sorry Now?* New York: St. Martin's Press, 1984.
Frank, Mary, and Lawrence Frank. *Your Adolescent at Home and in School*. New York: Viking, 1956.
Franklin, Penelope, ed. *Private Pages: Diaries of American Women, 1830s to 1970s*. New York: Ballantine, 1986.
Freud, Sigmund. "The Development of the Libido and the Sexual Organizations." In *Introductory Lectures on Psychoanalysis*, edited by Angela Richards, translated by James Strachey, 397–420. Harmondsworth, UK: Penguin Books, 1974.
———. *Dora: An Analysis of a Case of Hysteria*. Edited by Phillip Rieff. New York: Collier Books, 1963.
———. "Family Romances." In *The Freud Reader*, edited by Peter Gay, 297–300. New York: W. W. Norton, 1989.
———. "On the Universal Tendency to Debasement in the Sphere of Love." In *The Freud Reader*, edited by Peter Gay, 394–99. New York: W. W. Norton, 1989.
———. "The Origin and Development of Psychoanalysis." *American Journal of Psychology* 21 (April 1910): 181–218.
———. "Three Essays on the Theory of Sexuality." In *On Sexuality: Three Essays on the Theory of Sexuality and Other Works*, edited by Angela Richards, translated by James Strachey, 33–170. New York: Penguin Books, 1977.
Furlong, Andy. "The Japanese Hikikomori Phenomenon: Acute Social Withdrawal among Young People." *Sociological Review* 56 (2008): 309–25.
Gale, Harlow. "A Typical Adolescent Religious Experience." *Journal of Adolescence* 1 (1900): 17–25.
Gesell, Arnold. *Youth: The Years from Ten to Sixteen*. New York: Harper & Row, 1956.

Gibson, H. W. *Boyology*. New York: Association Press, 1922.

Ginott, Haim. *Between Parent and Teenager*. New York: Macmillan, 1969.

Ginzberg, Eli. *The Unemployed*. New Brunswick, NJ: Transaction Publishing, 2004. First published 1934 by Harper & Brothers.

Glustrom, Simon. *Living with Your Teenager: A Guide for Jewish Parents*. New York: Bloch, 1961.

Goldstein, Emmanuel, ed. *The Best of 2600: A Hacker Odyssey*. Indianapolis, IN: Wiley, 2009.

Goodman, Irene. "Television's Role in Family Interaction: A Family Systems Perspective." *Journal of Family Issues* 4 (June 1983): 405–24.

Goodrich, Samuel. *Recollections of a Lifetime*. Vol 1. New York: Miller, Orton, 1856.

Gough, John. *An Autobiography*. Boston: self-published, 1845.

Gould, Shirley. *Teenagers: The Continuing Challenge*. New York: Hawthorn Books, 1977.

Grayson, Alice Barr. *Do You Know Your Daughter?* New York: Appleton-Century, 1944.

Greenacre, Phyllis. *Trauma, Growth, and Personality*. New York: International University Press, 1952.

Gross, Lynn, and R. Patricia Walsh. "Factors Affecting Parental Control Over Children's Television Viewing: A Pilot Study." *Journal of Broadcasting* 24 (Summer 1980): 411–19.

Gruenberg, Sidonie. *Your Child Today and Tomorrow*. Philadelphia: J. B. Lippincott, 1920.

Hall, G. Stanley. *Adolescence*. 2 vols. 2nd ed. New York: D. Appleton, 1904.

———. *Life and Confessions of a Psychologist*. New York: Arno Press, 1977. First published 1923 by D. Appleton.

———. *Youth: Its Education, Regime, and Hygiene*. New York: Arno Press, 1972. First published 1906 by D. Appleton.

Hall, Winfield. *The Biology, Physiology, and Sociology of Reproduction*. Chicago: Wynnewood, 1913.

———. *From Youth into Manhood*. New York: Association Press, 1925.

Hallowell, Benjamin. *Autobiography of Benjamin Hallowell*. Philadelphia: Friends' Book Association, 1884.

Hass, Aaron. *Teenage Sexuality: A Survey of Teenage Sexual Behavior*. New York: Macmillan, 1979.

Haupt, Enid. *The Seventeen Book of Young Living*. New York: David McKay, 1957.

Hemery, Michael. *No Permanent Scars*. Columbus, OH: Silenced Press, 2011.

Hess, Robert. "The Adolescent: His Society." *Review of Educational Research* 30 (February 1960): 5–12.

Hicks, Barbara. *Youth Suicide: A Comprehensive Manual for Prevention and Intervention*. Bloomington, IN: National Education Service, 1990.

Hicks, Seymour. *Difficulties: An Attempt to Help*. London: Duckworth, 1924.

Higginson, Thomas Wentworth. *Cheerful Yesterdays*. New York: Houghton Mifflin, 1898.

Hollingshead, August. *Elmstown Youth: The Impact of Social Classes on Adolescents*. New York: John Wiley & Sons, 1949.

Hollingworth, Leta. *The Psychology of the Adolescent*. New York: D. Appleton, 1928.
Holt, L. Emmett. *The Care and Feeding of Children*. New York: D. Appleton, 1894.
Hoover, Rupert. *Enjoy Your Teen-Ager*. New York: Abingdon, 1962.
Howard, Marion. *Did I Have a Good Time? Teenage Drinking*. New York: Continuum, 1982.
Howe, Julia Ward. *Reminiscences, 1819–1899*. New York: Houghton Mifflin, 1899.
Hull, Jerry. *No! The Positive Response to Alcohol*. Kansas City, MO: Beacon Hill Press of Kansas City, 1989.
Jenkins, Joan. *A Girl's World*. New York: Hawthorn Books, 1967.
Johnson, Franklin. "The Problems of Boyhood: A Course of Ethics for Boys in the Sunday School: IX–XII." *Biblical World* 43 (April 1914): 257–64.
Johnson, Mel. *How to Live with Your Teenager*. Tempe, AZ: Success with Youth, ca. 1970.
Jones, Rick. *Stairway to Hell: The Well-Planned Destruction of Teens*. Ontario, CA: Chick Publications, 1988.
Katz, Donald. *Home Fires: An Intimate Portrait of One Middle-Class Family in Postwar America*. New York: Aaron Asher Books, 1992.
Kelly, Margaret. *Starring You*. Chicago: Mentzer-Bush, 1949.
Kirkendall, Lester. "Sex and Social Policy." *Clinical Pediatrics* 4 (April 1964): 236–46.
Kirtley, James. *That Boy of Yours: Sympathetic Studies of Boyhood*. New York: Hodder & Stoughton, 1912.
Knott, Laura. *Vesper Talks to Girls*. New York: Houghton Mifflin, 1916.
Kuhlen, Raymond. *The Psychology of Adolescent Development*. New York: Harper & Row, 1952.
Landers, Ann. *Since You Ask Me*. Englewood Cliffs, NJ: Prentice-Hall, 1961.
Larcom, Lucy. *A New England Girlhood*. New York: Houghton Mifflin, 1889.
Lasch, Christopher. *The Culture of Narcissism: American Life in an Age of Diminishing Expectations*. New York: W. W. Norton, 1978.
Leigh, Geoffrey. "Adolescent Involvement in Family Systems." In *Adolescents in Families*, edited by Geoffrey Leigh and Garry Peterson, 38–72. Cincinnati: South-Western Publishing, 1986.
Levin, Jack, and Ernie Anastos. *'Twixt: Teens Yesterday and Today*. New York: Franklin Watts, 1983.
Lutes, Chris. *What Teenagers Are Saying about Drugs & Alcohol*. Wheaton, IL: Campus Life, 1988.
Lyle, Jack. "Television in Daily Life: Patterns of Use Overview." In *Television and Social Behavior*, edited by John Murray et al., 1–32. Washington, DC: Government Printing Office, 1972.
Lyle, Jack, and Heidi Hoffman. "Children's Use of Television and Other Media." In *Television and Social Behavior*, edited by Eli Rubenstein et al., 129–256. Washington, DC: Government Printing Office, 1972.
Maas, Henry. "Some Social Class Differences in the Family Systems and Group Relations of Pre and Early Adolescents." *Child Development* 22 (June 1951): 145–52.
Madison, Arnold. *Suicide and Young People*. New York: Clarion Books, 1978.
Malmquist, Carl. *Handbook of Adolescence*. New York: Jason Aronson, 1978.

Manatt, Marsha. *Parents, Peers, and Pot II: Parents in Action*. Rockville, MD: Government Printing Office, 1983.

Mander, Jerry. *Four Arguments for the Elimination of Television*. New York: Morrow, 1978.

March, Norah. *Towards Racial Health: A Handbook on the Training of Boys and Girls, Parents, Teachers & Social Workers*. New York: E. P. Dutton, 1919.

Marschak, Marianne. *Parent-Child Interaction and Youth Rebellion*. New York: Gardner, 1980.

Martinson, Floyd. *Infant and Child Sexuality: A Sociological Perspective*. St. Peter, MN: Book Mark, 1973.

———. *The Quality of Adolescent Sexual Experiences*. St. Peter, MN: Book Mark, 1974.

Mavor, William. *The Catechism of Health*. New York: Samuel Wood & Sons, 1819.

McCoy, Kathleen. *Coping with Teenage Depression: A Parent's Guide*. New York: Penguin, 1985.

McDonald, Daniel. "Generational Aspects of Television Coviewing." *Journal of Broadcasting & Electronic Media* 30 (Winter 1986): 75–85.

McKeever, William. *Farm Boys and Girls*. New York: Macmillan, 1913.

Meagher, John. *A Study of Masturbation and Its Reputed Sequelae*. New York: William Wood, 1924.

Melville, Herman. *Moby Dick*. New York: Penguin, 1972.

Miller, Dawn. *Our Time to Be Blessed*. Bloomington, IN: Xlibris, 2010.

Miller, H. Crichton. *The New Psychology and the Parent*. New York: Selzter, 1923.

———. *The New Psychology and the Teacher*. New York: Selzter, 1922.

Mitnick, Kevin, and William Simon. *The Art of Intrusion: The Real Stories behind the Exploits of Hackers, Intruders and Deceivers*. Indianapolis, IN: Wiley, 2005.

———. *Ghosts in the Wires: My Adventures as the World's Most Wanted Hacker*. New York: Little, Brown, 2011.

Moll, Albert. *The Sexual Life of the Child*. New York: Macmillan, 1912.

Mudge, E. Leigh. *The Psychology of Early Adolescence*. New York: Caxton, 1922.

Nabokov, Vladimir. *Lolita*. New York: Vintage, 1997.

Nichols, Mary Gove. *Mary Lyndon, or Revelations of a Life*. New York: Stringer & Townsend, 1855.

Nowlin, William. *The Bark Covered House, or Back in the Woods Again*. Edited by Milo Quaife. Chicago: Lakeside, 1937.

Olson, G. Keith. *Counseling Teenagers: The Complete Christian Guide to Understanding and Helping Adolescents*. Loveland, CO: Group Publishing, 1984.

Oraker, James, and Char Meredith. *Almost Grown*. San Francisco: Harper & Row, 1980.

Osborne, Ernest. *Understanding Your Parents*. New York: Association Press, 1956.

O'Shea, Michael. *The Trend of the Teens*. Chicago: Frederick J. Drake, 1920.

Overton, Grace. *Living with Teeners*. Nashville: Broadman, 1950.

Partridge, E. DeAlton. *Social Psychology of Adolescence*. New York: Prentice-Hall, 1939.

Pechstein, L. A., and A. Laura McGregor. *Psychology of the Junior High School Pupil*. New York: Houghton Mifflin, 1924.

Pemberton, Lois. *The Stork Didn't Bring You*. New York: Hermitage, 1948.

Pepis, Betty. *Be Your Own Decorator*. New York: Pyramid Books, 1961.
Piaget, Jean, and Barbel Inhelder. *The Growth of Logical Thinking from Childhood to Adolescence*. New York: Basic Books, 1958.
Poland, Scott. *Suicide Intervention in the Schools*. New York: Guilford, 1989.
Post, Emily. *The Personality of a House*. New York: Funk & Wagnalls, 1935.
Powell, Marvin. *The Psychology of Adolescence*. New York: Bobbs-Merrill, 1971.
Prentiss, Elizabeth. *Stepping Heavenward*. New York: Randolph, 1880.
Pringle, Ralph. *Adolescence and High-School Problems*. New York: D. C. Heath, 1922.
Pryor, Sara. *My Day: Reminiscences of a Long Life*. New York: Macmillan, 1909.
Puller, Edwin. *Your Boy and His Training: A Practical Treatise on Boy Training*. New York: D. Appleton, 1916.
Purtell, Thelma. *The Intelligent Parents' Guide to Teen-Agers*. New York: P. S. Eriksson, 1961.
Ragaway, Martin. *How to Get a Teenager to Run Away from Home*. Los Angeles: Price Stearn Sloan, 1983.
Reuter, E. B. "The Sociology of Adolescence." *American Journal of Sociology* 43 (November 1937): 414–27.
Richardson, Norman. *The Religious Education of Adolescents*. New York: Abingdon, 1918.
Richmond, Winifred. "Sex Problems of Adolescence." *Journal of Educational Sociology* 8 (February 1935): 333–41.
Riddell, Newton. *Child Culture*. Chicago: Riddell Publishers, 1915.
Riemer, Svend. "The Family and Its Home." *Marriage and Family Living* 4 (November 1942): 77–79, 84.
———. "Sociological Theory of Home Adjustment." *American Sociological Review* 8 (June 1943): 272–78.
Riley, John, et al. "Some Observations on the Social Effects of Television." *Public Opinion Quarterly* 13 (Summer 1949): 223–34.
Ripley, Eliza. *Social Life in Old New Orleans: Being Recollections of My Girlhood*. New York: D. Appleton, 1907.
Rockwell, A. D. *Rambling Recollections: An Autobiography*. New York: Paul B. Hoeber, 1920.
Rogers, Dorothy. *Adolescence: A Psychological Perspective*. Monterey, CA: Brooks/Cole, 1972.
Roosevelt, Theodore. *Theodore Roosevelt: An Autobiography*. New York: Charles Scribner's Sons, 1922.
Salinger, Adrienne. *In My Room: Teenagers in Their Bedroom*. San Francisco: Chronicle Books, 1995.
Sananda, *Satan's Drummers: The Secret Beat of Evil Satan Is Alive and Well*. Phoenix, AZ: Phoenix Source Distributors, 1995.
Schaefer, Dick. *Choices and Consequences: What to Do when a Teenager Uses Alcohol/Drugs*. Minneapolis, MN: Hazelden Publishing, 1987.
Scheer, Henry, et al. "Events and Conscious Ideation Leading to Suicidal Behavior in Adolescence." *Psychiatric Quarterly* 35 (July 1961): 507–15.

Schubert, Paul. *The Electric Word: The Rise of Radio*. New York: Macmillan, 1928.

Schwab, Sidney, and Borden Veeder. *The Adolescent: His Conflicts and Escapes*. New York: D. Appleton, 1929.

Schwartz, Barry. "The Social Psychology of Privacy." *American Journal of Sociology* 6 (May 1968): 741–52.

Sherman, Steve. "A Set of One's Own: TV Sets in Children's Bedrooms." *Journal of Advertising Research* 36 (November-December 1996): 9–12.

Simpson, Bobby. *Dear Bobby Simpson*. New York: Dell, 1984.

Sinclair, Upton. *The Autobiography of Upton Sinclair*. New York: Harcourt, Brace & World, 1962.

Slater, Philip. *The Pursuit of Loneliness: American Culture at the Breaking Point*. Boston: Beacon, 1971.

Slattery, Margaret. *The Girl in Her Teens*. Philadelphia: Sunday School Times Company, 1910.

Slaughter, J. W. *The Adolescent*. New York: Macmillan, 1915.

Smith, Richard. *Twigs for Nests, or Notes on Nursery Nurture*. London: James Nisbet, 1866.

Smith, Thomas. "Influence in Parent-Adolescent Relationships." In *Adolescents in Families*, edited by Geoffrey Leigh and Garry Peterson, 130–54. Cincinnati: South-Western Publishing, 1986.

Sorensen, Robert. *Adolescent Sexuality in Contemporary America: Personal Values and Sexual Behavior, Ages Thirteen to Nineteen*. Cleveland, OH: World Publishing, 1973.

Spanogle, Howard, ed. *Teenagers Themselves*. New York: Adama Books, 1984.

Sparks, Beatrice, ed. *Jay's Journal*. New York: Times Books, 1979.

Spock, Benjamin. *Baby and Child Care*. 5th ed. New York: Pocket Books, 1963.

Stanton, Anna. *My Autobiography*. Des Moines, IA: Bishard Brothers, 1908.

Starr, Louis. *The Adolescent Period: Its Features and Management*. Philadelphia: P. Blakiston's Son, 1915.

Stone, Joseph, and Joseph Church. *Childhood and Adolescence*. New York: Random House, 1968.

Strain, Bruce. *Teen Days: A Book for Boys and Girls*. New York: D. Appleton-Century, 1946.

Strang, Ruth. "The Transition from Childhood to Adolescence." In *Understanding Adolescence*, edited by James Adams, 13–42. Boston: Allyn and Bacon, 1968.

Strom, Kay, and Lisa Strom. *Mothers and Daughters Together: We Can Work It Out*. Grand Rapids, MI: Baker Book House, 1988.

Subcommittee on Juvenile Justice, *Federal Role in Addressing the Tragedy of Youth Suicide*. Washington, DC: Government Printing Office, 1985.

Talmey, B. S. *Genesis: A Manual for the Instruction of Children in Matters Sexual*. New York: Practitioners' Publishing, 1910.

Taylor, Katharine. *Understanding and Guiding the Adolescent Child*. New York: Grosset & Dunlap, 1938.

Teo, Alan "A New Form of Social Withdrawal in Japan: A Review of Hikikomori." *International Journal of Social Psychiatry* 56 (2010): 178–85.

Thom, Douglas. *Child Management*. Washington, DC: Government Printing Office, 1925.

———. *Guiding the Adolescent*. 2nd ed. Washington, DC: Government Printing Office, 1946.

Todd, Mabel Loomis, Papers. Yale University Library and Archives.

Tracy, Frederick. *The Psychology of Adolescence*. New York: Macmillan, 1920.

Trumbull, H. Clay. *Hints on Child Training*. Philadelphia: John D. Wattles, 1891.

US Attorney General's Commission on Pornography. *Final Report of the Attorney General's Commission on Pornography*. Nashville: Rutledge Hill, 1986.

US Children's Bureau. *The Adolescent in Your Family*. Washington, DC: Government Printing Office, 1954.

———. *Moving into Adolescence*. Washington, DC: Government Printing Office, 1970.

———. *Your Child from 6 to 12*. Washington, DC: Government Printing Office, 1972.

US Commission on Obscenity and Pornography. *The Report of the Commission on Obscenity and Pornography*. New York: Bantam Books, 1970.

US Department of Commerce. *Demographic Trends in the Twentieth Century*. Washington, DC: Government Printing Office, 2002.

———. *Historical Statistics of the United States, Colonial Times to 1970*. Washington, DC: Government Printing Office, 1975.

———. *Statistical Abstract of the United States*. Vol. 105. Washington, DC: Government Printing Office, 1984.

———. *Statistical Abstract of the United States*. Vol. 131. Washington, DC: Government Printing Office, 2011.

US Department of Education. *Educational Longitudinal Study of 2002: A First Look at 2002 High School Sophomores 10 Years Later.* Washington, DC: National Center for Education Statistics, 2013.

Vandenbergh, Richard. "Loneliness: Its Symptoms, Dynamics, and Therapy." *Psychiatric Quarterly* 37 (July 1963): 466–75.

Watson, John. *Psychological Care of Infant and Child*. London: George Allen & Unwin Limited, 1928.

Weiss, Brett. *Classic Home Video Games, 1985–1988: A Complete Reference Guide*. Jefferson, NC: McFarland, 2012.

White, John. *Parents in Pain*. Westmont, IL: InterVarsity Press, 1979.

White House Conference on Child Health and Protection. *The Adolescent in the Family: A Study of Personality Development in the Home Environment*. New York: D. Appleton-Century, 1934.

Wile, Ira. *The Challenge of Adolescence*. New York: Greenberg, 1939.

Williams, Frankwood. *Adolescence: Studies in Mental Hygiene*. New York: Farrar & Rinehart, 1930.

Williamson, Audrey. *Your Teen-Ager and You*. Anderson, IN: Warner Books, 1952.

Wilson, Brian. *Wouldn't It Be Nice: The Creative Genius behind the Beach Boys*. New York: Harper Collins, 1991.

Winch, Robert. *The Modern Family*. New York: Holt, Rinehart and Winston, 1963.
Winn, Marie. *The Plug-In Drug*. New York: Viking, 1977.
Winterburn, Florence. *From the Child's Standpoint*. New York: Baker and Taylor, 1899.
Wood, Edith. "The Statistics of Room Congestion: Purpose and Technique." *Journal of the American Statistical Association* 23 (September 1928): 263–73.
Wood, John Allen. *The Autobiography of John Allen Wood*. Chicago: Christian Witness Company, 1904.
Wooden, Wayne, and Randy Blazak. *Renegade Kids, Suburban Outlaws: From Youth Culture to Delinquency*. Belmont, CA: Wadsworth, 2001.
Yates, Alayne. *Sex without Shame: Encouraging the Child's Healthy Sexual Development*. New York: William Morrow, 1978.
Yeomans, Edward. *Shackled Youth*. Boston: Atlantic Monthly Press, 1921.
Zim, Herbert. *Science Interests and Activities of Adolescents*. New York: Ethical Culture Schools, 1940.

CD/DVD-ROMS

Rolling Stone Cover to Cover: The First 40 Years. DVD-ROM. Bondi Digital Publishing, 2007.
Watchtower Library 2007. CD-ROM. Watch Tower Bible and Tract Society of Pennsylvania, 2006.

CONTEMPORARY FIRSTHAND ACCOUNTS

Adrienne Salinger (Northern California)
Amelia Eve (Northern California)
Anne (Northeast US)
Anthony Bernier (Los Angeles)
Bill Hendley (Los Angeles)
Bob Peticolas (El Paso, Texas)
Casey Calloway (Cumming, Georgia)
Douglas Mitchell (Wilmette, Illinois)
Greg (Blaine, Minnesota)
Jeff Steele (Corvallis, Oregon)
Jorge Oliveras (Miami, Florida)
Laurel (San Jose, California)
Leslie (Nampa, Idaho)
Nancy (Utica, Michigan)
Paul Fassbender
Paul Hoffman (New Jersey; California)
Roger (Irving, Texas)
Tiffany Hauck (Vancouver, Washington)
William Geurts (Portland, Oregon)

FILMS

Back to the Future, Universal, 1985.
Cooley High, MGM, 1975.
Elephant, Warner, 2003.
Endless Love, Universal, 1981.
Failure to Launch, Paramount, 2006.
Fast Times at Ridgemont High, Universal, 1982.
Freaky Friday, Disney, 2003.
Gidget, Sony, 1959.
Gimme Shelter, Warner Brothers, 1970.
Keep Off the Grass, Sid Davis Productions, 1969.
Parenthood, Universal, 1989.
Saturday Night Fever, Warner Brothers, 1977.
The Snob, Centron, 1958.
Social-Sex Attitudes in Adolescence, Crawley, 1953.
Teddy, Extension Media Center, 1971.
WarGames, Twentieth Century Fox, 1983.
Woodstock, Warner Brothers, 1970.

MUSIC

"Among My Souvenirs," Connie Francis, MGM Records, 1959.
"Brian Wilson," Barenaked Ladies, *Gordon*, Reprise/Sire, 1992.
"Camarillo Brillo," Frank Zappa and the Mothers of Invention, *Over-Nite Sensation*, DiscReet, 1973.
"Hello Walls," Faron Young, Capitol, 1961.
"If My Pillow Could Talk," Connie Francis, MGM Records, 1963.
"In My Room," Beach Boys, *Surfer Girl*, Capitol, 1963.
"Institutionalized," Suicidal Tendencies, *Suicidal Tendencies*, Frontier, 1983.

NEWSPAPERS

Alton Telegraph (Alton, IL)
Anderson Daily Bulletin (Anderson, IN)
Anniston Star (Anniston, AL)
Atlanta World
Austin News (Chicago, IL)
Bakersfield Californian
Brainerd Daily Dispatch (Brainerd, MN)
Capital (Annapolis, MD)
Charleston Gazette (Charlestown, WV)
Chicago Defender

Chicago Sun-Times
Chicago Tribune
Christian Science Monitor [*CSM*]
Chronicle Telegram (Elyria, OH)
Daily Chronicle (Centralia, WA)
Daily Courier (Connellsville, PA)
Daily Herald (Chicago, IL)
Daily Intelligencer (Doylestown, PA)
Daily Reporter (Dover, OH)
Daily Sentinel (Sitka, AK)
Daily Times-News (Burlington, NC)
Danville Register (Danville, VA)
Davenport Democrat and Leader (Davenport, IA)
Dominion-News (Morgantown, WV)
Frederick News (Frederick, MD)
Frederick News-Post (Frederick, MD)
Frederick Post (Frederick, MD)
Galveston Daily News (Galveston, TX)
Hammond Times (Hammond, IN)
Hays Daily News (Hays, KS)
Holland Evening Sentinel (Holland, MI)
Index-Journal (Greenwood, SC)
Indiana Gazette (Indiana, PA)
Iowa City Press Citizen (Iowa City, IA)
Journal News (Hamilton, OH)
Lima News (Lima, OH)
Los Angeles Sentinel
Los Angeles Times
Milwaukee Journal
Milwaukee Journal Sentinel
Morgantown Post (Morgantown, WV)
Mountain Democrat (Placerville, CA)
Newark Advocate (Newark, NJ)
News Journal (Mansfield, OH)
News-Palladium (Benton Harbor, MI)
New York Times [*NYT*]
Oakland Tribune
Odessa American (Odessa, TX)
Ogden Standard-Examiner (Ogden, UT)
Olean Evening Times (Olean, NY)
Panama City News (Panama City, FL)
Paris News (Paris, TX)
Pittsburgh Post-Gazette

Port Arthur News (Port Arthur, TX)
Post Crescent (Appleton, WI)
Post-Standard (Syracuse, NY)
Reading Eagle (Reading, PA)
Record Eagle (Traverse City, MI)
Reno Evening Gazette (Reno, NV)
Salina Journal (Salina, KS)
Santa Cruz Sentinel (Santa Cruz, CA)
Sheboygan Press (Sheboygan, WI)
Chicago Heights Star (Chicago Heights, IL)
Suburban Economist (Chicago, IL)
Sunday Journal & Star (Lincoln, NE)
Sunday News and Tribune (Jefferson City, MO)
Syracuse Herald-Journal (Syracuse, NY)
Times Recorder (Zanesville, OH)
Traverse City Record Eagle (Traverse City, MI)
Tri-City Herald (Pasco, WA)
Tyrone Daily Herald (Tyrone, PA)
U.S. News & World Report [*USN&WR*]
Van Nuys News (Van Nuys, CA)
Wall Street Journal [*WSJ*]
Washington Post [*WaPo*]
Youngstown Vindicator (Youngstown, OH)

PERIODICALS

Boys' Life
Analysts Journal
Billboard
Business Insider
Changing Times
Co-ed
Computerworld
Consumer Reports
Dealerscope
Ebony
Ebony Jr.
Financial Analysts Journal
Harper's
House & Garden [*H&G*]
Jet
Ladies' Home Journal [*LHJ*]
Laugh
Life

Mother's Magazine
Mother's Nursery Guide
Newsweek
New York
New York Times Magazine [*NYTM*]
New Yorker
Now
Parents' Magazine
People
Playboy
Popular Mechanics
Popular Science
Printers' Ink
Rotarian
Seventeen
Spin
Sports Illustrated
Television Week
Time
Variety
Wireless Age

TELEVISION

The Adventures of Ozzie and Harriet, ABC, 1952–1966.
The Aldrich Family, NBC, 1949–1953.
The Brady Bunch, ABC, 1969–1974.
Clubhouse, CBS, 2004–2005.
The Cosby Show, NBC, 1984–1992.
Desperate Housewives, ABC, 2004–2012.
Devil Worship: Exposing Satan's Underground, NBC, 1988.
The Donna Reed Show, ABC, 1958–1966.
Father Knows Best, CBS/NBC, 1954–1962.
The Goldbergs, CBS/NBC/Dumont, 1949–1954.
Leave It to Beaver, CBS/ABC, 1957–1963.
The Life of Riley, NBC, 1949–1950/1953–1958.
Make Room for Daddy, ABC/CBS, 1953–1964.
The Roosevelts, PBS, 2014.
Roseanne, ABC, 1988–1997.

VIDEO GAMES

Super Columbine Massacre RPG, developed by Danny Ledonne, 2005.

WEBSITES

A.V. Club, http://www.avclub.com.
Baby Boomer HeadQuarters, http://www.bbhq.com.
Historic New England, http://www.historicnewengland.org.
Internet Archive, http://www.archive.org.
Kaiser Family Foundation, http://www.kff.org.
National Sleep Foundation, http://www.sleepfoundation.org.
Penn State Division of Student Affairs, http://studentaffairs.psu.edu.
Teen Chicago, http://www.teenchicago.org; site now discontinued.
US Census Bureau, http://www.census.gov.
YouTube, http://www.youtube.com.

II. Secondary Sources

Arnett, Jeffrey. "Adolescents' Uses of Media for Self-Socialization." *Journal of Youth and Adolescence* 24 (October 1995): 519–33.

Belle, Deborah. *The After-School Lives of Children: Alone and with Others while Parents Work*. Mahwah, NJ: Lawrence Erlbaum Associates, 1999.

Bailey, Beth. *From Front Porch to Back Seat: Courtship in Twentieth-Century America*. Baltimore: Johns Hopkins University Press, 1989.

Barfield, Ray. *A Word from Our Viewers: Reflections from Early Television Audiences*. Westport, CT: Praeger, 2008.

Bederman, Gail. *Manliness and Civilization: A Cultural History of Gender and Race in the United States, 1880–1917*. Chicago: University of Chicago Press, 1995.

Benfield, G. J. Barker. *The Horrors of the Half-Known Life: Male Attitudes toward Women and Sexuality in Nineteenth-Century America*. New York: Routledge, 2000.

Bowden, Sue, and Avner Offer. "Household Appliances and the Use of Time: The United States and Britain since the 1920s." *Economic History Review* 47 (November 1994): 725–48.

Braden, Donna. "The Family That Plays Together Stays Together: Family Pastimes and Indoor Amusements, 1890–1930." In *American Home Life, 1880–1930: A Social History of Spaces and Services*, edited by Jessica Foy and Thomas Schlereth, 145–62. Boston: Northeastern University Press, 1992.

Brown, Brooks, and Rob Meritt. *No Easy Answers: The Truth behind Death at Columbine*. New York: Lantern Books, 2002.

Brumberg, Joan Jacobs. *The Body Project: An Intimate History of American Girls*. New York: Random House, 1997.

Buchholz, Esther, and Rochelle Catton. "Adolescents' Perceptions of Aloneness and Loneliness." *Adolescence* 34 (Spring 1999): 203–13.

Burnham, John. *How Superstition Won and Science Lost: Popularizing Science and Health in the United States*. New Brunswick, NJ: Rutgers University Press, 1987.

Burnham, Van, ed. *Supercade: A Visual History of the Video Game Age, 1971–1984.* Cambridge, MA: MIT Press, 2001.

Calvert, Karin. "Children in the House, 1890 to 1930." In *American Home Life, 1880–1930: A Social History of Spaces and Services*, edited by Jessica Foy and Thomas Schlereth, 75–93. Boston: Northeastern University Press, 1992.

Chinn, Sarah. *Inventing Modern Adolescence: The Children of Immigrants in Turn-of-the Century America*. New Brunswick, NJ: Rutgers University Press, 2009.

Chudacoff, Howard. *Children at Play: An American History*. New York: New York University Press, 2007.

Clark, Clifford. *The American Family Home, 1800–1960*. Chapel Hill: University of North Carolina Press, 1986.

Cohen, Lizabeth. *A Consumer's Republic: The Politics of Mass Consumption in Post-war America*. New York: Alfred A. Knopf, 2003.

Coontz, Stephanie. *The Social Origins of Private Life: A History of American Families,1600-1900*. New York: Verso, 1988.

Corsano, Paola, et al. "Psychological Well-Being in Adolescence: The Contribution of Interpersonal Relations and Experience of Being Alone." *Adolescence* 41 (Summer 2006): 341–53.

Cromley, Elizabeth Collins. "A History of American Beds and Bedrooms, 1890–1930." *Perspectives in Vernacular Architecture* 4 (1991): 177–86.

Cross, Gary. *Kids' Stuff: Toys and the Changing World of American Childhood*. New York: Harvard University Press, 1997.

Cullen, Dave. *Columbine*. New York: Twelve, 2009.

Danesi, Marcel. *Cool: The Signs and Meanings of Adolescence*. Toronto: University of Toronto Press, 1994.

Demos, John. *A Little Commonwealth: Family Life in Plymouth Colony*. New York: Oxford University Press, 2000.

Devlin, Rachel. *Relative Intimacy: Fathers, Adolescent Daughters, and Postwar American Culture*. Chapel Hill: University of North Carolina Press, 2005.

Douglas, Susan. *Listening In: Radio and the American Imagination*. Minneapolis: University of Minnesota Press, 1999.

Dudden, Faye. *Serving Women: Household Service in Nineteenth Century America*. Middletown, CT: Wesleyan University Press, 1983.

Easttom, Chuck. *Computer Crime, Investigation, and the Law*. Boston: Cengage Learning, 2011.

Eskridge, Jane, ed. *Before Scarlett: Girlhood Writings of Margaret Mitchell*. Columbia: University of South Carolina Press, 2000.

Fass, Paula. *The Damned and the Beautiful: American Youth in the 1920s*. New York: Oxford University Press, 1977.

Fischer, Claude. "Touch Someone: The Telephone Industry Discovers Sociability." *Technology and Culture* 29 (January 1988): 32–61.

Forman-Brunell, Miriam. *Made to Play House: Dolls and the Commercialization of American Girlhood, 1830–1930*. New Haven, CT: Yale University Press, 1993.

Foucault, Michel. *Discipline and Punish: The Birth of the Prison*. Translated by Alan Sheridan. New York: Vintage Books, 1995.

Friedman, Ted. *Electric Dreams: Computers in American Culture*. New York: New York University Press, 2005.

Gaines, Steven. *Heroes and Villains: The True Story of the Beach Boys*. New York: Da Capo Press, 1995.

Gelatt, Roland. *The Fabulous Phonograph, 1877–1977*. New York: Macmillan, 1977.

Gittleman, Peter. "The Gropius House: Conception, Construction, and Commentary." MA thesis, Boston University, 1996.

Grayson, Jane. *Vladimir Nabokov*. New York: Penguin, 2001.

Hadju, David. *The Ten-Cent Plague: The Great Comic-Book Scare and How It Changed America*. New York: Picador, 2009.

Hafner, Katie, and John Markoff. *Cyberpunk: Outlaws and Hackers on the Computer Frontier*. New York: Touchstone, 1995.

Hale, Nathan. *The Rise and Crisis of Psychoanalysis in the United States*. New York: Oxford University Press, 1995.

Harris, Richard. "The End Justified the Means: Boarding and Rooming in a City of Homes, 1890–1951." *Journal of Social History* 26 (Winter 1992): 331–58.

Hayden, Dolores. *The Grand Domestic Revolution: A History of Feminist Designs for American Homes, Neighborhoods, and Cities*. 4th ed. Cambridge, MA: MIT Press, 1989.

Hergenhahn, B. R. *An Introduction to the History of Psychology*. 5th ed. Belmont, CA: Thomson-Wadsworth, 2005.

Herman, Leonard. *Phoenix: The Rise and Fall of Home Videogames*. Union, NJ: Rolenta, 1994.

Hulbert, Ann. *Raising America: Experts, Parents, and a Century of Advice about Children*. New York: Alfred A. Knopf, 2003.

Hunter, Christine. *Ranches, Rowhouses, and Railroad Flats: American Homes: How They Shape Our Landscapes and Neighborhoods*. New York: W. W. Norton, 1999.

Hunter, Jane. *How Young Ladies Became Girls*. New Haven, CT: Yale University Press, 2002.

Ierley, Merritt. *Open House: A Social, Technological, and Architectural History of the American Home*. New York: Henry Holt, 1999.

Jackson, Kenneth. *Crabgrass Frontier: The Suburbanization of the United States*. New York: Oxford University Press, 1985.

Jacobson, Lisa. "Revitalizing the American Home: Children's Leisure and the Revaluation of Play, 1920–1940." *Journal of Social History* 3 (Spring 1997): 581–96.

James, Kandy. "I Just Gotta Have My Own Space!" *Journal of Leisure Research* 33 (January 2001): 71–90.

Jones, Kathleen. "Mother Made Me Do It." In *Bad Mothers: The Politics of Blame in Twentieth Century America*, edited by Molly Ladd-Taylor and Lauri Umansky, 99–125. New York: New York University Press, 1998.

———. *Taming the Troublesome Child: American Families, Child Guidance, and the Limits of Psychiatric Authority*. Cambridge, MA: Harvard University Press, 1999.

Kaestle, Carl. *Pillars of the Republic: Common Schools and American Society, 1780–1860*. New York: Hill and Wang, 1983.

Kenney, William. *Recorded Music in American Life: The Phonograph and Popular Memory, 1890–1945*. New York: Oxford University Press, 1999.

Kent, Steven. *The Ultimate History of Videogames: From Pong to Pokemon and Beyond*. Roseville, CA: Prima, 2001.

Kerber, Linda. "The Republican Mother: Women and the Enlightenment—An American Perspective." *American Quarterly* 28 (Summer 1976): 187–205.

Kett, Joseph. *Rites of Passage: Adolescence in America, 1790 to the Present*. New York: Basic Books, 1977.

Kirk, Carolyn, and Gordon Kirk. "The Impact of the City on Home Ownership: A Comparison of Immigrants and Native Whites at the Turn of the Century." *Journal of Urban History* 7 (August 1981): 471–98.

Kleinberg, S. J. "Gendered Space: Housing, Privacy, and Domesticity in the Nineteenth-Century United States." In *Domestic Space: Reading the Nineteenth-Century Interior*, edited by Inga Bryden and Janet Floyd, 142–61. New York: St. Martin's Press, 1999.

Krabill, Ron. *Starring Mandela and Cosby: Media and the End(s) of Apartheid*. Chicago: University of Chicago Press, 2010.

Ladd-Taylor, Molly, and Lauri Umansky. Introduction to *Bad Mothers: The Politics of Blame in Twentieth-Century America*, edited by Molly Ladd-Taylor and Lauri Umansky, 1–28. New York: New York University Press, 1998.

Lapsley, Phil. *Exploding the Phone: The Untold Story of the Teenagers and Outlaws who Hacked Ma Bell*. New York: Grove, 2013.

Laqueur, Thomas. *Solitary Sex: A Cultural History of Masturbation*. New York: Zone Books, 2003.

Larson, Reed. "Secrets in the Bedroom: Adolescents' Private Use of Media." *Journal of Youth and Adolescence* 24 (October 1995): 535–50.

Larson, Reed, and Maryse Richards. *Divergent Realities: The Emotional Lives of Mothers, Fathers, and Adolescents*. New York: Basic Books, 1994.

Leach, William. *Land of Desire: Merchants, Power, and the Rise of a New American Culture*. New York: Vintage Books, 1993.

Leaf, David. *The Beach Boys*. Philadelphia: Courage Books, 1985.

Levy, Steven. *Hackers: Heroes of the Computer Revolution*. Cambridge, MA: O'Reilly Media, 2010.

Lingeman, Richard. *Sinclair Lewis: Rebel from Main Street*. New York: Random House, 2002.

Livingstone, Sonia. *Young People and New Media: Childhood and the Changing Media Environment*. London: Sage, 2002.

Lupton, Ellen. *Mechanical Brides: Women and Machines from Home to Office*. Princeton, NJ: Princeton Architectural Press, 1993.

Martin, Linda, and Kerry Segrave. *The Servant Problem: Domestic Workers in North America*. Jefferson, NC: McFarland, 1985.

———. *Anti-Rock: The Opposition to Rock 'n' Roll*. New York: Da Capo, 1993.

May, Elaine Tyler. *Homeward Bound: American Families in the Cold War Era*. New York: Basic Books, 1999.

McLeod, Jack. "Television and Social Relations: Family Influences and Consequences for Interpersonal Behavior." In *Television and Behavior: Ten Years of Scientific Progress and Implications for the Eighties*, edited by David Pearl et al., 272–86. Washington, DC: Government Printing Office, 1982.

McMurry, Sally. *Families and Farmhouses in Nineteenth-Century America: Vernacular Design and Social Change*. New York: Oxford University Press, 1988.

McRobbie, Angela, and Jenny Garber. "Girls and Subcultures." In *Resistance through Rituals: Youth Subcultures in Postwar Britain*, edited by Stuart Hall and Tony Jefferson, 209–22. London: Hutchinson, 1976.

Millard, Andre. *America on Record: A History of Recorded Sound*. New York: Cambridge University Press, 1995.

Miller, Russell. *Bunny: The Real Story of Playboy*. New York: Holt, Rinehart and Winston, 1985.

Mintz, Steven. *Huck's Raft: A History of American Childhood*. Cambridge, MA: Harvard University Press, 2004.

———. "Sources of Variability in Rates of Black Home Ownership in 1900." *Phylon* 44 (4th quarter, 1983): 312–31.

Mintz, Steven, and Susan Kellogg. *Domestic Revolutions: A Social History of American Family Life*. New York: Free Press, 1988.

Mitchell, Claudia, and Jacqueline Reid-Walsh. *Researching Children's Popular Culture: The Cultural Spaces of Childhood*. London: Routledge, 2002.

Modell, John. *Into One's Own: From Youth to Adulthood in the United States, 1920–1975*. Berkeley: University of California Press, 1989.

Monkkonen, Eric. *America Becomes Urban: The Development of U.S. Cities and Towns, 1780-1980*. Berkeley: University of California Press, 1988.

Neuman, R. P. "Masturbation, Madness, and the Modern Concepts of Childhood and Adolescence." *Journal of Social History* 8 (Spring 1975): 1–27.

Norton, Mary Beth. *Liberty's Daughters: The Revolutionary Experience of American Women, 1750–1800*. Ithaca, NY: Cornell University Press, 1980.

Nye, David. *Electrifying America: Social Meanings of a New Technology, 1880–1940*. Boston: MIT Press, 1990.

Palladino, Grace. *Teenagers: An American History*. New York: Basic Books, 1996.

Paris, Leslie. *Children's Nature: The Rise of the American Summer Camp*. New York: New York University Press, 2008.

Peel, Mark. "On the Margins: Lodgers and Boarders in Boston, 1860–1900." *Journal of American History* 72 (March 1986): 813–34.

Peiss, Kathy. *Cheap Amusements: Working Women and Leisure in Turn-of-the-Century New York*. Philadelphia: Temple University Press, 1986.

Read, Oliver, and Walter Welch. *From Tin Foil to Stereo: Evolution of the Phonograph*. New York: Bobbs-Merrill, 1976.

Reese, William. *America's Public Schools: From the Common School to 'No Child Left Behind.'* Baltimore: Johns Hopkins University Press, 2011.

Richardson, James. "Satanism in the Courts: From Murder to Heavy Metal." In *The Satanism Scare*, edited by James Richardson et al., 205–20. New York: Aldine de Gruyter, 1991.

Rose, Al. *Eubie Blake*. New York: Schirmer Books, 1979.

Rotundo, E. Anthony. "Boy Culture." In *The Children's Culture Reader*, edited by Henry Jenkins, 337–62. New York: New York University Press, 1998.

———. "Romantic Friendship: Male Intimacy and Middle-Class Youth in the Northern States." *Journal of Social History* 23 (Autumn 1989): 1–25.

Rudel, Anthony. *Hello, Everybody! The Dawn of American Radio*. New York: Harcourt, 2008.

Ryan, Mary. *The Cradle of the Middle Class: The Family in Oneida County, New York, 1790–1865*. New York: Cambridge University Press, 1981.

Sanchez-Eppler, Karen. "Marks of Possession: Methods for an Impossible Subject." *PMLA* 126 (January 2011): 151–59.

Schiffer, Michael. *The Portable Radio in American Life*. Tuscon: University of Arizona Press, 1991.

Schrum, Kelly. *Some Wore Bobby Sox: The Emergence of Teenage Girls' Culture, 1920–1945*. New York: Palgrave Macmillan, 2004.

Simon, Roger. "Housing and Services in an Immigrant Neighborhood: Milwaukee's Ward 14." *Journal of Urban History* 2 (August 1976): 435–58.

Smith, Daniel Scott. "Family Limitation, Sexual Control, and Domestic Feminism in Victorian America," *Feminist Studies* 1 (Winter–Spring 1973): 40–57.

Smith, Ronald L. *Cosby*. New York: S.P.I., 1993.

Smith-Rosenberg, Carroll. "The Female World of Love and Ritual." *Signs* 1 (Autumn 1975): 1–29.

Snyder, Thomas. *120 Years of American Education: A Statistical Portrait*. Washington, DC: Government Printing Office, 1993.

Spigel, Lynn. *Make Room for TV: Television and the Family Ideal in Postwar America*. Chicago: University of Chicago Press, 1992.

Stansell, Christine. "Women, Children, and the Uses of the Streets: Class and Gender Conflict in New York City, 1850–1860." *Feminist Studies* 8 (Summer 1982): 309–35.

Stearns, Peter. *Anxious Parents: A History of Modern Childrearing in America*. New York: New York University Press, 2003.

Stearns, Peter, et al. "Children's Sleep: Sketching Historical Change." *Journal of Social History* 30 (Winter 1996): 345–66.

Steele, Jeanne, and Jane Brown. "Adolescent Room Culture: Studying Media in the Context of Everyday Life." *Journal of Youth and Adolescence* 24 (October 1995): 551–76.

Stengers, Jean, and Anne Van Neck. *Masturbation: The History of a Great Terror*. New York: Palgrave, 2001.

Sterling, Christopher, and Michael Keith. *Sounds of Change: A History of FM Broadcasting in America*. Chapel Hill: University of North Carolina Press, 2008.

Stoops, Nicole. *A Half-Century of Learning*. Washington, DC: Government Printing Office, 2006.

Sutherland, Daniel. *Americans and Their Servants: Domestic Service in the United States from 1800 to 1920*. Baton Rouge: Louisiana State University Press, 1981.

Tichi, Cecelia. *Electronic Hearth: Creating an American Television Culture*. New York: Oxford University Press, 1991.

Victor, Jeffrey. *Satanic Panic: The Creation of a Contemporary Legend*. Chicago: Open Court, 1993.

Ward, Peter. *A History of Domestic Space: Privacy and the Canadian Home*. Vancouver: University of British Columbia Press, 1999.

Whitaker, Mark. *Cosby: His Life and Times*. New York: Simon & Schuster, 2014.

Wright, Bradley. *Comic Book Nation: The Transformation of Youth Culture in America*. Baltimore: Johns Hopkins University Press, 2001.

Wright, Gwendolyn. *Building the Dream: A Social History of Housing in America*. New York: Pantheon Books, 1981.

———. *Moralism and the Model Home: Domestic Architecture and Cultural Conflict in Chicago, 1873–1913*. Chicago: University of Chicago Press, 1980.

Zaretsky, Eli. *Secrets of the Soul: A Social and Cultural History of Psychoanalysis*. New York: Alfred A. Knopf, 2004.

Zelizer, Viviana. *Pricing the Priceless Child: The Changing Social Value of Children*. New York: Basic Books, 1985.

Index